John Birmingham tells stories for a living. For doing so he has been paid by the *Sydney Morning Herald*, the *Age*, the *Australian*, *Penthouse*, *Playboy*, *Rolling Stone*, *HQ*, *Inside Sport* and the *Independent Monthly*. He has also been published, but not paid, by the *Long Bay Prison News*. Some of his stories have won prizes including the George Munster prize for Freelance Story of the Year and the Carlton United Sports Writing Prize. *Leviathan*, John's fifth book, was first published in Knopf hardback in 1999. His earlier works are *He Died With a Felafel in His Hand* (now being made into a feature film starring Noah Taylor), *The Tasmanian Babes Fiasco*, *How to be a Man* and *The Search for Savage Henry*. He lives at the beach with his wife, baby daughter and two cats. He is not looking for any more flatmates.

Also by John Birmingham

JOHN BIRMINGHAM

Leviathan

the unauthorised
biography of Sydney

V

VINTAGE

A Vintage Book
Published by
Random House Australia Pty Ltd
20 Alfred Street, Milsons Point, NSW 2061
http://www.randomhouse.com.au

Sydney   New York   Toronto
London   Auckland   Johannesburg

First published in Knopf hardback in 1999
This Vintage edition first published in 2000

National Library of Australia
Cataloguing-in-Publication Entry

Birmingham, John, 1964- .
   Leviathan : the unauthorised biography of Sydney.

   Rev ed.
   Bibliography.
   Includes index.
   ISBN 0 091 84203 4 (pbk.).

   1. Cities and Towns - New South Wales - Sydney - Growth.
   2. Immigrants - New South Wales - Sydney. 3. Aborigines,
   Australian - New South Wales - Sydney - History. 4. Police
   - New South Wales - Sydney. 5. Crime - New South Wales -
   Sydney. 6. Sydney (N.S.W.) - History. 7. Sydney (N.S.W.) -
   Environmental conditions. 8. Sydney (N.S.W.) - Social
   life and customs. I. Title.

994.41

Extracts from *Green Bans, Red Unions* by Meredith and Verity Burgmann
reproduced with kind permission of UNSW Press. Extracts from *Weevils in the
Flour* by Wendy Lowenstein reproduced with kind permission of the author.

Cover painting by Kevin Connor
Cover design by Greendot Design
Internal design by Yolande Gray
Typeset in Sabon by Midland Typesetters, Maryborough, Victoria
Printed and bound by Griffin Press Pty Ltd, Netley, South Australia

10 9 8 7 6 5 4 3 2 1

In memory of Pat Bell.
Drinker, smoker, talker, friend.
A great loss to the city.

Acknowledgements

A lot of innocent people suffered to make this book happen. I owe them all thanks, beers and a friendly squeeze on the rump. In a mate-to-mate sort of way, you understand. So present tooshies ...

Annette Hughes for all sorts of nifty bayonet work in the trenches; Caitlin Lye and Shelly Horton for some sterling efforts on the sick-making microfilm readers at State Library; Andrew Hollis at the Bureau of Meteorology, for his detective work on the weather records; Ross Fitzgerald for casting a gimlet-eyed gaze over the Rum Rebellion section, when my first choice, Grafton Everest, was caught indisposed at the last moment; Ross Pogson and friends at the Australian Museum for help with ... uhm, really old stuff; all of the staff at the State Library of NSW, especially the crew at the Mitchell and Dixson, and the gang in the Glasshouse for keeping me thoroughly caffeinated. A jittery salute too, to the boys at Due Mondi for the double, triple and quadro espressos which kept me awake, alert and jittering at warp speed in the Mitchell during a thousand long, long afternoons. And hell, while I'm at it, thanks to everyone at Gusto in Bondi for the brekky rolls and toasted croissants which pushed me into the day in the first place; Neville Wran for enduring half an hour of my ranting questions about the power structure of the city at the end of a very

ACKNOWLEDGEMENTS

long day; Michelle Jeuken, Les Wales and all the crew at the Macquarie Fields cop shop; Gordon and Wendy Gallagher for taking me into their confidence at the worst possible time; Bronwyn Ridgeway, Rowan Cahill and Bill Langlois for help with the green bans; Liz Wynhausen, Judith Elen and Paul Fraser for delving into the bowels of the News Ltd library; Michael Pawson for smoothing my troubled passage through maritime history; Bryce Wilson, Laltu and Mr Kang for help with the slave cases (which never made it to print thanks to our enlightened defamation laws); Tony Hughes for a champion effort on the photocopiers and for the research papers he knocked out on my behalf; the Monday lunch crew for six hundred chicken curries; the hard chargin' bitches of the Valerie's Surf Club for not cancelling my sorry butt when I had to skip a whole season while on deadline; Dinh Tran and Hiep Chi Phan for enduring my dumb questions with superhuman patience; and Anne-Maree Whitaker for making sure the dead stayed that way.

And two big tooshy squeezes for the following colourful Sydney writing identities for their stand up efforts above and beyond the call of duty. From Random House the fabulous Jane Palfreyman, the awesome Ana Cox and the bodacious Jody Lee. From somewhere in the forest, the spookily perceptive and always three-steps-ahead-of-me Julia Stiles. From the back paddocks of Warwick the long suffering, pants backwards nine hundred bucks richer but wishing he'd never touched my filthy money Peter McAllister. And from just across the brown couch, via two cats and a Jane Austen novel, my amazing wife Jane.

I luvs yooz all.

JB

There Leviathan
hugest of living creatures, on the deep
stretched like a promontory sleeps or swims,
and seems a moving land ...

John Milton, *Paradise Lost*

Contents

1
The Long Goodbye

Make a hole with a gun perpendicular
To the name of this town in a desktop globe
Exit wound in a foreign nation.

Ana Ng, They Might Be Giants

Dinh Tran's city was dying. People ran through the streets, terrified, aimless, spooked by the rumble of distant artillery and the crash of rockets falling nearby. They ran under hot grey skies, unnerved by short bursts of remote gunfire. Some had gone mad. You could see them here and there, mostly frail-looking older men, quiet and trancelike in the midst of the stampede. Dinh picked his way carefully through the crowd, dismounting and pushing his old bicycle through the worst of the chaos, around those few cars and trucks that had been abandoned in the crush, adding to the confusion. A scared, thin young schoolteacher, he was headed, like many, for the port of Saigon. He hoped to find a friend there who might deliver his family to the safety of the American fleet waiting offshore. But Dinh's escape, like the Americans' own, was confounded by the speed and violence of the city's collapse.

He was staying with relatives in the second district, a faded gem of French colonial rule close to the waterfront. His parents had sold most of their property ten days earlier, intending to flee as four divisions from the north, supported by heavy armour and artillery, tripped over a few battered, lightly armed units of what mained of South Vietnam's army at the hamlet of Xuan Loc.

The Long Goodbye

The battle for Xuan Loc, the last great engagement of the war, was fought less than seventy kilometres from the Trans' front step, and when the killing was done with, South Vietnam was no more. Dinh and his family had followed the disintegration as best they could. Some omens could be read easily in the closure of local shops and businesses, violent chaos spreading through the streets in defiance of a military curfew, whole families vanishing from the neighbourhood, garbage rotting in the streets, power failures, tracer fire arcing through the night sky, flashes and rumbles over the horizon. Other events only whispered their message, their meanings transmitted through rumour and low-grade intuition – the flight of Vietnamese government figures from the US air base at Tan Son Nhut; mass desertions of armed forces personnel; the machine gunning of fleeing civilians on the river barges; the resignation of President Thieu, his late-night dash to the air base, escorted by American spies toting machine guns and hand grenades, all of them expecting to be pulled over and shot by South Vietnamese troops.

The communists had surrounded Saigon by then. Up to twenty divisions with armoured support. They even had a small air force composed of southern mutineers which bombed the city on the day after the President's escape. The raid touched off wild rumours of a coup, or perhaps the first dread footfall of the North Vietnamese Army within the city itself. But that was one more day away. Even so, Dinh could hear the war getting closer every minute, could feel it through his feet with the explosions of rockets and tank fire in the city precincts, could smell it in the dark oily smoke which boiled up from warehouse fires and intermittent shell bursts. The air in his chest thudded to the beat of evac choppers, while American gunships and navy jets flew shotgun overhead.

'The soldiers of the Republic had abandoned the army,' said Dinh. 'They had abandoned their arms and uniforms. People were panicking and running around, trying to find a way to escape.' He leant forward as he said this, holding the memory within himself. He seemed to stare into and through the photographs arranged in front of him, dozens of them, spread across two coffee tables, pressed between glass and tabletop, tracing the pilgrimage of the Tran family from Saigon to Sydney; family snaps in refugee camps, tragic 1970s fashions in Villawood, flares and body shirts in front of the first car, the first house in a new country, the first high school dance. A slow but unmistakable accretion of security and wealth. From the photograph of a small, fragile family group standing in the dust of a Malaysian resettlement camp, through to a beaming, healthy new daughter in ski parka and boots up in the Australian Snowy Mountains.

'I used my bicycle to get to the port of Saigon,' Dinh recalled quietly. 'On that day people were moving around everywhere, not knowing where to go or what to do. Just walking and riding. Not much traffic, but people everywhere. On the twenty-ninth there was some bombing. We heard the noise of tanks moving and some gunfighting. There weren't too many people in the heart of Saigon. Very few soldiers. But there were probably a few thousand people running around the port. They just ran around in panic trying to escape. I saw some navy boats in the river, but nobody on them.'

The smell of steamed rice crept in from the kitchen. We sat in Dinh's living room and sipped a sickly sweet fizzy cola while Saigon burned and died behind his eyes. The room was not very big. Apart from a small black lacquer wall-hanging with an opal outline of Vietnam, it contained few signifiers of the cultural shift wrought on Sydney by the Vietnamese who settled there after the war. Escape had been closer that afternoon than Dinh realised. While he noticed only a few small abandoned navy craft at anchor in the river down at the port, around a bend at Khanh Hoi lay two huge barges, tugged there as part of an abortive American effort to move 30 000 high-risk Vietnamese out of the city. The barges were massive, with sandbag redoubts along the sides, harking back to their previous role, ferrying militia forces up the Mekong to Phnom Penh. There was no government presence of any sort at Khanh Hoi the afternoon Dinh went looking for an escape route. Anyone who cared to step onto the barges could have done so unchallenged. They pulled away from the docks, half empty, as evening fell and Dinh's family gathered together in their small room in the second district to await the arrival of the communists.

It was not long in coming. Next morning, NVA General Tran Van Tra ordered his army to advance into Saigon an hour after the last American chopper lifted off the roof of the embassy. It was a disastrous, humiliating exit for the superpower. Thousands of Vietnamese crawling and scrambling over the embassy fence, looting and burning the snack bar and warehouse, letting off small arms, chanting anti-American slogans and driving the embassy vehicles in mad slashing circles on the ruined lawn. Revolt everywhere, except for the local fire brigade who had volunteered to stay and fight the blaze, expecting in vain to be picked up by the Americans.

Totalitarian regimes aren't big on entertainment. Lots of parades and a constant subcutaneous frisson of terror just about covers the options. Thus at nine in the evening of 15 April 1980, when Dinh

Tran, his wife Phong and their two daughters stepped out through the door of the small closed-up shop where they'd been living since the communist takeover, they presented a weird picture to the deserted streets of Saigon, or Ho Chi Minh City as it had become. A young, neatly dressed family stepping out on the town where there was nowhere to go and nothing to do. They hailed a passing cyclo, the ubiquitous three-wheeled taxi which had survived the end of the war, and directed the driver to take them to a closed riverside market about twenty kilometres away.

They rode quietly through the mostly deserted streets, an anxious trip of about half an hour, through intersections guarded by sleepy, disinterested policemen. Finally stopping amongst the shuttered market stalls, Dinh paid off the cyclo jockey and ushered his family into the shadows. He was frightened and tense and torn up inside. Just before leaving home he had leaned forward and kissed his frail father's shaking head. 'I have to go now, Daddy,' he'd said, squeezing out the words. After Dinh turned his back to leave, he knew he would not see his father again. There was, however, no time for dwelling on such things. Dinh hustled everyone dockside and down to the end of a jetty. A fishing boat lay tethered there, low in the water but otherwise no different to any other in the small fleet bobbing slowly about in the dirty, foul-smelling river. They climbed aboard and – one, two, three, four – they dropped out of sight. The dock was still again; hot, quiet, dark and deserted. It remained so for a short time until an engine started up with a very faint, throaty growl and the little vessel into which the Trans had disappeared slowly pulled away from the dock and out into the river.

It was close and rank down in the boat's hold, pitch black and claustrophobic. Dinh could sense rather than see the press of thirty,

The Long Goodbye

maybe forty other bodies in the confined space. Hard to tell in that inky gloom. He kept Phong and the girls nearby, huddled tight, just as he had pressed close to his own parents and siblings on their flight out of North Vietnam twenty-six years earlier. He thought sadly of his father who was simply too old and weak to attempt this sort of adventure again. The other runaways whispered softly as the trawler slipped quietly downstream, stopping now and then to pick up more people who dropped into the hold through the tiny hatch which Dinh saw only as a square of lighter darkness. 'It is like they fall down from the sky,' he thought.

They motored along, stopping and starting, until dawn, by which time there were nearly sixty people below decks. In the cabin above, the crew ran up the government flag to establish their bona fides as honest toilers of the People's Republic. They ploughed on for a few more hours, picked up more human cargo, this time actually dressed like fishermen. Then the engines started to vibrate and roar and everyone in the hold felt the trawler lean back on her heels and pick up speed. They were away. Relief washed through the densely packed band of refugees. The little boat started to pitch and roll as she punched into the swell of the South China Sea.

Dinh relaxed a little; but while he took comfort in the long curling rise of the waves beneath the keel he could not let go completely. This was his third attempt to escape from Vietnam and now, having made the open sea, the most dangerous. Although thousands had made it out of Vietnam, thousands more had died trying. The fast inshore gunboats of the regime were perhaps the least of their worries. If caught they might be sent to a prison camp, a marginal threat when the whole country was effectively a prison anyway. There were other terrors ahead: storms, freak waves, shipwreck, thirst, starvation or madness. The sea might deliver them up to freedom, or into the hands of Thai pirates who would most likely murder them, after indulging in a few hot, slow days of rape and torture. If they avoided all that and made it into international waters, they might be run down by a supertanker. The boat might fall apart. The sea could swallow them up without trace. Or the crew might just get a hundred kilometres offshore and force them all over the side at gunpoint. Although Dinh had helped put this escape network together, he had bitter experience of the mendacity of his fellow man.

His brother had escaped via a secret network some years before. Dinh spoke to the smugglers, who said they could repeat the getaway at the cost of all the family's savings. A tall, well-built Kampuchean picked them up from their house at four in the morning. No baggage, no possessions. Normal street clothes for the long sea journey. They were crammed into a small sclerotic Honda, and driven to a province about 200 kilometres from Saigon. They pulled up to a stall at dawn, a hut beside the road with a very old table and some chairs. An old man ran the store, sixty years of age, thin and very poor. The driver asked them to wait while he picked up some other passengers for the next stage of the journey. He would return in an hour. They waited for three.

'They abandoned us,' he muttered fiercely, his voice quavering. 'They tricked us. We were nearly captured. We sat there, my wife and my small children and, at the table next to us, two more people. Two other escapees, disguised like poor people, labourers or peasants. Only at the end, as we all became very frightened, did we know the truth. We sat in this hut watching the dirt road out the front, cars and trucks and carts rolling by, until we gave up and returned to Saigon.'

The Long Goodbye

After another unsuccessful attempt Dinh knew he had to organise his own escape network. He approached one of the few people
he trusted outside his own family, another teacher at his school,
his best friend Cuong. Cuong and Dinh worked hard at being good
fanatical comrades during the day. So diligent were they about
maintaining their facade that the school's principal, an informer,
trusted them implicitly, never imagining that the atlases, encyclopaedias and English language textbooks they gathered were to be
used for anything more than school lessons. 'They never thought
we would escape,' said Dinh with more than a touch of satisfaction. 'During the day we worked very hard and contributed everything we could to the school. But outside, at night, we prepared
our escape.'

Cuong had many relatives in the fishing industry. They helped
the teachers buy a twelve-metre fishing boat with a covered hold
and a simple wheelhouse, helped them install the equipment and
plan the provisions needed for a sea voyage. Cuong and Dinh
pored over the old encyclopaedias after dusk fell, studying the
oceans and currents and consulting Cuong's closest relatives for
more specific details about the coastal waters. They knew that
when they left they would have to sail due east from Saigon,
directly into the South China Sea on a heading for the military hot
zone of the Spratley Islands. They would never make it there, they
hoped. April's prevailing winds and currents should, over the slow
beat of many hundreds of nautical miles, drag the little boat and
its seventy-three passengers around in a wide arc down towards
the joining waters of Singapore, Malaysia and the Philippines.

On the evening of the first day the boat hit a sandbank and
stuck fast. A terrible shudder ran through the hull as they fetched
up on the submerged hazard. Worried murmurs filled the darkened

hold as the engines cycled up to no effect. The boat would not move. Finally word came down for all the men aboard to climb over the sides and push the stranded craft off. A bizarre scene ensued as two dozen Vietnamese men, all in their casual street clothes, surrounded by miles of ocean, laboured at the sides of the vessel, while far away on the horizon the lights of the coast shimmered and winked. It took half an hour to work the vessel free.

There was no food on that first day because, apart from the incident on the sandbank, nobody was allowed above decks. They waited until they were several hundred kilometres beyond Vietnam's territorial waters before relaxing the rule. And even then, with so many people squeezed into such a small area, it was not safe to have more than two or three people moving around at any one time. Everyone sat very still for a week and a half, fearful that movement might capsize the boat. Rice was cooked in little petrol burners up on deck and passed from hand to hand below. Foreign ships passing close by made no move to assist them.

'We sailed for nine days,' recalled Dinh. 'Moving in the immense space of the ocean. We had to restrict the water and food, having nearly run out. Then a Singaporean warship came to us and everyone cheered and welcomed them. They pulled alongside, this ship was huge above ours. We begged them to help us into Singapore. The captain called a few of us into his ship, so myself and Cuong climbed up the ropes they dropped down. A very long climb as I remember. The captain was about twenty-eight. Very young and handsome. He wore an immaculate white navy uniform but, strangely, with the cheap sandals of a farm labourer.'

Dinh and Cuong were escorted to the control room where the young captain softly interrogated them. He offered to provide dry food, water and petrol if they continued on past Singapore. The

The Long Goodbye

two starving, exhausted men begged him to help them into Singapore. He demurred quietly at first, but as they persisted his demeanour changed. He grew hard and angry, eventually barking at his men to throw the teachers over the side. They had to run from the bridge and scramble quickly from his ship to their own. The Singaporeans did give them some food and water, but as the stores were being transferred, the sailors attached a thick tow rope to the trawler. The warship cranked up its turbines, churning the water at its stern into a minor maelstrom as it put on speed and towed the refugees away. 'We were like a leaf caught behind them,' says Dinh. 'Very fast in the water, skiing on their wake. Bouncing and smashing on their white wake.'

They were finally cut loose and warned not to venture near Singapore. Six, maybe seven hours later they met with an Indonesian vessel. Civilian this time. The Indonesians made it clear their government's welcome would be no more inviting. Later still the Malaysian navy appeared on the horizon. Ten warships in a line which the tiny fishing vessel could not hope to pass through. As night settled over the boat on the tenth day, the senior men gathered for a meeting in the wheelhouse. A small lamp threw a very weak glow over their sombre faces.

'We knew we could not get in anywhere legally,' said Dinh. 'So we decided to enter anywhere we could. The first place we found. There was a weak source of light some distance ahead so we made for that. Then we saw a mountain growing up over the horizon. We had decided to force a landing and damage the boat so we could not be towed again.'

As the distant whisper of surf grew to the roar of waves upon rocks, fear and excitement coursed through the refugees. Dinh's heartbeat gathered speed and strength, slicing through the pressing cramp of exhaustion and hunger, his skin suddenly greasy with cold sweat. The boat began to turn and roll more violently than it had at any time since leaving Vietnam. The floor below them tilted one way and another, pitching everyone into each other in the dark, more dramatic than any carnival ride.

They hit the Malaysian coast at two in the morning with a sick scream of wrenched and tortured wood. Sharp black rocks clenched the vessel all around, making it difficult and dangerous to jump off. Dinh gathered up his daughters in his arms. They clung fiercely to his neck as he leapt into the churning waters and sank immediately up to his chin. He struggled through the surf, waves rushing and dumping the three of them onto the sharp rocks. His daughters did not cry out, just clung more tightly. Around him others struggled through surf towards the beach. It took over an hour to get everyone safely ashore. Then the men waded back into the water with hammers and stones and broke up the boat so they could not be put to sea again.

At first the adventure of Dinh and his family seems so unusual and exciting, so far removed from the prosaic daily narrative of an average Sydney resident as to be truly alien. And yet when you pause and let your gaze traverse the city, say from the window of an Airbus bringing hundreds of new visitors and settlers to the folds of the harbour, the Trans' story resolves itself into a pattern of movement and experience so common that it stands as a leit-motif within the city's deeper history. Below you, along hundreds of kilometres of beach and foreshore, in houses and streets stretching way back over the plains, climbing gradually into the dark blue haze of the mountains, there live hundreds of thousands of people with personal tales just as extraordinary as the Trans'. Casting wider, taking in familial history, you net millions of stories, all

The Long Goodbye

similar in their elements of flight and redemption, for unlike the great cities of the old world, Sydney is almost wholly a migrant creation.

Conceived of as a place where people would go and never come back, it has grown alongside eruptions of insensate violence, oppression and dislocation elsewhere in the world. Asian wars, European wars, Middle Eastern wars, depressions, recessions, pogroms and revolutions, all have delivered millions of travellers and refugees into the fetid holds of small boats and the uncertain mercies of the open sea. Across thousands of miles, down through hundreds of years they have arrived willingly or otherwise, fleeing or cast out of one home and forced to build another. Some have amassed fantastic wealth, some have died broken and alone. It is the nature of individual stories to vary so. However it is the common threads weaving through the city's tapestry which stand out. The way the stories of Cockney pickpockets, Irish rebels, German Jews, Italian fishermen and Vietnamese schoolteachers all wind through and around each other in recurring patterns.

When Dinh Tran was finally released from the migrant hostel he made six trips shuttling back and forth between Villawood and the small flat on the beach at Cronulla which would be his family's first real home in Australia. This last part of his escape from Vietnam was attended by the same gnawing doubts about providing for his family which had assailed their earlier moves. They were launching themselves into a new world with little property or income and virtually no English. Without a car or suitcases, Dinh used a small beaten up plastic shopping trolley to move everything they owned. Clothing, books and shoes, it all went into old plastic shopping bags which he piled into the trolley before wheeling it a few kilometres away to Leightonfield train station. He'd catch a train to Central, wrestle the trolley off the carriage and onto an interchange for Cronulla. It was a long, tiring journey, repeated many times, but it marked the point in the Trans' story where anomie gave way to action. 'I had to concentrate on what to do', said Dinh. 'I stopped worrying. I started English classes. Then I found work.'

It was a path walked by millions before them; Jews fleeing the Holocaust, Italians escaping postwar chaos and poor British migrants attempting to break with an oppressive class system. Like them, Dinh and his wife Phong took what work they could and bent themselves to the task of settling into a new country. Husband and wife found jobs at an aluminium plant in Caringbah. They worked a split shift for six months. Hard, continuous labour. Dinh, a small man, spent his day lugging big aluminium panels through the foundry and lifting them onto moving hooks. 'We would finish heaving it onto the hook when another length would come through and we'd have to do it again', he said. 'All day. It never stopped, very heavy work.'

Eventually he moved to a press section where he made sure the melted aluminium ran smooth and flat on the runners. Between each hot, rumbling slab he had a break of fifty seconds, during which time he'd study the English notes he had written at two or three the previous morning. The machine-like routine of his work life was matched by the larger cycles of his day. Night shift at the factory, home in the wee hours, correcting his wife's English assignments and his children's homework until just before dawn, then writing out his own lessons for the next day. 'I'd take ten small note pages a day,' he remembered. 'Enough to put in my front pocket. I would have a new word, a definition and some phrases with the word every day. I did this for a long time, the whole time I was in the press section.'

The Long Goodbye

By July 1985 his English language proficiency was sufficient for him to pass the government's public service exams, a test failed by many native-born English speakers. Living in Bankstown in the dark brick bungalow with cool, white tiled floors, he hoped his children would graduate from university and move into an occupation where they could be of service to his new city and country. 'I educate them to become good citizens and support this society in the future,' he says. 'Not just to do everything they can to earn a high income. That is necessary for their family, but it is not the number one priority. Besides earning wealth, they must do something useful.'

While the Trans are a small but emblematic success, the city is not always so kind to its newcomers. Many of Dinh's countrymen have exchanged one form of oppression for another, escaping political tyranny for an economic one. If they are ambivalent or unhappy about their new home, the city too has reservations. For a place created by migrants it seems increasingly unwilling to contemplate a future in which they play a role. At times the look it turns on them is cold and guarded and deeply mistrustful and you have to wonder how such animosity came to be. But this is an old story, Sydney's first, and it begins with the story of her mother city, London.

Solitary, poor, nasty, brutish and short. Had Thomas Hobbes lived to witness the struggle for life by the underclass in Georgian England, he would have recognised his 'war of all against all' in a grim, skeletal form. The poor of that era were not the poor we know now. They were not just disadvantaged or underprivileged. They did not eke out dissolute, meaningless lives on welfare, fast food and daytime TV. They were the wretched of the earth, their existence every bit as woeful as the children who scramble over huge, smouldering hills of garbage in Jakarta today.

For respectable society – the emerging commercial classes and the hereditary, land owning elite who lived as a corpulent tick on the body of the rural masses – the sufferings of the poor were, as the magistrate Sir John Fielding put it, less observed than their misdeeds. Their struggles for subsistence went unnoticed, except when they ground up hard against the property and sensibilities of the lucky few. 'They starve and freeze and rot among themselves,' wrote Fielding, 'but they beg, steal and rob among their betters.' Nearly 100 years later, with the industrial revolution under full power, Friedrich Engels thought the poor 'a race wholly apart from the English bourgeoisie'. The latter had more in common with wealthy foreigners than the workers from whose labour they profited. Engel's contemporary, Henry Mayhew, a pioneer journalist, sociologist and founder of *Punch* magazine, wrote a long and vivid account of the lower classes called *London Labour and the London Poor*. He admitted himself at a loss as to how to systematically approach his huge investigation, being wholly unacquainted with the objects of his inquiry; '... for each day's investigation brings me incidentally into contact with a means of living utterly unknown among the well fed portion of society.'

The forces of history which produced these inequalities were the same as those which threw British naval and military might across the vast penumbra of the oceans, which filled the Thames to choking point with thousands of creaking, bobbing traders' vessels and awoke the countless millions whose ancestors had slumbered for centuries in the darkness of a peasant's life. The convergence point of these snaking, humming lines of social and economic

The Long Goodbye

energy was London, the centre of an empire, the home of the Royal Court and Parliament, the seat of financial power, of the nation's manufacturing industries, of its trade and communications. By 1750 one person in ten of all Great Britain's population lived there. (In contrast, Paris could claim only one out of every forty Frenchmen.) It was more than ten times larger than Norwich, the second city of the realm. As the focal point of the British Empire, London became the centre of the known universe, its policies and adventures determining the fate of nations. For some, however, it was just the worst place in the world.

For those who could not rely on the wealth of vast inherited estates, London life was a contingent, anxious proposition. The working folk of the city, and even the lower middle classes who depended on their custom, were roughly tossed about by chance. England was more often at war than peace between 1695 and 1815, and its economy constantly ground gears between the two. Even in settled times the average Londoner was subject to the cold winds of economic change which blew through the city every year.

Virtually all work was seasonal. Shipping, the foundation of the whole economy, was less a bedrock than a chimera. Before steam power liberated seamen from the fickle winds, thousands of families whose daily bread depended on finding work at the docks could be reduced to starvation by a mild change in the weather. In the months when the rich deserted the town, economic activity came to a standstill and whole classes of tradesmen were thrown onto their wits to survive. Of the thousands of house painters in 1740s London, one observer wrote that there was 'not bread for one third of them' and they were idle at least four or five months in the year. 'Their work begins in April or May, and continues till ... winter, when many of them are out of business.' The two or three shillings a day a man could earn was 'but a poor and precarious bread' and the itinerant workers who followed this uncertain trade were 'the dirtiest, laziest, and most debauched set of fellows in and about London'. The tailors of the same period were 'as numerous as locusts, out of business three or four months of the year, and generally as poor as rats'. Under these circumstances even solid, bourgeois pursuits such as shopkeeping and school teaching were not to be relied on. Henry Mayhew described the moneyed attitude to such people, eerily anticipating the fashionable economics of the present day.

> Such a labourer commercially considered is, as it were, a human steam engine, supplied with so much fuel in the shape of food, merely to set him in motion. If he can be made to perform the same amount of work with half the consumption, why a saving one half the expense is supposed to be effected. Indeed the grand object in the labour market of the present day appears to be to economise human fuel.

Mayhew considered the dock labourers of London to be the highest expression of this principle, 'a striking instance of mere brute force with brute appetites'. Dock work was then largely unskilled, needing neither references nor training, only arms and legs. Being suited to any sort of man it drew every sort. Mayhew met decayed and bankrupt master butchers, publicans, grocers, old soldiers and sailors, refugees, broken down gentlemen, discharged law clerks, suspended civil servants, beggars, pensioners, servants and thieves; that is, the same tattered grab bag of human tailings and misfits first disgorged from the rotting prison hulks of the Thames in 1787 to build a city on the other side of the world.

The Long Goodbye

Mayhew estimated that 20 000 such men made their living among the forest of masts and snapping, coloured flags each day. He moved among them with pen and paper, noting the surrounding factories with monstrous iron wheels arching through their roofs and clouds of black smoke vomiting from tall chimneys. Here came a group of men with faces stained bright blue with indigo; there went barrel gaugers carrying long brass tipped poles, dripping with the spirits of a cask just measured. Flaxen-haired German sailors mixed it up with turban wearing Arabs. A blue-smocked butcher with a tray of fresh meat and a box of cabbages on his shoulder, followed by a ship's mate with a cage of green birds passed a sorrowful young woman with new bright cooking tins at her feet, an emigrant preparing for her voyage, perhaps to Sydney. The air was pungent with a thousand conflicting odours; tobacco, rum, rich coffee and spices mingled with the stench of rendered animal hides. It rang to hammers on nails, coopers pounding at their casks. Yankee sailors sang Negro spirituals as they hauled away at rattling chains and creaking ropes. Water splashed. Animals bleated and moaned while empty casks rolled down the quay like 'stones with a heavy drum-like sound'. However, the richness of dock life contrasted sharply with the precarious returns of dock work. Whilst all this treasure seemed as boundless as the sea itself, Mayhew endeavoured to impress upon his readers the desperate nature of the struggle for life in its midst:

> Until I saw with my own eyes this scene of greedy despair, I could not have believed there was so mad an eagerness to work, and so biting a want of it, among so vast a body of men.

19

At seven thirty each morning thousands would gather at the entrance to the docks, waiting for the calling foremen to arrive. A sudden current running through the crowd signalled the start of a ghastly humiliating fight for work. All the men scuffled and scrambled and threw their arms into the sky to catch the eye of the foremen handing out the day's casual positions. Some jumped up on the backs and shoulders of those in front of them, trying to draw a favourable glance. All of them shouted, some the foreman's first name, some his last, some their own names. As the minutes passed, the contest became fiercer still, fired by the knowledge that hundreds assembled there would go without.

> To look in the faces of that hungry crowd is to see a sight that must be ever remembered. Some are smiling to the foreman to coax him into remembrance of them; others with their protruding eyes eager to snatch at the hoped for pass. For weeks many have gone there, and gone through the same struggle – the same cries; and have gone away, after all, without the work they had screamed for.

Mayhew at first imagined the work they sought so eagerly must be particularly pleasant or light, when in fact it was so heavy and continuous that he quickly came to think only the fittest and best fed could stand it. Even those who did not make the first call often waited in their hundreds in the holding yards on the off chance of a stray ship appearing unheralded in port. Each day the scene repeated itself. Mayhew met some in the waiting yard who had been six weeks without work, living on scraps of bread thrown to them by luckier labourers who knew their own turn in penury would inevitably come. One fallen businessman he came across had been reduced to scouring the streets for rags and offal. He was one small step removed from the lowest of the street grubbers, the turd scavengers who hunted up dog shit to sell to the city's tanneries. His main source of income was gathering discarded cigar butts, drying them out and selling the tobacco at half a penny per ounce to the thieves in his lodgings.

At this level there was little separating the poor from the criminal classes, as they were imagined. Mayhew numbered hundreds of common thieves amongst the supplicants of the dockyards' foremen. They lived heaped upon each other in sprawling slums, in cramped and winding rows of badly constructed terraces, often in damp, unlit mud lined cellars. The streets in these parts of town were almost always unpaved open sewers which on dry, windy days gave off thick clouds composed of pulverised horse and cattle dung and further contaminated with a silt of rotting fruit and offal and human sewage. A horrific fetid stench pervaded these neighbourhoods at all times, the constricted buildings allowing little, if any, ventilation. Good weather meant simply that the narrow lanes were used for drying masses of wet clothes on lines strung between the tightly packed dwellings.

Through much of the eighteenth century these streets were awash with a violent, hard running tide of alcoholism. Parliament encouraged gin distilling to eat up the island's mountainous surplus of corn production. (A lot of it produced on members' estates, coincidentally.) So liberal were the gin laws that nearly every shop and business in London was free to deal in the rough, fiery spirit. Many of the distillers were themselves hopeless drunkards whose stills often exploded and sent fire racing through the old wooden quarters of the town. Official figures estimated that by 1725 every fifth house in the city was selling gin. This was probably an underestimate which did not take into account the huge number of street vendors and freelance grog merchants. 'All chandlers, many tobacconists, and such who sell fruit or herbs in stalls and wheelbarrows sell geneva, and many inferior tradesmen begin now to keep it in their shops for their customers,' declared an investigator's report. It was impossible to go about your day without confronting the opportunity for cheap drink and constant imprecations to partake. By the 1730s over eighty trades including barbers, tailors, labourers, weavers, dyers and shoemakers were retailing the stuff. Many workers were encouraged by their employers to take their pay in gin, inevitably finding they had nothing to take home at the end of the week.

The orgy of spirit drinking was a public disaster, greater – by several orders of magnitude – than the troubles visited on the late twentieth century by heroin, amphetamines or indeed all of the legal and illegal drugs combined. Cheap, ubiquitous, warm and numbing, it was especially ruinous for the poor. During the worst years of the epidemic three quarters of their children died before the age of five. Those who were consigned to the parish workhouse had even less chance. The mortality rate for children taken in under the age of twelve months was ninety-nine percent. The ravages were not restricted to a general depression of already marginal living standards. The drink inflamed terrible passions. In 1750 Judith Dufour strangled her two-year-old child to death and threw the body in a ditch so she could sell the clothes for gin. Although reforms in the middle of the century put an end to the worst excesses, the mortality bills still reflected an increased death rate from the long binge fifty years later. Many of the first convicts were raised in this debauched environment.

In the 1840s Friedrich Engels dived into the underworld to describe the rookery of St Giles, an infamous den surrounded by

The Long Goodbye

the rich environs of Oxford Street, Trafalgar Square and the Strand. He found:

a disorderly collection of tall, three or four-storeyed houses, with narrow, crooked, filthy streets, in [which] there is quite as much life as in the great thoroughfares of the town, except that here, people of the working class only are to be seen. A vegetable market is held in the street, baskets with vegetables and fruits, naturally all bad and hardly fit to use, obstruct the sidewalk still further, and from these, as well as from the fish-dealers' stalls, arises a horrible smell. The houses are occupied from cellar to garret, filthy within and without, and their appearance is such that no human being could possibly wish to live in them. But all this is nothing in comparison with the dwellings in the narrow courts and alleys between the streets, entered by covered passages between the houses, in which the filth and tottering ruin surpass all description. Scarcely a whole window-pane can be found, the walls are crumbling, door-posts and window-frames loose and broken, doors of old boards nailed together, or altogether wanting in this thieves' quarter, where no doors are needed, there being nothing to steal. Heaps of garbage and ashes lie in all directions, and the foul liquids emptied before the doors gather in stinking pools.

Engels, as industrious and sympathetic an observer of the poor as his class enemy Mayhew, agreed with the magazine publisher that these crowded slums were as great a source of moral corruption as they were of diseases such as scrofula and typhus. He sermonised that there is a degree of misery, a proximity to sin which virtue is rarely able to withstand and which the young cannot resist. In such circumstances the progress of vice is almost as certain and rapid as that of physical contagion. In slums like St Giles lived 'the poorest of the poor, the worst paid workers with thieves and the victims of prostitution indiscriminately huddled together'. Those who hadn't drowned in the whirlpool of moral ruin which surrounded them sank daily deeper, progressively losing their power to resist 'the demoralising influence of want, filth, and evil surroundings'. Engels wondered that there was not much more crime emanating from these human waste dumps.

Popular mythology would not have Sydney founded by such people. Rather, goes the fairytale, the city fathers were honest starving farmers and hapless Irishmen down on their luck and forced to steal to feed their sooty-faced urchins. Unfortunately, not everyone was exiled for making off with a loaf of bread or a guvnor's silk hanky. The common British trait, shared by all classes, of sneering at Australians' criminal origins has a solid basis in fact. Many of those transported to the colony were serial offenders, the natural end product of an undeclared class war which raged across the landscape of Britain like a giant threshing machine, chewing up and spitting out hundreds of thousands of lives to feed a fantasy of the propertied classes: that crime was a moral contagion which could be cut from the flesh of the lower orders and cast away to rot on the hot, fatal shore of the antipodes. The main point of transportation, as Robert Hughes put it, was not what happened to the criminals once they were *there*, but that they would no longer be *here*. It was a delusion based on the false premise that crime had no external causes such as grinding poverty, starvation and despair. Instead it sprang in every case from the contaminated soul as an act of free will.

In truth criminality, like greatness, was a contingent affair. Some were born to it, some achieved it, and the rest had it thrust rudely

The Long Goodbye

upon them. The forlorn extremes of the latter in no way detracted from the lusty embrace of lawlessness by the former. Mayhew met bands of thieves who were proud of their profession and took imprisonment as a sign of achievement; rather foolishly, given the savage nature of the legal system at the time. Eighteenth century English justice encompassed punishment cut from the cloth of the Dark Ages, including amputating hands, slicing off ears, slitting nostrils, branding and whipping, often served up as an entrée to the state's main course of vengeance, death by hanging. The law itself was confused, stitched together from a patchwork of ancient Roman doctrine, a great unwritten mass of mediaeval common law, and the formal codified statutes dating from the reign of Edward I at the end of the thirteenth century. The result was an ambiguous and contradictory body of laws with barbaric ambitions and arbitrary effects. Many judges and juries actually used this to mitigate the cruelties of the system. Charges of many First Fleet convicts were worded so as to attract the lesser penalty of transportation instead of execution.

None of which seemed to affect the thinking of those criminals who still revelled in their own infamy. Interviewing a large party of thieves, Mayhew found they cheered each other on as each replied to questions about how many times he had been jailed. One junior desperado, who claimed to have been locked up twenty-nine times in his nineteen short but action-packed years, drew a long thunderous standing ovation from dozens of his mates. A seaman ordered to draw up a list of the occupations of the convict ship *Recovery*'s transportees in 1819 reported back to the surgeon-superintendent that three quarters of their charges claimed to be nothing more than thieves. Scratching his head, and providing an insight into the accuracy of convict records, he asked whether he should just list them as 'labourers', one of the most common job descriptions of the men sent out to Australia. In 1797, in *A Treatise on the Police of the Metropolis*, Patrick Colquhoun described a whole underground society of idle and disorderly mechanics, labourers, pilferers, embezzlers, coiners, receivers of stolen goods, spendthrifts, rakes, and 'giddly young men . . . in the pursuit of criminal pleasures'. They were 'profligate, loose and dissolute characters . . . seducing others to intemperance, lewdness, debauchery, gambling and excess . . .'

They really were a sorry lot and they tried the patience of those appointed as their moral guardians. Surgeon Haslam's attempted reforms fell on arid ground. He tried to educate the convicts in the hulks about 'the beauties and conveniences which the light of truth and rectitude of conduct would present' in contrast to the infamy and contempt they then wallowed in. They were having none of it. 'My admonitions,' Haslam lamented, 'were drowned in a roar of blasphemy.' The Reverend Bedford of Hobart Town was subject to the gross indignity of being mooned by a group of uppity female convicts who drew up their skirts and smacked their arses as he attempted to tell them off. Some just admitted defeat; the Reverend Richard Johnson regretted on his departure from Sydney that the convicts had not been improved at all by their odyssey. They were still indulging themselves in sloth and idleness, engaging in most 'profane and unclean conversation, and committing abominations which it would defile any pen to describe'.

Contrary to the hopes of those in the United Kingdom who thought transportation a salutary and reforming example, the likelihood that the blinking, benighted creatures who stumbled from the convict transports in Port Jackson were hard core criminals actually increased over time. Reforms to the English legal system saw exile to the colonies progressively reserved for more and more

The Long Goodbye

serious offences. The system which consigned the first convicts to Australia was much more ferocious and haphazard, however, and some really were exiled for petty misdeeds born of want and desperation.

The convicts were not alone in their exile. Having volunteered for the adventure of the First Fleet, Ralph Clark, a newly-wed second officer of His Majesty's Royal Marines, found himself haunted and depressed at the prospect of a long separation from his home and family. Clark took time to set down his feelings as Arthur Phillip's squadron weighed anchor and set course for a brisk run down the Solent, a deep strait which bends sharply, just like a boomerang, between the low broken shoreline of Hampshire and the steeper, chalky northern coast of the Isle of Wight. As watery daylight leaked into the world, the estuaries of the Medina, the Newton and Yar Rivers slipped by on the port side and then Hurst Castle loomed, a grim sixteenth century fortress squatting at the end of a long, thin pebble bank jutting out into the channel. The castle's contribution to English penal history – King Charles was held there after the civil war before being removed to Westminster for trial and execution – meant little or nothing to Clark. He was busy imploring God to allow the fleet to put in at Plymouth so he could see his 'dear friend and affectionate Alicia' and their 'sweet son'. Sadly the Lord wasn't taking requests that morning and a little further on, as England receded, Clark wailed, 'O my God all my hoppes are over of seeing my beloved wife and son'.

He was an attentive diarist but a bit of a hypocrite. His journal is replete with furious references to the female convicts, abandoned trollops who were not to be compared with the lovely lost Alicia.

LEVIATHAN

A few days after sailing from Tenerife four tradesmen aboard Clark's vessel, the inappropriately named *Friendship*, broke through a bulkhead to get to the female convicts. They were discovered in bed with Sarah McCormick and three Elizabeths: Pulley, Dudgens and Hackley. There had been similar trouble in Portsmouth, and Pulley and Dudgens had previously been confined to irons for fighting. Clark wrote that they were greatest whores who ever lived and blamed some nascent industrial action amongst the ship's civilian crew on their influence. His pen dripped venom at their every mention. On their release from irons Clark predicted a ready return to confinement. 'I am convinced they will not be long out of them,' he wrote. 'They are a disgrace to their whole sex, bitches that they are. I wish all the women were out of the ships.'

When the *Friendship*'s carpenter, boatswain, steward and a seaman were transferred to the fleet's command vessel, the *Sirius*, after breaking through to the women that second time, all but the carpenter were whipped. Clark was disappointed that the women were only returned to irons. Were he the commander, he wrote, he would 'have flogged the four whores also'. When one of these 'damned whores', Elizabeth Dudgens, was finally flogged for abusing the captain, Clark worked himself into a righteous lather as a marine corporal flayed her back with the whip. He did not play with her, the young officer noted, 'but laid it home, which I was very glad to see'. Dudgens was then tied to the ship's pump to ponder and repent. Clark, bitter at being forced into close communion with such degraded creatures – so inferior to his own good and graceful wife – felt not a whit of compassion. The prisoner 'had been long fishing' for such a violent correction and now she had it 'until her heart's content'. What delicious irony then that

The Long Goodbye

Lieutenant Clark, loving husband and father and stern unbending moralist should later be found on Norfolk Island shacked up with the teenaged Mary Branham, a thief and housebreaker and mother to his bastard child.

Ralph Clark's mood may have been amongst the worst affected by the fleet's separation from home. Others testified to an adventurous spirit below decks, a sense of anticipation and an eagerness to be done with the Old World which had manifestly failed most of the travellers. *The Voyage of Governor Phillip to Botany Bay*, a contemporary account cut and pasted from Phillip's despatches, described the convicts as 'regular, humble, and in all respects suitable to their situation'. Watkin Tench, a young captain of the marines, wrote in his journal that during the two months spent at anchor after their rendezvous at the Motherbank 'the ships were universally healthy and the prisoners in high spirits. Few complaints or lamentations were to be heard among them and an ardent wish for the hour of departure seemed generally to prevail.'

Tench had the 'tiresome and disagreeable' duty of inspecting all the letters written to or from his charges. He found it a heavy burden but centuries on he provides a useful glimpse into those hearts and minds held shackled and mute in the darkness below decks. The great number of letters surprised him, and though the tone varied 'according to the dispositions of the writers' they all worried about 'the impracticability of returning home, the dread of a sickly passage and the fearful prospect of a distant and barbarous country'. Tench, a sympathetic observer of human frailty, was certain that this 'apparent despondency proceeded in few instances from sentiment. With too many,' he argued 'it was, doubtless, an artifice to awaken compassion and call forth relief, the correspondence invariably ending in a petition for money and tobacco.'

The arc of these lives, over 1000 convicts and their keepers, had been entirely deflected from their normal course on 18 August 1786, when the Home Secretary Lord Sydney wrote to the Treasury authorising the first unsteady steps on a journey to the far side of the world. While Sydney's memo formally set the creaky wooden engines of state to work on founding a jail within the harbour which would bear his name, history had channelled events towards that point many years earlier. When George Washington and crew kicked King George III's worthless royal butt out of North America they not only fathered the United States but also became distant uncles to Australia. No longer able to export its criminal classes to the American colonies, the British government annexed a whole continent for a prison.

Some writers have tried to decode a secret history within the white settlement of Australia, peering beyond the cover story to discern deeply buried strategic agendas: a bid to deny the French a stranglehold over the Pacific, a supply base for pine and flax, a naval station to harass the Spanish off South America. In writing to request the East India Company's help in mounting the First Fleet, Lord Sydney did say the colony would help prevent the emigration of other European powers to the area, an occasion 'which would be attended with infinite prejudices to the Company's affairs'. But whilst some strategic, military and commercial considerations no doubt played upon the minds of those planning the colony, a stone cold fact remains at the heart of any retrospective embroidery: the city was not established as a military stronghold or a commercial depot but as a far flung desolate jail.

The involvement of the insanely powerful East India Company –

The Long Goodbye

the Microsoft of its day – was not unusual. No permanent naval body was ever created to manage the business of convict transportation to Australia. The government contracted out each convoy and shipment to private enterprise, the rationale being that commercial vessels could dump their human cargo then pick up a paying consignment of tradeable goods such as tea or spices on the way home, offsetting the cost of a global journey. Thus, when the government first settled on the idea of unloading its surplus criminal population they approached the directors of the East India Company to tender for the job. The company was certainly large enough to handle the assignment and its charter seemed to indicate that New South Wales fell within the territory ceded to it anyway. On 19 September 1786, they accepted the First Fleet contract.

The fleet initially consisted of ten vessels: two warships, the *Sirius* on which the commander's flag flew and *Supply*, an armed tender; five prison ships: *Alexander*, *Charlotte*, *Friendship*, *Scarborough* and the slow-moving, clumsy *Lady Penrhyn*; and three freighters, *Borrowdale*, *Fishburn* and *Golden Grove* to carry the bulk of the colonists' stores and provisions. Another convict transport, the *Prince of Wales*, with its consignment of forty-nine females and one lone, lucky captive male – a burglar named George Youngson – was added later.

These ships were no wind driven racing chariots. They were young, strong vessels – three were launched in 1786, the year the fleet was conceived – but they were nothing like the sleek, fast clippers which ran between Portsmouth and Sydney in later years. They were small, tiny in fact, given the scale of the undertaking. *Alexander*, the largest, measured just over thirty-four metres in length and nine across. And that was an extreme measurement which overstated the actual space available to her passengers.

LEVIATHAN

Supply, the minnow of the fleet, stretched all the way out to twenty-one metres, confining her travellers to a space little bigger than a cricket pitch. Blunt-nosed, fat-bellied and flat-bottomed, the fleet ships would wallow in the high seas like hapless wooden whales.

Into their holds went convicts, marines, officers, seamen, wives and children along with the food, stores and equipment needed to sustain so many lives for two years. Phillip did not think the months spent at anchor taking on these supplies excessive, and indeed when he gave the signal to weigh anchor and lay on sail for the great unknown, there were still serious shortfalls in the inventory – notably, adequate clothing for the female prisoners and ammunition for the marines. That there were such shortfalls should not be surprising. The ships were already crammed to bursting point. From dawn until dusk, for week after week, convoys of heavily laden ferries and barges had trawled back and forth to service them as they lay off Portsmouth, settling lower and lower into the water. Jammed up hard against the human travellers were scores of penned animals, sheep, pigs, chickens and geese. Those passengers with the freedom to move around had to squeeze past forty-five tonnes of tallow, eight hundred sets of bedding, hundreds of boxes of seeds, ten blacksmiths' forges, seven hundred steel spades, seven hundred iron shovels, seven hundred garden hoes, seven hundred felling axes and two hundred canvas beds. Dozens of scythes for hacking through weeds and wheat were hauled over the sides with dozens of razors for scraping off stubble. Beef, bread, potatoes and pease porridge came on board with coal, tents, boots and bayonets. Ten thousand bricks, eight thousand fish hooks and three quarters of a million nails were packed in tight with thousands of boxes and bags of sundry items.

The Long Goodbye

The claustrophobic crush was made worse by the renovations carried out to turn mercantile traders into secure, sea-going prisons. Philip Gidley King, second lieutenant of the *Sirius* and later a governor of the colony described the security. Very strong, thick wooden walls, studded with nails and punctuated by loopholes to fire through in case of 'irregularities', were run across the lower decks behind the mainmast. The hatches were secured by crossbars, bolts and heavy oak stanchions. Above, in the fresh air, a wooden barricade about a metre high 'armed with pointed prongs of Iron', divided the soldiers and ship's company from the convicts. Sentinels and armed guards hovered around hatchways and up on the quarterdeck to 'guard against any surprise'. Watkin Tench reported that as the convicts were embarked the opportunity was taken 'to convince them in the most pointed terms that any attempt on their side either to contest the command or to force their escape should be punished with instant death'. Cannons loaded with grapeshot and pointed down the hatchways into the prisoners' quarters backed up the stern words.

In spite of all this, a rough sort of egalitarianism prevailed. The convicts may have been manacled to each other below decks, but by some measures the marines were little better off. In mid-April their commandant, Major Ross, wrote of grave concerns for his troops aboard the *Alexander*, many of whom were afflicted with a terrible illness. The trouble, thought Ross, lay with their quarters, which were located beneath the seamen's, thereby cutting them off from any fresh air. Their berths were suitable only for storing provisions, he wrote. They lived in a funk 'rendered putrid' long before they breathed it in. Apparently even convicts couldn't be stashed away down there. During the last week and a half in March the ship was evacuated and cleaned out.

LEVIATHAN

On 7 May, when Phillip arrived from London keen expectation swept through the assembly whose enthusiasm had been blunted by previous delays. Officers and common men bent themselves to their tasks with renewed vigour. But when at last, on the morning of 12 May, the fleet commander ran up the flags to signal departure, nothing happened. The ships' masters had withheld many months' pay from their men, hoping to gouge them with inflated prices for supplies bought from ships' stores whilst at sea. A day was lost sorting out the dispute, with some of the men being put ashore. At three in the morning the next day, Phillip tried again. This time the sailors followed the signal flags aloft. Their shouts mingled with the rumble of unfurling canvas and, escorted by the frigate *Hyena*, the eleven groaning wooden buckets with their burden of outlaw pilgrims dipped their bows to the waters of the Solent and began to crawl slowly into the west.

John Hunter, Phillip's second-in-command, reported light breezes and fair pleasant weather through the Channel but was mortified to discover that two of the transports sailed 'exceedingly bad'; one of them, the *Charlotte*, had to be towed by *Hyena*. Watkin Tench, finding no comfort in his own thoughts, took a midmorning stroll down past the *Charlotte*'s barricades to see how the convicts were faring. With most 'their countenances indicated a high degree of satisfaction, though in some the pang of being severed, perhaps forever, from their native land could not be wholly suppressed'. He found the men affected more badly than the women, only one of whom appeared upset. Borrowing from *Paradise Lost*, another tale of man's fall from grace and journey into banishment, he wrote: 'Some natural tears she dropp'd, but wip'd them soon'.

Good weather and a change of scene, however, soon brought

The Long Goodbye

forth some cheer and acceptance of 'a lot not now to be altered', according to Tench. Adding to the lighter mood came an order from the *Sirius* that the convicts' chains be struck off. Tench took great pleasure in extending 'this humane order' to all the prisoners under his control. In the evening of that same day, with a high sea running so strongly that Phillip, a very salty old sea dog, could not even sit properly at his table to write, the *Hyena*'s crew gave three cheers and withdrew from the convoy carrying some hastily scrawled dispatches.

One of these letters briefly mentioned an attempted mutiny on board the *Scarborough*. Apparently the marines' stern warnings backed up by cannon and bayonet hadn't been enough to dissuade some of the convicts from attempting a revolt. Hunter thought that Phillip's order to strike off the convicts' fetters may have encouraged them. A number of prisoners on the *Scarborough* had hoped to overpower their guards and sneak away from the fleet at night. Given away by a snitch, two ringleaders were taken aboard the *Sirius*, severely flogged and returned to heavy irons. It was the first major excitement of the voyage, although there had already been some minor personal dramas.

Two days after the Isle of Wight fell away beneath the horizon, a marine corporal named Baker took a loaded musket from an arms locker and laid it down for inspection. The gun discharged, firing its ball through his right ankle. The bullet shattered the bones and deflected with enough force to carry on through a cask full of beef and two geese on the other side of it. The geese did not make it to Australia but Baker recovered, returning to duty with full use of the joint just three months later. It was a small, slightly ridiculous harbinger of the dangers and mishaps which lay in ambush over the next eight-and-a-half months.

LEVIATHAN

Some like Ishmael Coleman, went quietly into their good night. Fleet Surgeon John White reported that eight days after *Hyena* had peeled away, Coleman 'departed this life . . . worn out by lowness of spirits and debility, brought on by long and close confinement'. The surgeon recorded that the patient resigned his last breath 'without a pang'. Others were not so fortunate. Jane Bonner, a convict on the *Prince of Wales*, was crushed by a longboat which rolled from its booms and jammed her 'in a most shocking manner' against the side of the ship. She lingered in agony through the night, dying before White could reach her. Thomas Brown, 'a very well-behaved convict' by White's own testimony, fell from a bowsprit where he had been hanging washing. The *Charlotte* hove to at once and *Supply*, realising what had happened, bore down as well. But Brown disappeared before help could reach him. Crewmen on the forecastle who saw the accident said the ship ran him down. White's journal is replete with such mishaps, but not all of the victims were innocent. On New Year's Day, with landfall in Australia less than a month away, the boatswain on the *Fishburn* climbed aloft with a head full of grog. The ship was labouring in heavy, chaotic seas and inevitably the fool toppled from high up in the rigging and 'bruised himself in a dreadful manner'. Already suffering badly from scurvy, his wounds soon mortified, and he died about half an hour after White clambered over the side to attend him.

Diseases such as scurvy and dysentery were much more of a threat to the wellbeing of the convict ships than drownings, shipwreck or accident. Most of those committed to the deep between Portsmouth and Sydney were simply devoured by sickness. Surgeons were constantly scanning their charges for any sign of illness. Sometimes an outbreak was entirely avoidable as when, in mid-July after crossing the equator, several mariners and convicts

The Long Goodbye

aboard the *Alexander* suddenly took ill. White climbed into the *Charlotte*'s rowboat and made another of his many difficult shuttle visits, immediately discovering where the problem lay: the ship's bilge water. A filthy toxic swill of human waste, rotting food, decaying animals and sea water sloshing around in the lowest parts of the vessel, it had risen high enough to lap over into the living areas. So poisonous was the atmosphere below deck that it turned the brass buttons on the officers' tunics black, and when the hatches were taken off the stench was so powerful the seamen reared back in disgust, scarcely able to stand over them.

The privations of a long sea journey in the late eighteenth century, the fierce environment, the cramped, primitive conditions and the crude nature of medical science all conspired to kill off large numbers of unhealthy travellers. The First Fleet, however, had an excellent health and safety record in comparison with later convoys. The Second Fleet, for instance, lost hundreds of their male passengers en route and more again in the months following their arrival in Sydney. The hot, dark wet weeks spent traversing the equatorial Atlantic were some of the worst, dreaded by medical staff. Wrote White:

Every attention was … paid to the people on board the *Charlotte* and every exertion used to keep her clean and wholesome between decks. My first care was to keep the men, as far as was consistent with the regular discharge of their duty, out of the rain; and I never suffered the convicts to come upon deck when it rained, as they had neither linen nor clothing sufficient to make themselves dry and comfortable after getting wet: a line of conduct which cannot be too strictly observed, and enforced, in those latitudes.

Even in the best maintained vessels the atmosphere below decks was still humid and awful. Despite his efforts Surgeon White was called on a number of times to put down eruptions of fever and diarrhoea. One epidemic which appeared a month before Christmas carried off Daniel Cresswell, a marine, who suffered the most acute, agonising pain White had ever witnessed.

In some ways the First Fleet women were in a worse position than the men. Their irrepressible sexuality and the grim prudishness of their masters meant they were boxed up at night in even the hottest climes. At one point White describes an evening rumbling with distant thunder 'and the most vivid flashes of lightning I ever remember'. The weather was so hot that the female convicts, 'perfectly overcome by it, frequently fainted away; and these faintings generally terminated in fits'. Unfortunately for the women, the fleet's commanders took such a dim view of 'the warmth of their constitutions' and 'the depravity of their hearts' that the hatches over their bunks remained battened down through the night lest they make their way to the seamen's quarters to take their warm, depraved hearts' delight. Their desire to be with the men was so strong that neither shame – considered a negligible modifier in matters of erotic hunger amongst the lower orders – nor the fear of punishment – somewhat more effective – could deter them.

Not that White could talk. Like many of his peers he enjoyed the indulgence of a breathtaking double standard. As Aveling points out, it wasn't the sexual activity of the women which offended the officers. It was their lack of 'deference'. Most of the officers took a mistress from among the 'clean' and 'well behaved' females and a selling point of White's journal was the detail provided of the sexual escapades accessible to His Majesty's far flung

The Long Goodbye

officer corps. After docking at Tenerife, a hot dry volcanic island off the north west coast of Africa and the first of three ports of call on the journey, those officers not concerned with restocking the fleet's fresh food and water supply took their liberty in the town. White seems to have been a little unlucky in his wanderings. He testily recorded that the women of the Spanish port were 'so abandoned and shameless' that it would do an injustice to the prostitutes of London 'to say they are like them'. Someone had told him all the women of Tenerife had 'an amorous constitution' and were addicted to 'intrigue', by which White seems to mean semisecret carnal encounters. The sort, that is, which he seems to have gone without.

At Rio de Janeiro, the next port, thousands of miles south and across the other side of the Atlantic, White mentions the flogging of Cornelius Connell, a private in the marines, 'for having an improper intercourse with some of the female convicts'. Shortly afterwards he regales us with his trip to a festival on shore, a noisy colourful affair at a church. A band 'exerted themselves with might and main to please the surrounding audience'. Fireworks and rockets concluded the evening at about ten o'clock, after which White speculated, 'some intrigues' followed. Both he and Watkin Tench acted on the advice of Daniel Solander, a naturalist on Cook's voyage, who wrote that Rio women exposed themselves at their doors and windows as soon as it became dark, 'distinguishing, by presents of nosegays and flowers, those on whom they had no objection to bestow their favours'. Walking through the town each night, White and Tench waited for the flowers and the favours to descend. Sadly it was not to be. Tench retained his humour at being misled by Solander's tale. 'We were so deplorably unfortunate as to walk every evening before their windows and balconies without being honoured with a single bouquet,' he wrote, 'though nymphs and flowers were in equal and great abundance'. White meanwhile spent more time describing the *señoritas* than the port itself. The sense of a slightly desperate, long deprived sailor stepping ashore with a whole lot of loving to give comes through strongly in his narrative.

The women, when young, are remarkably thin, pale, and delicately shaped; but after marriage they generally incline to be lusty, without losing that constitutional pale, or rather sallow, appearance. They have regular and better teeth than are usually observable in warm climates, where sweet productions are plentiful. They have likewise the most lovely, piercing, dark eyes, in the captivating use of which they are by no means unskilled.

He was particularly taken with the local women's fashion of growing their thick, black hair to prodigious length. They wore it plaited and tied up in a kind of club or large lump, which did not complement their delicate and feminine appearance, according to White. However, he did convince a local gentleman he was visiting to have his wife untie her braids which cascaded down and dragged upon the floor as she walked. White offered his services to tie them up again and the mind boggles at the effect on this randy old goat as he ran his gnarled hands through the lengths of sweet, thick, lustrous femininity after months at sea. One can only hope that for the sake of the Royal Navy's honour he kept any excitement to himself.

Whilst at Rio the convicts were strengthened with a daily serve of rice, fresh meat and a generous allowance of vegetables. The tropical port also abounded in fresh oranges, an unbelievable

The Long Goodbye

luxury for the outcasts of London's slums and an excellent defence against scurvy. Phillip took the opportunity to make up his inventory shortfall by purchasing extra musket balls for the marines and one hundred sacks of tapioca which came in tough, coarse burlap bags. Just the thing for the female convicts to wear as their own clothing rapidly disintegrated.

At least one convict, Thomas Barrett, demonstrated similar enterprise, minting his own coins below decks and passing them off on unsuspecting Brazilian slaves as legal tender. Barrett, given ninety-nine years for absconding from a previous sentence of transportation, had somehow rigged up a coin press in the bowels of the *Charlotte*. A genuine alchemist, he had turned some old buckles, buttons and pewter spoons into quarter dollars. The finished work was so authentic that had his raw materials been superior, he could have minted himself a fortune. This ingenuity extended beyond counterfeiting to subterfuge. A painstaking search failed to find any trace of his coin press and the officers were left to ponder how Barrett and his accomplices had pulled it off as they were never allowed near a fire, a guard constantly watched over their hatchway and officers walked through the area every ten minutes or so. White was so impressed by their 'cunning, caution, and address' he could only wish 'these qualities had been employed to more laudable purposes'. Some evidence of collusion with their overseers came later in the month when a marine received 200 lashes for trying to pass off one of the fake coins on shore.

The fleet departed Rio on 4 September, arriving in Table Bay, Cape Town, on 13 October. Phillip reported a 'prosperous course' which carried them to the edge of European culture without 'any extraordinary incidents'. Of course the ghost of poor Thomas

Brown who went to hang out his washing and never came back, might disagree. In contrast with the sensual *carnivale* of Rio, the dusty, drought-locked Dutch settlement at the hard southern nub of Africa presented a threadbare farewell to civilization. But a farewell it was. David Collins, the colony's first law officer, admitted to a melancholy reflection on the prospect before them – the abandonment of polite society for the world of savages. Who knew for how long? Years at the very least. All communication with families and friends now unalterably cut off, they sailed into a state unknown and ominous. Their decks and holds were packed even tighter than when they had left Portsmouth. The hard bargaining Dutch, who had initially expressed fears of being unable to supply the English because of a recent famine, eventually produced the desired plants, seed and livestock at a grossly inflated price.

On board the *Sirius* John Hunter took note of his extra passengers: six cows with calf, two bulls and numerous sheep, goats, hogs and poultry. Throughout the remaining ships no less than 500 animals had been squeezed on – rams, stallions, mares and colts – creating a vision which 'excited the idea of Noah's ark'. Cramped passageways were blocked by sacks and barrels of seed and plants, the first wave of a botanical invasion to complement the white man's conquest of Australia: cotton bushes, coffee and banana trees, oranges, lemons and guava, tamarind, prickly pear, bamboo, Spanish reed, sugarcane, grapevines and apple trees, pear trees, strawberry, oak and myrtle. If these preparations were not enough to impress upon the travellers' minds the fundamental nature of the void which loomed, on the evening of their first day out of Cape Town a ship from London passed. For Collins, this last chance encounter with an agent of their native country, 'its pleasures, its wealth and its consequence', presented a striking contrast

The Long Goodbye

to the destiny which rolled towards them on the precipitous blue waves of the southern Indian Ocean.

A week of gales and monstrous seas welcomed the adventurers to the underside of the globe. The livestock taken on in Cape Town were so unnerved by the violent roll and pitch of their new world that Hunter feared they would perish long before wobbling ashore in New South Wales. Suggestions to sling them in harnesses, to let them ride out the wild buffeting in a sort of bovine hammock, were dismissed because of a fear their legs would atrophy from lack of exercise. The animals were not the only ones suffering. Hardened sailors who had spent their lives fighting the cruel seas of the North Atlantic could not have seen waters so uniformly huge and unremitting as those they sailed into from Africa. In that part of the world – a massive band of deep ocean circling the planet between the latitudes 40° and 60° south – dry land accounts for but three percent of the earth's surface. The howling westerly winds which blow all year round pick up great volumes of water and push them along at staggering speeds for thousands of kilometres. A tiny vessel like *Supply*, struggling up the windward slope of one of those immense, cobalt blue rollers, would have been like a child's toy set on the side of a hill. With dense streaks of foam breaking and streaming along in the wind, with the crests of other waves tumbling and toppling and spinning away, with yawning black chasms opening up in the waters all around, it was not uncommon for the seamen on one vessel to lose sight of nearby ships, hidden behind roiling towers of salt water. Sometimes a ship would tip over a crest, skiing down the black face of the wave which would then detonate right over it, sending roaring geysers down through the ships' innards, washing marine, convict and officer, and man, woman and child alike from their beds.

LEVIATHAN

Wrestling these seas twelve days out of Cape Town, with the fever which did for Daniel Cresswell running hot through his shipmates, Phillip decided to transfer command from the *Sirius* to the hardier, faster *Supply*. He had carpenters, sawyers and blacksmiths transferred to the best ships in the fleet – *Supply, Alexander, Scarborough* and *Friendship* – and ordering the other vessels to follow him, split the convoy in two. His own leading detachment was expected to arrive at least a fortnight earlier and prepare a landing site. John Hunter, who could still see *Supply* a day later, took the slower, wallowing whales south with *Sirius* where they picked up even stronger winds and a large following sea to unknowingly keep pace with the fast squadron.

On 9 January 1788, with the gloomy mist shrouded forests of Van Dieman's Land hiding somewhere off the port bow, Edward Johnson, once of Dorset, paid the ultimate price for the ill-conceived act of larceny which had seen him sentenced to transportation. On a dark hazy day assailed with random, contrary winds, Johnson, 'worn out with a melancholy and long confinement' simply closed his eyes and expired. White, who attended him, thought it a pity 'as he seemed sensible of the impropriety and imprudence of his former life, and studious to atone for it'. A day later the sea threw one last trial at Johnson's surviving companions. A sudden violent white squall blew up from nowhere, ripping the *Charlotte*'s mainsail like tissue paper and carrying off the *Prince of Wales*'s mainyard.

The tag end of the First Fleet was spared any further excitement and ten days later they swung left into Botany Bay, where Phillip had only just preceded them. A voyage of mythic stature was over. Eleven vessels, thrown over 24 000 kilometres of poorly charted, angry seas to lodge upon the fringe of an invisible, fantastic land.

The Long Goodbye

Even with the tremendous task in front of them many of the First Fleet diarists still had time to marvel at their fortune. Although so many had started the voyage sick and undernourished, only a small fraction had been cut away by death. No ships had been lost, contrary to expectation. Gazing at the drab, unpromising shores which encircled their battered armada, they were right to give thanks. But they were the only ones doing so. Collins noted that as Phillip moved along the coast towards Port Jackson and the founding of Sydney, 'the natives everywhere greeted the little fleet with shouts of defiance and prohibition'; the words *warra warra* – go away, go away – resounding wherever they appeared.

The first white man officially acknowledged as being killed by native Australians was Peter Burn, transported for stealing a thirty-six gallon barrel of beer. The thirst which cost him his liberty lost him his life four months after he arrived in New South Wales. Burn and another convict, William Ayres, had wandered away from the main camp late in the day looking to gather sarsaparilla herb, a common substitute for tea and coffee in the starving, isolated settlement. They walked around to Woolloomooloo Bay, then a broad shallow valley drained by a fresh-water creek, and cut off from the camp by the hilly terrain and wild scrub. When the natives attacked, Burn and Ayres might as well have been a thousand miles from help.

Ayres crawled back to the Cove after nightfall and was carried into the hospital with a barbed spear thrust deep into the flesh between his shoulder blades. Burn had abandoned him, running off after he'd been hit. The natives quickly surrounded Ayres and stripped him. Burn meanwhile did not get far. Wounded, bleeding and terrified, Ayres saw him captured a short distance away. The war party were dragging him off, kicking and screaming, his head already bashed and pulped. His clothes were discovered a few days later, torn and rent by spears, tacky with dried blood.

A week later two more convicts were killed in the same area. The whites were not of one mind about who to blame. Phillip wrote to Lord Sydney that he had not 'the least doubt of the convicts being the aggressors'. Judge Advocate David Collins, however, thought Burn 'had fallen a sacrifice to his own folly and the barbarity of the natives'. The colony was lucky to have in Phillip a restrained leader, acutely aware of the balance of power between white and black in the earliest days. Frequently marching out to treat with the natives, he knew the chances of his own community surviving would be limited without the Aborigines' tolerance. The marines, with their musketry, drill and brightly coloured uniforms were no match for the Iora's bush skills and spears. As Robert Hughes points out, a proficient warrior could put four spears into a soldier in the time it would take the white man to fire off one ball and reload. By December 1790 seventeen Englishmen had been killed or wounded in attacks by Aborigines, none of whom had been captured or killed in return.

Phillip himself was speared in a botched encounter at Manly Cove, although his liberal policy was not affected by the incident. He understood that the man who speared him acted in self-defence, assuming as Phillip advanced on him with his open upturned palms that he was about to be snatched up and carried away. In the Governor's opinion most of the native violence involved either misunderstanding or justifiable retaliation. For instance, the convicts were in the habit of stealing the Aborigines' canoes and spears, making it necessary for Phillip to publish decrees, enforceable

The Long Goodbye

under pain of death, to stop his people from interfering with the locals. He explicitly banned any revenge raids on Iora camps and, recognising their prior claims over the land's resources, ordered that fishermen encountering any Aborigines on the harbour should hand over a portion of their catch.

However, when his gamekeeper McEntire was killed, Phillip finally authorised a large posse to track down those responsible. McEntire had trekked over to Botany Bay with two other convicts and a sergeant of the marines, hunting kangaroos to restock the colony's depleted larder. They bashed out through the scrub along the northern arm of the bay, making camp at a small hut recently erected on the peninsula for just this purpose. A rustling noise in the bushes awoke the sergeant with a start around one in the morning. Assuming some kangaroos had wandered up close, he called to the others, who quickly roused themselves. Peering into the obsidian blackness of the Australian night, they were alarmed to spy five natives advancing on them with spears at the ready. McEntire, who was more familiar with the bush and its indigenes than his companions said, 'Don't be afraid, I know them'. He laid down his rifle, stepped forward and spoke in their language. They began to withdraw, McEntire following and chatting as he went. Then, without warning, one of the 'Indians', as the colonists then called them, leapt onto a fallen tree and loosed his spear at the advancing white man. It pierced his chest with a sick wet crunch, the barbed wooden head driving hard between two ribs and puncturing the left lung. Prematurely but presciently McEntire cried out, 'I am a dead man!'

He staggered back to the hut, where someone broke off the protruding shaft while the others chased his attackers. The Indians, however, were too swift, too agile and too much at home in their own world and their pursuers soon gave up the trail. McEntire, awash with his life's blood, begged them not to let him die in the woods. A large, muscular type, he dragged himself back to Sydney where the surgeons could only tell him that yes, he was a dead man. Watkin Tench, who would soon be appointed to lead a revenge party, described the change which came over the once fearsome gamekeeper as he received the news.

The poor wretch now began to utter the most dreadful exclamations and to accuse himself of the commission of crimes of the deepest dye, accompanied with such expressions of his despair of God's mercy as are too terrible to repeat.

As he lingered on the tables of the rugged camp hospital for the next three days a number of Aborigines made their way in to see him. They seemed to know what had happened and when surgeons made signs of extracting the spearhead, still lodged tightly in the swollen, supperating wound, they gestured violently. Death would quickly follow any attempt at removal. The medical staff demurred, and on 12 December they removed the spear's head. Out came a large wooden barb with several smaller stone spikes fastened on with yellow gum. However most of the spikes tore free with the force of extraction and remained embedded in the gamekeeper's flesh. This primitive surgery did not really help. McEntire had already seen his last Christmas and on 20 December he died.

Governor Phillip ordered a patrol of fifty marines to kit up and search out the tribe from which the murderer hailed. At the same time he expressly forbade any unauthorised attacks on the Aborigines. He called in Tench and tasked him with a three-day march 'to bring in six of those natives who reside near the head of Botany

The Long Goodbye

Bay; or, if that should be found impracticable, to put that number to death'. Tench had wrangled the body count down. Originally the young captain was to execute ten and bring more back as prisoners. They 'were to cut off and bring in the heads of the slain; for which purpose hatchets and bags would be furnished'. But no signs of friendship or invitation were to be used to lure the victims into a trap. Phillip thought such conduct treacherous, giving the natives reason to distrust the English in the future. So it was to be an honest, straightforward killing, a thoroughly British massacre. Phillip explained to Tench his reasons for ordering the strike; seventeen colonists had been killed or wounded by the natives; he thought the Bideegal tribe to be the principal aggressors and he was determined to strike a decisive blow, to convince them of English superiority 'and to infuse an universal terror, which might operate to prevent further mischief'. His observations of the natives had led him to conclude that although they did not fear death individually, a tribe found its strength and security in its numbers; hence the necessity of decimating the whole rather than just punishing the individual. Phillip told his subordinate he had long held off violent measures, believing that in every former instance of hostility the Aborigines had acted out of misunderstanding or in retaliation.

'To the latter of these causes,' said Phillip, 'I attribute my own wound, but in this business of McEntire, I am fully persuaded that they were unprovoked, and the barbarity of their conduct admits of no extenuation.'

Tench, on being asked whether he saw any way around the impending action inquired whether, instead of destroying ten people, the capture of six might suffice, 'as out of this number, a part might be set aside for retaliation' and the rest released some time later to spread the word. Phillip agreed, adding that if six couldn't be taken, Tench should ensure that number were shot.

Thus at four in the morning on 14 December, Watkin Tench strode to the head of a column consisting of another captain, two lieutenants, two surgeons, three sergeants, three corporals and forty enlisted men. Loaded down with heavy packs, canteens, bayonets and firearms clanking in the dawn and clouds of dust billowing up around their boots, they clomped south; a 'terrific procession' Tench called it, neatly anticipating the clumsy, impotent lunge of another technologically advanced but hopelessly misplaced army in the jungles of Vietnam a hundred and seventy years later. Reading Tench's caustic, self-aware narrative of the hunt for McEntire's killers, it is hard to shake a sense of strange familiarity, some exotic kin to deja vu as the lost patrol drags itself through an unpleasant alien landscape suddenly devoid of all sign of the enemy, in fact of all sign of life. The soil was shallow and sandy, 'and its productions meagre and wretched'. When forced to quit the sand, they had to drag themselves through deep crevices and 'clamber over rocks unrefreshed by streams and unmarked by diversity'. Tench wrote that by nine o'clock they had reached the peninsula at the head of Botany Bay, 'but after having walked in various directions until four o'clock in the afternoon, without seeing a native', they halted for the night, exhausted.

Come daylight the British stretched stiff, aching limbs, noisily emptied their bladders, hauled their packs up from the ground and started out again, marching into the morning sun, hoping to make the south-west arm of the bay, about five kilometres from its mouth. Tench was going to rake over the area then sweep around to the northern arm to complete the search. Unfortunately the guides were off and at half past seven they suddenly came upon the shore at the head of the peninsula, between the two arms. Five Indians were gathered about the shore and the troopers moved quickly to surround them. In vain, however, as

> ... they penetrated our design, and before we could get near enough ... ran off. We pursued; but a contest between heavy-armed Europeans fettered by ligatures, and naked unencumbered Indians, was too unequal to last long. They darted into the wood and disappeared.

The alarm being given, they moved rapidly to a little village of five huts which stood nearby. Before they could reach it, however, three canoes filled with Aborigines were seen paddling with great haste to the opposite shore. Exhausted and sweating, the avengers could only search the huts for 'weapons of war'. They found none. Knowing the chances of surprising anybody were gone, at least for that day, Tench ordered the men to return to their baggage. After a rest they marched for two hours in the afternoon, finally camping at a swamp. Wasted by fatigue and heat they settled down for the night but found no real respite as black clouds of mosquitoes and sandflies fell on them. They hauled themselves back into Sydney the following day.

Phillip ordered them out again, this time at night. Hoping to fool the natives, they pretended to prepare a raid on Broken Bay to capture the man who had thrown a spear at the Governor a little earlier. They marched out under a full moon three days before Christmas, proceeding to the river they had waded through on the return leg of the last mission. The tide forced a halt to any advance until quarter past two in the morning. Dropping all their equipment except firearms and ammo boxes – which they tied fast on top of their heads – they waded across. Six short men and one sergeant, 'who from their low stature and other causes were most likely to impede our march', were left to guard the equipment train.

Tench ordered the guides to move out as quickly as possible, without regard for terrain. They hurried alongside the river for three quarters of an hour, suddenly stopping by a creek about fifty metres wide 'which extended to our right and appeared dry from the tide being out'. Tench consulted the guides, asking whether the bed could be crossed safely, or whether it might be better to walk around the head of the water course, a few hundred metres away. The guides indicated it would be a dangerous crossing but feasible. And so Tench's second expedition teetered on the edge of disaster. Pressed for time, he ordered his men over. Within a few minutes they began to sink into the creek bed.

We were immersed nearly to the waist in mud so thick and tenacious that it was not without the most vigorous exertion of every muscle of the body that the legs could be disengaged. When we had reached the middle, our distress became not only more pressing but serious, and each succeeding step buried us deeper. At length a sergeant of grenadiers stuck fast, and declared himself incapable of moving either forward or backward; and just after, Ensign Prentice and I felt ourselves in a similar predicament, close together.

Men cried out in distress all around. Tench did not know what to do. With every moment the danger increased. Luckily, those at the rear of the column, warned by the soldier's shouts, moved towards the head of the creek and passed over safely.

The Long Goodbye

Our distress would have terminated fatally had not a soldier cried out to those on shore to cut boughs of trees and throw them to us – a lucky thought which certainly saved many of us from perishing miserably; and even with this assistance, had we been burdened by our knapsacks, we could not have emerged; for it employed us near half an hour to disentangle some of our number. The sergeant of grenadiers, in particular, was sunk to his breastbone, and so firmly fixed in that the efforts of many men were required to extricate him, which was effected in the moment after I had ordered one of the ropes, destined to bind the captive Indians, to be fastened under his arms.

Congratulating each other on a close escape, the soldiers cleaned their rifles of mud, formed up and pushed on. They found themselves a few hundred metres from the village half an hour before sunrise. Tench split the command into three squads and ordered them to charge the settlement in perfect silence. Despite the long, tiring march through the dark and the terrifying episode at the creek bed, the marines executed his design perfectly, converging on the village from three different directions at exactly the same moment. 'To our astonishment, however,' wrote Tench, 'we found not a single native at the huts; nor was a canoe to be seen on any part of the bay.'

At first he thought they had arrived perhaps thirty minutes too late. But the camp fires were cold and no fresh food could be found. The natives, Tench concluded, had decamped a number of days earlier and had not returned. Another abject failure. Tench considered letting his disappointed men refresh themselves with a swim, but the tide was turning and if they did not leave immediately, they would be cut off from their baggage and with it food and water. Alternately running and walking, they made the creek in time, but it was hard on the men, several of whom simply collapsed and refused to go on, a telling indication of their weariness, considering the savage discipline of the British army in those days. Tench, no martinet, was mindful of their plight. He was sorry that all he could do 'for these poor fellows was to order their comrades to carry their muskets, and to leave with them a small party of those men who were least exhausted, to assist them and hurry them on'.

They rested through the heat of the day, continuing their mission at four in the afternoon. They marched until sunset, seeing no natives, only miles of 'high coarse rushes, growing in a rotten spongy bog, into which [they] plunged knee-deep at every step'. One final push, in the wee hours of the next day, ended like all the others in failure and despair. Come nine in the morning they turned north to Sydney. While McEntire's killers were not caught, the tired bitter men of Tench's patrol did come across a group of black potato thieves on the way back. A sergeant and some privates gave chase and Tench reported that their rage at the previous days' frustrations 'transported them so far that, instead of capturing the offenders, they fired in among them'. Some women were captured but the men escaped.

One of the men, a native called Bangai, was hit, a mortal wound to the shoulder. Surgeon White, on hearing of this, took three Aborigines from Sydney with him to see if he might be able to save the man. But on reaching the spot where he was last reported they were told that he had died and the body was being tended to about a mile off. They found it near a fire, covered in green boughs. The face was hidden behind a thick screen of woven grass and ferns. A strip of bark hung around the neck and a stick had been stripped and bent into an arch over the body. None of the natives who had taken White to the spot would touch the corpse, or even approach it, saying the *mawn* would come; literally that 'the spirit of the deceased would seize them', an ancient belief with some real-world efficacy, although sadly for the first inhabitants of Sydney Harbour they did not understand how much.

The white men who hunted the Aborigines carried a far deadlier weapon than their clumsy, single shot muskets. They stepped down from the weathered wooden decks of their ships with flintlocks and cannons but their blood and tissue were to prove much more efficient at destroying the local community. The British were crawling with viruses and bacteria against which the quarantined natives of the harbour had no defence. The men, women and children who made it across the oceans came bearing a cocktail of smallpox, syphilis, measles, whooping cough and influenza. Bred up through hundreds of years in the filthy, crowded cities of Europe, these invisible attackers fell ravenously upon their new, unprotected hosts.

Smallpox was the mass killer. It was already burning at the edge of the Iora when Tench and his patrol set out for Botany Bay. The English blamed La Perouse and his crew for introducing the fearsome disease, but every European who penetrated the harbour was effectively bearing a death sentence with them. Smallpox was particularly well adapted to its new home. A stable virus which can live outside the body for months in dust or clothing, it has a long incubation period of up to two weeks, during which time the new host is infectious without showing it. A contaminated hunter could travel hundreds of kilometres, meeting others and passing on his gift. The virus cooked up and gathered strength within the warm, dark oven of the victim's organs and, when it was ready, announced itself with a burst of unpleasant symptoms: fever, head-ache, muscle pain, nausea and vomiting.

Taking to his bed, fussed over by the women of the tribe, the hunter would break into a rash two or three days later; a flat spot, or macule, changing into a blister – clear at first – but soon filling with a rich contagious pus. Another week or so and scabs would form and fall off; although at the extremities, the hands and feet by which a hunter lives, they were longer lasting because of the tougher skin. The scabs left ugly scars, or pockmarks, by which the disease is known. However, with no natural immunity to draw on, unable to hunt or gather because of the painful eruptions, and with the tribal structure collapsing around them, the Iora hunters had more to be concerned about than their good looks. They were in the first stage of being annihilated.

By the 1850s a few hundred remained in bands scattered over the entire Sydney plain. A Russian naval officer, Pavel Mukhanov, describing a visit to Sydney in 1863, recounted a meeting with Ricketty Dick, the 'last survivor of the aboriginal tribe who used to be masters of this district'. Mukhanov found him sitting by the road at the gate of a wealthy farm, grunting two or three English words, begging for alms. He was a small brown crippled man with long matted dreadlocks. The Russian thought his every line was imprinted 'with stupidity and hopelessness' and pondered whether nature was right, to condemn 'this pitiful race' to extinction. Echoing the fashionable theories of the time, he predicted that Dick's brothers would soon simply vanish, without explicable cause, leaving in their place a 'strong and vigorous British race'. Mukhanov threw the old beggar a shilling by way of recompense.

The Long Goodbye

We do not have to look so many years ahead of Phillip's time to find evidence of the Aborigines' decline. Their ancient civilization had been thoroughly debased and overcome by the convict state within a few years of the First Fleet's arrival. It often took the unbiased eye of a foreigner such as Mukhanov to bear witness and take note. In April 1792 Judge-Advocate David Collins remarked favourably on the integration of black and white cultures or, more accurately, on the assimilation of the former by the latter. He noted that the natives had not recently launched any hostilities against the settlement and several of their younger people lived in the township, which was visited in turn by their relatives. In 1796 he thought the two races were getting along famously, the 'friendly intercourse ... so earnestly desired' having been established, 'these remote islanders have been shown living in considerable numbers among us without fear or restraint; acquiring our language; readily falling in with our manners and customs; enjoying the comforts of our clothing; and relishing the variety of our food ...'. They had always been their own masters, wrote Collins, and 'by slow degrees we began eventually to be pleased with and to understand each other'.

To throw a less rosy tint on the state of the Iora we have to look to the journals of other Europeans travellers. Men such as the Spanish naval captain Alessandro Malaspina di Mulazzo who berthed in Sydney Cove between March and April 1793. His mission included preparing secret strategic reports on the state of Russian and English settlements in the Pacific. Malaspina saw Sydney primarily as a military threat. Spain, with her South American holdings, still saw the Pacific as her own private lake, and Malaspina thought that by setting up a penal colony the English were gathering a formidable collection of desperadoes who would menace the entire world with their depredations. Some might find that wryly amusing, perhaps even a little cool, but the Spaniard cut much closer to the bone when dissecting the Aborigines' future.

Tranquil inhabitants of its immense shores ... how can you imagine at this moment that the present of a few ribbons and Trinkets, the useless gift of a few domestic animals, and astronomical observations a thousand times repeated, will very soon have brought you to a scene of blood and destruction? You will see your fields laid waste, your huts overrun, your women violated, your very lives snatched away in the flower of their youth and joys, solely to feed new Buccaneers ...

Malaspina had his own blind spot of course – the appalling record of the Spanish in the Americas – but he was right in seeing through Collins' idyll. The peace between the old and new civilizations was a matter of brute power, not cultural refinement. 'They keep generally good harmony with the Europeans,' he wrote, because

... punishment has made them cautious in this regard; there are very few tribes which do not maintain a strict subordination to the English, and the inequality in arms has extinguished or removed the discontented. The mere sight of a musket, the appearance of the uniform of a soldier, would scatter an army of natives, who with signs of peace and submission take pains to capture their goodwill ...

By 1819, when Frenchman Jacques Arago visited Sydney, he was surprised to find a fully grown city 'of admirable design'. It seemed to Arago to have been growing for centuries rather than three short decades. He may have spent a little too much time at sea. His enthusiam for the new city led him to imagine that the 'best architects had deserted Europe and come to New Holland to reproduce their most elegant mansions'. However, the bright march of European architecture stood in contrast to the absence of enlightened human virtue.

Visiting an influential merchant and his family for dinner, Arago was horrified to find the family's young ladies watching a group of Aborigines, all naked and 'presenting all the outward signs of the most revolting misery', drawn up to amuse the colony's new elite with a gladiatorial contest. In Roman style it was to be a fight to the death. Covered with old scars, and armed with spears and clubs, the blacks had already been rewarded for their preliminary 'capers and grimaces' with some glasses of wine and brandy and a few pieces of bread which they still held under their arms. Arago watched with dawning horror as the alcohol took effect on the warriors.

Their gestures soon became more violent and their speech more raucous, all talked at once and all shook their murderous weapons fiercely. Attracted by the uproar the master and the mistress of the house and their guests hurried to the scene and invited me to await the issue of this commotion. I agreed readily, convinced that license could go no further and almost certain that the ladies and girls would leave us alone to enjoy this sight. I was mistaken in my expectation, and on the contrary their light voices stimulated the courage or rather the ferocity of the actors. But when these poor wretches had ended the prelude to their bacchanals, their clubs, swung with greater force and skill, began to fall on nearby fences as though practice were needed to make their aim sure: and these hapless people whose gaeity at first had been so peaceful, at length belaboured each other soundly; two fell dangerously wounded and a third was killed outright. The gins, who until then had taken no part in the action beyond encouraging the combatants, now rose, quietly carried off the victims, perhaps their fathers or their brothers, and disappeared with their burdens.

He marvelled that such a display could take place in the heart of a civilized city with respectable merchants and such elegant, accomplished young ladies as the spectators. But it was not the first such scene he had witnessed. A small inn had laid on similar entertainment for the Spaniards just a few days before. Arago noted that all quarrels seemed to end in such ways for the blacks, but he recognised that this brutality did not come naturally to them. Most often it was the whites who encouraged them with 'bottles of strong drink'.

Scarcely have the fumes mounted to their heads when they breathe battle and utter war cries. They are eager to slay, seeking out antagonists, provoking them by fierce war songs and asking for death in the hope of giving it. They find only too easily the opportunities they provoke, and their war whoops are answered by other whoops no less terrible. Then the combatants, drawn up in two lines about twenty paces apart, begin to threaten each other with their long pointed spears; they are soon throwing them with marvellous skill and force, and finally attack each other with formidable heavy clubs. Limbs are broken, bones crushed, heads split; no cry of pain escapes the breast of these

The Long Goodbye

savage beasts; the air only resounds with frightful
vociferations ...

It was a long fall from the judicious rule of Arthur Phillip. His
lighter hand was stayed by the idea of the noble savage, a notion
which was still working its way through the Age of Reason when
Cook sailed up the east coast and found a race neither civilised
nor corrupted. They may have appeared to his crew 'to be the most
wretched people on Earth, but in reality,' wrote Cook, 'they are
far more happier than we Europeans'. They lived a tranquil existence; everything needed for life was provided in abundance by the
earth and the sea. The fine climate meant they had little need of
clothing and 'they seemed to set no Value upon anything we gave
them, nor would they ever part with any thing of their own for
any one article we could offer them'. After being threatened by a
couple of natives on the shores of Botany Bay, Cook wrote, 'All
they seem'd to want for us was to be gone'. A wise response,
thought the mariner, who challenged anyone to tell him 'what the
Natives of the whole extent of America have gained by the commerce they have had with Europeans'.

Cook was writing at a time when two strains of thought were
contending for the issue; the older, noble view of primitivism; and
what Glyndwr Williams calls the chillier assumptions of the four-
stages theorists who arranged societies in an order dependent on
their form of subsistence, with the Aborigines at the bottom. The
unstoppable advance of European colonialism seemed to confirm
the prejudices of the latter school who saw indigenous societies
around the globe destroyed by white civilization. In the new
rational sciences which sought to explain everything in terms of
the interplay of natural, identifiable forces – and especially in terms

of Darwin's theories of natural selection – nineteenth century Europeans had an armoury of reasons, excuses and justifications for the demise of those civilizations which seemed to shrivel up and die at first contact with their own. This frame of mind certainly informed Mukhanov's journal when he wrote of Australia's black race being displaced by a virile English yeomanry as a natural event. Even Cook's journal, which was not to be published in full for nearly 100 years, was infected by the new thinking. His observations of the Aborigines, previously excised, were first read in 1893 when the editor, a cretinous oaf named Captain Wharton, thought it necessary to remedy Cook's woolly headed liberalism with the following:

> The native Australians may be happy in their condition, but they are without doubt among the lowest of mankind. Confirmed cannibals they lose no opportunity of gratifying their love of human flesh. Mothers will kill and eat their own children ... Internecine war exists between the different tribes [and] ... Their treachery, which is unsurpassed, is simply an outcome of their savage ideas.

Henry Reynolds has identified two approaches to the Aborigines, growing like stunted trees from these intellectual roots: (i) the Aborigines were not human and so could be treated as beasts, and (ii) they were innocent but ignorant and thus the colonists had a humanitarian duty towards them. The latter viewpoint was only slightly more generous. It still encompassed the inevitability of their disappearance, killed off or bred out of existence. It did, however, have one practical consequence: as a comforting theory, denied to whites in America and Africa, it helped defuse, to a certain degree, white antagonism. At no stage, after the first few desperate months were survived, did the transplanted British state think itself mortally or even seriously threatened by the natives. So secure was their hold on the new colony, in fact, that they could indulge themselves in a contented hypocrisy. Governor King wrote about the natives to his successor, the *Bounty*'s William Bligh, in 1806:

> Much has been said about the propriety of their being compelled to work as Slaves, but as I have ever considered them the real Proprietors of the Soil, I have never suffered any restraint whatever on these lines, or suffered any injury to be done to their persons or property.

Of course, King's charitable admission that the Aborigines were the real owners of the land did not survive as official policy.

When Tench and his marines had marched off to Botany Bay, seeking the killers of Phillip's gamekeeper, the young captain had thought them a wonderful sight. In reality of course they were woefully ill-equipped for their search and destroy mission. While their muzzle-loading, Brown Bess muskets were elegant examples of nineteenth century weapons design, the long heavy flintlock rifles were best deployed at very short range by massed ranks of British foot soldiers against massed ranks of hapless Frenchmen on the fields of Europe. They were no good at picking out individual targets over great distances and the soldiers who used them were untrained and poorly outfitted for campaigns of rapid movement through rugged terrain against fleet-footed opponents who melted into the countryside. Even the tight, bright uniforms of which Tench was so inordinately proud acted against the marines, restricting their movements, sapping their energy in the harsh, hot weather and giving early warning of their approach through the drab scenery of the Australian scrub.

Over time, of course, the tactics of the white warriors improved, as did their technology, but the undeclared war against the natives continued long after their dispersal from the Sydney Plain. For many it continues today, the same patterns of conflict repeating and renewing themselves with each generation. Two hundred years after Tench's dawn patrol had left Sydney Cove with hatchets and hessian sacks to bring back the heads of some recalcitrant tribesmen, another group of raiders set out in the bleak hours before sunrise in search of another black man who'd killed one of their own. On Monday 24 April 1989 a young police constable named Alan McQueen had been shot and fatally wounded by an Aboriginal man, John Porter. Recently released on parole from Long Bay Prison where he'd pulled an eight year stretch for armed robbery, Porter was the natural consequence of two centuries of grim work by the white power structure; mad, bad and, as it transpired, genuinely dangerous to know. Porter had fired on the police who'd originally taken him down for armed robbery. When they subdued and searched him they found another gun in his underpants, a knife strapped to his leg, another knife hidden in his car and a shotgun buried in his garden. He was a violent man who drew down on McQueen and blew him away without warning, putting a few holes in his partner Jason Donnelly, a probationary constable trying to get through his first day on the job, for good measure.

Three days later six SWOS teams gathered in the canteen at Redfern Police Station a few minutes shy of four a.m. A list of

The Long Goodbye

some sixteen possible boltholes for Porter had been pared back to six addresses, which were all to be raided by the force's elite paramilitary units on the stroke of six that morning. Each team leader received an envelope with a search warrant, photos of Porter, a map and operational orders. Teams One through Three also had rough sketches of the floor plans for the premises they were to hit. Detective Sergeant Charles Brazel of the Special Weapons and Operations section addressed the assembled officers, telling them not to let their emotions get the better of them and stressing that although they had been assigned to numbered teams each of the targets was equally important. Porter was as likely to be found at any of the half dozen flats and houses and the risks were as great for Team Six as for Team One.

While that may have been the party line, the eight members of Team One, which included Brazel himself, thought differently. They were all permanently attached to SWOS, unlike some of the part-timers in the other squads. They spent all of their time either training for or actually carrying out extremely dangerous missions. Some 'relaxed' off duty in the Army Reserve. The Royal Commission into Black Deaths in Custody described them as the crème de la crème of the Special Ops section. They were assigned to raid an old shop which had been converted into a house at 193 Sydenham Road in Marrickville. It was Brazel's personal understanding that Porter had been hidden by friends at this property after shooting McQueen and Donnelly.

Brazel had formed this opinion after talking to either Graham Watson or Terry Dawson, two other members of Team One. Watson, who would be first through the door later that morning, had joined the force in 1975 and SWOS ten years later. A qualified instructor in the use of weapons and building entry techniques, he had been involved in armed raids at least three times a month during his attachment to SWOS. He thought of Sydenham Road as 'the priority address'. Dawson, a detective sergeant and the third man through the door, had joined the force in 1966. He had also qualified as a SWOS field commander, a marksman and a weapons instructor and he too thought it most likely the fugitive would be found at Sydenham Road.

The other members of Team One agreed. Senior Constable John Rhodes – an expert marksman and anti-hijacking specialist who had effected more than 600 entries over the years and who would go in second after Watson – thought it more likely his unit would encounter the cop killer than any of the others. Senior Constable Graham Bateman, a member and instructor of the Police Assault Group, who charged in behind Sergeant Brazel, did so expecting to confront Porter and possibly any number of armed associates. Behind Bateman came Constable Bruce Marshall, number six through the door and the least experienced police officer. He had joined the force only two years previously, but gave nothing away in ability, having racked up six years of active army service with the SAS and 1 Commando Company. Bringing up the rear were Constables Martin and Whittaker who would be responsible for handcuffing any offenders found inside.

When the Redfern briefing had wrapped up, each team received their tactical kit. Everybody in Team One was fitted out with a bullet-resistant vest, and all, except for the sweepers Martin and Whittaker, also picked up a Remington pump action shotgun with a torch attached to the barrel. Everybody carried handguns, either .357 magnums or 9 mm pistols. Eye goggles, digital radios, a sledgehammer, crowbar, cans of mace and flexicuffs were issued. With twenty minutes to kill before kick-off, Team One drove to the nearby Newtown Police Station. They transferred to a van and moved to the form-up point, a street corner about 200 metres from the house. Just after five a.m. the Central District Ambulance Service was placed on alert. An ambulance officer who asked what sort of injuries they might have to deal with was told 'gunshot wounds'.

Two hundred years had taught the white authorities not to tele-graph their punches. Tench's black quarry had probably known his men were on their way days before they arrived. John Porter too would have known he'd gone to the top of the SWOS hit list the second he pulled a pistol on Alan McQueen. He had been at Sydenham Road a number of times in the previous weeks. But he was not there when Detective Sergeant Brazel's men came calling. The only people resident were an Aboriginal family – David Gundy and his son Bradley Eatts – and two friends, Richard McDonald and Marc Valentine. They slept as Team One left the form-up point and moved down Sydenham Road, an empty school play-ground sliding past the van on the right, a row of small workers' cottages renovated in postwar migrant kitsch on the left. As highly trained, as well equipped, as finely honed a strike force as Team One were, especially compared with Watkin Tench's sorry crew, the outcome of their mission was to be just as disastrous. With one major difference. Whereas Tench's assignment had taken nearly two weeks to break down, the SWOS raid on 193 Syden-ham Road unravelled in less than two minutes. The end result was the same however. One dead Aboriginal man and a further poi-soning of the already treacherous relationship between black and white.

As all six teams formed up around the city, in Marrickville, at Bondi and Petersham, in Summer Hill and Newtown, they radioed in to the command post at the Sydney Police Centre that they were ready. Warrants for the raids had been issued with an entry time of six a.m. However, by ten to six all the teams were in place and three minutes later the CP advised them to move at their own discretion. Team One's van moved off from the street corner by Marrickville High School. It travelled 200 metres, pulled up in front of the old converted shop and disgorged eight armed men into the quiet dawn. Whittaker stood by the door with his sledge-hammer at the ready. The other men, guns cocked, safeties released, formed up around him. Brazel signalled Whittaker who smashed the door open with one blow and Team One poured through the breach yelling, 'Police! Police!' After that there was no set plan. The men's training came to the fore as they adjusted to the layout of the building and the discovery of its various inhabitants. It was dark. The team moved quickly, illumination provided by the crisscrossing shafts of light coming from the torches attached to their shotguns. In the front room, which ran the length of the building, they found McDonald lying on three armchairs which had been pushed together. Watson, first through the door, covered the dazed man with his shotgun, shouting, 'Police! Stay down! Get your hands up!'

Rhodes passed him, charging across the lounge room to a set of two improvised steps in the far corner. He entered a corridor which ran down the left-hand side of the house, and spun into a bedroom where he found another man, Valentine, lying in bed and a small boy, Bradley Eatts, standing alone. Terry Dawson passed him on his way up the hall. Behind him, Brazel made for the kitchen at the rear of the building. The rest of Team One were in the lounge room by now, already handing over their captives to the sweepers. Watson, who had covered McDonald, left him to

The Long Goodbye

Martin. He then made for the rear of the house where Terry Dawson had just kicked open David Gundy's door and moved into the gloomy bedroom.

Gundy had been taken from his family in the early 1960s, shuffling between various institutions and foster parents. He was, unsurprisingly, a troubled child, although his clashes with the law did not extend beyond a few stealing charges. He found work in 1975 and a devoted girlfriend, Dolly Eatts, a year later. Gundy had worked hard. He studied to advance himself and he took care of his young family. For the past eight years of his life he had had no trouble with the police. When he next encountered them, however, he had only a few moments to live.

There was a bed behind the door which Dawson had kicked in, some other pieces of furniture scattered around, and a man clad only in underpants, yelling, 'You cunts! You cunts!', coming at Dawson through the gloom. David Gundy grabbed at the barrel of the shotgun, either to push it away or perhaps to try to wrestle it free. Dawson, who had been trained to retain control of his weapon above all else, was yelling, 'Police! Don't!' It mingled with Gundy's shouts and with the other incoherent yelling and screaming throughout the house. Then the shotgun discharged.

The Remington 870 is a big, heavy-hitting piece of artillery. Adapted for the US Marine Corps at the height of the Vietnam War it was just about perfect for the requirements of the Special Ops section. When fired it unleashes a super-hot wad of eighteen lead pellets at a muzzle velocity of over 1200 feet per second. These pellets spread out from the mouth of the gun at a rate of about one inch for every yard travelled. It is an excellent firearm for clearing constricted spaces in close urban combat. Its utility for subduing confused angry young men in their underpants is more problematic. Gundy was immediately subdued, but only because the fiery blast atomised a twenty-three centimetre long chunk of his wrist and left arm. It also disintegrated his watch band, embedding small pieces in the wall behind him. But the fatal wounds were elsewhere. Two of the pellets which emerged last from the barrel had bumped into the spray of bone, tissue and metal and deflected into Gundy's abdomen where they passed through his lungs, pulmonary artery and heart. He staggered backwards, one arm hanging uselessly by his side, the other still raised as he shook his fist at the intruders. Bateman had entered the room behind Dawson by now. He placed his shotgun on the ground and moved around behind the wounded man to grab him. They fell to the bed in a tangle. Whittaker entered and 'cleared' the room, assuring himself there were no other occupants. He flicked on the overhead light and moved to the bed to give first aid while Watson called for the ambulance. From street corner to deathbed had taken 110 seconds.

Instantaneous rage convulsed the city's black population, mirrored in the wider community by a deep sense of disquiet. It didn't help the police that none of the places they raided that morning were occupied by cop killers. The team which hit a boarding house in Darley Street at Newtown charged down a seventy-four-year-old pensioner, Bob Salisbury, who thought hooligans were trying to break in when his door crashed open. Salisbury told reporters he might have had a go at protecting himself if he'd been a bit younger. Luckily for him his fighting days were over and all he could manage was to stumble blearily to his door, which flew open, smacking him in the face and knocking his glass eyeball clear out of his head. He scrambled around on the floor looking for it while black-clad SWOS men danced around him yelling, 'Stand back! Stand back!' Three doors down, Beryl Walsh, a tea lady at

The Long Goodbye

Grace Brothers Broadway department store, was having a quiet cuppa before heading off to work when her door exploded inwards and over half a dozen heavily armed men burst into her hallway. Beryl, who was recovering from a heart attack she'd suffered three weeks earlier, went into shock. Detectives attached to the SWOS team made her a cup of coffee and told her to fix up her front door and send them the bill. Amidst this lowbrow farce Gundy's wife Dolly Eatts returned from a trip to Queensland, took one look at their gore-soaked mattress and demanded to know why there was blood all over their bed. The police had said David stood up and struggled. But all she knew was that there was blood on the bed, not the walls.

She did not trust the police to investigate themselves and she was not alone. As inaccurate and premature details of the shooting appeared in the press, the force began to face insinuations of a payback execution. Gundy's relatives made a late submission to the Black Deaths Royal Commission which all but accused the force of a premeditated killing. The two fatal shotgun pellets, they argued, had not been deflected on their path. Their track through David Gundy's body had been 'true trajectories'. The victim had not been standing and struggling when shot, but sitting on the bed,

his body half turned towards the light from the shotgun at his left, his arm thrown up to a raised position with his arm slightly bent from the wrist to shield his eyes from the light from the gun. Half awake, his arm was near to or touching the end of the weapon, and the shot blasted his lower forearm, sending body tissue and blood onto his face over the left eye area.

It was a desperate thesis, demonstrably wrong, which grew out of

200 years of bitter, impacted frustration. But that did not matter. What mattered was that Gundy's people knew in their *hearts* that the white invaders had once again despatched their warriors to exact vengeance for the loss of one of their own. Phillip had sent Tench out with his muskets, machetes and sacks to bring back six of Botany Bay's natives 'or, if that should be found impracticable, to put that number to death'. For Sydney's surviving Aborigines, the capture and punishment of a real renegade having proved impractical for whitey, another black man had simply died in his place. Again.

It was expected that the inquest into Gundy's death would open these raw psychic wounds to painful scrutiny. Nobody could have expected, however, that on the first day of the inquiry – scheduled, coincidentally, for National Aboriginal Day – that the police would further inflame matters by conducting another armed raid, this time on an Aboriginal children's sports carnival in Alexandria Park, Redfern. A report prepared by the Aboriginal Legal Service stated that somewhere between five hundred and one thousand Aborigines, at least sixty percent of them children, were at the carnival when six white men in civilian clothes entered the park with guns drawn but without immediately identifying themselves as police. While searching for an Aboriginal man on a couple of outstanding warrants, two of the men suddenly discharged their weapons. A bystander wrestled one of the officers to the ground; but the others, seeing the man they were after making a getaway in a truck, fired, despite there being a number of children on the back of the vehicle.

It would be a remarkable event in any other setting, say at a sports carnival organised by a private boys school on the North Shore, but in the context of Redfern's indigenous history it is an old story. In the

The Long Goodbye

months following Gundy's death large groups of armed police swept through the district, culminating in a maxiraid in Eveleigh Street in February 1990. One hundred and thirty-five police, many of them Tactical Response Group officers kitted out for a riot in helmets and flak jackets, kicked down the doors of ten houses in the black ghetto at four in the morning. Out of this massive show of force came three arrests for property offences and one for possession of a bong. Two people were detained in connection with unpaid warrants and another two in relation to warrants for breach of bail and for 'being under the influence of intoxicating liquor on the railways'. Leaning precariously over a sizable credibility gap, Superintendent Alf Peate and Inspector Alan Peek said the action had been taken in response to 'a despairing cry' from the local Aboriginal community for a strong response to increasing rates of drug-related crime. The Bureau of Crime Statistics and Research subsequently analysed crime figures from the month of the operation and for seven following months. It concluded there was no evidence of a decrease in crime in the area. Obviously that bong seized by the TRG wasn't missed. Chief Inspector Peek provided a more revealing justification of the raid to the State Ombudsman when he argued that it had made the local community realise that unless there was a decline in trouble from their more rambunctious members, operations like this would recur. Like the punitive expedition ordered by Governor Phillip, it may not have been totally successful in terms of its immediate goals but at least they had 'struck a decisive blow', convinced the blacks of the white authorities' superiority, and perhaps even infused a 'universal terror, which might operate to prevent further mischief'.

The treasure stolen from the Aborigines – their 'proprietorship of the soil' – was rich enough to lift another benighted people, the convicts and the poor of England, from wretchedness and want. Convict transportation – established to terrorise a whole class into submission, or simply to amputate from the social body those who refused to be cowed – perversely came to represent the best hope for some of the lowest, most debauched lumpenproles in Britain. The British government hoped the system would largely pay for itself. By exploiting the wealth of an 'empty' continent and working its soil with slave labour, the Empire turned a neat trick of exchanging its unwanted criminal garbage for gold, wheat, wool and a thousand lesser riches.

The workers who ripped this bounty from the soil were the same men and women who had grubbed for their livelihood, such as it was, in the towns and countryside of Britain. From stealing food and clothes, picking pockets and gathering dog turds for a living, they went to a place where their labour was very much in demand. The carrot held out was freedom – a ticket of leave – and the chance to work for themselves, to shave off a thin leaf of fortune denied them at home. Each day spent toiling for the State, or advancing its interests in servitude to private landowners and colonial businesses, moved the convicts closer to that freedom.

After finishing their sentence, most could not afford the return passage, but most would probably not have cared. Years of hard work, fuelled by a healthier diet, had generally left them stronger and more capable of fending honestly for themselves. Chronic labour shortages ensured that their trades, either brought with them or learned in the colony, commanded good wages. The majority of the convicts were male and aged between seventeen and thirty; and as Manning Clark wrote, they were right for the task at hand – in the prime of their life and physical strength and not too old to adjust to strange surroundings, climate and a new social setting. For the thieves and other criminals

> despite the rage, the filth, the wretchedness of their external environment, and beneath the crude jokes and the carelessness with which they comported themselves, Australia was their one hope of deliverance from their degraded position: If he could go to Australia, a young thief told Mayhew, he would be very glad; as if he stopped in England he feared he should do nothing but thieve to the end.

The colony which grew out from Sydney simply could not afford the luxury of being sniffy about its members' past. Everyone who stepped off the transports was a resource, a pair of arms and legs to clear forests, till soil, tend beasts or keep office. The police force was staffed by former criminals. Many of the public buildings which so impressed Jacques Arago were designed not by the finest French draughstmen but by an exiled English forger. In *Letters to the Right Hon Robert Peel MP*, Edward Eagar, a disgraced attorney, testified that 'a reward for merit very rightly exists, in that convicts who have served their time can prosper'. Far from heaping poisonous middle class obloquy upon the fallen professional, as would have been required in England, Governor Macquarie wrote that Eagar was a man 'of strong, sound good sense and superior understanding ... extremely well informed as to the resources of this colony and to the general disposition of its inhabitants, their views and interests'.

As long as an individual, however recalcitrant, had something to offer and was willing to fit into the machine, he had a future. Frederick Thomas, a teenage swindler, fought the system for years and paid. Fifty lashes in 1836 for absconding. The next year spent in irons. Seventy-five lashes in 1839, another twelve months in irons for larceny after that. Caught stealing in 1842, he had another fifteen years dropped onto his sentence, to be served in an even harsher penal settlement, Tasmania. Then, at last, he got a break. After he saved the life of an officer's child, the system cut him some slack and by 1849 he had his ticket of leave, a wife and a job as a draughtsman in the Department of Public Works in Hobart, where he was eventually promoted to Clerk of Public Works. He arrived back in Sydney in 1870, a successful architect with six children.

These sort of stories did not sit well in the United Kingdom. Resentment and envy gathered around the tales of criminals made good. In 1855 Geoffrey Mundy neatly summed up for the prosecution in *Our Antipodes*.

> The virtuous operative of the Old Country is too often ill-fed, ill-lodged, ill-clothed and at his wits' end to save himself and family from the workhouse; while his fellow-villager, who has been transported for repeated offences, finds himself, after a short probation, allowed to work for his own livelihood, in a cheap country, with a splendid climate, and at a rate of wages unheard of in England.

The discovery of gold encouraged witnesses appearing before British parliamentary committees on crime and punishment in the 1850s to predict that some would be tempted into law-breaking by the prospect of a free trip to El Dorado. The Molesworth Inquiry – another investigation of the convict system, this one in the 1830s – denounced the freed convicts, called emancipists, some of whom 'are very wealthy, and have accumulated immense fortunes'. In most cases they made their wealth, according to Molesworth, by selling sly grog and lending money to obtain land and large herds of stolen cattle. The former governor, Sir Richard Bourke, rejected the slander. The estimates of their wealth he dismissed as being 'much beyond the truth' and Molesworth's statement about how they obtained it 'mere gossip upon which no reliance can be placed'. While admitting some may have profited by dishonest means, Bourke defended the efforts of the rest.

> The circumstances of the Colony have afforded to all the power of realising property by habits of probity, industry and frugality. By such means many persons who have been convicts and many Gentlemen who came out as inferior officers in the Navy and Army or as civilians have amassed fortunes beyond their most sanguine hopes.

The chance to carve a new life out of virgin territory was not restricted to the convicts. Their children were even more likely to thrive in the strange new environment. Mundy, who bemoaned the relative deprivations of honest workers in the old country, wrote of a twelve-year-old waiting on tables in a hotel, a four-year-old carpenter's apprentice, and Joshua Holt making £60 a year as an overseer of a gang of twenty convicts. He was just thirteen years old. As soon as a boy could swing an axe, carry water or lead a horse, the colony would call on him for work which most modern men would consider beyond their own powers. Charles Macallister, a boy of ten, regularly drove a bullock team into the dangerous wastelands between Sydney and Goulburn, hundreds of kilometres away. Young women worked just as hard in domestic service.

For them, marriage was virtually a contract to provide free labour and sex.

The responsibilities laid upon the city's youth quickly pressed their childhood out of them. The government recognised this in its own census records, generally treating anybody over twelve as an adult until 1841, when the cut-off point was raised to a wizened old fourteen. Many observers were shocked not just by the independence and maturity of the first native-born white Australians but by their strength of character as well. That 'stern and uncompromising moralist' Reverend John Dunmore Lang was 'happy, indeed, to be able to state' after ten years in the colony, that the young were nothing like the revolting, licentious drunks who had raised them. Far from being a nation of pirates as Malaspina had predicted, the convicts' children were, if anything, a sober, law abiding and reasonably censorious group. Upwards of ninety percent of them were born to criminal parentage, so the note of surprise in Commissioner Bigge's character sketch, included in his *Report on Agriculture and Trade* of 1823, is understandable.

The class of inhabitants that have been born in the colony affords a remarkable exception to the moral and physical character of their parents: they are generally tall in person and slender in their limbs, of fair complexion and small features. They are capable of undergoing more fatigue, and are less exhausted by labour than native Europeans; they are active in their habits but remarkably awkward in their movements. In their tempers they are quick and irascible, but not vindictive; and I only repeat the testimony of persons who have many opportunities of observing, that they neither inherit the vices nor feelings of their parents.

The Long Goodbye

Molesworth had painted the colony as a sinkhole of depravity and vice. Like Malaspina he feared the creation of a rapacious, bandit nation. The truth could not have been more removed from their lurid fantasies. In 1840 Sir William Westbrook Burton, a Supreme Court judge of the colony, penned an article to refute the slurs of Molesworth's report. Presenting three years' statistics from Sydney Gaol, he showed that the vast majority of offenders were convicts or former convicts. Those native-born white Australians who did appear before him generally faced trifling charges. He never passed the death sentence on any of them, or even heard of any crime being committed which justified it.

A rider to all of this cheeriness was that the colony's women did not share nearly as freely in its plunder. Sydney the penal colony was a place created in the male image, a military world of violence and control where everyone bent to the demands of the system. A system run by men for men, with women included as a sexual afterthought. Georgian and Victorian society had a horror of homosexuality, made all the more compelling by its ubiquitousness. The women of the First Fleet, and those who followed them, were sent out not simply because they had sinned but because they could do so again, this time in the service of the Empire. It was a bit rich for Ralph Clark and John White to come over all chaste and sanctimonious when writing about the convict women; particularly as Clark took a concubine from amongst them. The women's role was explicit. Their presence was required to stymie any outbreak of 'perversion' amongst the salty, long deprived men of the fleet. This conception of female immigration as a sort of sexual safety valve still held fast decades later when officers and enlisted men were allowed to take female 'servants', a quaint euphemism exposed by TW Plummer who wrote to Governor

Macquarie in 1811 that officers, noncommissioned officers, privates and settlers were all taking female convicts 'not only as servants but as avowed objects of intercourse, which is without even the plea of the slightest previous attachment as an excuse, rendering the whole colony little less than an extensive Brothel'.

In 1831 the Colonial Office settled on a plan for financing free emigration to Australia, paid for by the sale of land in the colony. From 1832 to 1836 much of the money raised by this scheme funded the shipment of thousands of single women to correct the gender imbalance caused by many years of predominantly male convict transportation. It was not the first time authorities had formed a nexus between land and marriage. A few years earlier Governor Ralph Darling had encouraged a plan to give the marriageable young ladies of Sydney and beyond a dowry in the form of a generous land grant. Darling hoped to provide for several very large families made up mostly of daughters who, though respectable, possessed no property and thus no prospects. But, wrote Darling,

The addition of 1300 acres of land to a man who has already received all he has a claim to, and which he could not obtain except by purchase, will it is hoped, act as an inducement to the young settlers to marry.

Nearly 30 000 acres were allotted under the scheme, mostly to the daughters of the administrative and military classes. It ceased in 1831, having become a source of deep resentment amongst the less well connected who were kept from the trough.

The migration scheme funded out of land sales was not well thought out. Hoping to siphon off huge numbers of their 'redundant' poor, Britain shipped south thousands of unemployed

The Long Goodbye

labourers and women. An economic boom in Australia during the 1830s hid some of the problems. With the colony's insatiable appetite for immigrant labour and single women, many of the migrants were quickly absorbed. But when, in the latter part of the decade, a land bubble burst, combined with a credit squeeze in London and a drought in the colony, the economy imploded. So severe was the damage that rice, maize and wheat had to be imported again. Because of problems with the migration scheme, poor planning by colonial authorities and the time lag imposed by the brute fact of distance, Sydney began to fill up with sick, starving English migrants.

The trouble with the scheme of the 1830s was that the migrants were not necessarily chosen for their suitability. Many were pushed onto the boats by parish authorities seeking to ease the drain on their poor funds. Like the convicts arriving from the hulks before them, they were often in no state to travel and the death rate, especially amongst the children, was appalling. From 1838 to 1839 one child died out of every eleven making the voyage.

As ignorant and hypocritical as ever, Sydney's God-botherers and moralists worked themselves into a lather over the poor character of the women, whilst commercial interests complained that the men were unsuitable for hard frontier work. In 1835 Governor Bourke suggested the bounty system, where colonists would be paid by the government to bring out the type and number of immigrants they needed. It seemed rational, shifting control of the system to the point of delivery. However, England was still too far away for the colonists to exercise any real command over the initial selection and they came to rely on immigration and shipping agents. The bounty permits were progressively transferred from Sydney back to London, into the hands of the shipowners. When the bounty payments were increased, moving immigrants became a very profitable business and the system fell into open abuse. Shippers received £38 for a man and wife under forty years old, £19 each for a single man or woman, and £10 for children. Inferior boats were packed tight with as many migrants as possible. The system began to groan under the pressure, increased mortality en route just one sign of the coming disaster.

As with their convict predecessors, a long slow grind of attrition rather than spectacular catastrophes accounted for most of the migrants' deaths. Children and babies died because the conditions on board seemed almost calculated to kill them. John Dobie, surgeon on the *Duncan*, reported that nineteen children died of marasmus on his vessel. They just wasted away after foul weather during six weeks of the voyage 'necessitated locking the passengers below with the hatches battened down'. Even on a passage blessed with calm weather, the crowded holds were great incubators of disease. Smallpox took ninteen children aboard the *Amelia Thompson*; scarlet fever killed thirty-five on the *Maitland*; while parents on the *Layton* buried seventy of their children, killed by a measles epidemic. After the *Lady MacNaghten* arrived in February 1837 carrying ninety cases of typhus, the quarantine officer, James Stuart, reported that when the luggage and bulkheads were cleared away he found 'every sort of filth, broken biscuits, bones, rags and refuse of every description; putrifying and filled with maggots'. Demonstrating an awesome inability to learn from the past, the shipowners had placed poorly sluiced toilets in between decks where they polluted the air to the point where it was 'almost insufferable'.

Fourteen adults and fifty-three children died aboard the *Lady MacNaghten*, finally forcing authorities to reduce the proportion

The Long Goodbye

of children allowed on migrant ships. That restriction merely split families, with many youngsters aged seven and less orphaned on the docks as their parents were told they could not take them. No formal machinery existed in Sydney for receiving the migrants. When the recession hit hard in the early 1840s, families already torn by separation and death were further oppressed by the cruel demands of the time. Landowners would not employ large families because the children were an unproductive drain on their resources. The Benevolent Society, which was empowered to break up families, put many children into its orphanage while their parents worked in the bush. These children became another lucrative form of cheap labour. They were apprenticed for up to seven years, until they reached twenty-one, receiving no wages until the last three. Nor was that money paid directly to them. Employers deposited their young workers' earnings into a bank. That was often as close as the youngsters ever came to it. And if a girl married before turning eighteen, her employer did not have to pay her anything.

The immigrants' woes were attended to in the end not by colonial authorities – who in a spirit of ferocious social Darwinism thought migrants had no right to call on the support of the state – but by a private citizen, a woman named Caroline Chisholm. She overcame entrenched misogyny and sectarian ignorance to effectively become Australia's first immigration department. A Catholic in a place where the Roman Church was regarded with suspicion if not outright hostility by the ruling classes, she burned with a fierce inner light – one of those few people truly affected by the suffering of others and, even more rarely, one driven to do something about it.

Arriving in Sydney late in 1838 from Madras in India where she had established a school for the wild, untutored children of the British garrison, Chisholm settled into a quiet cottage life at Windsor, far from the bustle of the city's heart. Her husband, Captain Archibald Chisholm of the East India Company, had come south for his health and the short time they spent at Windsor before he was called back to the company's service in the first Opium War was the last period of private respite they would enjoy for many decades. The wave of good economic fortune, on which rode the fate of so many individuals in the colony, was cresting and breaking even as Captain Chisholm took sail for China to prosecute his drug-dealing employers' turf war.

As in every collapse before and since, asset prices, which had climbed stratospherically on the folly of investors who could not believe they would ever move in the other direction, suddenly did just that. Catastrophically. Horses going for £70 when Caroline Chisholm settled in Sydney could fetch no more than a tenth of that price two years later. By 1842 so many investors had become ruined debtors that a Bankruptcy Act was passed allowing them to remain free if they handed in their estates. The prison colony's own jails would otherwise have been insufficient to contain the defaulters.

Exacerbating the problems was Governor Gipps's decision at the very tail end of the boom to issue a huge number of bounty immigration orders at the urging of landowners and businessmen who feared a labour shortage with the imminent winding down of convict transportation. Combined with troubles in Canada which would have diverted a large number of migrants to Sydney in any case, Gipps's order saw the number of migrants jump from 6500 in 1840 to just over 20 000 the following year. With no work available and no formal structure for coping with the arrivals, the city was overwhelmed. A shanty camp of tents and humpies and open air fires sprang up. Hundreds of young women roamed the streets, sleeping in doorways and under trees, turning to prostitution for their subsistence.

Chisholm took a number of these women back to Windsor, gave them food and shelter and sought employment for them. But she knew that the magnitude of the disaster gathering in the streets of Sydney called for a much greater response. She was particularly aggrieved by the condition of the young women who were easy prey for any man with a few coins in his pocket. She lit upon the idea of founding a home for these women but was beset not only by official prevarication but also by the active opposition of her own Church. Chisholm was well aware of the sort of prejudice which would be inflamed by a woman, especially a Catholic woman, engaging in public activity, but she vowed to help all regardless of their faith. In response, she later wrote, several leading Church figures put every possible obstacle in her way and she was relentlessly entreated to give up her mad scheme.

As her biographer Margaret Kiddle points out, Caroline was essentially a very conventional woman, but one who took the teachings of the Christian faith seriously, unalloyed by hypocrisy or intolerance. She did not want to rebel but was forced to by the failure of her betters. She was so tortured by the opposition of Church elders that she resolved to take a few days' solace and contemplation in Parramatta to examine her conscience.

Whilst there she was walking by the river when she came upon a 'frail beauty' whom she was surprised to discover she already knew. A beautiful Highland girl named Flora, Caroline had last seen her in the tent city near the immigration barracks where she had drawn the eye of a wealthy married man. Chisholm had tried to warn the girl but this cad had 'ruined' and abandoned her. Now spastic with rum and rage and bitter self-loathing, Flora had determined to drown herself in the river. Caroline walked and talked with her for an hour, up and down a sandy little beach, comforting the girl and easing her suicidal passions. In doing so she rid herself of any doubts about the rightness of her own cause or the arrogant dimness of her opponents, and she returned to the city with all her fears burned away by righteous certainty.

With the crisis worsening daily in the city's centre public indignation was finally stirring. In early September of 1842 the *Chronicle* reported that another 2500 migrants had poured into Sydney in the last fortnight and reported the story of one, Mary Teague, who was placed in the stocks for drunkenness. She had been found collapsed in a ditch, but from hunger not rum, having been turned off her ship a day before with no food and nowhere to go. Chisholm redoubled her efforts in an increasingly receptive climate. She had already had an audience with Gipps, who had expected to be harangued by a wizened old biddy in a white cap and granny glasses. 'I was amazed,' he wrote, 'when my *aide* introduced a handsome, stately young woman, who proceeded to reason the question as if she thought her reason, and experience, too, worth as much as mine'.

Amazed though he was, the Governor agreed to another meeting at some stage in the future. When the future arrived with starving Englishmen and women ranging through his streets like Indian beggars, he was forced to agree to his stately young visitor's request for access to the disused immigration barracks. Ever the bureaucrat, however, he made her sign an undertaking that her scheme would not cost the government one penny.

And so, in the last days of October 1841, Caroline Chisholm

The Long Goodbye

moved into the small wooden storeroom, a little over two metres square, crawling with vermin, where she built the basic machinery of Australian immigration. She later recalled the horrors of her first night. Weary, after a day of heavy labour, she had just laid down her head and put out the light when she was assailed by such a racket that she thought wild dogs had broken in and were planning to eat her. She relit her candle to find the floor of her cramped little cabin crawling with giant rats.

What I experienced at seeing rats in all directions I cannot describe. My first act was to throw on a cloak, and get at the door with the intent of leaving the building. My second thoughts were that, if I did so, my desertion would cause much amusement and ruin my plan. I therefore lighted a second candle, and seating myself on the bed, kept there until three rats descending from the roof, alighted on my shoulders. I felt that I was getting into a fever, and that in fact, I should be very ill before morning, but to be outgeneralled by rats was too bad. I got up with some resolution, I had two loaves and some butter (for my office, bedroom and pantry were one). I cut it in slices, placed the whole in the middle of the room, put a dish of water convenient, and, with a light by my side, I kept my seat on the bed, reading and watching the rats until four in the morning. I at one time counted thirteen, and never less than seven did I observe in the dish, during the entire night.

The barracks were soon full of indigent young females. Chisholm moved quickly to disperse them through the countryside, where there was always work to be done in spite of the depression gripping the city. She sent questionnaires out to determine the needs of settlers in the various districts, quizzed her charges closely about their own skills and backgrounds, and matched up each up with the other. She received permission to use bullock trains, returning to the bush after dropping their load of wool, to transport her colonists to their new employers. Riding her white charger Captain, she took convoys of women into the bush where there was no shelter, often no road, and no protection from native attack or bands of bushrangers. Her fame soon spread, however, and her wagon trains were never molested.

Whilst her first concern had been for the young women scavenging in the streets of Sydney, she did not forget the children, the young men and the families still being deposited in their thousands at Circular Quay and around the Rocks. She believed that if only a little more logic and forethought could go into planning mass migration, it still offered the best hope for the colony and the poor of Great Britain. To this end she established her own settlement at Shell Harbour, south of Sydney; she initiated the prosecution of the captain and surgeon of one particularly awful immigrant ship; she established the Family Colonisation Loan Society to replace the network of corrupt and hopeless agents in Britain; and she gathered stories of those who had successfully made the transition from the old country to the new. These voluntary statements, as she called them, many of which she took in fields and farmhouses throughout the vastness of the bush, served to counteract some of the grim economic news filtering back to London, but also cast an objective light on the shameless boosterism of the immigration agents' propaganda. She is supposed to have addressed the House of Lords and, when challenged on some point of fact, glanced briefly at the sceptic, untied a large sheaf of papers, and begun to read case after case from the voluminous

The Long Goodbye

files she had gathered to support her arguments. Further moves towards her files were enough to quickly kill off any ill-mannered interruptions after that. Caroline Chisholm toured the United Kingdom seeking potential immigrants, introducing them to each other before the voyage, attempting as far as possible to draw groups of colonists from extended support networks of friends and relatives within small local areas. She sent her own ships out from England, the first two full of children previously abandoned at the docks by their parents. She scoured workhouses all over the country looking for them, and when they sailed it was under the curling blue banner of the Family Colonisation Loan Society.

By 1845 she had placed 11 000 migrants into work, reunited 600 broken families, and built a huge network for moving and supporting her people in the outback. Her genius lay in administration and perseverence but she also brilliantly intuited certain patterns which were natural to successful migration. In seeking to gather colonists from neighbouring regions and groups she anticipated the chain migration which would characterise nearly 200 years of human movement into Sydney. As it would be later with Greeks, Italians and Vietnamese, so it was first with the English: small groups of the adventurous and the desperate striking out across the seas to establish a base for their families and neighbours who followed.

Not everybody agreed with Chisholm that the colony's future depended on mass immigration. Workers benefited from labour shortages during boom periods, demanding and receiving much better wages than they could ever hope to achieve in the UK. The migration of large numbers of impoverished British workers threatened to undermine the locals' position during the good times and to destroy their livelihood in the bad. Government assistance for immigration came under sustained pressure from the working class during economic downturns such as that which afflicted the city in the late 1850s. Agitation and large, frequent public meetings calling for an end to assisted passages led the government to briefly curtail assistance in June 1860.

Before the late 1870s this anti-migrant feeling was largely confined to periods of economic distress. After that the disparate, largely working class anti-immigration forces set themselves to the task of eliminating government assistance for migration and did not rest until they saw their goals achieved. In 1886 the Premier Sir Patrick Jennings finally promised to cut the immigration item from the New South Wales budget. Macquarie Street had long resisted all approaches on the issue, but the combination of massive public pressure, a drought and large scale unemployment forced their hand.

Throughout these years of agitation, the anti-immigration movement had never objected to the migrants themselves. A large percentage of the colony's population had been born in the UK and were unlikely to find fault with migrants who were cut from the same cloth as them. Their objections were simply economic; an oversupplied labour market could not keep the Australian working man in the style to which he had become accustomed. In 1878, however, in the early days of the concerted push to close off British access to local jobs, another migration issue arose which had little to do with rational economic or political debate. In November of that year a strike broke out on the Sydney waterfront which soon spread around the country. The summer winds of 1878 blew hot with racism and hatred and the seeds of the White Australia Policy.

* * *

The Long Goodbye

The *Journal of the Royal Australian Historical Society* recounts the arrival of the Chinese in Australia's metro centres as an alien invasion, more curious than threatening to begin with, as though some fantastic plant or animal had sprung fully formed from the ruptured earth of the first gold diggings. Their disturbing *otherness* could only increase with their numbers and growing impact on the goldfields. Hailing from 'a grimly Malthusian setting where thrift and industry were essential for survival', the southern Chinese were a remote and perplexing yet universal feature of the countryside during the rush years. They were a race apart, remarked the *Journal*, and intended to remain so. On the fields they camped together, remained aloof and laboured in concert, a massive hive of worker bees swarming over the tailings with unbelievable patience and brutal unremitting toil. Surviving on the thinnest of margins, they could earn a living off fields abandoned by the whites as unprofitable. In the process they also earned the undying enmity of the diggers. Fears that the Chinese would undercut local working conditions and somehow eat up all the gold in the ground by themselves, combined with darker fears of being overrun and bred out of existence by the 'yellow hordes'.

Before the gate was closed on them, the Chinese constituted by far the largest non-European migrant group in Australia. Three separate phases had marked their coming. Before the discovery of gold a small number of indentured rural peasants arrived to work the land; they were followed by two massive waves of gold seekers. Sailing from Kwangtung Province in South China, they poured into Victoria and later into Queensland. The census of 1853 showed the Chinese population of Victoria at 2000. Two years later, when the Victorian Parliament passed laws restricting their entry, they numbered 17000. Harsh as they were, the laws failed to stop the numbers of Chinese swelling to 40 000 within another two years. New South Wales passed its own anti-Chinese statutes in 1861, but the petering out of the gold rush was a more effective deterrent. Contrary to popular fears, the Chinese were not really interested in staying, and as the opportunities for profiting on the goldfields disappeared, so did they, only returning in great numbers with the discovery of more gold reserves in Queensland.

In the mid to late 1860s both Victoria and New South Wales repealed laws passed to staunch the Chinese inflow, leaving their people feeling exposed when the Chinese reappeared on northern goldfields in the 1870s. The national industrial dispute which started with seamen in Sydney Harbour, however, was not directly related to trouble on the diggings; instead it arose from general fears of economic and racial displacement which crystallised around the issue of Chinese sailors being employed by an Australian shipping company in local waters. Although the strike by workers of the Australian Steamship Navigation Company (ASN) began as a fairly simple action to protect local jobs, sparks from the clash soon lit upon a tinder-dry undergrowth of xenophobia.

The employment of non-Europeans was mostly restricted to the tropical north, which had a severe labour shortage and needed workers 'biologically adapted' to the extreme conditions. British migrants were more suited to southern business and industry, generally made up of small concerns which could not afford to import labour in any case. ASN was a bit different. Based in Sydney but running services right up the east coast and deep into the Pacific, it had access to cheap skilled Chinese seamen and the capital to employ them in significant numbers. It was also in direct competition with the Hong Kong-based Eastern Australian Mail Steamship Company, which already employed Chinese and so could

The Long Goodbye

undercut ASN. Under the chairmanship of George Dibbs, later a premier of New South Wales, ASN replaced European workers with Chinese on three ships in April 1878.

The union movement reacted as a whole, the Seamen's Union gaining the support of the Trades and Labor Council for a campaign seeking the legislative restriction of any Chinese immigration. Ann Curthoys, who sketches a brief but comprehensive outline of the ensuing battle in *Who Are Our Enemies?*, writes that this strategy was in line with earlier responses to Asian immigration which thought that 'the best solution to Chinese economic competition was to exclude Chinese from the colony altogether'. At that time trade unions were small bodies, representing skilled urban tradesmen, but they were growing in sophistication and power. The Sydney Trades and Labor Council (TLC), which had been formed in 1871, gained experience in campaigning against assisted British immigration in 1877.

Within a year the prospect of otherwise respectable British workers supplanting locals from their jobs had been replaced by the alarming spectre of millions of 'flat-faced, flat-footed heathen Chinese' driving the white race out completely. That at least was the awful vision tormenting those who attended a rally on 23 July to protest all Chinese immigration. There were just under 1000 Chinese resident in Sydney then, considerably less than the 1500 working men who squeezed into the city's guild hall, with many more spilling out onto Castlereagh Street. Sydney's Chinese community, almost entirely male, lived crammed into small dank terraces around the inner city. Some were market gardeners, exercising a skill – farming in dry, poor soils – of great use and some mystery to white Australians. Many others were employed in the furniture trade, centred on George Street, arousing the rally's indignation on behalf of white cabinet-makers driven out of their trade by 'coolie labour'. Most of the evening's considerable heat and anger was not generated by economic debate but by the belief that the Chinese were inherently immoral and a danger to the virtue of the city's females. Curthoys records that by November 1878, 181 European women were married to Chinese men, a further 171 were 'living in sin' with them. These outrageous liaisons had also brought forth 586 Anglo-Chinese children. The 'twin issues of economic competition and immorality' were only exacerbated by the fact that 'Chinese arrivals were again, for the first time since 1861, exceeding departures'. Although the vast majority of the Chinese were to be found in remote mining districts and although, almost to a man, they wished only to build up a very small pile and return home, their passage through the metro centres, the small remnant populations they deposited there, and the memories of earlier bloodshed on the goldfields had snagged like a fishhook in the national psyche.

The angry tradesmen were addressed by Seamen's Union reps and a group of anti-Chinese politicians, including Angus Cameron, a carpenter and a member of the Legislative Assembly who was one of the original organisers of the push against British migration. To roars of approval, he denounced the Chinese invasion, proclaiming, 'We came here to better our position and we will not have this moral pestilence – we will have none of them!'

A little earlier Thomas White, the President of the Seamen's Union, had first linked their dispute with ASN to the wider issue of Chinese immigration. White's was one of the wilder performances that night. He told the crowd that he had seen 'old schoolmates and young girls with whom he had gone to church' fallen into depravity in the Chinese dens of the city. He tore into the

The Long Goodbye

newspapers, most notably the *Herald*, for going arm in arm with the Chinese merchants responsible for importing the 'pestilence'. And he referred to the parliamentary report on common lodging houses, saying it was not possible for a man to read the evidence of witnesses like Inspector Seymour without disgust. Cameron, who had chaired the committee which produced the report, described its findings as loathsome and beastly, but nothing compared to what the audience might see for themselves in the Chinese quarter that very night. Whipping his listeners into a frenzy, he declared that the Chinese did not just threaten their individual livelihoods but the nation's very character, along with the virtue and character of their wives and daughters. 'Their presence here means moral and political degradation in every sense of the term'.

Some of the audience who were not in the habit of keeping up with Parliament's publications were very keen for the offending passages to be read out. And they were especially keen to hear from Inspector Seymour. Given the fevered atmosphere, White and Cameron were probably wise in recommending that the men read it for themselves later. Seymour, an 'Inspector of Nuisances' for the city council, had spent a good deal of time amongst the Chinese and was not shy about passing on his findings. Asked simply whether he knew if the Chinese kept lodging houses in the city, Seymour peeled off into a long colourful diatribe about the conditions to be found in opium dens, some of which were just down the street from the guild hall.

The Chinese live eight or ten in a room and lie on stretchers ... I have gone into a room and found a small lamp in the centre, and a Chinaman with a woman between his legs, naked all but a petticoat, and another Chinaman in the same

95

position on another part of the stretcher; in the next room the same and in the next the same. These were white women, some of them married women, and others women of the town. I have found another Chinaman lying with his arms around a woman, one hand on her bosom, and his other hand under her legs, pulling her parts about like a dog. In another place there was a Chinaman had a girl on the table, sitting up, with his trousers down, and one of the girl's legs over his shoulder; she was under the influence of opium, and he was using her – having connection with her – and seven or eight Chinamen waiting at the door to do the same to this woman.

Seymour went on to explain that he found scenes of this sort repeated up and down Cyrus Lane, the girls telling him that they were enslaved to the Chinese through their addiction to opium. The smokers' dens could be found all through the central city, in dangerous, filthy warrens like Abercrombie Lane and Rowe Street and throughout Surry Hills, where many of the Chinese lived. It was enough to drive God-fearing white men to violence. However, the Inspector of Nuisances may not have taken into account that many of the couples – 181 of them at least – whose boudoirs he had happily barged into were married. And the rest, 'women of the town' as he called them, were unlikely to be the object of societal concern under normal circumstances. Elsewhere in the report the witnesses and their parliamentary questioners are less solicitous of the city's 'lowest sort' of women. When shacked up in cheap lodgings with poor white trash they were little better than Ralph Clark's abandoned trollops. Only when they started snorting up drugs and throwing their legs over Chinamen's shoulders was there any concern expressed for their 'virtue and character'.

The Long Goodbye

It seems that the workshop was not the only place where white men had to worry about the special skills of the Chinese.

Curthoys writes that while Thomas White briefly described Chinese labour as unfair competition, because they could live on virtually nothing and had no families to support, he canvassed non-economic objections to the Chinese at length; the dangers of cohabitation with young white women, the dangers to British institutions of secret tribunals and societies, their lack of respect for the law. Whereas twelve months previously he had decried the assisted migration of British workers to Australia, he now told the meeting he would 'rather see all the convicts of Great Britain in New South Wales than one Chinaman'. The *Evening News* reported that a rousing cheer went up as he said he would be the first to shoulder a musket to prevent the Chinese coming to drive out the Caucasian race. When the Anglo-Saxon smelt blood there was no holding him back, he declared, adding quickly that he hoped it wouldn't come to that. But he continued that he also hoped decent people would decline to travel in any ship where Chinese were employed, or dine in a hotel where they ate, or buy furniture from a factory where they worked. The crowd erupted again when he said it was their duty to shove aside any Chinaman they encountered on the footpath.

In the months leading up to the November strike, meetings like this were a regular feature of the city's night-life. The machinery of the movement had already been built for the campaigns against assisted British migrants. Whilst that had largely been a working class affair, opposition to the Chinese crossed class boundaries and left the shipping company largely isolated, save for lukewarm encouragement from the *Herald* and the Chamber of Commerce. Their argument that the Chinese were an inferior race whom working men could exploit, thus improving their own position, was recognised and denounced for the self-serving tosh that it was. A number of non-union and middle class organisations had grown out of that first anti-immigration meeting sponsored by the TLC in 1877. They included the Working Men's Defence Association (WMDA) and the Political Reform Union (PRU), the latter becoming a focal point of anti-Chinese agitation, organising most of the public meetings which took place each Saturday in Hyde Park and Haymarket.

In early August the WMDA called its own public meeting, attended by about 250 people. Several speeches denounced 'the Chinese variously as inhuman, immoral, incapable of becoming civilised, and loathsome'. A much larger meeting about a fortnight later raised a petition, eventually carrying thousands of signatures, which was presented to the Legislative Assembly on 6 November, two weeks before the seamen walked off the job. In the meantime Thomas White had led a delegation to the Colonial Secretary, Michael Fitzpatrick, to present demands for legislative action. Fitzpatrick demurred, pointing out that not many Chinese had arrived and many who had were on their way somewhere else. He also had to consider British imperial obligations, 'which involved a reluctance to offend China'. At this point, despite the anger and anxieties of the general populace, the TLC seemed to have lost. The decision to strike from 18 November, after another 109 Chinese had arrived to man five ASN ships, changed everything.

Although the strike was principally designed to force ASN's hand, it also revived the wider anti-Chinese movement. The *Evening News* reported that Angus Cameron received a wild, cheering reception when he addressed a 'monster' gathering in Castlereagh Street on the first day of the walkout. Cameron admitted

The Long Goodbye

that Chinese labour might be excused under strict free-trade principles, but 'in the eyes of God and man they had just grounds for rejecting these people'. Hard as it was, he could justify simple competition between Englishmen and Orientals, but 'all the powers between heaven and earth could not justify the prostitution and the disease of their female population; the curse and the dregs of infamy which the Mongolian bore in his face when he came amongst us'. Previously the industrial issue of the Chinese seamen had been lost in this sort of rhetorical tumult over opium dens, disease, secret societies, down-breeding and the curious preference of some white women for yellow men. But with increasing numbers of idle ASN ships filling the harbour, the whole city could see the tangible effects of racial conflict. As the confrontation escalated it dragged in more and more people – waterside workers, businessmen, shopkeepers and finally, as the city's commercial arteries clogged up, the public themselves. The action spread to Newcastle and Brisbane within four days and ASN quickly found it did not have enough Chinese to replace the nearly 800 seamen and wharf labourers on strike.

On 19 November at a meeting between the union executive and company directors the union argued that the Chinese would cost all of their members their jobs and that they should be sent home. The directors refused to negotiate while the union was on strike, saying they were breaching their contracts, that ASN had been forced into this position by their competitors, and that the Chinese were only to be used in tropical waters, to which they were more suited than whites. The company thought the union would cave in under financial pressure and on 28 November it knocked back an offer by the seamen to pay the fares of the returning Chinese and to enter into a £500 bond not to strike for a year. A shareholders meeting the next day strongly supported the directors who announced they would use volunteers on their ships from 2 December and, far from backing down, they would now be sending to Hong Kong for another 300 Chinese.

The company was both overplaying its hand and underestimating the level of support for the strikers. The Queensland Government announced it would withdraw ASN's mail subsidy if it continued to use Chinese labour. Spontaneous donations from the public and from unions as far away as New Zealand poured thousands of pounds into the TLC's fighting fund while few volunteers materialised to help out the company. Tension climbed through the summer. A severe heatwave in the bush triggered the migration of millions of insects which descended on Sydney as the two sides geared down for a long and bitter confrontation. Residents in Ashfield were driven to hide in their houses as plagues of locusts and flying ants swarmed over their suburb. But even greater consternation was aroused by the approaching swarm of 300 Chinese, their progress charted in regular press reports. Public meetings grew in size and volatility. A speaker by the name of Stedman inflamed a meeting of 250 in the Oddfellows Hall at Balmain, telling them that the Chinese picked up dead and decaying dogs to eat, and that some even threw 'the remains of children' into their cooking pots. Whilst 500 listened to the usual suspects at a Political Reform Union meeting in Woollahra, two men were taking more direct action in Essex Street where they attacked a man named Ah Gee with a hammer, smashing him about the head and face before being driven off by a cab driver. Indeed, a lot of people took to heart Thomas White's advice about shoving Chinamen out of their path. The *Herald* published a growing stream of letters detailing attacks on Chinese residents throughout the city.

The Long Goodbye

One reader described seeing 'a respectably dressed Chinaman' try to hail a cab, only to be clouted in the face with the driver's whip. A crowd of up to 1000 materialised around the post office after a young man had intervened to protect a Chinaman from assault by 'a number of roughs'. The good Samaritan was himself set upon and had to be escorted away by police. Another mob of 'thirty or forty lads' chased a single Chinese man up William Street, pelting him with such a shower of stones that passersby had to duck and run for their own safety. One woman who argued with a member of the crowd was told, 'the Chinamen are taking our country from us and we must kill them'.

In spite of White's inflammatory speeches, most press reports were careful to separate this anarchic, spontaneous violence from the actions of the striking seamen. The *Evening News*, a great supporter of the anti-Chinese movement, deplored the attacks, editorialising that they would rather have a population of Mongolians than a city full of these 'low brutal fellows'. Even the *Herald*, which supported the ASN and the city's mercantile interests against the union's claims, described the strikers' overall behaviour as sober and orderly, only turning on them when a riot broke out on the afternoon of Saturday 9 December.

Half a dozen mounted police and up to sixty uniformed and plain-clothes police were patrolling Lower George Street around ASN's wharf. A crowd of a few hundred had gathered there to harass a smaller number of strikebreakers due to leave the company's premises after four o'clock. The police directed the men to leave via a small street which ran beside the Mariner's Church, but no sooner had they stepped out than the crowd rushed them, screaming abuse. The police formed a thin shell around the workmen and attempted to move into George Street, the crowd tearing along after them 'hustling, jeering, hooting and attempting to seize and assault some of the workmen'. The paper described the crowd as ferocious and their victims as being in great fear despite the armed escort.

> If any of them happened for an instant to get away from the side of those who were protecting them an attempt was made, with what can only be compared to the ferocity of wild beasts, and when one of them, in deadly fear of a repetition of a brutal beating he had received the previous day, ran a little in advance of the crowd and the police for a cab ... a number of his persecutors broke from the crowd, chased him and clambered about the cab as though they would pull the driver from his seat and demolish the vehicle rather than be baulked of their prey.

Distinctions between the mob, the police and the strikebreakers became confused, the violence cranking up as they surged and fought. At Charlotte Place the police suddenly regrouped, turned on the attackers and charged into them with whips and billy clubs. The *Herald*'s man watched as 'the blows of the police fell fast and heavy', unleashing panic and confusion amongst the 'roughs' who scattered 'like chaff' in their attempts to flee, quickly leaving the scene deserted save for the police, their charges and a score of injured bystanders. The *Evening News* reported that after the skirmish such fears were held about an assault on the company's property that No. 2 Battery of the Permanent Artillery was issued with rifles and live ammunition, marching from Victoria Barracks in Paddington to put down any trouble.

The idea of the military being called into the streets to fire on the populace was considered a routine, if regrettable, precaution.

The Long Goodbye

Just a few days previously an ugly mob had broken away from a huge congregation in Hyde Park to rampage through the city attacking any Chinamen they could find. The night-time rally, complete with burning torches and 'the ascent of a rocket' to draw a crowd of 10–15 000, had dispatched a deputation to Parliament with another petition calling for legislative action to ban Chinese from the colony. Many of the protesters were described as 'larrikins', an all-purpose label for the thousands of shiftless, teenaged criminals who haunted the city streets. These were the 'low brutal fellows' who had been increasingly drawn to the anti-Chinese movement by the opportunity it presented for a spree of community-sponsored violence. At least 2000 of them left the Hyde Park demonstration to trawl the city in packs, seeking out victims. With large numbers of plain-clothes police on patrol around the park, one group of larrikins made their way at 'full speed' to Lower George Street where many Chinese merchants and warehouses were located. Lit by burning branches, they gathered stones to hurl against the walls and shuttered windows of the shops while a smaller party charged the premises of a furniture maker called Ah Toy. They tried to hurl their torches inside the building, where dozens of Chinese lived and worked, but were thwarted by a nearby constable. More police appeared, formed up and charged. The *Herald* reported that the riot line 'unmercifully' laid into the seething, raucous mob 'with whip, staves and sticks', driving them back up George Street.

These scenes did not discourage the leaders of the anti-Chinese movement. After a delegation of Chinese merchants and their supporters called on the Colonial Secretary demanding protection from the attacks, Angus Cameron addressed another big public meeting, describing the move as 'a dodge' by ASN. There was no reason to invoke extra protection, he said. 'The assaults of which they had read so much had been tortured and twisted and magnified tenfold to do injury to the men who had so nobly resisted a momentous evil.' The attackers were most likely 'little boys' aroused by the righteous indignation of their parents' dinner table conversation about the Asian invasion. Any slurs against the strikers or other supporters of the movement were a perversion of the truth. So the meetings continued.

When the strike spread to the mining industry after the Seamen's Union asked coalminers not to service ASN vessels, the company rolled over. It had lost a fortune by miscalculating the strength of opposition, both to its immediate scheme and to the perceived implications for the wider community. The *Sydney Morning Herald* was its most enthusiastic backer in the press, and that enthusiasm was lukewarm at best. Other papers such as the *News*, whilst criticising the violence of sections of the movement, were otherwise bombastic in their support. They never turned any serious forensic gaze on the records, the agenda or the performance of men like White and Cameron. They were acting on very strongly held beliefs, but that was not enough to stop them from indulging in naked power plays and demagoguery. Cameron, most prominent of a number of parliamentary activists, played a very important part in pitching the anti-Chinese message beyond the limits of the aggrieved working classes.

When increasing numbers of parliamentarians, mayors and aldermen appeared on platforms with the representatives of small business, middle-class reformers and the union movement, the forces arrayed against ASN and its supporters in the Chamber of Commerce became unstoppable. Drawing support from around

The Long Goodbye

the nation, the anti-Chinese movement crossed boundaries of geography and class. It forged alliances between shopkeepers and criminals, bosses and workers, Irish and English, migrant and native born. According to Curthoys it demonstrated 'the political impossibility of importing cheap Chinese labour, and so laid the basis, more clearly than any other single event, for the weakening of capital's interest in the Chinese as a source of cheap, or even simply extra, labour'. The colonial ministry, which had been crippled through the period of the strike by a conflict over land law, collapsed in late December, about the same time ASN's 300 approaching Chinamen were shipwrecked without loss of life. The new ministry, led by Henry Parkes, quickly announced that it would introduce laws restricting Chinese immigration. Parkes, who thought of the Chinese as a 'degraded race' which would 'always pull down the superior British race morally, intellectually and even physically', had to fight big-business representatives who clung to the dream of importing cheap Asian labour. But with another surge in Chinese migrant numbers in 1881 being blamed for a smallpox epidemic, and with extra-parliamentary agitation continuing, conservative resistance was overcome. It was the end of this interest in the Chinese as a cheap, superexploitable labour source which laid the basis 'for the emergence of a nationally supported White Australia Policy'.

Racism was officially sanctioned and organised along twin tracks in Australia for much of the twentieth century. The White Australia Policy attempted to hold off the Asian hordes to the north, while the local Aborigines were to be humanely bred out of existence through the happy coincidence of high mortality rates amongst the adult population and a stealthier program of state-sanctioned child stealing. While such policies were sustainable in a world dominated by European and anglophone powers, they faltered under the banzai charge of Imperial Japan and later collapsed with the exposure of Nazi Germany's racist insanities, the dismemberment of the British Empire, the decolonisation of Africa and Asia, the emergence of the civil rights movement in America, the richly deserved demonisation of apartheid South Africa and, of course, the rapid dilution of Australia's own Anglo homogeny.

This latter process did not run altogether smoothly. For instance, the contribution of European Jews to postwar reconstruction was not appreciated by all. In February 1947, HB Gullet, a Liberal member of parliament wrote to the *Argus* in Melbourne describing the arrival of Jewish refugees from Europe as the beginning of a national tragedy and an act of gross deceit by the Immigration Minister, Arthur Calwell. Gullet said the Jews, an Eastern race, had swarmed all over Europe, owing loyalty and allegiance to nobody. They were rife in New York where they owned practically everything and in an accusation which could have come straight from the tombstone of Joseph Goebbels, he argued that: 'They secured a stranglehold on Germany after the last war during the inflation period, and in very large part brought upon themselves the persecution which they suffered'. If the policy of allowing them entry was continued the country would, he thought, 'bitterly rue the day'.

Most of the friction which arose as millions of European refugees poured into the cities of Sydney and Melbourne to rub up against the old British monoculture took the form of this sort of low-grade resentment and irritation. Born of ignorance and hopelessly disconnected from the brute facts of Australia's place in the

The Long Goodbye

world, it could not resist the force of realpolitik. Gullet, for instance, could have drawn little succour from the victory of his own conservative party in the federal election of 1949. Under Menzies the great postwar tide of migration continued unabated. In the space of one generation it completely transformed the Australian nation and that transformation was felt nowhere more keenly than in the metro centres where most of the newcomers settled. Before the Second World War the 'British' proportion of Australia's population was about ninety percent. By 1971 Sydney and Melbourne were ranked among the ten largest Greek cities in the world.

Given the deeply rooted xenophobia of the nineteenth century Australian character it may seem surprising that this massive conversion – from a mono- to a multi-cultural, or if you prefer from a provincial to a cosmopolitan society – should take place without the sort of convulsions which had attended previous migration waves. There were no Klan-like processions down George Street to beat up the aliens and burn down their homes and businesses. Not that the base level of paranoia was any less. With Australia having just closely escaped national extermination at the hands of Imperial Japan, and living under the shadow of a looming confrontation with the Communist bloc, the national psyche was raw and fearful.

But it was, ironically, the existence of this universal dread which allowed the dramatic metamorphosis to proceed without fracturing the Australian social contract. Australia's population almost doubled in one generation, but unlike America in the 1920s, or Great Britain at the end of the Empire, the new arrivals did not fundamentally threaten the dominant culture. They were different of course. The Poles, Yugoslavs, Czechs, Greeks and Italians who began to fill up Sydney's old inner city terraces brought new languages, customs, histories, food, art, literature, taboos and religion – their culture, in other words – which had defined their forebears' lives over thousands of years; a very different tapestry from the one stitched together by Sydney's Anglo-Celts in the previous century and a half.

It was not so different, however, as to undermine the basis of white civilization. As exotic as an Italian Jew or a Slavic peasant may have appeared to a fifth generation resident of Rose Bay or Manly, their histories intersected at many points in a common European narrative. Many of the Greeks who clustered together supportively in Redfern, Newtown and Erskineville had come from the hot, limestone island of Ithaca, which generations of English schoolchildren knew as the mythical home of Ulysses, and from Levkas, which some scholars think more likely to have been his home turf. They could see the democratic traditions of their ancestors transplanted to Australian institutions. The works of their ancients, of men like Plato and Hippocrates, were the bedrock upon which Western society rested. The Italians who arrived on the same migrant ships brought with them the history of Rome, which was synonymous with the history of Europe for 1000 years and of England for nearly 500. Roman rule gave birth to civilized England. Its language, religion, science and history – the machinery of national creation – were all shaped by Roman hands. Thus, 2000 years after Julius Caesar took his legions across the English Channel, Australian and Italian Catholics could find themselves worshipping the same God, in the same language, in a church built to principles laid down by Greek architects over two millennia earlier.

Coming hard on the end of a desperate war, the advent of mass

The Long Goodbye

European migration did not undermine the nation's sense of identity. In fact, as Sandra Rennie explains, it supported the existing cultural architecture. Still dealing with the recent prospect of annihilation, and no longer able to hide behind the skirts of Mother England, Australia was forced to recast its identity from being British to European, Protestant to Christian, and Anglo-Celtic to merely white. In doing so the country avoided the hysteria which had attended increased migration to America from similar sources after World War One. The US had restricted immigration in 1924 after growing panic about being swamped by the 'primitive Slavic races' who were pouring into Chicago and New York from the political sinkholes of old Europe. Identifying with Nordic culture generally and Anglo-Saxon in particular, and traumatised by the disappearance of the frontier upon which so much their mythology was based, American intellectuals and proles alike viewed the growth of the huge industrial cities and ethnic slums with alarm. After the attack on Pearl Harbor, isolated and sparsely populated Australia could not afford the same indulgence.

While the integration of European migrants progressed with remarkably few major problems, for Aborigines, Australia at the start of the 1950s fulfilled all of Jonathan Rauch's criteria for an oppressive society: direct legal and governmental discrimination, denial of political franchise, systematic denial of education, impoverishment and a long-established pattern of human rights violations without recourse. Asian Australians, with the exception of a few small remnant Chinese communities, did not exist. By the end of the 1960s however, White Australia's fortifications were crumbling and would soon be reduced to rubble by a remarkably bipartisan pincer movement from the major political parties. Unfortunately the renovations to the political superstructure did not alter some of the darker cultural foundations on which racist policies such as White Australia and Aboriginal child stealing had been erected. So while postwar economic success enabled Australian society to comfortably welcome millions of new arrivals from previously alien cultures, the retreating waters of official discrimination left behind a few stagnant pools of racism in which the pond scum clung tenaciously to life. The 1972 election which delivered the reforming Whitlam government also marked the first reappearance in the Western world of a Nazi party, the National Socialist Party of Australia, openly running, in jackboots and swastikas, on a crazed crank-up-the-gas-ovens platform.

Until that point the genteel face of racism had been maintained by Eric Butler, Australia's foremost anti-Semite and Nazi apologist. Butler was the long-time chief of the League of Rights, and from 1934 the publisher of a journal called *New Times*, which enthusiastically reported on the progress of Adolf Hitler's daring social experiment. After that experiment was rudely interrupted by the Second World War, the League changed tack, but only slightly. It declared that (i) the Holocaust was a fraud, (ii) the Luftwaffe was controlled by the Jews, (iii) the Nazi Party was controlled by Jews and (iv) Jews had engineered the war to make themselves look good. The League is still rattling along today, desperately trying to hitch itself to the One Nation bandwagon and still quietly maintaining that the Luftwaffe was controlled by the Jews.

National Action is another group of hard core right-wingers who have been busy cosying up to Pauline Hanson's populist movement. A very dubious bunch of Aryan enthusiasts, these guys spent a lot of their political gestation period thrashing about in impotent rage until the arrival of Dinh Tran and his fellow refugees gave them a hook on which to hang their fright masks and

The Long Goodbye

secondhand SS helmets. In 1979, when the first great wave of Vietnamese refugees broke on the shoreline, Sydney's right-wing extremists plastered the inner city with leaflets and stickers, the central theme of which could be summed up in the slogan 'Stop the Asian Invasion'. They received hundreds of initially sympathetic inquiries about their campaign, which unsurprisingly came to nothing when their true nature became obvious. Years later in the early 1980s about fifteen to twenty disgruntled right-wingers gathered around a few beers at a sharehouse in Glebe. They all agreed the revolution had been 'this close' but perhaps they shouldn't have booked the oompah band for their victory celebrations so quickly. Mainstream Australia just wasn't aware of the threat it faced from the Asian hordes. They would have to be led to that knowledge. To that end the activists founded a new party, National Action, which described its politics as the Third Way; neither capitalism nor communism but revolutionary nationalism. Spokesmen repeatedly stated they were not anti-Asian, merely opposed to the 'Asianisation' of Australia, and insisted that some Asian immigrants were acceptable as long as they assimilated.

Within a year, independent of developments in Glebe, the media began to run a hostile line against overseas students, particularly Asians. Sensing their time had come, National Action plastered campuses and the streets of Sydney with stickers and graffiti. In their own dim, pointy-headed way they had actually tuned into a powerful shift in the city's cultural and economic structure. The city's old north-south divide was rapidly mutating into an east-west schism. More than a decade later researchers from Sydney University's Planning Research Centre would describe the end point of this accelerating mutation: a bifurcated city 'with a band of middle-income suburbs standing in between what looks like two armies confronting each other'. Furthermore, by the late 1990s the geographical divide was amplified by a growing economic and racial chasm, with poverty strongly ethnicised along the city's south-west frontier and marked, according to a Monash University study, by 'the emergence of a potentially huge underclass in Sydney, concentrated in such areas as Fairfield, Auburn, Canterbury and Bankstown'.

For every Dinh Tran who carved out their own version of the Australian dream, there is a Nguyen or a Wang trapped in the gears of an economy grinding its way out of the past. Globalised production, often said to have exported low-skilled Australian jobs to places like Indonesia and China, has in fact imported the work practices and 'efficiencies' of the Third World to the suburbs of Sydney, nowhere more so than in the clothing industry, one of the biggest employers of migrant women. Typically working between twelve and eighteen hours a day, seven days a week, for three dollars an hour or less – a return to the practices of a hundred years ago, when the trade exploited Sydney's poor white working girls in much the same manner – they are at the sharp end of massive changes which have overtaken the local clothing industry in the last decade or so. They are also emblematic of the dark side of increasing economic efficiency. While improving productivity would seem to be a motherhood issue, it is also, as Henry Mayhew explained, a matter of economising human fuel. Isolated, desperate for work, often with poor language skills and unaware of their rights, the outworkers fall prey to the lowest sort of operators. Whole families work and eat at their sewing machines, living in their garages and sheds for days at a time to complete large orders. One woman who rang the Textile, Clothing and Footwear Union had worked unpaid for eight months. When she approached her employer about her money, he punched her and took her receipt book – the only evidence she had of the work she had done. Another woman contacted the union after working an incredible 150 hour week then being told that because of a mistake in the sewing – a flaw she had identified but been told to ignore – she would not be paid.

Throughout the 1980s a booming economy masked the social consequences of this deep tectonic rupture within the city's demographics. While shareholders, CEOs and property owners in Sydney's east and north gorged themselves on the proceeds of profit growth and asset inflation, hundreds of thousands in the city's south and west were chopped into a fine mince by the same economic system. Ethnic atomisation complicated the process, with poor families from Lebanon, Vietnam, Turkey, Cambodia and Laos displacing hundreds of thousands of poor whites on the urban fringe, the latter decamping for the coastal strip north of the city. And while the achievements of some Asian-Australians taunted those trapped in relative or even absolute poverty the failure of many others to cope with the transition to Sydney's rapidly globalising economy has provided legions of bitter recruits to the army of the underclass.

Taken in isolation any one of these developments could drastically destabilise a society. At their point of confluence they were potentially tragic. This may be the point Geoffrey Blainey was trying to make in 1984 when he ignited the national race debate. Whatever his intentions though, simply positing a connection between race, culture and social crisis proved to be a self-fulfilling prophecy. Corrosive anxiety about massive economic change suddenly fused with fears of racial and cultural change and National Action unexpectedly found itself called upon to explain its position. These paragons of the master race denied they were in any way racist. National Action didn't believe in the superiority of one race over another. It simply believed that the Anglo-Celtic culture of Australia should not be endangered. As more people noted what they were saying, *Ultra*, the party's internal bulletin, announced that the time had come for taking it to the streets.

Student unions noted an escalating number of bashings of Asian students after dark, both on campus and around the inner city. There was a shift not just in the frequency of political violence, but also in its intensity and focus. The targets began to change. The party bulletin *Audacity* featured a regular 'filth file' in which critics of the party would find their name, phone number and address published with an invitation to the 'curious and adventurous' to dish out a little nationalist justice. Journalists such as Gerard Henderson, Andrew Olle and Adele Horin who covered the immigration debate or related topics in an unsatisfactory manner began to receive phone calls and death threats late at night. Academics and unionists found their car tyres slashed and graffiti daubed on their houses. Greenpeace and Community Aid Abroad shops were broken into and looted.

Subverting the dominant paradigm doesn't come cheap, however, so in early 1984 a scam was cooked up to rip off the GIO and raise money to buy all the shotguns and balaclavas they would need to make people understand the righteousness of their cause. A woman who rented a room at National Action headquarters came home one day to find the place ransacked, her jewellery gone and party member Jim Saleam shaking his head. Later the woman overheard Saleam talking about 'sharing out the insurance money' with another party member. He was found guilty of insurance fraud in 1987. His appeal failed in April 1989 and he was later jailed as Jewish Luftwaffe veterans everywhere chuckled

The Long Goodbye

quietly into their glasses. Saleam ate another big bowl of Her Majesty's porridge after a bungled terror attack on Eddie Funde, a representative of Nelson Mandela's African National Congress. A few months before his failed appeal a couple of NA storm troopers covered the licence plates of their car, drove over to Funde's place, pulled on balaclavas and pumped a couple of rounds through the front door. The shooter and his driver were tumbled and rolled over, but Saleam put the Crown through the inconvenience of trying him for supplying the shotty and organising the job before they could lock him up again.

Regardless of Saleam's personal travails the wider Asian immigration debate continued, often with no real refinement of the sort of arguments which had so inflamed Sydney's rougher element a hundred years earlier. Emboldened by mainstream support for their position – if not actually for them – National Action began working its way down the enemies list, widening their focus from vulnerable students and the occasional journalist to gays, lesbians, Aboriginal, peace and anti-apartheid groups, academics, liberal congregations such as the Pitt Street Uniting Church, the Antidiscrimination Board, union activists and, somewhat recklessly, a couple of Special Branch cops who had been assigned to their case. After National Action raided the meeting of a gay migration lobby group the hammer came down.

Having suffered through months of harassment the gays were ready for a fight. Their resistance seemed to unnerve the storm troopers and a handful of hysterical pansies and angry dykes proceeded to bitch slap them out of the room. Special Branch quickly obtained a search warrant and charged over to a house in Petersham used as an alternative headquarters by NA. They found a tape recording and photographs of the raid. Most of the those who took part were arrested and charged. The cases were heard in Glebe local court and attended by observers from a resistance group called Community Alert Against Racism and Violence. 'It was unbelievably pathetic,' said CAARAV's Betty Hounslow. 'Shane Rosier, one of their big men, was just this really pathetic bloke in his late forties who was, you know, a bit chubby. He wore these brown trousers that kept riding up the back and an old yukko-looking brown cardigan. They found a lot of weapons in his house ... coshs, chains, and studded balls. And his story to the magistrate was that the weapons were part of his collection. He'd always been interested in weapons, he said. His grandfather was a famous gun collector. He and his dad had always wanted to have a gun collection just like old Granddad's, but they'd never had enough money to collect guns so they had to collect cheaper, working-class weapons. And this was why he had all these things. He said the tape of the raid was left on his doorstep one morning. Like a little abandoned baby.'

The pressure told and the right-wing extremists turned on each other as deeply repressed suspicions and rivalries burst through to the surface. Everybody seemed to accuse everyone else of being police spies and sexual deviants. The final slide into ignoble collapse was marked by the gunshot murder of Wayne 'Bovver' Smith in National Action headquarters at Tempe a few years later. It was an almost perfect example of the hapless farce which so often attended the adventures of National Action in the 1980s. Bovver, twenty-five years old and already weighing 108 kilos thanks to the three or four stubbies of beer he'd consume for breakfast each morning, was shot eight times with a sawn-off .22 rifle by Perry Whitehouse, ten years his senior but less than half his size, during

The Long Goodbye

a drunken, confused and basically pointless argument. When Whitehouse blew him away, Bovver was wearing a singlet bearing the message: Say No To The New Gun Control Laws.

National Action's failure could be sheeted home to a number of factors – besides their being totally fucked. The anti-Chinese movement of a century before had enjoyed widespread parliamentary and political support. Most importantly the union movement provided a well-organised structure for protest and, in the dispute over Chinese seamen, had a single, easily exploitable focus for a mass campaign. Also, the press on the whole supported the protesters. A hundred years later there was no single flashpoint from which to launch a mass campaign. The middle classes had no readily discernible problems with Asian migration and had in fact benefited from the contribution of Indochinese settlers to the diversification of inner urban culture – even if this was merely a superficial enjoyment of increasing numbers of Asian restaurants. Until the arrival of Pauline Hanson and One Nation there was no significant parliamentary support for the reintroduction of racist policy making, although Liberal leader John Howard did cause himself considerable difficulties by trying to tap into the anxieties which Geoffrey Blainey identified. National Action also erred in their eagerness to open hostilities against a rainbow coalition of gays, blacks, unionists and the like. As much as these interest groups may have offended the sensibilities of the respectable right there was simply no constituency outside the clubhouse at Tempe for saddling up and charging after them with shotguns and firebombs.

Obscured by all this, however, is the simple fact that like most pseudo-revolutionaries, Sydney's extremists simply could not tear themselves away from the comfortable inner suburbs where their favourite pubs were always close at hand. Had they ventured beyond the cafe zone they would have found more fertile ground for their seed. Out in suburbs like Macquarie Fields, St Marys and Mount Druitt where three generations of one family can be found scratching by on welfare, the likes of Australians Against Further Immigration, and more recently One Nation have found a receptive audience for their slightly more sophisticated protofascism. For despite the abject failure of National Action the past two decades have been characterised by the disintegration of postwar consensus over migration as the threat of cultural annihilation from outside is forgotten and the strain of economic inequality increases.

People who feel themselves threatened, who think they are getting less than they deserve, inevitably cast about for an explanation. In the end that's all Pauline Hanson offered, although she added the force multiplier of blame. Not just blame of the Government or Opposition who are mostly remote media figures, electrons and sound bites, but blame of tangible, immediately accessible human beings. That Vietnamese baker. Those threatening black teenagers. That rich Chinese businessman in the silver Mercedes. Whatever becomes of Hanson, the economic conditions and policies which gave rise to her and fellow travellers like Saleam persist. It may be then that Sydney's first story, a 200-year-long epic of successful migration, is over. And the wealth which was so ruthlessly taken from the first inhabitants will not be so readily handed over to the next.

2
The Virgin's Lie

There shall broad streets their stately walls extend,
The circus widen, and the crescent bend;
There, ray'd from cities o'er the cultur'd land,
Shall bright canals, and solid roads expand ...

ERASMUS DARWIN, 'Visit of Hope to Sydney Cove', 1789

And her five cities, like five teeming sores
Each drains her; a vast parasite robber state
Where secondhand Europeans pullulate
Timidly on the edge of alien shores.

AD HOPE, 'Australia', 1955

The morning after the Russians crashed a plutonium-powered Mars probe into the ocean off Chile I awoke before six. It was light, with summer on us and, unable to sleep, I decided on a walk around the cliffs at South Bondi. Bad cabin fever can set in when you're writing a long book and it's a good idea to get out every now and then, breathe some air, maybe talk to somebody. My friend Peter Robb, who was finishing *Midnight in Sicily* while I was trudging through the research for *Leviathan*, told me that he worried he had become strange and eccentric as he sank deeper into the project. I was aware of something similar within me as the weeks and months wore on and the keyboard time started to stack up. So I forced myself to leave the flat occasionally. Just enough to stay in practice.

The weather had been foul at the start of that summer, making my confinement even more severe. The previous week, while friends back in Brisbane had complained of stifling forty degree days, I had hurried, shivering, down Campbell Parade to the Noodle King wearing black jeans, two jumpers and a greatcoat. A few other fools hurried along with hands thrust deep into the pockets of their heavy coats, some of them nuzzling into bulky scarves or clapping gloved hands together. This was summer at

The Virgin's Lie

Bondi, I kept reminding myself over a huge bowl of hot chicken laksa as the wind blew folding sheets of salty rain and sea spray around.

However, this morning dawn had come hard and bright with only a fresh breeze to take the edge off the promise of a warm day. I had a heavy schedule that week and had already shot Monday to hell, sleeping in then ditzing about on the Net for hours looking for celebrity porn. Waking early on Tuesday, I figured on a walk down the beach to check out the surf and clear my head before a big writing session. I'd become a little more attuned to the vagaries of the surf over the months I'd been living at the beach. I was never much of a swimmer, especially in the ocean, but I'd had a bodyboard years ago and still remembered the reassuring, if misleading sense of control it gave me out in the breakers. I bought another one after moving to Bondi, thinking I could use it to get a little exercise, to temper the effects of a sedentary lifestyle. You'll understand the extent of my cluelessness when I say that I planned to hit the beach and catch tubes every day in summer. It didn't occur to me in any real way that the surf was a living thing, with arbitrary, lethal moods. It was an idea I was familiar with, having grown up in Australia, but not one I understood in my bones. I had never been sucked out to sea by a rip, never been driven into the sand like a tent-peg by a mean, beach-breaking dumper. I knew intellectually that the sea was capricious and uncaring, but she hadn't had her evil way with me and so I didn't really understand.

That changed when I took my walk that morning. I was only a minute or two's stroll back from the strip at Bondi and I could tell something was different as soon as I left the flat. It wasn't just the fine weather. There was something below that, something deeper.

After a few moments of idling along, I realised with a start that I could hear the roar of something big over the rise at the end of the street. I'd grown used to the background noise of the surf, especially late at night or now, early in the morning, when there was no traffic to mask it. But this was different. Hurrying a little, I wondered if maybe I should have fetched my board. I realised as soon as I made the rise what a fool idea that had been.

The entire bay, nearly a kilometre across, was alive with snaking ridge lines of cold, green salt water. They were immense, ungodly things, deformities in the surface of the world, piling up and up until they were taller than some of the old apartment blocks clustered around the far side of the bay. They raced in towards the crescent of the beach in sets of seven, eight or nine. Because Bondi's shoreline is turned in at about forty-five degrees, with the northern end of the bay cradled behind the massive rocky outcrop of Ben Buckler, it is the southern reach which normally gets the clean rolling swells loved by surfers. But an intense storm which had swept across the coastline 300 kilometres to the north during the night and spent itself out at sea had drummed a berserk, frenzied rhythm into the surface of the Pacific and that wild energy had travelled back to land in the form of these behemoth waves. There was no sheltered water anywhere in the bay. It had become a giant cauldron awash with precipitous walls of spray and spume, with foaming canyons and cold boiling turmoil.

It was all the more astounding for the still, pleasant nature of the morning. No clouds or smog haze sullied the powder blue sky and the sun still hung low, burning with a fierce white light which the deeper, calmer waters caught and threw off as a silver sheet too painful to look into without squinting. So vast and dense were the waves closer in, however, that as they built up then collapsed in on themselves, they formed cavernous inky-black tunnels which admitted no light. I turned to walk back to the beach as a monstrous wall of water smashed into a rock ledge way below, throwing a geyser into the air above me.

Across the bay white water burst over the rocks at Ben Buckler, churning and billowing and erupting again in time with the pulse of the waves. One huge black rock stood out on the shelf below, big as a truck, unaffected by the millions of tonnes of water slamming into it. It looked fixed and utterly immovable, as though it had been there 10 000 years before Arthur Phillip rowed past and would be there another 10 000 years from now. There is a bronze plaque on that rock, fixed into the face turned away from the waves.

This rock, weighing two hundred and thirty-five tons, was washed up from the sea during a storm on 15 July, 1912.

Locals appear to have had trouble convincing visitors that the sea actually spat up this giant, lifted it three metres from the ocean floor and carried it another fifty metres across the rocky shelf which juts out from the base of Ben Buckler. The plaque was set on the rock in March 1933, but the intervening years had allowed some doubt to set in. Residents said the rock had been used as a makeshift changing area before the turn of the century. However, photographs taken in the 1880s and held by the State Library show the area to be clear and so it seems that a furious sea did in fact disgorge the brute one night before the First World War.

I'll admit I became a little obsessed with that rock. There was something in its legend which muttered to me of our sense of place, a fear that the land itself might just be malevolent, waiting for a chance to do us wrong. The civilized mind's response to Australia's vast ageless spaces has always been deeply anxious; an uneasy awe which local artists have touched to great effect, in *Picnic at Hanging Rock* for instance, or in Nolan's Ned Kelly paintings, those alien landscapes peopled by strange, disturbing figures, filling the hollow places of your heart with dread and desolation. The land was as much the enemy of Watkin Tench and his revengers as the blacks whom they had set out to slaughter. The 'Indians' seemed to disappear into it, while the white men nearly disappeared under it when they blundered into that muddy riverbed. Its thin sandy clays begrudged the first settlers even a subsistence crop. Its heat baked and finished off the foolhardy and well prepared alike. Its snakes and spiders and slithering things could kill a man with one bite, or drive him mad with a hundred nettlesome stings. Axes which bit hungrily into sturdy English oaks rang impotently on the ironbark. And the sea, which surrounded them and separated them forever from Mother England, seemed to contain as many terrors as the jungles of Africa.

A couple of guys at the University of Wollongong – Professors Bryant and Young – enlivened my search for information about the big rock at Bondi when I came across their papers on the incidence of tsunamis along the New South Wales coast. They fronted up to the 13th Australian Geological Convention in 1996 to argue that catastrophically large waves had struck the coast around Sydney on six occasions over the past 8000 years. The most recent, between 250 and 300 years ago, topped out at 110 metres and was powerful enough to roar over the cliffs and punch inland for five kilometres. To appreciate the effect of such a monster coming ashore today, you would need to imagine a wall of water sweeping up Pitt Street about level with the thirtieth floor

The Virgin's Lie

of Governor Phillip Tower. Such a wave, it seemed to me, wouldn't have much trouble tossing around a marble like the big rock at Bondi.

Except of course the Bryant–Young tsunamis were not brewed up by a storm. More likely they were caused by some cataclysmic event like a sea floor collapsing at the edge of the continental shelf. It would not be the only recorded instance of such a disaster in the Pacific region. Something similar probably caused the Lanai Event which threw debris over 300 metres up the steep sides of that Hawaiian island 100 000 years ago, while a landslide in an Alaskan fjord in 1946 caused a wave which deposited debris as high as 524 metres above sea level. The waves which battered the coast of Sydney in 1912, however, were simply generated by bad weather in the Tasman Sea.

Luckily, an authoritative contemporary account survives, delivered to the Royal Society of New South Wales by Carl Sussmilch just one and a half months after the freak storm. A balding guy, with a smile which beamed out from behind rimless spectacles, Sussmilch was a chubby-faced, eloquent geologist intimately acquainted with Sydney's coastal environment. Visiting Bondi Beach a short time after the storm, he was instantly struck by the extent of the damage. He had seen nothing like it in fifteen years of study. Sussmilch described the devastation for the other members of the society: large boulders thrown two to three metres up a rock shelf, some sixty metres from their original resting places; huge rocks split as though by dynamite; massive scarring of the sandstone platform, and more marine denudation above the high-water mark 'during the few hours of this one storm than the cumulative results of many previous years'. Sussmilch told his astounded audience that besides being lifted and carried over fifty metres, the big rock had been completely turned over, as evidenced by the marine life now growing on what had been its top. There was no doubt some heavy shit had gone down at Bondi. The *Sydney Morning Herald* had also reported, just after the storm, that swimming baths were swept away, along with changing sheds, refreshment rooms and, at the northern end of the beach, everything but one brick house.

Spectacular as the tempest of 1912 was, the last great inundation to drastically affect the city's coastline was not Sussmilch's freak storm, or even one of Bryant and Young's monster waves, but the rapid rise of the seas about 10 000 years ago. Giant ice sheets had previously locked up much of the world's fresh water, but with the warming of the planet they melted and the seas rose by about sixty-five metres, advancing over the area's broad coastal plains at a rate of about two metres a year. The process stabilised only 6000 years ago. Aborigines had been making their homes in the valleys and plains of Sydney for much longer than that, possibly for more than 40 000 years, and so bore witness to this event, rapid in geological time but just gradual enough in human terms to be manageable.

It was not the first time the area had been drowned. The seas had advanced and retreated through the valleys which now form Sydney Harbour up to eight times in the last 700 000 years, sometimes dropping 100 metres below their present level, opening up stretches of gently sloping, grassy plains where the Pacific now marches off towards the horizon; sometimes submerging vast tracts of currently high, dry and valuable real estate. The city's singular geography assisted in these repeated inundations. Lying in a sort of elongated sandstone bowl, Sydney occupies ground which has remained relatively unscathed by the changes which tore at the rest of the seaboard as the continent floated around, bumping into

The Virgin's Lie

other land masses, grinding together to form the mega-continent of Gondwana before being torn asunder again.

Geologists like to describe this bowl, the Sydney basin, as Permo-Triassic in origin, meaning that basically it didn't exist as a structural entity until about 250 million years ago. At that time Australia lay in the south east corner of the supercontinent known as Gondwana, slotted in between Antarctica and India. As the forebears of the dinosaurs and later mammals began to evolve, the future site of Sydney, a flat featureless sort of place, started to sink. It was as though an irascible God, unhappy with his first try, had reached down and pressed his thumb onto the coast, leaving a rim at the edge of the land just high enough to keep out the sea. As long as the sea didn't rise of course. This shallow depression had the good fortune not to be badly folded or warped over the next couple of hundred million years. Around it, however, change was taking place. Mountain ranges raised up from the earth's crust to then be worn down over hundreds of millions of years, their coarse quartz sediment carried into the shallow bowl by streams and rivers and deposited in thick beds on the floors of swamps and lakes. Great arcs of time passed as the massive tracts of golden sandstone and later shale were laid down and compressed to form the future city's foundations.

Even with this activity the topography of the basin remained fairly boring until about one million years ago when gentle movements in the earth's crust gradually lifted the sandstone beds nearly 230 metres above sea level. The soft, sandy *tabula rasa* cracked and was then gouged and eroded by rivers and streams to a depth of 190 metres. The islands and bays of Sydney Harbour were created as glaciers melted and the seas flooded into these deep river valleys, some reaching back as far as fifty kilometres inland. To the south, however, in Botany Bay, the site of the First Fleet's abortive initial landing, the plains had not been raised by folding of the crust before the Ice Age. Indeed the area had sunk a little as the Blue Mountains wrenched themselves skywards, with an extensive flood plain being eroded between the Georges and Cook Rivers. This too was then drowned with its sister harbour 10 000 years ago.

It's not known exactly when the first human footprints were pressed into the soft muddy shores of the harbour. Chances are the ancestors of the Iora walked down through the steep-sided river valleys which became the upper reaches of Port Jackson and Broken Bay whilst they were still dry, forested hollows. The coastal plains on which they hunted and lived now sleep beneath the rolling swells of the Pacific, and any trace of the ancients' passing has long since been obliterated. Pressed by the rising seas and climate change, the Aborigines retreated and adapted where other species died off. Giant kangaroos and wallabies, many times larger than their present-day descendants, disappeared along with the fierce leopardlike *Thylacoleo carnifex*, a carnivorous relative of the possum, and the slow, hulking Diprotodon (think of it as a sort of long-necked rhinoceros wombat). Unlike their human competitors, the extinct marsupials relied on the incremental adjustments of evolution to fit them out for a rapidly changing world. The Aborigines however didn't need to wait a thousand generations to grow claws and fangs to tackle the likes of *Thylacoleo*. They didn't have to sprout a thick, furry pelt to keep out the cold. They could shape a spear or light a fire and change the world itself.

For James Cook, Australia was a 'continent of smoke'. As the *Endeavour* sailed slowly up the eastern coast, both Cook and botanist Joseph Banks scratched frequent notes into their journals

The Virgin's Lie

about the fires which burned on shore. Every day seemed to bring more of them, from the small twinkling campfires which appeared at dawn and dusk, to huge perplexing conflagrations which filled the sky with ash and embers. Fire, which they never seemed to lose sight of in the following months, was in part responsible for the careworn visage the continent turned towards the sailors. Banks wrote that the country, although 'well enough cloth'd appear'd in some places bare'. It reminded him of the back of a hungry cow, 'cover'd in general with long hair', but scraped clean by 'accidental rubbs and knocks' wherever her scraggy hip bones had stuck out further than they should.

When they finally landed in Botany Bay, the English stepped into a land transformed. For thousands of years the Iora and their cousins had set the firestick to small patches of ground, to individual trees, to single gullies or hillsides to clear ground for easier travel and hunting, to kill vermin and to regenerate plant stocks for themselves and for the kangaroos which played such an important role in their economy. They used fire to limit the growth of rainforest, which was unusable to them. When the First Fleet's officers pushed out past the picket lines of their little settlement to explore the country beyond Sydney Cove, they found charred or smoking trees every kilometre or so. They recognised the hand of the natives but did not understand the extent of their influence. The firestick kept the forests clear of choking undergrowth and promoted plants which responded to fire as a natural part of their life cycle. When the Aborigines were driven away, this ecological regime, thousands of years in the making, was disastrously undermined.

Fuel loads were the problem. Fuel loads and human folly. It was many generations before the white man learned to imitate the firestick's effect by burning off small patches of land. Sir Thomas

Mitchell, New South Wales's Surveyor-General in the 1830s and 1840s, illustrated the change when he wrote that without the 'natives to burn the grass', thick forests of young trees had sprung up 'where, formerly, a man might gallop without impediment and see whole miles before him'. Those thick young forests, rather than being thinned by small, periodic burn-offs, grew even denser and more tangled. Leaves, branches and dead trunks compacted into a dry, incendiary carpet on the forest floor as lantana wound itself through the impenetrable undergrowth. Long hot summers baked every trace of moisture from the scrub, which intermittently exploded in vast apocalyptic firestorms. At first these wildfires were only a problem for the country folk who lived and worked within the mutating bush; but as the coastal cities sprawled into forested hinterlands, more and more people built their homes inside the doors of the furnace. Seventy-one of them died in Victoria in January 1939 when bushfires destroyed 1000 homes across the state. Another seventy-two perished in the Ash Wednesday blaze of 1983. In between, smaller catastrophes carried off the forgetful and unwary; sixteen in January of 1952, five in the Blue Mountains in December 1957, and another three fire-fighters and a hundred houses in October 1968.

Unfortunately the lamentations of the dead spoke only fitfully to the living. While the professional fire-fighters who routinely bore the brunt of summer's burning came to understand the bush and its demands, most who chose to live at the city's edge did not learn the lesson. In January 1994 the effects of two centuries of this folly was concentrated within the folds of a long, deep, riotously overgrown valley near the juncture of the Georges and Woronora Rivers in Sydney's southern suburbs. Just a few kilometres from the immense sweep of the Royal National Park,

The Virgin's Lie

Como, Jannali and the neighbouring suburbs of Menai, Illawong and Bangor are a fine example of the deal Sydney has struck with the bushland at its edge. Here ridgetop development wraps sinuously around quiet river bends and along the scarps of plunging valleys. These valleys are themselves choked with matted scrub, their deepest reaches largely inaccessible. It is striking scenery, even stunning in the right light.

The morning of Saturday 8 January found these suburbs, found all of Sydney in fact ringed by fire. Hot dry winds had been streaming towards the coast from the dead centre for many days. Averaging twenty knots, gusting to forty, the breath of the desert parched everything it touched. The sun shone as a small red dot through thick roiling masses of smoke which rose from over two hundred fires around the state, many of them raging out of control and threatening to join together in a repeat of the disasters of 1939 and 1983. City dwellers, whose only usual contact with the annual cycle of calamity was through the news media, found themselves running through their own suburban streets as trees and houses exploded in flame. Roads were cut, ash fell on beaches, fire-fighters died and thousands fled. In the week before that Saturday most of the action had been played out across the city's north and in the mountains to the west. There were fires in the south, however, and hundreds of men and women fought them just as desperately, a little resentful at times of the attention paid to the suffering of the media's favourite demographic north of the Harbour Bridge.

A huge fire had broken out in the Royal National Park on Wednesday, quickly threatening the small townships of Maianbar and Bundeena on the shores of Port Hacking. About six o'clock the following evening, while the brigades were heavily committed in the national park, John Hay, a constable at the small roadside police station in Menai a few kilometres away saw fire break out in the scrub nearby and hurried over to stamp it out. At that time it was only three or four metres in diameter and the flames were crackling low to the ground. It was more than one man could handle, however, and it soon set off for the south-west, pushed along by strong winds and feeding hungrily on the scrub which is so common in that part of Sydney. That fire would grow and burn fiercely through the streets and back blocks of Menai, but by midnight the local bushfire brigade had it calmed down to a charred ground of smouldering tree stumps.

It flared again the next day as the wind picked up embers and dropped them all over the suburb. By three it was burning so ferociously in Menai's tangle of cul-de-sacs, dead-end streets and loop roads that fire-fighters had given up battling it directly and had shifted instead to the protection of life and property. Gale-force winds whipped twisters of fire high into the sky, walls of flame blew vertically over the roofs of houses and the scorching air was alight with flying debris. As dramatic as these scenes were, the worst was still to come, for this blaze was tearing over ground where the fire brigades and those home owners who elected to stay could still stand and fight. A few hundred metres away yawned the maze of deep valleys which had drawn so many residents to the area. The massive system of interlinked canyons, some kilometres across and hundreds of metres deep, was heavy with millions of tonnes of tinder-dry fuel which had been sitting, baking in the sun and high wind, waiting for a spark.

It should never have happened. It was not as though people hadn't been warned. Sutherland Council, the authority responsible, had filed away numerous letters from the local bushfire brigade about the ominous build-up in fuel loads since the late 1980s.

The Virgin's Lie

Weather constraints, funding problems and resistance to indiscriminate burning from environmentalists combined with simple inertia to see the warnings ignored for five years. Across the river, in Como, in a yawning, steep-sided gorge known as the Glen Reserve, the situation was even more precarious.

Glen Reserve lies in a corridor running from the head of Bonnet Bay between a hilltop labyrinth of winding avenues (curiously, all named after American presidents) and a soaring, heavily wooded cliff face, above which sit Lincoln and Woronora Crescents. Like the valleys across the river, the Glen Reserve had not been cleared or backburned for a long time. Like them it had been flagged as a serious flashpoint for many years, this time by the NSW Fire Brigade rather than the volunteers of a local bushfire outfit. For years Sutherland Council had been filing correspondence from residents and fire-fighters requesting action to reduce the hazard in the reserve. No action was ever taken. One and half kilometres long and nearly three hundred metres wide, it had become, by January 1994, an enormous firepit. It sat at the mouth of a giant funnel formed by the canyons across the Woronora River. And when the conflagration which tore through those canyons finally spat a burning branch across the river over the heads of the men in the fireboat, it went up. Not like the fire which Constable Hay had tried to stamp out – slowly at first and building over a period of days. This one went up like a bomb.

The sort of bomb it resembled actually has a name: a fuel-air explosive device. These were developed by the Americans as a sort of poor man's nuclear warhead. Put simply, this device sprays an extremely flammable, superfine mist over a wide area, which it then ignites in one stroke. Nature conspired with about five years of half-witted bureaucratic docility to create a fuel-air explosive in the bushland below Lincoln and Woronora Crescents on the afternoon of 8 January. Besides the incredible tonnages of dry plant matter resting on the floor of the reserve, there were hundreds if not thousands of living gum trees. Of the many species which have adapted to the Aborigines' fire regime, the *eucalypti* are arguably the most successful. They have no lower branches to burn during smaller ground fires. Their base is protected by thick flame resistant bark. This shelters little buds which sprout like a bright green stocking after a larger fire, sustaining life while the eucalypt regrows its major limbs. In stronger fires long strips of bark conduct the flame quickly up to the forest canopy where the leaves exude a fine oily mist which explodes on contact with the flames, carrying the fire through the canopy in such a rush that most of the tree is left unscathed.

This inflammable mist lay heavily over the Glen Reserve as the Menai fire approached. However, it was a long, long fall from Lincoln Crescent to the floor of the reserve and many residents were out on their verandahs or walking the ridge line that Saturday afternoon, taking in the spectacular scenes, little worried by the time bomb lying at their feet. Not that they were completely sanguine. At one o'clock Alan Subkey, a fire brigade officer, arrived in Lincoln Crescent with a lighting truck and a brief to stand watch in case the Illawong fires should jump the river. A number of locals stopped to voice their fears to Subkey about such an eventuality but, with the Emergency Services' communication channels already heavily overloaded, he did not pass their concerns on to his superiors. He was relieved by another fireman, Tom Mood, about half an hour later. Mood parked in front of number 39 and while on lookout chatted with the two young girls who lived at that address, ten-year-old Catherine Dickin and her thirteen-year-old sister

The Virgin's Lie

Kylie. About quarter past two Tom Mood was ordered down the hill to Jefferson Crescent where a fire had broken out, threatening a number of homes. As Mood and his partner drove away they saw no immediate danger to Lincoln Crescent and in that they were supported by Catherine and Kylie's dad, Richard. The Dickins watched TV during the afternoon and wandered out to the verandah occasionally. There they could see increasingly thick smoke billowing up from the Illawong fires, as well as a number of their neighbours, out on their own verandahs or walking the street, taking in the same view. None of them had been warned about the disaster which was about to engulf them. Nobody had been around to advise on evacuation plans or even the rudiments of preparing their homes for what was coming.

It was inevitable. In a submission to the coronial inquiry into the fire, one expert witness, Dr Edmund Potter, said that if ever there was a case for selective evacuation, Lincoln Crescent was it. He wondered how any responsible official with even 'a smattering' of common sense could have failed to anticipate what would happen in the Glen Reserve. They did, sort of, which is why Subkey and Mood were sent to watch over it. But the Emergency Services' failing communication systems, combined with conflicting lines of authority, the extreme demands of the situation and the simple element of human frailty ensured that when tragedy did strike there were no assets in place to cope with it. Recognising the inevitable, however, did not require Dr Potter's twenty-twenty hindsight. At eleven that Saturday morning John Benson, a resident of Woronora Crescent and an off-duty fire officer of many years experience, had stood on the bluff high above the Glen Reserve watching the fires across the river. He was so sure the blaze would make it over the water that he rang his boss and requested to be placed back on duty. But, according to Potter, none of the authorities higher up the chain of command 'was watchful and in readiness . . .'.

Shortly before four o'clock the bomb went off. The same hot, dry westerly winds which appeared almost every day during the fire crisis materialised at two p.m. They blew directly over the scorched ground where Constable Hay had stamped out a fire two days earlier, and swept down into the burning maelstrom of the Illawong valley system. The fire-fighters working deep inside that cauldron noticed the change immediately. Walls of flame grew higher and moved faster. Burning embers and branches and storms of hot ash flew thicker and faster. At two-thirty Carl Caterson, visiting his parents' home, the last in Sproule Road, Illawong, saw a large fire jump a break prepared by navy personnel down near the river and travel a hundred metres towards his house in five seconds. The Caterson house had a good view of the Woronora River and Carl watched the fire tear around the face of the ridge and make for the water.

There was a bushfire brigade launch down there, on standby at the mouth of Bonnet Bay. Deputy Captain Peter Carter, who had felt the rapid increase in wind speed, watched a seven-metre tall wall of flame accelerate through bushland he and mate Scott Ireland had recently hosed down. Around three-thirty they saw the fire make the jump. The burning sparks arced over eight hundred metres to land in the dry brush. A spot fire burst into life. It was about the size, Carter thought, of a family car. Then *whooomph!* Within seconds it had detonated into a furious blaze as big as three football fields, and the whole hill beneath Woronora Crescent was alight.

Spot fires had broken out elsewhere in Como as well. As Carter and Ireland watched the start of the Glen Reserve holocaust, about two kilometres away hot ash and smoke were rising from behind the Jannali High School. This outbreak quickly spiralled out of control and engulfed twenty houses and the Como West Public School. Called to Woronora Crescent by a radio message for urgent assistance, Detective Sergeant Beresford saw a huge fireball come barrelling up from the valley below to roar over a couple of police vehicles and ignite trees on the other side of the road. At one minute to four the main body of the fire leapt right over the massive cliff face and fell on the undefended street. It took out the church down near Bindea Street first. A fire-fighter named Reid who had driven about three hundred metres along Lincoln Crescent saw that the houses at numbers 36 and 38 were going up. He travelled another fifty metres to park outside number 19. Monstrous liquid rivers of flame were pouring over the ridge line at eighty kilometres an hour and the sky was a blanket of fire three metres above him. Visibility shrank to less than two metres and spot fires ignited three houses in a row. Home owners and fire-fighters extinguished them, but then number 27 exploded in a massive roiling plume which could not be doused.

Up at 39, Richard Dickin had watched the deteriorating situation with alarm. When he saw the geyser of flame, maybe sixty metres high, which burst over the crest of the hill to incinerate the church down the street, he told his wife Mary and the two girls to get ready. They were out of there. Their house, which Richard had spent some time preparing just in case, was one of the sturdier homes in a street which still contained numerous fibro cottages from the postwar boom. It was a brick dwelling of two storeys on a strong base of Hawkesbury sandstone. It was solid, much loved and kept in immaculate condition. It would not last more than a few more minutes. Suddenly the windows blew out of neighbour David Kelk's place. Kelk, who had put considerable energy into his own precautions, rushed from the house, which was instantly filled with smoke and hot ash, to find all of the trees in his garden alight, along with his eaves and fibro fence. It was an awesome sight, but nothing compared to Dickin's house. That was an inferno. Driven back by the blistering heat, Kelk was quickly found by a couple of fire-fighters and ushered away with his wife.

Inside 39 the family and their two dogs piled into the car for a quick escape. As the garage door opened however, they were confronted by the savage cremation of the front of their house which David Kelk had just seen. A ute at the top of the drive had gone up and the furious torrent of fire blasting up from the reserve was driven right into their faces by the wind. Richard Dickin hurriedly shut the door and they fled back into the house, sheltering inside the bathroom. Knowing they couldn't stay there, Dickin went to search for an escape route through the back yard. While he was away fire burst from Catherine's bedroom. Mary, Catherine and Kylie ran from the house to follow Richard who had been forced into the pool by the intense heat. Everything that could burn was afire; trees, bushes, the house, the fencing and a pergola in the back yard. Mary, the girls and their pets ran, terrified, to the pergola where the dogs suddenly burst into flame. Richard screamed at them to get in the pool and they sprinted over, diving in and swimming for the deep end. Only Catherine and Kylie made it to Richard. As they yelled for help Mary floated a few metres away, dead from smoke inhalation.

Fire had cursed the mysterious southern land in European imagination long before it did so in any European's experience.

The Virgin's Lie

Thousands of years before Dutchman Dirck Hartog nailed a plate to a tree on the western coast of Australia, a Greek author named Theopomus had written confidently of a continent on the far side of the world 'which in greatness is infinite and unmeasurable'. He pictured a utopia of green meadows and pastures, tended by mighty beasts and gigantic men, of numerous cities governed by civilized laws and ordinances. Pliny the Elder and Pomponius Mela of Rome had no doubt this place was as thickly peopled as the Mediterranean and the rest of Europe, but they were convinced no conversation would ever take place between north and south because of the tropic seas which, wrote Pliny, are 'burnt and cremated by flames, scorched by the near sun'. To Mela they were an impossible barrier, a burning zone.

Fantastic reports from Carthaginian sailors who braved the West African coast as far south as Sierra Leone in 500 BC lent credence to these alarums. Hanno's crew told of ugly, wild men, incredibly strong and covered with coarse black hair, calling themselves 'gorillas'; of entire lands consumed by unceasing fire; a world rendered unfit for human life by the terrible heat. The Atlantic Ocean, shrouded by heavy fogs and dust storms, was christened the Sea of Darkness while 'scorching winds from the Sahara confirmed the opinion that the Tropics were an eternal barrier to human travel'.

Greek and Roman knowledge of the wider world shrivelled at the hot touch of these winds, dying out long before the equator. The furthest reach of the European mind in its first flowering was Sri Lanka, and even that was but lightly brushed and deeply misunderstood. In a map drawn by Ptolemy in the second century AD the Asian land mass continues south-east for thousands of kilometres before turning west, back towards Africa, which it rejoins.

Ptolemy thus made the Indian Ocean a land-locked sea – like the Mediterranean minus the Straits of Gibraltar. Its southern waters lapped at the shores of Terra Incognita, the unknown land, at around about the same point where westerly winds pile the big breakers up against the white beaches of south-western Australia.

It wasn't until Hartog and his countrymen started bumping into West Australia in the early 1600s that Europe began to seriously consider the strategic and economic implications of a vast, uncontested land in the southern reaches of the world. The dead grey hand of the Church had smothered intellectual inquiry during the Dark Ages, consigning the work of Ptolemy and his peers to the forbidden realms of heresy. Imperial Rome had sought out distant lands and bent them to its will by force of arms. Holy Rome denied such places could even exist and bent everyone to its delusions by a reign of terror. The Bible had nothing to say about the antipodes or its inhabitants. They lay outside God's great scheme and thus they did not exist.

While Ptolemy was either reviled or forgotten, Pliny's bedtime stories fared a little better as harmless popular tales. The wastes of southern Africa served as a useful sort of allegorical tool, an imagined hell on earth with which to frighten the faithful into submission. There, where the Pope's word meant nothing, abominations were not just commonplace, they were the rule. People 'lived on the milk of dog-headed apes'. Others had four heads each, or just one eye in the centre of their foreheads, or giant feet under which they could take shade from the relentless punishing heat. It was a Godforsaken wasteland of inversion and madness. Much later even Dante took the cue, emerging from 'the horrid circles of hell', he finds himself 'in the Antipodes, exactly opposite Jerusalem'.

The Virgin's Lie

It took greed, a force as powerful as religious oppression, to break the Church's shackles. From 1615 captains of the Dutch East India Company's vessels had orders to sail a fixed course, east from the Cape of Good Hope until they found themselves below the Sunda Strait, where they were to steer north for the company's factories in Batavia. The company had calculated this route as the most likely to exploit prevailing winds and currents, but in the early seventeenth century it could not yet provide its sailors with the means to fix their positions with any real accuracy and at any rate the winds and currents were liable to shift on a whim. The result was an increasing number of lost and confused Dutchmen ploughing along the western coast of Australia, the unknown land which Ptolemy had mapped out millennia before.

The sick, sand-blasted wilderness they found seemed to bear out the ancients' warnings. It looked utterly desolate. Then Abel Tasman's epic voyage around the southern coast, Tasmania, New Zealand, Tonga, Fiji and New Guinea raised the prospect that New Holland, as it was becoming known, might produce something more useful than lonesome despair. There might even be two continents there: the wasteland in the west and a more temperate and fertile sister in the east. Alexander Dalrymple, an eighteenth-century Scottish geographer and first hydrographer of the British Admiralty, thought the land might stretch across thousands of miles, through a full 100° of longitude, making it bigger than the whole civilized part of Asia, from Turkey to the eastern extremity of China. Dalrymple was a passionate advocate of the idea of a huge, populous Great South Land, so rich that the merest scraps from its table would be 'sufficient to maintain the power, dominion, and sovereignty of Britain, by employing all its manufactures and ships'. Sir George Young echoed the sentiment, writing that the variety of climates sure to be found in such a great continent would provide Britain with 'almost all the different Productions of the known World' in just one united land. Even Joseph Banks, who had first-hand knowledge of Australia's less than ideal conditions, thought a land 'which was larger than the Whole of Europe' would furnish all manner of spices, crops and precious metals. Even so Banks was not the naive optimist those who followed him to Sydney Harbour later thought. He said it was the most barren country he had ever seen and although he recommended settlement at Botany Bay, with its plentiful supplies of fish, its fresh water and good soil 'capable of producing any kind of grain', he tempered his enthusiasm with advice that any colonists would need to carry at least a year's supplies to provide for themselves.

It turned out to be sound advice. When the First Fleet dropped anchor in Botany Bay in the first days of 1788, their initial joy at having made the dangerous passage without severe loss of life soon curdled into disappointment that the fine meadows and babbling streams of Banks's and Cook's journals seemed to be a chimera. The earlier navigators had arrived during a particularly wet week in autumn, while the First Fleet, long delayed in Portsmouth, dropped anchor during the hottest, driest part of a very hot, dry year. On 19 January, with only the *Supply*, *Scarborough*, *Alexander* and *Friendship* in the bay, Governor Phillip took a small boat about ten kilometres up a river which drained into the northwest of the bay and found 'the country low and boggy with no appearance of fresh water'. They retreated to try their luck with another inlet in the south-west, rowing ashore for a lunch of salt beef and porter at which they drank the health of absent friends before trekking inland. This time Phillip and his men found just 'one little rivulet of fresh water'. These were the first hard lessons

The Virgin's Lie

in a re-education which would take more than two hundred years. They were not in England any more and could not look at this land through a glass tinted by life in a cold, wet climate. When Phillip took some marines ashore to begin clearing ground, to rip up the grasses and hack down the trees which held the thin soils in place, the natives, with whom they'd had good dealings so far, turned ugly. Perhaps they understood, even if intuitively, the dire results of the white man's behaviour.

Surgeon John White, who wrote that the safe arrival of all the ships on 20 January 'was a sight truly pleasant, and at which every heart must rejoice', soon complained that their anchorage didn't deserve any of the praises 'bestowed on it by the much-lamented Cook'. It was 'sandy, poor, and swampy, and but very indifferently supplied with water'. Of Cook's fine meadows, White could see none, though he assured his readers he 'took some pains to find them'. Hunter surveyed the bay for anchorages, finding a few of good depth but exposed to the easterly winds which blew straight in, setting up 'a prodigious sea'. And those few places which were sheltered from the rough swell were too shallow to be of much use.

That evening Arthur Bowes Smyth, a surgeon on the *Lady Penrhyn*, dragged a fishing net around the north side with some success. But after just a short time in the country he was sanguine. This might seem a fertile spot, he suggested, with 'great numbers of very large and lofty trees reaching almost to the water's edge', and with the space between those trees seemingly covered by grass; but closer inspection revealed the grass to be 'long and coarse, the trees very large and in general hollow, and the wood itself' to be fit for nothing but the fire. The soil which supported this poor verdure was really nothing but sand, teeming with huge black and red ants which were inclined to inflict a painful bite on the curious and unwary. By the time the mullet and bream which Bowes Smyth had hauled up were finished and the last bones picked from his shipmates' teeth, Phillip had concluded that Botany Bay was unsuitable for settlement and was planning to move north to Port Jackson where, despite their initial disillusionment, the English were once again quickly charmed and just as quickly misled by appearances.

John Hunter, who had joined the little boats of Phillip's exploratory mission, thought the northern harbour very unappealing at first. Peering in past high rugged cliffs he could see the big ocean waves which tossed them about so roughly go rolling away to break on the far shore, completely unimpeded. But when they rowed through the heads and saw the water turn south into a deep, calm, well-protected shelter, he was mollified. Dozens of little bays and inlets, all safe from the depredations of the high seas, wound away as far as he could see, while the land rising up from them appeared 'superior in every respect to that around Botany Bay'. Phillip could envision a thousand of His Majesty's ships arrayed there in perfect safety. John White's first impression was even more hyperbolic. He described it as the finest and most extensive harbour in the universe, a port which could provide safe anchorage not just for every British ship of the line but 'for all the navies of Europe'.

The safety offered within its enfolding arms impressed a number of diarists, not least those who left Botany Bay with the fleet's rear guard and almost came to grief within sight of their destination. Poor lonely Ralph Clark, who was so underwhelmed by their first landfall he thought the whole colony would be dead within a year if they stayed there, was almost dead within the day. Wallowing in vicious seas and contrary winds, his vessel, the *Friendship*, nearly ran onto rocks at the mouth of the bay before actually crashing into the *Prince*

The Virgin's Lie

of Wales, then the *Charlotte*. Screams and shouts rose above the howl of the wind, the roar of wild surf and the sick-sounding crack of timber as booms were snapped off, sails torn and the carved woodwork on the *Charlotte*'s stern pulverised. Clark confessed himself terrified and almost certain of drowning. After considering the barren prospects on dry land and such a close shave on the waters of Botany Bay, he found himself not surprisingly 'much charmed' with the secure, untroubled anchorage in Port Jackson. Safely ensconced he wrote to his wife Alicia, saying he had kissed her picture and read his Bible lesson for the day, as always, before dining alone and, no doubt, reflecting on the Lord's good grace in sparing him. So taken was he with his first impressions of Sydney Cove he told Alicia he would not wish to return home, if only she and their son were with him. He also remarked, offhand, that the few small tents which had been erected on shore looked very pretty amongst the trees.

Behind Clark's relieved appreciation of the city's first nightfall we can spy a vision of an empty, pristine land which would affect European understanding of Australia in practical, poetic and often destructive ways for the next 200 years. As the Bicentennial History explains, the British were self-consciously going about 'the great business of creation itself'. God had 'wrought cosmos out of primordial chaos' and a rough band of criminals and jailers scrambling out of their fetid wooden boats might just do the same. White men's eyes saw no evidence of Aboriginal tillage and husbandry and thus the cove and all the continent behind it seemed 'a Virgin Mould, undisturbed since the Creation'. The flimsy tents pitched at the edge of primordial woods, alive with weird, even monstrous life forms; the cries of unfamiliar birds; the strange fierce light of day; the cold alien stars at night, they all spoke to Clark and his contemporaries of a new Eden and a celebration of the eighteenth-century Enlightenment spirit, the belief that the story of man was one of improvement and progress. Phillip himself best expressed it when stealing a rare moment from the demands of his work to ponder its meaning. There were few things more pleasing to the Governor than contemplating 'order and useful arrangement arising gradually out of tumult and confusion'. And nowhere was the satisfaction more felt than on a distant 'savage coast' where a civilized people were struggling to lodge themselves.

> The wild appearance of the land entirely untouched by cultivation, the close and perplexed growing of trees, interrupted now and then by barren spots, bare rocks, or spaces overgrown with weeds, flowers, flowering shrubs, or underwood, scattered or intermingled in the most promiscuous manner, are the first objects that present themselves; afterwards, the irregular placing of the first tents which are pitched, or huts which are erected for immediate accommodation, wherever chance presents a spot tolerably free from obstacles, or more easily cleared than the rest, with the bustle of various hands busily employed in a number of the most incongruous works, increases rather than diminishes the disorder, and produces a confusion of effect, which for a long time appears inextricable, and seems to threaten an endless continuance of perplexity. But by degrees large spaces are opened, plans are formed, lines marked, and a prospect at least of future regularity is clearly discerned, and is made the more striking by the recollection of former confusion.

The views of the convicts who were exiled to this savage coast weren't sought and aren't recorded but many of the officers wrestled with their creative mission. Incapable of dealing with the land on its own terms, all perceived it through a prism of past experience and inherited taste. Hunter thought the woods resembled a deer park which could be quickly stripped of wood and put under the plough. Arthur Bowes Smyth gazed around to find lawns, grottoes and plantations of tall stately trees as fine as any 'nobleman's grounds in England'. Bowes Smyth went on to trill his enchantment with the flights of 'parraquets, lorrequets, cockatoos, and maccaws' and his awe at the stupendous rocks hanging over the water's edge. He admitted he could not do justice to the beauty and usefulness of the many 'commodious quays by the water'.

The references to gardens were not completely whimsical. At the time English aesthetics were being reworked in a confrontation between landscape designers and the philosophers from whom they drew their inspiration. Some of the tensions and sensitivities this produced can be found in the First Fleet writings, albeit in a less calculated fashion. If Hunter and Bowes Smyth were not personally familiar with deer parks and noblemen's grounds, they were certainly mindful of the work of men like Lancelot 'Capability' Brown, a hugely popular and influential landscaper who favoured improving on nature's disorganised forms to impart a sense of tranquillity with simple, almost formal arrangements of 'a small number of natural elements – a grove of trees, a pond, the slight curve of a hill'. At the end of the eighteenth century Brown's school, very much a product of the Enlightenment, was challenged by the Picturesque movement whose champions, such as Sir Uvedale Price, preferred the riots of nature. Price's gardens were described as 'wild, dramatic, and unkempt'. The Picturesque movement, just one strand of the nineteenth century's emerging

Romantic reaction against the Age of Reason, celebrated nature in all her 'horrid graces'. Intimations of this revolution can be found in the reactions of men like Hunter, Bowes Smyth and his fellow surgeon George Worgan. The latter found within the harbour 'a variety of Romantic views, all thrown together into sweet confusion by the careless hand of Nature ... Here a romantic, rocky, craggy Precipice over which, a little swirling stream makes a cascade. There a soft vivid-green, shady Lawn attracts your eye.' Lieutenant Southwell from the *Sirius* wrote that nothing could 'be conceived more picturesque' than the landscape of Sydney.

> The land on all sides is high, and cover'd with an exuber'n of trees; towards the water, craggy rocks and vast declivity are everywhere to be seen. The scene is beautifully height'ed by a number of small islands that are dispers'd here and there on which may be seen chrm'g seats, superb buildings, the grand ruins of stately edifices ... at intervals the view being pr'ty agreeably interrupted by the intervention of some proud eminence, or lost in the labyrynth of the inchanting glens that so abound in this fascinating scenery.

The harbour's Picturesque characteristics were all there – its 'roughness, sudden variation and contrast' – but the awful truth was sinking in too: the implications of surviving in such a primitive, unpredictable environment. As taken as he was with the scenery, Southwell finished by warning that: 'Tis greatly to be wished these appearances were not so delusive as in reality they are'. The virgin land, it transpired, was not a fertile young maiden but a withered old crone. Major Ross, the marines' cheerless commandant, wrote to London that it was the worst country in the world and it would be cheaper 'to feed the convicts on turtle and venison at the London Tavern than be at the expence of sending them here'. For a truly melancholy sketch, however, we turn inevitably to Ralph Clark. Having written Alicia that first optimistic report of his new home, he followed it in July of 1788 with a letter in which those high hopes thudded back to earth with a plume of parched red dust. Like Hunter, Ralph also thought it 'the poorest country in the world', and its inhabitants the most miserable set of wretches under the sun.

> There is neather [sic] river or Spring in the country that we have been able to find ... all the fresh water comes out of swamps which the country abounds with ... the country is overrun with large trees not one Acre of clear ground to be seen ... the Thunder and Lightning is the most Terrible I ever herd [sic], it is the opinion of every body here that the Government will remove the Settlement to some other place for if it remains here this country will not be able to maintain its self in 100 years ...

Alicia's husband and his fellow colonists had been rudely disavowed of their first generous impressions within days of arriving at Sydney Cove. The new-born settlement was quickly forced to grapple with two serious challenges to its survival – Australia's barren soils and its weird violent weather. The former were a result of the continent's slumber through great stretches of geological time. Without the calamitous tectonic disruptions which chewed up the crusts of other lands, Australian rocks tended to sit and bake under the sun for billions of years at a time. They were worn away very slowly by wind and water, their precious constituent minerals leached from the ground by time's plunder. In the Sydney basin this was exacerbated because the sandstone bed laid down so many hundreds of millions of years before was never going to break down into anything fertile. The potatoes and cabbages which Phillip ordered planted with all despatch either flourished for a short time before weakening and dying or simply died straightaway. With scurvy and dysentery spreading through the population, the Governor established small plantations of ginger, oranges, lemons and limes, all to no avail. There was little in the thin, swampy ground for their roots to fasten onto. The rich deposits of elements which made the soils of England so fruitful – the thick potage of nitrogen and phosphorus, the abundance of potassium, calcium, magnesium and sulphur – were missing from the sucking mud banks of Sydney Cove.

The parsimony of the soil reached beyond the wavelets lapping at the harbour's edge. Without a generous transfer of nutrients from the land to coastal and esturine waters, any hopes of supplementing a diet of salt provisions with fresh seafood proved as illusory as had hopes of establishing little English market gardens on shore. The transplanted subjects of mad King George saw vast stretches of unexploited coastline and unexplored harbour and could not help thinking of their fertile traditional fishing grounds in the North Sea and English Channel. But after initially amazing the Iora with the power of their nets, the white men soon found this source of nutriment petering out too. During the day the *Sirius* worked up and down the harbour with a large net, dragging it clean. Tench was sent out at night with a small fishing party, and despite working till after dawn and scouring dozens of bays and inlets, he barely returned with enough fish to replace the energy expended in catching them. More plentiful were the delicately flavoured oysters which could be plucked in their hundreds from the

The Virgin's Lie

branches of mangrove trees and small rocks at the harbour's edge. However, as their shells could be ground up and fired for limestone, which the settlement lacked, the oysters' best days – like the Iora's – were behind them.

Even had the ground at Sydney Cove been more fertile, like the floodplains of the Hawkesbury River or the Hunter Valley where the colonists did eventually turn over sods of good brown earth, it may have made little difference in those early days. The fleet arrived at the height of summer, with the best growing months missed because of delays in leaving Portsmouth. Then, in 1789, with a storeship carrying sorely needed rations from England wrecked near the the Cape of Good Hope, and with the *Lady Juliana*, the first ship of the disastrous Second Fleet already under sail, drought descended and any colonists who thought they had the measure of this hard barren land were in for one of those unpleasant shocks their new home seemed so adept at providing. Temperatures climbed and milky white skin blistered and burned as El Niño turned it on for the newcomers, warning them that a strange powerful force drove the weather on this side of the globe.

It was as though Pliny's tales of mythical burning waters contained a metaphorical truth. Europeans who understood weather in terms of four reliable unvarying seasons were unprepared for the chaotic conditions of life in the southern Pacific. Here the weather was as much a plaything of chance and probability, of the vagaries of huge drifting bodies of warm sea water, as it was of the planet's regular tilting towards and away from the sun. Since this haphazard routine emerged into public consciousness as El Niño after the monstrous drought of 1982–3 it has often been referred to as an abnormal weather pattern. But there is nothing abnormal about El Niño. It has followed the same rough disordered pattern for thousands of years and is as much a part of life on the Pacific Rim as monsoons and vulcanism. However, it is only in the last fifteen years or so that we have come to understand it in anything more than a fragmentary fashion.

Cook and Banks viewed Botany Bay through a different prism in the autumn of 1770. The lush pastures they observed must have compared favourably with the dying fields of an English autumn. Here it seems the warm Pacific breeze promised to keep the savageries of winter at bay. Unfortunately they knew nothing of El Niño or its related Southern Oscillation. The land they saw had not suffered a severe El Niño event since 1716 – an unusually long interval – and they were seeing it at its best. Neither they nor anybody on the convict ships which followed was equipped to understand the phenomenon.

Indeed, although the first evidence of El Niño seems to have been recorded in Peru in 1525 by the expedition of the Spanish conquistador Francisco Pizarro, more than four hundred years would pass before Jacob Bjerknes, a Norwegian meteorologist working at the University of California, had the data and technology to piece the story together. Bjerknes was standing on the shoulders of a British scientist, Sir Gilbert Walker who, as head of the Indian Meteorological Service in 1904, had been handed the task of working out some way of predicting monsoons, after their failure in 1899 had led to famine on the subcontinent. In the course of his research Walker discovered a link between changes in ocean temperature and rainfall in South America. This in turn seemed to be connected to air pressure readings taken at Darwin and Tahiti. Walker's numbers seemed to indicate that as pressure rose at Tahiti it fell in the Northern Territory. He called this seesawing the

The Virgin's Lie

Southern Oscillation and wondered at what seemed to be a weird link between these barometric changes, Australian droughts, the Asian monsoon season and mild Canadian winters. In the days before satellites, electronic ocean buoys and supercomputers Sir Gilbert was widely thought of as a crank. The idea that bushfires in New South Wales and famine in India might be related to the failure of Peruvian fishing grounds was a mad suggestion, as preposterous to all right-thinking scientists in the early twentieth century as had been Ptolemy's map to the Church in the Dark Ages. Unable to prove his theory, Walker remained convinced he would be vindicated when high atmosphere wind patterns could be routinely measured. Fifty years later Bjerknes had the wherewithal to do just that and to draw a connection between ocean temperatures, air pressure, rainfall and wind patterns. More than just a connection in fact, they were all components of the same system, the El Niño Southern Oscillation effect or ENSO.

When ENSO is not having its evil way with Australian farmers, a satellite image of the Pacific Ocean will show a huge area of warm water in the west, washing up against Indonesia; a cold tongue of nutrient-rich waters in the east, and the same trade winds which pressed hard against the canvas of HMS *Endeavour* blowing strong and true from east to west. These are thought of as 'normal' conditions. Roughly two years out of seven, however, the pattern reverses itself and all hell breaks loose.

What happens is this. Normally the waters at the equator are warmed by the sun and moist air rises from them, cooler air is then sucked in from the subtropics in its place. The Coriolis effect, that force generated by the earth's rotation which makes water spin down the sink differently depending on whether you are north or south of the equator, kicks in. Above the equator it sends this mass of air east. Below the equator it moves west, giving rise to the trade winds. So steady and powerful are these winds they push the warm water on the surface of the Pacific Ocean left, actually piling it up against Indonesia so that the sea level is about fifty centimetres higher there. The water warms even further as it travels through the tropics, the air above it becoming saturated with moisture which rises higher and higher, only to fall on South East Asia during the yearly monsoons. The damp, warm, rising air strengthens the westerly drive of the trade winds. Its power projects way into the upper atmosphere where it shapes the flow of the jet stream, much as a rock in a fast-moving river distorts the waters which have to rush around it. The tracks of great storms are determined by the contours of this flow, the weather patterns for a huge portion of the globe riding upon its anguine, sinuous forms.

Back east meanwhile, off the coast of South America, cold water wells up from the depths to replace those warm streams which headed west. Rich in nutrients, these colder seas support abundant bird and fish life and, not incidentally, the fishermen of Peru. For years at a time they haul up nets straining with anchovies destined for the world's pizzas and pet food tins. But every now and then, around Christmas time, the nets come up empty. The warmer waves have not migrated west. They lap against the edge of the boats, which drift around on a huge bath of tepid sea water. El Niño, the Christ Child, has arrived. The gusting trade winds slacken then turn. All of that warm water heaped up on the coast of Indonesia comes rolling back across the Pacific, taking with it the moist rising air. The jet streams buckle and deform. Twelve thousand metres above sea level new highways are blasted through the atmosphere, jet streams strong enough to shoot across Central America and on across the Atlantic, strong enough to decapitate

The Virgin's Lie

big roiling thunderheads on the east coast of the US before they can mutate into hurricanes. Monsoonal rains which would have irrigated Asia's rice paddies and Australian wheat fields now fall uselessly in mid-Pacific. Coral reefs off the Galapagos Islands die back in balmy, arid shallows. Tens of millions of boobies, cormorants and pelicans starve to death off Ecuador. Seal pups in California perish as storms flood their beaches. Malaria, dengue fever, and encephalitis spread as mosquitoes breed in stagnant pools in Sri Lanka. And in Australia farmers load their guns to cull dying stock as bushfires rage at the edge of Sydney.

Why? Because nothing lasts forever. The exchange of heat between air and water which is the engine of our weather has been described as a dance, but with one partner waltzing quietly whilst the other madly tangos. 'Ocean temperatures drive winds; winds drive ocean currents; ocean currents redistribute heat over sea surfaces; and the new pattern of ocean temperatures drives new winds.' But air and water never find a balance 'because the ocean moves heat around far more slowly than the atmosphere'. So El Niño is not an abnormal event. Rather it is commonplace, mundane even, except for those who have to live with it.

Tim Flannery's popular study of Australian ecology, *The Future Eaters*, describes the pattern of adaptations forced on the continent's plants and animals by the harsh reign of El Niño as 'parsimony born of resource poverty'. Nomadism became endemic, with birds, marsupials and early humans all chasing the rains across the country. Unable to follow them, Australia's plants responded by growing short rigid leaves and small internodes and remaining relatively small in size. In turn animals adapted to these thin pickings by becoming 'energy misers' – sitting still, like the koala, for great stretches of time, dozing through the heat of the day and paring back reproduction rates. Unprepared for such tight margins of existence, the plants in Governor Phillip's garden scarfed up all the nutrients from the poor sandy soil, then withered and died. The livestock the English had brought with them found the local weeds a poor substitute for the lush grasses of home. They either turned up their hooves from starvation or hovered on the edge of it, unable to produce enough dung to fertilise their masters' little plantations.

The strange wiry plants of the harbour also proved useless for shelter. The fleet had brought a small supply of building materials from England – some bricks and lime, lots of nails and a surfeit of window glass – in the expectation of using local materials to supplement them. But Sydney's timber proved no better than the soil and water, Surgeon White complaining that it was fit for little but burning. In a familiar refrain he thought it the worst 'that any country or climate ever produced'. Planks cut from those few trees which looked promising quickly warped and turned brittle when sawn and exposed to the sun. Removing the trees was still hard, frustrating work. Blackbutt and red gum soared up to forty metres above the floor of the valley which climbed away from the mouth of the fresh-water stream Phillip had discovered. Without machinery or dynamite a dozen men could take a week to dig out their trunks and roots. An axeman standing at their base would often find the uppermost branches obscured by clumps of swamp mahogany and bangalay. Below them acacias, yellow tea-tree and paperbarks struggled for a foothold alongside Port Jackson figs and cabbage tree palms. This last tree at least proved useful, with a trunk which could be split into serviceable logs and planks, soft as they were. It was best woven in between tougher timber then smeared over with mud and clay to keep out the wind, a method of hovel building tracing its roots as far back as the Iron Age. Convicts also wove the palm's fronds into hats to keep the blistering southern sun off their heads, and the camp's hogs weren't averse to snacking on its pith. Rushes from the mud flats and the stalks of the blackboy were initially lashed together and thrown onto the crossbeams of the crude little huts for thatching. Later the she-oak was found to provide good roofing shingles and the women were set to whittling out thousands of them.

It was some time, however, before the tents Ralph Clark found so fetching were replaced with more permanent shelters. In fact their influence on the form of the city persists. When Phillip swept his arm around the curve of the bay, saying he wanted the convicts and marines settled on the rocky western banks while he and the officers would take the gentler, more open slopes to the east of the stream, he fixed a division between class, power and wealth which has survived to this day, with disastrous consequences for the environs of western Sydney and the lives of those born into its hardest stations. The tracks tramped into the earth between the little clutches of tents and humpies eventually became the skeleton streets around which the body of the young city would grow. The rock- and root-strewn path which made its way from the convicts' bedraggled encampment, past the marines' infinitely tidier parade square and tents, alongside the bank of the stream and then out to a desolate brick pit about a kilometre or two back from the harbour, eventually became George Street. Another trail, which veered off to the left, across a little wooden bridge over the stream to the more salubrious officers' marquees and the Governor's house, in time became Bridge Street.

Phillip gave the convicts enough leisure time to grow their own vegetables and build their own shelters, were they so inclined.

Some weren't of course. Long after the first hospital had been erected, Surgeon Arndell's servant, Samuel Chinery, was still bunking down in a hollow tree nearby. Another couple of old lags named Owen and Turner lived under a rock at Millers Point. (They were well suited as flatmates – Turner had gone down for thieving, Owen for receiving.) By way of contrast, a fellow thief, James Tenchal – alias Tenninghill – took advantage of the Governor's ruling and by April of 1790 was the proud owner of a one-room home with a lockable door. It didn't stop William Chaaf, an unreformed burglar, from trying his hand though. Chaaf, who had been hired to thatch Tenchal's roof, crawled in through an incomplete section with mischief on his mind. Through his trial we learn a little of convict domestic architecture: Tenchal's windows had wooden shutters, fixed by a bolt; the straw thatching was laced to the rafters; the floor was tramped earth, and the only furniture was a table, a bed and a couple of chests. Most of the little huts were also built with hearths and chimneys, but so prone were they to catching fire that regulations were quickly passed to curb their use. Although all of the early convict dwellings were pulled down to make way for commercial development as soon as the city's economy took off, this simple style of lower-class dwelling survived until quite recently. My old friend Pat Bell, who kicked around Paddington in the 1960s, told me of visiting two- or three-room shacks in that suburb in which the floors were still just stamped earth.

Phillip's own house was a prefab unit shipped out with the fleet and thrown up in a week. It was the finest structure in the land, but that wasn't saying much. Constructed of wood and canvas, its best feature was that it didn't collapse in the first storm like many of the camp's bark lean-tos and mud huts. Like James Tenchal,

The Virgin's Lie

Phillip dreamt of solid walls and a stout door, but being governor he had the wherewithal to make it happen much sooner and on a slightly grander scale. In May of 1788, while Phillip hunched over his first official despatch to Lord Sydney – complaining of a pain in his side from sleeping on the ground, the colony's lack of any botanical experts, the need for more females to be sent out for the men, and the inability of his canvas house to protect him from the wind and rain – a team of convicts set to work on the first permanent governor's residence. The bricks and lime brought from England were supplemented by clay bricks fired at a pit back up in the hinterland, near what would later become Central Station. Phillip's house was modest: two storeys built along stolid Georgian lines, with very little ornamentation. Although there was an abundance of rich sandstone available for building, the lack of lime for mortar restricted its use. Indeed most of the early buildings were set close to the ground with thick walls because of this. Phillip's house was a simple symmetrical arrangement with three bays gazing over his struggling garden beds down to the Cove. The centre bay was topped by a pediment, the front door by a semi-circular fanlight. (You can walk through a ghost structure of the house in the forecourt of the Museum of Sydney.) Although the view to the water from its 'most exalted station' is now partly blocked by a hotel and office block, it doesn't take too great a leap to imagine the gulf between this first Government House and the sorry hovels of the lower orders.

Separated by more than 200 years and insulated by the comforts of the digital age, it is difficult for us to comprehend the burden shouldered by the men who raised that first substantial home. The clay which provided bricks for the house may have lain only a kilometre or so inland but it was a very different kilometre from the smooth graded roads you would take today. Sydney's furrowed brow has been smoothed by time. The land over which the convicts scrambled was infinitely more precipitous and disjointed, piled up with ragged broken ridge lines and steep hills, shot through with deep valleys and abrupt cliffs. All movement was by foot; the only power that which came from the bent backs and straining muscles of the men. And with dysentery, scurvy and starvation stalking the colony, even the strongest backs could not bend that far. Muscles fluttered and grew weak. Shoes rotted and fell away from swollen feet which struggled for purchase on stony ground. There were no beasts to pull the carts from the brick pits, so the men themselves were harnessed. A dozen of them would drag carts laden with hundreds of bricks to and from the brick fields five times a day. The terrain was so rugged that thousands of bricks were broken and pulverised during the trip. As the colony grew this sight became more common, not less. In 1793 David Collins described hundreds of men so yoked, hauling great loads of timber and stone around the town's many building sites.

Famine and disease sapped the energy of the settlement for these works during the first years. In the few months before work commenced on Phillip's house, hundreds had fallen ill and taken to their cots and tents. Everyone left standing was assigned to scrounging for food or building a large timber hospital. However, these early troubles actually turned out to be something of a left-handed gift because when the bulk of the Second Fleet arrived that hospital became the centre of colonial activity. By then, June of 1790, Phillip had split his command, sending one detachment to colonise Norfolk Island and another up river to establish a farm on the relatively fertile alluvial plains at Parramatta, or Rose Hill as it was first known. Unlike Sydney, which simply grew up around the contours of the first tents and the local topography, Rose Hill was planned. Phillip laid out a wide central street, running west from the riverbank to a small cottage he built as a second governor's residence. Large free-standing huts were run up on either side of the thoroughfare, each separated from its neighbour by up to eighteen metres. Phillip was mindful of the immediate dangers of fire spreading through the satellite township, but he also had one eye to the future by leaving plenty of room for uncluttered development. He had drawn up similarly ambitious plans for Sydney Cove but, anticipating two centuries of unplanned, untrammelled growth, these died a lingering death over the next twenty years, taking another governor, William Bligh, down with them.

When the *Lady Juliana* rolled through the heads in June, the population of Sydney Cove was much diminished by these developments. Over 200 convicts and marines had sailed for Norfolk. Hundreds more were wrestling with the vagaries of the local soil and climate on farms up the Parramatta River. The harbourside town was a quiet place, where sickly administrators bent over their papers, brick-makers tended their kilns and a few sawyers their tools. The camp, according to George Worgan, had a 'villatick' appearance. Many tents and humpies remained, especially among the boulders above the white beaches of the western headland, but they were outnumbered by thatched huts with little gardens struggling along behind wobbly picket fences. The tenor of the town was grim. Real hunger pinched at the guts of everyone from the Governor down. Thin rations were cut and cut again. Depression and lassitude, the boundary riders of starvation, were given free rein in the minds and journals of the officers. In March 1790, after *Sirius* and *Supply* left for Norfolk Island, Collins wrote:

the whole settlement appeared as if famine had already thinned it of half its numbers. The little society that was in the place was broken up, and every man seemed left to brood in solitary silence over the dreary prospect before him.

For the usually cheery Watkin Tench they were 'days of despair' when 'the hearts of men sunk'. Glowering storm clouds, fat with cold rain hung low in the sky, occasionally bursting over the hamlet, destroying huts, washing out the foundations of larger buildings, and 'filling up every trench and cavity which had been dug about the settlement'. A small boy fell into a flooded clay pit and drowned. Starving thieves braved execution to steal melons and pumpkins from ruined gardens. In April, just a few days after yet another reduction in the rations and working hours, the *Supply* returned with news that the *Sirius* had been wrecked.

All hopes rested on the horizon, but no relief appeared over the next two months. One young man wrote home describing poor wretches gazing ardently out to sea whilst starving mothers wept 'upon the infants at the breast'. Little surprise then that when the signal flags for a strange ship where hoisted in the afternoon of 3 June women ran into the streets with babies in their arms 'congratulating each other and kissing their infants with the most passionate and extravagant marks of fondness'. Marines wrung each others hand's, unable to speak, tears streaming down their faces. The news first burst on Watkin Tench 'like meridian splendor on a blind man'.

The colony had not been forgotten, just dreadfully unlucky. A supply ship called the *Guardian* had struck an iceberg off South Africa the previous December and been forced to return to the Cape. It was a great loss. The ship had been hauling tonnes of

The Virgin's Lie

flour and meat, along with livestock, clothing, medical supplies, fruit trees and farming equipment. Twenty-five convict farmers and tradesmen had been aboard the *Guardian* with seven overseers. Two were drowned, more were missing and the balance had been detained at the Cape. *Juliana* brought some of the stores salvaged from the wreck but she also arrived with nearly 250 female convicts and news of another 1000 convicts on the way. Collins was mortified to find 'a cargo so unnecessary and unprofitable' as the women dumped on the colony. But the stores they brought alleviated some the town's suffering and the women were to prove much easier to assimilate than the Second Fleeters who followed them.

Unlike the First Fleet, which rode well under the firm hand of Phillip, the second suffered from uncertain lines of command and slipshod organisation. The voyage of the *Juliana*, which left well before the rest of the fleet, had been overseen by William Richards, the same contractor who had outfitted the First. Unfortunately for the bulk of the Second Fleet convicts, the capable Richards was replaced as contractor by the slave traders Camden, Calvert and King, who were more concerned with turning a profit on the voyage than delivering healthy prisoners. Their charges were shackled in heavy irons, confined below decks, and fed a diet almost totally lacking in vitamin C and calcium. Fist fights and pistol duels erupted between the ships' captains and the officers of the New South Wales Corps, who had been embarked with the convicts.

By the time the transports *Surprize*, *Neptune* and *Scarborough* dropped anchor in Port Jackson, nearly one third of their passengers were dead and most of the survivors were sick; men, women and children unable to walk or even stand, hoisted from stinking beds and flung over the side of the ships like baggage. Some fainted at the first breath of fresh air, others died. The Reverend Richard Johnson described them lying on the shore, many unable to stir, some dragging themselves up the banks on their hands and knees, some carried on the backs of others. They were wretched scarecrow characters, with hollow cheeks, dark sunken eyes and sticks for limbs, covered in sores and ulcers and caked-on layers of excrement. Corpses, tossed from the transports on the very last leg of the voyage, bobbed up and down the length of the harbour, their obscene, bloated forms washing up on the foreshores to balloon out and burst as putrescent gasses rumbled inside them. At night, above the moans of the dying, dingoes could be heard tearing apart bodies hastily consigned to a mass grave dug near the present site of Wynyard Station. Tents reappeared around the Rocks as the hospital filled to capacity and beyond. Surgeon White's medical staff, themselves hard-pressed to survive just a few weeks earlier, now had 500 potential deathbeds to attend. Rampant scurvy was the least of their worries, with fever, violent diarrhoea and possibly typhoid to contend with. Wine, oatmeal and vinegar were the best medicines on offer at first as groups of relatively healthy First Fleet convicts were sent into the woods to search for acid berries, native spinach, sarsparilla and cabbage tree leaves.

Sydney's population had jumped from 591 in April to 1715 by July. Even if the newcomers had been in good shape, her sinews would have torn trying to accommodate such growth. Elizabeth Macarthur, who arrived with the Second Fleet, thought the place completely wretched when she disembarked.

The filthy ships in the Cove, the rude lines of sodden barracks, the tents that held the sick sagging in the downpour along the water

The Virgin's Lie

front; the night fires in the region of the Rocks, a sink of evil already and more like a gypsy encampment than part of a town ... the stumps and fallen trees, and the boggy tracks wending their way around rock and precipice; the oozy Tank Stream spreading itself over the sand by the head of the Cove ...

This was not a settlement equipped to cope with an invasion of the living dead. Phillip sent most of the healthy Second Fleeters – which largely meant Richards' *Juliana* women – out to the newly established village at Rose Hill. Another consignment was shipped off to Norfolk Island in August. As the sick lists grew shorter, through death or recovery, the city's greatest crisis since its foundation gradually ebbed back to manageable proportions.

One of the more pressing problems was water. The arrival of the Second Fleet coincided with the climatic chaos of yet another El Niño event. Elizabeth Macarthur wrote that December and January had been hotter than she could describe, infinitely worse than the fiercest summer day back home. Breezes brought no relief, only hellish hot gales which forced everyone to shut themselves up inside their makeshift cottages, trying 'to the utmost of our power to exclude every breath of air'. She had seen little rain since arriving and the soil of her garden was completely 'burnt up'. In March 1791, with the colony still struggling to accommodate its population explosion, Phillip wrote to England that rain had been so scarce since the *Juliana* arrived that most of the springs in the harbour had dried up. The little stream which divided the settlement at the Cove was 'much diminished', although still sufficient for cooking. The weather was only partly to blame. Land clearing by the English had shattered the frail architecture of sandstone and vegetation which delivered the rill of sweet spring water from its

165

catchment around the heights of Hyde Park and down through the valley now covered by Pitt and George Streets. Fringed by acacias, wild spinach, flowers and ferns, it meandered for nearly two kilometres around 'shelving rocks and pearly white sand beds'. Phillip had imposed an eighteenth century green ban on clearing scrub within fifteen metres of the banks but the decline had begun and the fall was inevitable. It is best summarised by PR Stephensen in his history of the harbour.

> In that spongy topsoil and in the porous sandstone subsoil were natural storages of fresh water that the removal of the trees and shrubs and smaller plants would quickly deplete. Soil erosion was not understood by the pioneers, who, bred in the lore of damp islands, believed that 'springs' of fresh water were perennial. Nor could they understand that the clearing of the trees and the 'underbrush' and the cultivation with spades and hoes of the shallow topsoil, would cause that topsoil to be washed away by heavy showers of rain, leaving the sandstone subsoil exposed. So British settlement in the Vale of Sydney quickly destroyed the 'spring' of fresh water and the fertility of the soil, two of the principal features that had caused Governor Phillip to decide to form the settlement there.

The settlers tried to augment their precarious water supply even as they so efficiently destroyed it. Phillip had a paling fence erected alongside the stream to prevent hungry stock from eating the shrubs on the banks and befouling the water. He then had deep tanks cut into the sandstone to catch and hold thousands of litres of water, as insurance against the droughts and baffling tricks of the local weather. These engineering works, which gave the Tank

The Virgin's Lie

Stream its name, sufficed for a time. But they filled with silt and sand as erosion denuded the parched and exposed landscape beyond the paling fence. When Phillip left the colony at the end of 1792, worn down by his burdens, power ebbed away from the governor's mansion, drawn to the twin poles of the officer class and the port's emerging trade barons who, more often than not, were one and the same.

The rambunctious, two-fisted rogues of the newly formed New South Wales Corps who had arrived with the survivors of the Second Fleet disembarked at Sydney Cove, squinted in the harsh unfamiliar light and, as their dark-adapted eyes slowly adjusted, they saw laid out before them an opportunity for plunder unmatched in the Empire. Here lay a world for the taking. Its indolent, backward indigenes could offer no resistance. They fled when anyone pointed a shovel at them, let alone a musket. Malaspina was right. Their fields would be laid waste, their huts overrun, their women violated and their lives snatched away. And when they were gone, those fields would be tended by a limitless workforce of state-supplied white slaves. You could say that when Phillip's ship sailed into the sea mists, bound for England in December of 1792, that all of the New South Wales Corps' Christmases were about to come at once.

With no real check on their power or appetites, the corps was pretty much free to do as it pleased; and it pleased more than a few of them to build their homes on the verdant slopes of the Tank Stream, to catch the breezes and views and give their livestock easy access to water and food. Hungry pigs and goats quickly broke through those fences which hadn't been torn down by their owners, stripped the banks of foliage and polluted the town's water supply with their prodigious output of faeces and urine. In addition to brazenly disobeying the orders Phillip had given to protect the water supply, the corps also flouted his town planning directions. Just before leaving, Phillip had drawn a line between the head of Woolloomooloo Bay, to the east of the cove, and Cockle Bay (which we know as Darling Harbour) to the west. Within this area, which constitutes most of the modern city's CBD, no land was to be granted or leased and all housing was to remain the property of the Crown. By this order Phillip hoped to ensure the orderly development of what would become one of the leading cities of the world. Unfortunately, the corps had as much respect for his claim on this land as they did for the Iora's. Under his immediate successors, Major Grose and Colonel Paterson, the degradation of the Tank Stream proceeded in tandem with the alienation of public land in the centre of the town.

With no effective constraints, growth spurted ahead in fits of uncontrolled demolition and construction which would make a modern developer weep with envy. Rough log cabins were haphazardly replaced by small brick cottages. Shingles and tiles took the place of reeds and straw. Barracks, storehouses and wharves occupied easier ground on the western reach of the cove, whilst the convicts' simple huts spread promiscuously on the heights above. When Malaspina's expedition arrived in 1793, the Spaniard expected to see rapid progress towards civilization but the vista disappointed him. He described 'land ill-cleared, fields little worked, wretched houses, and everywhere the marks of oppression and disgust'. Sydney, the hub of English commerce and administration in the Pacific, contained about 300 houses by his reckoning, a third of them still roofed with straw. They clustered together in apparent disorder, although Malaspina was assured everything had been arranged according to Phillip's grand plan. 'I managed to examine it,' he remarked dryly, 'and do not know how it operates ...'

It operated to enrich the officers of the corps. In the years after Phillip's departure the military handed itself land grants and convict labour like cigars and port at a thumpingly debauched regimental piss-up. So profligate was the diversion of public resources to private ends that when the First Fleet's John Hunter returned to the colony as governor in September of 1795, he complained that he could scarcely round up twenty convicts from a population of thousands. The rest had been diverted into the personal service of the colony's leading lights. There was 'scarcely a pound of salt provisions in the store'; not one barn or granary had been built to hold the increasingly large harvest; the government's boats had 'gone to ruin and decay'; numberless houses, once public property, had been leased into private hands; and the roads had fallen into such disrepair that they were often useless.

Neither Hunter nor his successor, Philip Gidley King, were able to take the measure of the corps. They were caught between the leverage of men like the warrior-capitalist John Macarthur, and the indifference of a home government preoccupied by great power politics on the Continent. Hunter managed some running repairs, despatching work gangs to the oyster beds to gather shells for plastering the town's buildings against the elements. But it was a dilatory business, and when a string of violent storms fell on Sydney in June 1799, they thoroughly smashed the place, demolishing windmills, church towers, and private homes. Hunter was forced to virtually plead for the help of the town's leading citizens and officers in rebuilding. They readily gave their agreement, then withheld any significant material support. Hunter was only too aware of how much power had slipped from the governor's hands since the time of Phillip. Writing to the Duke of Portland a month after the devastation, he glumly described his failure to curb the rapacious dealings of the corps by way of public orders: 'you will see, my Lord, that where I must depend for their due execution on persons interested in their failure, how little is to be expected from such Orders'.

When Governor King arrived to replace the vanquished Hunter, he came packing a determination that 'the public shall not be cheated; and ... the King's authority shall not be insulted'. His mission was not a pleasant one, he wrote to Sir Joseph Banks:

> the obnoxious character of a reformer is not calculated to appear often on the theatre of this world. I have had the most flagrant and dishonourable abuses to do away; and I have succeeded, but at the expense of being hated by those whose interest has been hurt ...

Much of his energy, like Hunter's, went into the continuing struggle against the trading elite's 'monopoly and extortion'. Suffering from the labour shortages and restricted budgets of his predecessors, there was little scope for King to radically redesign the fabric of the town's man-made environment. He built a church, jail and brewery at Parramatta, and flour mills, a tannery, a guardhouse and bridge, amongst other sundry works, in Sydney itself. Private capital went into Campbell's Wharf – the best in the country when completed in 1803 – whilst the town's finest buildings, such as Captain William Kent's Palladian mansion, Simeon Lord's four-storey townhouse and Robert Campbell's colonnaded

The Virgin's Lie

Indian bungalow, were all commissioned by wealthy merchants.

Meanwhile a growing population pushed further up the reaches of the Tank Stream, along the road out to the brick fields. Difficult topography helped sandwich the advance between high ridge lines running back from the Rocks and Government House. Within that conduit the destruction of any forest remnants accelerated. In 1802 a visiting Frenchman, Charles Leseur, prepared a map of the settlement which identified 260 houses. This number had increased to nearly 700 within two years as cross-streets like Hunter and King emerged from the arbitrary confluence of design and circumstance which shaped the city's framework. As Peter Bridges points out in *Foundations of Identity*, his elegant study of early Sydney, despite the steadily increasing number of private buildings which transformed empty lots and isolated shanties into continuous rows of terraces, the town 'still had a down-at-heel appearance'.

Captain Colnett of HMS *Glatton* arrived in March 1803 to be grossly underwhelmed by this zircon in the crown of Empire. The poverty of the soil was obvious, the town looked like nothing more 'than a miserable Portuguese settlement', and some lazy swine had heightened this picture of dilapidation by allowing the flagstaff 'on what was called a battery' to lean at least thirty degrees from the perpendicular. Colnett, who cultivated a serious feud with King during his stay in the port, lacerated the Governor for the poor state of his post. Although his opinions aren't always to be trusted, his observations of the port's decrepit condition sit comfortably alongside King's own complaints. The arrangements for watering his ship were eccentric at best, with Colnett forced to send a party over five kilometres away to fill three hundred tonnes worth of water casks. The casks then had to be rolled across hundreds of metres of mud flats and left, half submerged, in the stinking ooze until the tide rose high enough to float them off to the boat. The reservoirs which Phillip had cut into the Tank Stream's sandstone banks were full of silt. The wharf in front of the hospital at the Rocks was hopeless; a boat drawing more than a foot of water couldn't rest beside it at low tide. The Governor's Wharf on the other side was even worse, with no capacity to land goods of any weight. The *Glatton*'s seamen were forced to throw barrels of wine over the side of their launch and swim them to shore. Mooring chains lay rusting on the tidal flats and Colnett compared the dockyard on the north shore to a dog kennel. He confirmed that the only decent wharfing facility belonged to Robert Campbell, and it was in peril from the colony's gunpowder magazine which was kept nearby in an old hulk, swinging at anchor amidst open fires and crowded moorings.

Colnett was wrong in dumping the blame for this parlous state of affairs solely in King's lap. He'd proved much more effective at reining in the corps and its fellow travellers than had Hunter, and he was constrained by London's refusal to commit adequate resources to the colony or even to send him the sort of convicts who would be of most use. Despite his problems King did push through a major reform which laid a foundation for rational growth – of a sort – in the future. Much of the land within the limits of the town had been leased, bought, traded and sold with only the most cursory records being kept. In some cases a packet of land had changed owners a number of times by mere word of mouth. King ordered a town survey and created a register of leases and ownership, the first time any real order had been imposed on the frenzied derangement of Sydney's property market since Governor Phillip left.

Despite benefiting enormously from the regulation of property relations, the town's power elite refused to call a cease-fire in their sniping campaign against the Governor. He had curtailed the worst excesses of the corps, but their rancour hadn't been quelled, only forced underground. When their champion, John Macarthur, returned in triumph from banishment to England, the bell was tolling for King. If the British Government were hoping his replacement would make a better fist of ruling the anarchic outpost, they were to be sorely disappointed. If you were looking for someone to inflame the already aggravated situation, Captain William Bligh of the *Bounty* was your man.

The only Australian leader to be deposed by an armed uprising, he was initially warmly welcomed by the men who had seen off both Hunter and King. The popular image of Bligh is that of a stunted, foul-mouthed ogre with axes in his eyes, stalking the quarterdeck of the *Bounty* and being unconscionably rude to Fletcher Christian. In fact, Bligh's early period in the colony went well, even though he was a reformer cut from the same cloth as King. The causes of the coup which eventually unseated him were numerous, rooted in both systemic failure and personality clashes, but Bligh's vigorous prosecution of Governor Phillip's orders regarding leases inside the town certainly contributed. He demanded that any houses occupying Crown land should be vacated and demolished, but rather than treading softly on very dangerous terrain he cursed and swore and succumbed to violent fits of anger when challenged. His actions preserved a huge slice of the city, which now forms the Domain, Hyde Park and the Botanic Gardens, but it antagonised the same powerful interests that had destroyed his predecessors. For their part, the officers of the corps were to discover that their move against him, although immediately successful, contained the seeds of their own destruction, delivering to the colony a governor who was both willing and able to force their submission.

Lachlan Macquarie hailed from the risibly named Island of Mull in the Argyleshire Hebrides. His ancestors, chiefs of the Clan Guarie, had lorded it over the small isle of Ulva for some 900 years and bred from their fierce line a hard-set, self-willing soldier who distinguished himself in battle against the French in Egypt, the Dutch at Cochin and Colombo, and all sorts of uppity natives in India. In 1807, returning from the subcontinent, he was almost drowned in the Persian Gulf on his way to Basra. There, upon discovering that war had erupted between Turkey and the Czar, he collected despatches from Baghdad and struck off across Russia to St Petersburg and thence to London. Lachlan Macquarie was not a man to baulk at putting the slipper into a gang of mutinous rummies in Sydney.

On 1 January 1810, his first day in the governor's mansion, Macquarie issued a proclamation damning the renegades who had overthrown the King's last representative and announcing His Majesty's 'high displeasure and disapprobation' of their outrageous conduct. Three days later he put the corps to the sword, proclaiming that anyone appointed to public office since Bligh's removal were themselves to be removed and replaced by those they had usurped. Any grants of land or stock, or leases of houses made to officers of the corps in the same period were now null and void. The mutineers were to hand over all official papers, records and documents, along with any public money, stores or provisions. Any trials, arrests and investigations which had taken place since the mutiny were themselves declared illegal. Stripped of its power and wealth, the corps was sent packing a few months later, ironically in the same naval convoy that carried poor old Bligh back to England.

Shameless greedheads they may have been, but the exertions of

The Virgin's Lie

the corps did leave one positive legacy. Thanks largely to their villainous efforts, the human garbage dump envisioned by the punishment freaks of the 1780s had been transformed into a rising entrepot. For all its shortcomings and in the face of economic recession at home, Port Jackson had become the transit point for an increasing flow of colonial trade. Bullock drays tottering with loads of barley and wheat creaked and rumbled down George Street, raising billows of dust as they weaved around giant ruts and washouts in which packs of dogs fell upon unwary half-feral goats. Coastal packets plied the harbour with maize from the Hawkesbury or coal and limestone from Broken Bay. They dropped anchor off Campbell's Wharf next to Calcutta traders which sat low in the water, weighed down with spars of Indian timber and Chinese sandalwood, with hogsheads of *bêche-de-mer*, with salt pork and fish oil, cedar and barley, with sugar and tea and thousands of barrels of wine and spirits. American whalers called in on their way to and from the east coast of New Zealand; during one week three sealers arrived from there with 45 000 skins.

There were just over 6000 people resident in Sydney when Lachlan and Elizabeth Macquarie stepped ashore to review an honour guard of the 102nd Regiment. A salute boomed from the cannon of their ship and was answered by the guns on Dawes Point. Their new home stood out in the amphitheatre of the cove. It was still one of the biggest structures in the town, although the grand houses and stores of a few wealthy merchants dominated the bay's western shore, whilst two windmills and the intimidating bulk of Fort Phillip held the ridge above. Like a clutch of seashells scattered by a child's careless hand, the remaining cottages, their whitewashed features startling in the sun, either bunched up on the steep, rocky slopes above the western wharves or played themselves out in a thin, random scatter south along the line of George Street and the Tank Stream.

It was a pleasant enough vision of bucolic charm, but between the idea and reality fell the shadow. In Macquarie's first letter home he reported that the barracks were so decayed the 73rd Regiment had to be encamped in the fields at Grose Farm (where Sydney University now lies). The hospital was in a ruinous state, completely unfit for receiving the sick, and the colony's two boats were so rotten as to be useless. The occupants of those picturesque little cottages threw their offal and excrement directly into the streets, where it sat and baked in the sun until washed into the Tank Stream by a downpour or snaffled up by wandering pigs. After rain the streets were impassable and during it they could be lethal. A man and wife were drowned in Pitt Street in 1807 after being swept into a deep gutter during a storm. The Parramatta road, which Macquarie thought barely worthy of the name, was ineffectually kept in repair by an order which required travellers to collect rubble from the brick fields to dump into potholes so deep they could cripple a horse.

And running through the middle of this environmental disaster was the Tank Stream. Instead of the sylvan brook described by the First Fleet writers, Macquarie found an open drain, little better than a sewer in parts, polluted by wandering animals, industrial waste and ignorant householders who washed their filthy clothes in the sandstone tanks already befouled by the ashes and garbage they had dumped upstream. Gone were the little white beaches, the stands of acacia and bunches of wild spinach, replaced by toilets, slaughterhouses and tanneries. Having reimposed order in the civil universe, Macquarie bent to the same mission in the physical. He passed an order in February 1810 banning the use of the tanks for washing and authorising the seizure and forfeiture of any animal found wandering nearby. It had little effect and in September he was forced to issue a much longer order banning all animals, noxious trades and householders from use of the water. He further outlawed the dumping of rubbish in the streets, as it inevitably found its way into the town's only water supply, and ordered the magistrates 'to pay the strictest attention' to enforcing these edicts.

A month later the fluctuant, ill-contrived paths and trails over which passed all of Sydney's traffic, along which capered so many of its pigs and goats, and onto which was tossed so much of its garbage, were paid the honour of being officially turned into streets by a stroke of the Governor's pen. He had ordered them widened to fifteen metres, including a footpath on both sides, and banned the construction of houses without authorisation by the town surveyor. The same order attempted to round up the town's anarchic population of stray farm animals, authorised the constabulary to shoot any dogs found attacking people or horses, and for good measure reinforced the Governor's previous injunction against the general populace letting off their own firearms in and around the town, especially on Sundays. The main thoroughfare, leading from Dawes Point to the Brickfields and beyond – a riotous unfenced barnyard, the haunt of murderous packs of dogs and itchy-fingered gun-toting colonists – until then variously known as High Street, Spring Row and Sergeant Major's Row, was renamed George Street in honour of the colony's barking-mad sovereign. Street signs were erected along the unmade tracks and everybody was told to stop using their old names. The Governor announced that he intended to clear some ground near the administrative quarter, which would be called Macquarie Place, in line with his cheerful habit of naming everything he could get away with after himself. He moved the old overcrowded market square away from the Rocks back up George to Market Street, which would in turn run down to a new wharf at Cockle Bay. A swathe of open ground looking down on the town from the east became Hyde Park and the brick-makers in the adjacent pits were banned from digging for clay there.

These were all small but significant steps towards realising Phillip's vision of imposing 'order and useful arrangement' on a savage coast. By 1810 brute creation was no longer manifest in the wild land, untouched by cultivation, but rather in the 'tumult and confusion' wrought by the hands of men, by their greed and rampant appetites, checked by nothing more than the feeble angels of their better nature. Macquarie was both informed by Enlightenment ideals of reason and progress and driven by a baser personal desire to mould the coarse clay of this settlement into something finer, and preferably named after him. It was simultaneously a civilizing mission and a soothing balm for the soul of a proud man whose clan had ruled their own distant world for most of a millennium and only recently fallen from grace. Roads and bridges were just the start, the framework of the complex urban set piece he would will into existence.

Macquarie knew, however, that will was not enough. He would need skilled men to fully realise these dreams. In his first letter to London he had asked for a professional architect to be sent out, but none was forthcoming. Perhaps the closest thing he had at first was his own beloved wife Elizabeth, an adventurous, confident woman, who arrived in the colony as qualified as anyone in architectural design and probably more so in matters of taste and landscaping. A copy of Gyfford's *Designs for Elegant Cottages and Small Villas* had sailed with her to Sydney and from it came house

The Virgin's Lie

plans for the Judge Advocate and the Colonial Secretary. Her influence was important in shaping the Orphan School at Parramatta, the gardens of Government House and the design of the Domain, where generations of Sydneysiders have ambled along the roads she laid out and caught the breeze off the harbour from the sandstone bench which bears her name. But even her untutored gifts were not equal to the grand stage of her husband's vision and it was not until Lieutenant John Watts and the convict forger Francis Greenway arrived in 1814 that he could call on men whose talents matched his aspirations. Watts, a family friend, had been formally trained as an architect and the Governor quickly set him to work on military hospitals, barracks, a church and old Government House at Parramatta. But it was Greenway, the urger, the manipulator, the insolent, conceited, self-aggrandising genius, to whom Macquarie turned to realise his grandest schemes and, often, his biggest whitest elephants. Peter Bridges neatly abstracts their relationship in *Foundations of Identity*.

It was an odd partnership but one of mutual advantage, Macquarie had discovered in Greenway an architect whose skills and creativity were tuned to his own ambitions, and Greenway had a patron who could offer him opportunities for the realisation of his professional advancement. His position as a convict did not prevent him from freely proffering his professional advice and suggestions for all sorts of grand projects ... they shared a deep streak of vanity and tender self-esteem, both rejected opposition to their visions as obstacles created by plodding minds to be righteously rejected and failed to discern that the architect's more grandiose schemes were figments of an unreal ambition.

Macquarie's own imagination wasn't averse to the odd booby flight. One of Greenway's more important early tasks was to pronounce the last rites over a project the Governor had hoped would prove an immense ornament and benefit to the town, as well as to his own standing, but which degenerated into an embarrassing circus. In early November of 1810 the colony's Acting Commissary, a sort of chief storekeeper, had signed a contract with D'Arcy Wentworth, the Principal Surgeon and Superintendent of Police, and two merchants, Garnham Blaxcell and Alexander Riley, to build a new hospital on a site commanding the high ridge to the east of the town. It was a huge project for an infant colony, a monumental investment of scarce resources which would, when complete, overshadow and totally dominate the miniature village below. A structural symphony in three movements, the hospital consisted of a main building nearly ninety metres long with walls over half a metre thick, and two smaller but still substantial separate wings, which now serve as the Old Mint and the core of Parliament House on Macquarie Street. With hundreds of rude little mud huts and tumble-down, jerry-built cottages still blighting the face of the town, the hospital would sweep aside the doubtful, disreputable circumstances of Sydney's birth and carve a message deep into the ancient sandstone beds on which it lay: the might and power of Imperial Britain had arrived and none would stand before it. No warped, disjointed cabbage tree logs would go into this building. No greasy, leaf-choked mud would be smeared on its walls to keep out the wind and rain. Cedar, mahogany and cut stone would hold up the massive edifice and deny the elements. Wide verandahs would encircle the buildings, the upper level being supported by columns of solid stone, recalling the classical forms which adorned the first great Western city-states.

Convicts take a wagon down the track that became George Street. (*Courtesy of State Library of NSW*)

Almost one hundred years later the same street was jammed with traffic. (*Courtesy of State Library of NSW*)

Arthur Phillip: Foundation governor and forgotten hero. *(Courtesy of State Library of NSW)*

John Macarthur: Insatiable greed and a will to power. *(Courtesy of State Library of NSW)*

Lachlan Macquarie: The architect of civilised Sydney. *(Courtesy of State Library of NSW)*

Wentworth the Younger: Statesman, class traitor or hero? *(Courtesy of State Library of NSW)*

Versailles at Central Station. A 1908 proposal for urban regeneration which bit the dust.
(Courtesy of Sydney City Council Archives)

Circular Quay: From rat-infested sewer to Orwellian meta-space. *(Courtesy of Sydney City Council Archives)*

The Rocks and Darling Harbour in the years before the plague.

(Courtesy of Sydney City Council archives)

The Hotel Australia. An oasis in the wastelands.
(Courtesy of Royal Australian Historical Society)

The Virgin's Lie

At least that was the plan, for which the contractors received eighty oxen for slaughter and the exclusive right to import spirits into the colony for three years. Unfortunately none of them were builders. The only tradesmen they could find were totally unsuited to such a huge, complicated undertaking. Nobody had really mastered the difficulties of using local materials. And the town's other merchants went into a tailspin over the import deal, some of them already having valuable shipments on the way. Long story short? It was a cock-up, with the contractors losing money and the job itself botched beyond imagining. Garnham Blaxcell was so deep in the hole with his creditors over this and other failures that he took flight for England but fetched up in Batavia where he drank himself to death within a few months.

Nor did Macquarie escape unscathed. He was beset by critics on all sides – the skinflints in Downing Street who would have spent nothing on the colony if at all possible; the contractors in Sydney who were being ground into the earth by looming financial disaster; and those nattering pointyheads common in any small, isolated castaway society, especially one so thoroughly riven by factional warfare for most of its short and miserable existence. In April 1816 Macquarie turned to Greenway for help. The convict draughtsman inspected the works as part of a committee which reported that the contractors had committed a number of gross and 'most serious' violations of their agreement. The foundations of the main building, upon which the colossal weight of the whole rested, were in an appalling state. The basement wall, rather than being almost a metre thick, was only forty-six centimetres, and made of thin ashlar, much of which was already 'in a dangerous and mutilated state requiring immediate attention'. With water seeping into the basement the decay grew worse every day. The boundary wall was in a 'shattered state', with no level base ever having been laid and the whole length in danger of falling into ruin. Many of the stone columns were already split. Rather than being made of single continuous pieces, the roof beams had been cobbled together in three separate sections 'thereby making them quite useless'. If anything went wrong in the basement, as seemed inevitable, the roof, the walls and colonnade would come crashing down on the patients and medical staff. Other minor problems included dry rot in the floor, and gutters which were about to blister and crack in the sun. In the end, rather than recommending increased funding as requested by the builders, Greenway said they should pay a penalty of £10 000.

Greenway's own first foray into the built environment was on a much smaller scale but met with immeasurably more success. The lighthouse he raised in the form of a 'sturdy Doric tower' on South Head was far removed from the plain, utilitarian sentinels which guarded the coast of England. Immensely pleased that something was going to plan for a change, Macquarie granted his new architect a conditional emancipation. The tower, predictably, was named after the Governor. Greenway's first project within the town was the Hyde Park Barracks which still stands next to one of the old hospital wings he so ferociously criticised. When completed, the *Sydney Gazette* described it as a noble structure, beautiful at a distance but conveying a sense of towering grandeur on a closer approach. Greenway's clean lines and elegant dimensions, the obvious quality of his materials and the harmony they evoke between the art of design and the demands of execution are still a silent admonition to the dog's breakfast of the old hospital next door. Columns askew, brickwork confused, a mishmash of shoddy, half-arsed incompetence, the hospital benefits from recent

The Virgin's Lie

renovation and a heavy patina of old age which renders modern onlookers indulgent and less critical of an old trollop's charms, especially when viewed within the context of the ugly, neo-brutalist monster boxes which have stamped their heavy jackboots all over that part of the legal district in recent decades.

Between 1816 and 1819, when their whole act came to a shuddering halt, Macquarie and Greenway laboured mightily to remake Sydney's image in line with their own occasionally fanciful ideals. Greenway's pencils flashed over plans of churches, courthouses, barracks and a new, monumental Government House. Macquarie continually rode out to lay foundation stones, visit building sites and dedicate the ornaments to the civilization he was raising all around him. Jacques Arago, ploughing up the harbour with Louis de Freycinet's scientific expedition of 1819, was taken aback by the progress.

> The appeerance of homes standing in cultivated clearing on the harbour's wild shores recalled elegant chateaux in the neighbourhood of Bordeaux. European fruit trees and trim sweet smelling hedges had usurped the place of the Australian bush, and in the midst of prodigious and bizarre nature long avenues unfolded magically and led to small dwellings carefully embellished by ingenious art.

Arago thought that Sydney made 'a charming picture', its villas of cut stone, decorated with sculptures and fine balconies, contrasting strangely with the old wooden houses which were vanishing so quickly. Wandering around the better districts, the Frenchman could find nothing 'to proclaim that this town, already so beautiful, is the work of but a few years'. The flatteries of Arago were just what the dynamic duo liked to hear, but in the end the condemnation of the Bigge Report was what they got instead.

JT Bigge was a lawyer, a former chief justice of Trinidad and a scaly old toad. An arch-conservative, he was despatched to Sydney by the Colonial Office to investigate whether the convict system was still the 'object of real terror' originally intended. Well attuned to those wealthy landholders who saw the convicts as indentured slaves, Bigge stepped ashore a few weeks before Arago, cast his eyes over the same charming picture and enthusiastically took to it with a large ugly nail-studded club. Bigge knocked seven kinds of hell out of Macquarie's administration and one of his first targets was the Governor's public works program. In this he was ably assisted by the testimony, sworn or otherwise, of men like Gregory Blaxland and John Macarthur. Blaxland was all for building good roads to and from his own property but he 'saw little virtue in fine public buildings in a pioneer settlement'. They 'gave ships' captains entering the harbour a false impression of prosperity and hampered the establishment of a useful and profitable agricultural base on which to build the colonial economy'. They were simply 'not necessary for this generation', a view firmly subscribed to in London. Macarthur, whose habit of chewing up and spitting out difficult governors was becoming a little compulsive, employed 'all his influence in London to destroy the Governor's reputation in official circles and to precipitate his recall'. He relentlessly brown-nosed Bigge, who returned the favour by pushing Macarthur's line that New South Wales's future lay in the hands of wool producers, 'men of real capital, with estates of at least 10 000 acres each, who would maintain transported convicts as their labour force and keep them landless and in proper subjection'.

Macquarie, who had naively expected Bigge to vindicate his

administration, found himself increasingly marginalised and under attack. His relationship with Greenway deteriorated as the ego-maniacal architect unwisely tried to play both ends off against the middle. It was a great relief to the tired, dispirited Scot when he learned, at the end of 1820, that his third request to resign had been accepted. He and Elizabeth sailed for home in February 1822, waved off by huge cheering crowds of people who had benefited from his reformist programs. Greenway, who now had to face his legion of enemies without a protector, soon fell out of favour and was forced back into private practice. He wasn't what you'd call a people person and he struggled to make a living. He died farming poor swampy ground on the Hunter River and was buried without a tombstone or marker in a lonesome field outside East Maitland.

As Lachlan and Elizabeth Macquarie stood at the rails of the *Surry* to accept the best wishes of the town's lower orders they could at least take some consolation from the changes they had wrought on that strange remote little world. The life of the town was still cupped within the intimate folds of the valley which climbed away to the south. But where they had once surveyed a desperate, muddy outpost whose organising principle was the will to power rather than the rule of law, they left behind a well ordered, prosperous sea port. The imposing lines of the General Hospital which receded with each pitch and roll of the *Surry*'s deck may have reminded Macquarie of the perils of immoderate ambition, but for all its faults it marked out an axis along which layers of power were steadily accumulating. The colony's legal and medical professions were drawn there to the hospital and law courts. They built fine houses, chambers and offices around Hyde Park, and opportunistic merchants soon set up shop to serve them.

Further south commercial activity was accelerating at the intersection of Market and George Streets, where Macquarie had moved the town markets in 1811. Private warehouses spread along Sussex and Kent Streets to store the increasing volume of goods unloaded at Macquarie's Cockle Bay Wharf. In all, well over a thousand buildings covered the ground where black ghosts crept between the memory of trees, along the banks of the dying Tank Stream.

That much abused rivulet had withstood the depredations of the English for a little longer than its surrounding ecosystem or the Aborigines, but like them it was doomed. None of Macquarie's orders had arrested its decline, which accelerated on his departure. By 1824 Sydney's water supply had become a threat to public health. In February of that year an aging surveyor by the name of John Busby arrived to solve the crisis. It took him until 1837, by which stage he was over seventy years old. The tunnel which he drove through four kilometres of sandstone, from the Lachlan Swamps (now Centennial Park) to Hyde Park, meandered about like an old wino. Busby's critics said he didn't care to get down and dirty with his rough convict workforce and consequently the excavation's line of advance travelled along the path of least resistance, or in whichever direction the miners' noses were pointing when they swung their picks and shovels in the hot, cramped confines of their tunnel. Even after completion supply was never certain – especially when mains and public fountains were run off the bore – and the town's health suffered from the liberal use of lead piping. With the Tank Stream ruined there was no other source of fresh water until 1859. Indeed, the city's enormous thirst was not properly quenched until well into the twentieth century, with the construction of dams on the Upper Nepean. Until then the city's water supply was erratic at best and nonexistent at worst.

The Virgin's Lie

The failure of the system, particularly in summer, was not uncommon and when water did flow it was often discoloured, foul tasting and crawling with aquatic life. The Water Board's history quotes the example of a Canterbury man who kept a sieve on hand in the early 1930s because he 'received a supply of freshwater shrimps every time he turned on his tap'. Centipedes and eels were also frequent visitors to the kitchen sink, and in 1932 the *Telegraph* reported on a Paddington man whose tap emitted a giant wriggling 'Gorgian worm'.

Rogue prawns and giant worms were more inconvenient than life threatening. The leitmotif of nineteenth-century Sydney was much heavier: a parched, stinking city beset by desperate water shortages and choking under a mountain of human waste. With no universal sewerage system in place, thousands of cesspits dotted the landscape, often consisting of nothing more than holes dug into the porous topsoil, filled with fecal matter, topped off and started again a few metres away. In Waterloo the ground was so thoroughly contaminated by the 1870s that the Sewerage and Health Board predicted the whole district would soon be unfit for human habitation. Drinking wells were sunk into this spongy, poisonous earth and such sewerage outlets as existed vomited their noxious brown sludge directly into the harbour. The authorities were not unaware of the problem. In *Nineteenth Century Sydney*, David Clark reports the case of a Balmain man who escaped conviction on a charge of drunkenness because he told the magistrate he had nothing to drink but beer. The court considered this a reasonable excuse. (In an eye-bulging footnote Clark also tells the story of the Albion Brewery whose beer was much appreciated for its 'distinctive' flavour; a product, it transpired, of the hideously polluted ground water in the brewery's reservoir draining through the Devonshire Street Cemetery.)

LEVIATHAN

Notwithstanding the indulgences of Balmain magistrates, Sydney's awareness of its own physical degradation in the late 1800s seemed to have been clouded by wilful blindness, as the city tried to ignore the savage forces which burned at the heart of its fantastic growth. In 1878, when thousands of demonstrators rampaged through the Chinese quarter to protect their way of life from the yellow peril, a big wedge of the city's population already lived in conditions just as appalling if not worse than those found in any opium den. Like the underclass of London however, they were all but invisible to those who went about their lives in the better part of town. Even though their homes lay next to each other, and the stench of the lower orders must have wrinkled the noses of consulting surgeons in Macquarie Street and the well-to-do merchants of the Rocks, the city slums were simply allowed to fester for decades.

When Busby's bore was finished in 1837 it serviced a town not too dissimilar to the one Macquarie left behind. One major change was that Woolloomooloo Hill, which we know as Potts Point, had been carved from the bush atop soaring cliffs to the east of the Domain. It was Sydney's first suburb, an exclusive retreat for a handful of colonial worthies who could afford to remove themselves from the increasingly unpleasant atmosphere of the town. A number of conditions imposed on the landholders ensured that only the brightest stars in the colony's tiny firmament got to twinkle on the ridge. John Busby had an estate there, as did the Surveyor-General Thomas Mitchell, Supreme Court Justice Sir James Dowling and the colony's High Sheriff Thomas Macquoid. Each land grant was to have just one villa on it, worth no less than £1000, set back at least sixty yards from the road and facing towards Sydney. There was no artless Georgian false modesty about these buildings. Showpieces of a new indigenous elite, they proclaimed their owners' wealth and import with all the bombast and florid styling available to the designers-gone-wild of these Regency and Neo-Gothic piles. And just in case the unwashed masses huddled back in town didn't get the message, the Hill's stylish residents hacked away every vestige of native fauna so that their handsome temples shrieked their significance from a blinding canvas of bare sun-blasted rock. Thomas Shepherd, a landscape gardener, took his betters to task for their madness, saying,

> When you ... first got your estates, your ground was well furnished with beautiful shrubs. You ignorantly set the murderous hoe and grubbing axe to work to destroy them, and the ground that had been full of luxuriant verdure, was laid bare and desolate, and the prospect ruined.

The 'desart' of Woolloomooloo Hill, as it was known, would eventually be improved by carting in soil on which familiar English gardens could grow. In the town, meanwhile, growth and decay raced on in tandem.

With the notable exception of the upper-class decampment to Potts Point, the boundaries of Sydney did not move much during the 1830s or early 1840s. Feverish construction went on inside the town limits, however. British capital spun off the Industrial Revolution at home, funding the growth of the pastoral industry here and encouraging the migration of thousands of workers. The simple, primary structure of the city's economy evolved into denser, more complex forms as professionals, service workers, middlemen and ten-percenters all set up shop in the nooks and crannies of a maturing system. As land values climbed, the wide open lots of the town's early years were chopped and diced into smaller packets. Second storeys appeared above shops and offices, often providing living space for the proprietors working below. Footpaths were gradually eaten away as frontages crept out to claim all the available space. Mercantile power folded around the markets which Macquarie had moved south, animating the streets around the intersection of Market and George with an unrestrained, almost American energy.

James Maclehose's 1839 *Picture of Sydney and Strangers' Guide* left its readers in no doubt about the speed of the change overtaking the town. Maclehose wrote that 'up to a comparatively late period' Sydney was little more than an insignificant village of bark huts, themselves little better 'than the rude wigwams' of America's barbarian Indians, and certainly inferior to the huts of African savages. Maclehose defined the southern outskirts of the emerging city as 'a ridge of elevated land, known as the Surry Hills', and the western limits as 'a beautiful and extensive salt water lagoon' of more than two miles in length. Most of the city's industrial wealth was concentrated in Sussex Street, which ran alongside Darling Harbour. At least eight flour mills could be found on the harbour's western shore, while the east was taken up by ship- and boat-building yards and a dozen or so large wharfs, all of them constantly busy with vessels either landing or taking on cargo.

George Street, the retail corridor along which so much of this cargo would travel, had only recently been levelled and finished with granite. Its western reaches, past the markets, had been regraded to alleviate the problems of a dangerous climb and descent of Brickfield Hill. About 28 000 cubic metres of sandstone and soil was sheared off the top of the hill and used to lengthen the plane of ascent, all by manual labour. Running parallel to

The Virgin's Lie

George, Pitt Street displayed a dimorphic character, with the commercial sector near Market Street boasting 'three of the largest and most extensive Manchester warehouses in the colony'; while south of Park Street small cheerful cottages surrounded by bright gardens and shaded verandahs pleased the eye and recalled 'the rustic beauties of Old England'. Maclehose noted that the 'gentlemen of the law' found the southern end of Elizabeth Street 'to be very convenient' because of its proximity to the Supreme Court, and increasingly, although he does not mention it, because of the large number of taverns which had sprung up so the wig-wearing vultures could refresh themselves at their leisure. Of the city's poorer areas he had less to say. There were some fine merchants' villas in the Rocks, high up on the ridges where they were safe from sewerage run-off, but the rest of that district he dismissed in short order, saying that 'the roads and foot-paths are in such bad repair, and so filthy, that no respectable person will pass through them if avoidable'. And avoided they were. Many of the ramshackle huts which infested the rocky slopes had survived, sort of, since Macquarie's time or earlier. Essex Street was so steep as to be 'almost impassable for wheeled carriages' and in such poor repair that even pedestrians had to be exceedingly cautious when climbing it. Argyle Street's precipitous narrow passage was 'so completely overrun with the filth which is discharged from the upper streets' that it had been largely abandoned as a pathway with people 'generally preferring to go a distance, rather than encounter the abominable stench . . .'.

The retreat of the city's respectable classes from these slums, the way they held their breath and averted their eyes when passing was, in a sense, a remarkable triumph of will. By staring fixedly at their large and extensive Manchester warehouses, by tending the rose beds in their cheerful cottages and proudly surveying the mercantile fleets which plied the waters of the harbour, the better part of the city simply wished away the malignant chancre which had erupted on its own body. During the latter half of the 1840s the generous spreading of the city at its limits was accompanied by an intense compacting of its rotten core. Two maps prepared by William H Wells neatly illustrate this process. The first, drawn up in 1842, depicts the semi-rustic port of the Maclehose guides. Ninety percent of the built environment was contained within a long thin wedge running back from the harbour to Campbell Street. The elite enclave clinging to the heights of Darlinghurst was a major outpost. A couple of dozen desultory shacks stood around Surry Hills and a number of brewery workers' homes straggled out along the line of road we now think of as Broadway. For the most part, though, Sydney was still boxed up inside a tight grid of streets which never quite seemed to sort themselves into any sort of system. By December 1850, when Wells released another major map of the city, it had begun to metastasise. If his first chart presents a rough sketch of the future city, this latter one is closer to a formal blueprint. A great swathe of free ground still marked the Domain and Hyde Park, but the empty vistas which filled so much of his previous drawing had been buried under new streets and suburbs such as Chippendale, Kensington, Strawberry Hills, Balmain and Paddington, while the centre of town had become a dense, tangled warren with lanes and alleys driven into the core of city blocks by builders desperate for space.

The city's population had climbed towards 50 000. The luckiest of them lived in spacious villas with water laid on and servants to tend to those indelicate domestic duties, such as disposing of master's bodily wastes. The middle classes lived harder and closer in townhouses, cottages and terraces. With no staff to clean and carry for them a good deal of their time and money was spent procuring enough water to keep house in the modest but exacting style demanded by emerging Victorian morality. The rest of the population, the vast majority in fact, lived in dwellings squeezed onto the lower slopes of the Rocks, into the dark, threatening tenements of the city proper and around the emerging industrial zones to the west. In some parts of town, such as Sussex Street, the different classes were all tossed in together as the great black engine of capitalism progressively mowed down slum housing, replacing it with more valuable commercial and residential property. In one of a series of articles devoted to the state of Sydney's sanitation in 1851, the *Herald* described Sussex Street's appearance as grotesque. Handsome cottages with well-tended gardens were bracketed by rotting wooden shacks; while single-roomed hovels, little more than packing cases in the last stages of decay, rubbed up hard against luxurious newly built townhouses.

The relentless pressure of development bulldozed great heaps of the poor into increasingly filthy, crowded slums like Durands Alley. Forty squalid houses in an unpaved, undrained dogleg lane near the junction of Goulburn and Pitt Streets, the *Herald*'s correspondent described it as a 'vile place' fit only for keeping pigs. It appears on Wells's map as a narrow, crooked shaft bored deep into a dense mine of abysmal little hutches. It survives in skeletal form today as Cunningham Street, with the same broken V shape, the same claustrophobic atmosphere and just a hint of the original ambience provided by a brothel and Club X porno shack at the Pitt Street junction and, on emerging into Goulburn, a melancholy strip, home to the handjob specialists of the Eros Theatre.

The first inhabitants of Durands Alley – as many as eight of them sleeping in rooms less than four metres square – afforded the *Herald*'s man the grim pleasure of seeing just how low human beings could descend. He found them one Monday morning with bound-up heads, black eyes and bruised, smashed-in faces from their weekly boxing match held each Sunday in the thick sludge of decaying offal and shit which passed for a pavement outside their homes. Later on Monday they would creep down to the Haymarket to bash and rob bullock drivers and country folk in town for the sales. The *Herald* warned that, like 'certain loathsome reptiles', their sort 'only come out at night from these dark recesses'.

> Ask them a question in the daytime, and reptile-like, they hiss [at] you; unaccustomed to sympathy of any kind, they conclude your only object is to mock them in their misery. They feel ... that society has cast them from its bosom to perish in dirt and dishonour ... As they are not respected by society, so they have ceased to respect themselves – careless of life, and heedless of death, they sink into the grave leaving nothing behind them but a vicious example.

In a few short decades the enterprising colonists had managed to recreate, in places like Durands Alley, the very same conditions which had filled the English prison hulks of the 1780s. But for the middle and upper classes Sydney's slums were another country. As Henry Mayhew had written of the English lower orders, the degradation of their lives were 'utterly unknown among the well fed portion of society'. In February 1851 the *Herald* – already comfortably settled into its role as the mouthpiece of well-fed Sydney – said that one of the underworld districts it visited was as foreign to the city's respectable citizens as Peking 'or the Empire of Japan'.

The Virgin's Lie

This slum, whose ghosts now sleep beneath the massive concrete foundations of the Macquarie Bank and the neo-Romanesque marvel of Burns Philp's old headquarters in Bridge Street, was hemmed in by the rear of commercial premises on George Street and the last sad trace of the Tank Stream. The history of the stream seems to have been lost to the *Herald* by then, for nowhere does their writer refer to it as anything more than a wide open sewer. In it, bloated animal carcasses – mostly rats, cats and dogs – putrefied under the summer sun in a foul soup of human excrement and rotting garbage. The smell assaulted the senses from Hunter all the way down Spring Street to the quay.

The roving packs of dogs and hordes of near-feral goats which had driven Macquarie to distraction had not been in the least affected by his efforts. Thirty years after he left they still ruled the streets. Colonel GC Mundy, who arrived in 1846 as Deputy Adjutant General to the military forces in the Australian colonies, complained that the city's thoroughfares were 'infested by an innumerable host of apparently ownerless dogs' which ranged at will through the town, tormenting and terrifying all. Any horseman who rode at a pace faster than a trot was certain to draw a riotous pack of the 'lawless brutes' to his heels.

> Many a luckless wight have I watched flying along the street in a cloud of dust and dogs, fresh detachments of curs debouching upon him from every alley and court, until they vanished together round a corner, leaving me to imagine the finish. But more serious consequences arise sometimes from the stray dogs. Two or three times I have been the horrified witness of attacks upon children by large and fierce dogs, which would have ended fatally but for the prompt help of passers-by. I once saw a

powerful mastiff seize a horse by the throat, between the shafts of a gig, and pull it to the ground; nor did the ferocious beast quit its hold until killed by a blow with an iron bar.

Mundy, who served in the colony for five years, had been less than impressed during his early days ashore. In spite of the harbour's many charms, its lovely islands, its sweeping bays and headlands crested with handsome villas, there was, to his eye, 'something singularly repulsive in the leaden tint of the gum-tree foliage, and in the dry and sterile sandstone from which it springs'. Mundy conceded he would have been astonished at the wealth of George Street were it not for the earbashing he'd received from his fellow passengers on the way out. Natives of Sydney, they had sung its praises 'in so loud and high a key' that on arriving, Mundy could not help but be disappointed.

He also came, of course, with the impartial eye of a disinterested outsider. Unlike his fellow travellers, Mundy had no emotional investment in the young outpost and was only too willing to peer beyond colonial spin and boosterism. The lighting and paving of the streets were 'a disgrace' and the sewerage 'shamefully bad'. Hyde Park was 'merely a fenced common, without a tree or a blade of grass' and the barracks housed a bunch of flea-bitten crims rather than a proud regiment. The city was still overrun by goats; just one 'conspicuous item of the Sydney street menagerie'. Like the dogs they rambled everywhere, invading any garden with an unlocked gate. In a few seconds, roses, sweet peas and carnations were 'as closely nibbled down as though a flight of locusts had bivouacked for a week on the spot; the flower-beds dotted over with little cloven feet, as if ten thousand infantine devils had been dancing there . . .'.

The Virgin's Lie

An old India hand, he was also contemptuous of the local architecture which was totally unsuited to a semitropical climate. The houses of the respectable classes he dismissed in a withering blast as 'barefaced, smug-looking tenements, without verandahs or even broad eaves'. Even the most handsome and comfortable villas were crowded with expensive, overstuffed furnishing, as opposed to the practice in most warm countries of using only the plainest and hardest fittings in otherwise bare rooms. He found the view from his own quarters in the city's legal district most disagreeable

for they looked upon the backs of a cluster of St Giles-like tenements, across a piece of waste ground, unbuilt on because litigated ... where all sorts of rubbish might be shot, or at least was shot, from a load of soot to a proscribed cat or the decimated fraction of a litter of puppies. Here, in the warm summer nights, many a drunken outcast of the pot-houses took his rest without fear of the watch-house: nor had he much cause for fear; the solitary policeman crawling stupidly along the middle of the street, and the solitary lamp dim twinkling in the shadowy distance, were little likely to discover or disturb his slumbers.

Mundy was to overcome some of these initial misgivings about Sydney, however, conceding that the growth of the city during his first two years was enormous. A new suburb sprang up on either side of William Street where just recently 'the belated diner-out might have fallen among bushrangers'; whilst the valley of Woolloomooloo, which had contained just one large villa on his arrival, was soon overrun by 'a forest of chimneys ...'. The same chimneys impressed the hell out of George Butler Earp in 1853 when he remarked that the traveller landing in this new metropolis would find it hard to convince himself he was in a strange land, so faithfully did all these belching smokestacks recreate the industrial airs of home.

The thickening smoke which hung in the humidity of Sydney's long summers signalled the death of the old, intimately scaled town. More and more chimneys would climb skywards in the next decade, until Mundy's concrete forest had spread across the entire city, colonising it so completely that in photos of Sydney from that time the most striking feature is the amazing number of smokestacks befouling the air. Bent backs and straining muscles were quickly replaced by steam power in the city's economic engine room. Thousands of furnaces burned millions of tonnes of wood and coal as the industrial revolution, which had gestated for centuries in Europe, swept Sydney in a few short years, bringing with it the choking smog. The wealth of the continent was there to be stolen, and scores of new industries sprang up in response. Construction, manufacturing and transport, the sinews of a modern industrial state, all grew freakishly in size and complexity as the colonists created their replica of an advanced civilization on the rough foundations of Arthur Phillip's convict settlement.

While steam powered the changes of the next thirty years, they were paid for by gold and wool. The discovery of gold in particular jacked the Australian colonies into a wild, rampaging energy which lit up the southern skies and drew legions of the hopeful, the desperate and the crazed from the dark recesses of the old world. The national population more than doubled, from four hundred and eighty thousand in 1850 to over a million by 1858, with more migrants arriving in two years than had convicts in the previous seventy. This explosion of national wealth was reflected in the blossoming of the built environment. The rich still lavished their

The Virgin's Lie

treasure on luxurious private homes, but now they were so rich they could flaunt their power in the public sphere as well. Fantastic, raw, swaggering wealth declared its own glory in the granite and marble grandeur of the Commercial Banking Company's old premises in George Street at the bottom of Martin Place, in elegant glass-roofed consumer arcadias such as the Strand, and in the proliferation of gentlemen's clubs such as the Australian and the New South Wales at the big end of town. Macquarie Street, which housed the Australian Club, was adorned with a string of stylish Italianate terraces. John Askew, who visited the city just after Mundy left, described the area as the 'West-end of Sydney'. He liked to walk through the district of a summer's evening, 'about an hour after sunset, when the drawing-rooms are in a blaze of light'.

Then the rich tones of the piano, or some other musical instrument, are heard gushing forth from the open windows, accompanied by the sweet melody of female voices, plaintive, or lively, blending in the general harmony. Beautiful ladies, dressed in white, may be seen sitting upon the verandahs, or lounging on magnificent couches, partially concealed by the folds of rich crimson curtains, in drawing-rooms which display all the luxurious comforts and magnificence of the East, intermingled with the elegant utilities of the West ... Fairy like forms flit before the light, affording now and then a moment's pleasure by a glimpse of their lovely features 'ere they disappear. And the lightly sounding footfall, and the merry laughter of happy children, add still more to the pleasing variety of sounds which float upon the evening breeze ...

LEVIATHAN

Not to be outdone by these delicate urban harmonies, the State replied with its own powerful symphony of monumental design. Between 1864 and 1868 the Colonial Architect, James Barnet, completely reworked the diminutive Australian Museum into a massive public temple, fronted by soaring Corinthian pillars and finished with the sort of intricate, expensive detail which was bound to make a lot of know-nothing yahoos in Parliament squeal like stuck pigs. Barnet's museum redefined the dimensions of the city in a way not seen since Macquarie's ill-fated hospital, taking a smalltime provincial backwater into the big league. Then in 1866 Barnet started work on a project which would dwarf it completely: the General Post Office. Still a major landmark in a city which has grown exponentially, upwards and outwards, the GPO was an undertaking as important as Utzon's Opera House a hundred years later, and just as controversial. But it was even more significant in terms of the footprint it left on an infinitely smaller, simpler Victorian city. Here was proof – manifest in millions of tonnes of exquisitely carved rock raised over the grave of the Tank Stream – of the might and power of Imperial Britain, proof of the triumph of her people and their sciences over brute creation, and proof that the destiny of a small white Christian nation was to rule this giant land amidst a sea of lesser races. Those shameless self-promoters Macquarie and Greenway would have approved. Unlike them, however, Barnet was able to ride over the enemies who massed in front of him. When he was finally white-anted out of office in 1890, 1000 new buildings stood as monuments to his long career, from dozens of minor projects like suburban post offices and schools, to other major set pieces such as Customs House, the Lands Department Building, the Colonial Secretary's Building and the Exhibition Buildings in the Botanic Gardens, a wonder of their day and since lost to a fire.

The Virgin's Lie

The change in the face of Sydney over these years was not restricted to individual buildings. The boundaries of the city suddenly became incredibly mobile after decades of incremental advance. A feedback loop of increasing wealth, immigration and industrialisation pushed the envelope of settlement out over the dry horizons which had imprisoned the colony's first settlers. Steam-powered trains and horse-drawn trams delivered workers to the CBD from ever further away as the city splayed its fingers down the train line, opened in 1855, to Parramatta, south along Botany Road, north atop the ridge to Hornsby and out through Paddington in the east. Harbour-front suburbs such as Balmain, Glebe, Mosman and Watsons Bay grew in tandem with the private ferry services which made them possible, while Manly was established as a healthy retreat for the better-off. Their ranks swelled as the long boom filled the pockets of thousands of skilled tradesmen, professionals, merchants, miners, money-movers and industrialists, all of whom were as keen as mustard to get away from the city's slums. They enriched another group, real-estate speculators, who have plagued the city ever since. Those perennial winners, the old money families, who had grown fat on generous land grants, now lined up for a second bite of the cherry as they subdivided their estates and ran up thousands of terrace houses over their old cow pastures. Lines of terraces marching down a hill became a signature of Sydney at that time, from the mean, airless little prison cells knocked out for the lowest sort of workers to the grand, multistoreyed fancies of the nouveau riche. The fever of those times, the rocket-rush, head-spinning vitality of such growth was beautifully caught by James Inglis at the end of the 1870s in *Our Australian Cousins*.

LEVIATHAN

The overflow of bricks and mortar has spread like a lava flood, over the adjacent slopes, heights, and valleys, till the houses now lie, pile on pile, tier on tier, and succeed each other row after row, street after street, far into the surrounding country; and the eruption is still in active play, and everywhere the work of building and city extension proceeds at a rapid pace. The invasion of construction has bridged the harbour, and laid out streets innumerable on the North Shore: masonry crowns every island in the spacious basin – every projecting buttress of rock maintains a pedestal of wall and gable and roof. Verandahs overrun the heights, and chimney stacks peep out from the hollows. The sand drives are covered with cottages, the very marshes have a crop of dwellings, that are constantly springing up, like mushrooms ... Everywhere the sound of workmen's tools is heard, all through the busy day. Brickyards are worked to their utmost capacity; iron foundries are taxed to their greatest powers, sawmills and joinery establishments are in full activity, and at present the building trades are in constant and vigorous employment.

However, Inglis, unlike some of his contemporaries, was not completely blinded by this glorious display. He complained that land had become so valuable that open drains were boxed with timber and covered by little wooden cottages, 'nurtured in corruption and redolent of putridity and decay'. As the middle class raced away into the burbs, the position of the underclasses in the city centre grew worse, for even as the city's population was falling, its density was increasing. The abyss between the winners and the losers yawned wide, dark and deep. When Samuel Mossman was spruiking the advantages of colonial life to his London readers in 1862 he tempted them with descriptions of the lunchtime fare

The Virgin's Lie

available to Sydney's working men; 'soup and fish, roast and boiled, as much as any man can eat'; turtle from Moreton Bay; beef and mutton at twopence per pound; wild turkey from the plains; ducks and pigeons, rolling in fat; sweet and juicy vegetables; and smiling black-coated potatoes from Tasmania, the finest spuds in the world. Given the toxic swill which the workers of the old country had to force down – wilted, rotten vegetables and rancid meat (such as a pig, weighing ninety kilos, which was found dead and decayed, then cut up and exposed for sale by one butcher at Heywood) – it's not surprising Mossman should trumpet the tucker of the harbour city. But sadly, had he ventured from the cafes and dining rooms of George Street down into the warrens of the poor, he would have found a world remarkably similar to the worst rookeries and wynds of London or Glasgow.

The slums which the *Herald* had detailed during the early part of the 1850s had not been swept away by the subsequent decades' tsunami of affluence. In fact, they sank further into hopelessness, victims of official neglect and their own population boom. In *Nineteenth Century Sydney*, Max Kelly points out that even as settlement spread further from the city centre, the centre itself became more densely populated. Surry Hills, which had been a thinly populated sand-blown wasteland during Mundy's tenure, had a population of 23 000 by 1871, and 42 000 by '91. In the former valley of the Tank Stream, steeply rising demand for commercial property led to a rapid increase in land prices and forced a massive shift from residential to business use. And yet the numbers of people living within the city continued to grow, drawn by the wealth which was making their lives a misery. As the hovels of the working poor around Darling Harbour were razed to make space for new warehouses, shipping offices and bond stores, the poor just moved themselves into the nearest hovels which weren't being demolished.

Kelly describes it as a truism of the nineteenth century that as populations rose, the quality of inner-city residential life took a dive. The only qualification he makes is that Sydney had never housed its working population properly. The fetid slums of the city's golden age were not a case of once-adequate housing falling to pieces under pressure, because unfortunately most of the housing built from the 1850s through to the 1870s was crap even when it was new. Labour and materials were expensive; the economy was running at white heat; and most developers were building as quickly and cheaply as possible, for profit rather than posterity. The *Herald*'s 1851 exposé was just one of a series of investigations into the awful state of Sydney's housing, none of which, in the end, counted for squat.

In the late 1850s William Jevons, a gifted Renaissance type, made his own single-handed survey of the city's suburbs and housing. An economist, logician, meteorologist, photographer and writer, Jevons would take his notebook and camera on long solitary walks through the parts of Sydney most respectable folk studiously avoided. He found the same pinched, dirty faces in the same stinking back streets extensively chronicled by the *Herald* seven years earlier. The city authorities had done little or nothing to remove the canker from their midst. The lower streets of the Rocks were still a festering slum of 'horrible intensity'. Sewers and gutters were unknown and 'the drainage of each house or hovel simply trickles down the hill, soon reaching, as the case may be, the front and back of the next lower house'. More often than not it fetched up against the walls of the lower house, soaking through to the foundations and floors below. Some dug trenches around their homes to divert the sludge, effectively surrounding themselves with filth which brewed up in the sun's warmth every morning and which was kept 'in a constant state of moistness by new accretions of liquid filth'.

In Redfern he found that curious arrangement, so common in Sydney, of all the classes being thrown in together; tall, spacious terraces along Pitt and Cleveland Streets surrounded with native fig trees or Norfolk pines, wretched hovels lining Botany Road, log huts everywhere in between, and an entirely new suburb rising on the black sandy hills of Sir Daniel Cooper's Waterloo Estate to the south. This, he said, was something you could only see in the New World, the sudden appearance of a whole town, the boards of its houses still raw with sap and sharp splinters. Nowhere but Australia, however, could you find such a collection of 'hastily erected frail small habitations, devoid of even a pretence to ornament and in many or most cases belonging to, and built by those who inhabit them'. It looked more like a military camp than a permanent town or village. Most of the homes consisted of little more than two rooms and were constructed of rough timber, canvas, corrugated iron, rubble, packing crates and, in some cases, glass bottles. The one thing they had going for them was space. As long as there was enough distance between their flimsy walls to permit a free flow of air, disease and contagion were less likely to strike. Unfortunately, as the building of Sydney accelerated through the next thirty years, open space was quickly bought up and buried under ever-increasing tonnages of bricks and mortar.

A year after Jevons's freelance investigations, a Royal Commission parroted his findings. A year after that the Legislative Assembly despatched a committee to walk the same streets and come to the same conclusions. As Max Kelly wrote, there was no doubt that here were slums of the most abject kind. A lack of sanitary inspection and an absence of health laws, population pressure, land-sweating by landlords, rising rent levels and a falling supply of inner-city accommodation, all combined to deepen the slum problem. The committee's chairman, Henry Parkes, found working-class accommodation 'deplorably bad', with many of the older tenements being 'unfit for the occupation of human beings'. A section of Ultimo Road was described as consisting of 'human slaughter houses'.

Fast forward another decade and a half and the Health Board's report into Sydney's sewerage and water supply recounts the same depressing litany of overcrowded, tumble-down shanties tucked away within the folds of the emerald city. Decades of frenzied growth, the first burst of urban sprawl, had compacted life at the centre to a point where one house had a yard, a metre square, surrounded on three sides by seven-metre high walls. At the corner of Market and Clarence, the committee inspected a row of weatherboard humpies, variously used as a butchery, workshops and residential premises. If you wanted to know how long colonial timber could last until it decayed into powder, they quipped, these places would satisfy your curiosity. They contained just enough solid timber to keep them standing, but not a splinter more. One house in particular grabbed their attention, representing as it did 'the *ne plus ultra* stage of dilapidation'. It contained two small ground-floor rooms with a rickety ladder climbing into the darkness of a sleeping nook under the roof. Originally a weatherboard cottage, the inspectors couldn't say what it was now, so much rubbish having been tacked on during patchwork repairs. Boards eaten out by white ants had been papered over or covered by scraps of tin. Upstairs, countless layers of rotting wallpaper curled

The Virgin's Lie

down from the roof, a ruined tapestry clogged with cobwebs and dust. One sorry mattress lay on the floor, the only furniture in the house, which was otherwise crammed with piles of old clothes. Needless to say there was no drainage from any of these hovels. The city's poor were still swimming in filth. In Glebe, where the gutters were choked by dead dogs, cats and chickens, bones, offal and decaying vegetable matter, the committee found a three-room house with broken floorboards and scarcely a single pane of glass in any of the windows. The toilet had collapsed into its own cesspit. It had no door, not even an old sack, and anyone wishing to use it had to crouch over the spot where the seat used to be, holding onto the doorposts which remained, in full view of the neighbourhood.

The committee members, drawn from the ranks of Sydney's comfortable, self-satisfied burghers, found themselves mired in ever more horrifying sinks of poverty. Led by Professor John Smith, an expert chemist of 'cultivated intellect, extraordinary patience and industry', they plunged into a secret world, guided by missionaries and guarded by police. It was far removed from the liberal certainties of their lives. These were celebrated by the *Herald* on Australia Day 1876 when it preached about the rareness of poverty in a city, where 'the many have plenty as well as the few' and where 'we are not entirely free sometimes from the danger of having too much'. This land-of-plenty thesis ignored the pale riders of disease which stalked the city's poorest quarters. The 1870s witnessed an alarming rise in mortality rates, particularly amongst Sydney's children who were, according to the government statistician, 'literally decimated' by diarrhoea and atrophy, pneumonia and bronchitis, diphtheria, convulsions and measles.

The *Herald*'s bumptious optimism must have rung hollow to the committee as they picked their way through hundreds of treacherous alleys and lanes and 'rows of mean looking, ill-ventilated, poorly drained tenement buildings, all seemingly crammed to bursting with the city's poor'. Reading their reports, I was struck by how often their descriptions simply shuddered to a stop as the degradation overwhelmed their ability to describe it. Sometimes I could almost see them standing there, gape-mouthed in confusion, completely baffled by the awful scenes in front of them. One such occasion was at a house in Abercrombie Lane, an evil, constricted, otherworld passageway which the *Herald* had visited twenty-five years earlier and found as alien as the forbidden city of Peking. The *Herald* had been worried then by the prospect of some wild revolutionary fervour seizing the minds of the masses huddled within. They had been so completely cut off from 'the confident gospels of prosperity and order', so thoroughly debased by their miserable circumstances, that even this conservative broadsheet admitted they owed no loyalty to a system which thrived on their misery. Apprehensively entering the home of a cab driver named Ryan, they discovered him with his wife and three children in a room below the stairs. There were no windows to let through a breeze and consequently the atmosphere was dominated by the piles of human excrement which lay on the floor. Ryan and his wife were both drunk, the latter sitting on a wooden box with a child in her arms, mother and child completely naked. As the inspectors entered the room she simply drew up an old skirt from amongst the dung piles and held it against herself. The rest of the furniture consisted of a broken chair and a table on which a few cups and glasses lay beside a rum bottle. The couple were too drunk to answer any questions so Smith's men pressed on. Upstairs they found heaps of old rags and what might have been a mattress

The Virgin's Lie

but was now just a 'bundle of rotten flock and rags' with two women sleeping on it. An expedition into the kitchen was cut short by hundreds of fleas which suddenly swarmed over them. Their strait-laced Victorian minds reeled at such deviance. Wedded to the mythology of the times which emphasised the benefits of hard work, abstinence and submission to the strictures of a rigid hierarchy, they could only wonder, like many before them, at the evils which would germinate in such an environment. In the end, however, it was not a revolutionary malady but a physical one which came roaring out of these crowded, filthy slums. After decades of neglect and wanton folly in the high offices of the city, nature took its course. On 19 January 1900, the plague arrived in Sydney.

That Friday dawned bright and hard over a city which had sprawled out across two hundred and fifty square kilometres and which was climbing towards a population of half a million people. The sandstone basin which had lain empty and undisturbed for hundreds of millions of years was rapidly filling up. As the sun swept gently over Port Jackson's heavily wooded northern shores, a thin wiry man made his way from Ferry Lane in the Rocks down to the wharves and warehouses of Darling Harbour. Ferry Lane was, and still is, just a paper cut in the massive sandstone ridge overlooking Walsh Bay, and at that time 10 Ferry Lane – four rooms, an attic and a basement – was home to Arthur Payne, a thirty-three-year-old wagon driver of fair complexion and nervous temperament. Like many of the lower class he still lived within walking distance of his workplace, unable or unwilling to meet the price for a train or tram ride from the suburbs.

LEVIATHAN

Arthur had suffered no serious illnesses in the years leading up his appointment with history, so we can only guess at his reaction to being seized by dizziness, a headache and a sharp pain in his stomach as he manoeuvred a van through the city around about lunchtime on that very hot Friday. He was shaken badly enough to lie down for a spell when he reached the warehouse he'd been heading for, although he was not so badly affected that he couldn't finish his shift. Later that afternoon, still racked by gut cramps and a headache, he noticed a small lump high up on his left thigh, near his groin. He left work about an hour before sundown and, on reaching home, drank some castor oil, vomited prodigiously and took to his bed. There he lay, thirsty and feverish, with his head pounding and pain spiking through his stomach, while the lump in his groin ached continuously. The city's medical authorities, alarmed by the spread of plague in nearby Pacific ports, had been waiting for just such a case. The Board of Health's chief medical officer and president, Doctor John Ashburton Thompson, personally examined Payne three days after he had swooned at the reins of his wagon. He found a worrying mark just near the Achilles' tendon, 'a circular spot about 3 mm in diameter', coloured a dark, angry red. 'This observation,' he wrote, 'suggested that the infection had been communicated by puncture at this spot, and that the inoculation was most likely to have been effected there – at a part of the foot which was well covered by the boot the patient wore – by an insect, namely, by a flea.'

For Thompson, a world authority on leprosy who had fought an outbreak of dengue fever in Queensland and typhoid in Leichhardt, this was the moment of detonation. Sydney's slums, as Professor Smith's committee had discovered, were swarming with fleas, many of them resident upon the bodies of millions of giant,

The Virgin's Lie

happy, well-nourished rats. The collapse of the inner city's wharf districts' sanitation systems had provided an almost perfect environment for the mass production of these rodents. In describing their favoured hangouts Dr Thompson also described the conditions more than 100 000 people like Arthur Payne lived in. Rats prosper and breed in the dark and intricate recesses of ill-constructed or decaying buildings, he wrote. They burrow and play in warm piles of household refuse; in basements, cellars and storerooms where rotten flooring sits just above the natural soil; in stables and in dung heaps. They can always be seen at night in lanes and alleys, however well-paved, hunting for food in discarded refuse. They sneak inside the home through holes and gaps. Or they just march in through open doors and windows. They are attracted by heaps of lumber and organic refuse which, rumbled Thompson, are too often allowed by local authorities to grow like topsy in backyards and vacant lots. They always live amongst legions of fleas and bugs 'for dirt, decay, darkness and filth favour them at least as much as they favour the presence of rats ...'. And they threatened the occupants of every dwelling nearby, whether in good order or not. For while the plague took some of its victims from the sort of premises Thompson described, it fell on even more homes which were kept in a good and fair state but which were doomed by unsanitary methods of connection to the sewers, or even by simple proximity to them.

Despite Thompson's own confidence, the theory that fleas transmitted the plague bacillus was not widely adhered to in 1900. In fact in some circles it was considered kind of out there with the flat-earthers and moon-of-cheese crowd. Rats were acknowledged carriers of the plague, but the juggernaut of Victorian science hadn't quite made up its mind whether the illness travelled by air, water or simple touch. Thompson, however, was as sure of the flea's role as he could be, and he thought that the city's best long-term defence lay not in the wholesale slaughter of rats – although this was important – but in attacking the man-made conditions which allowed them to flourish.

In spite of Thompson's best efforts, the attack was a little slow in starting. The city's medical practitioners were asked to imme-diately report any cases of plague or anything even resembling plague. During an inspection of the wharves on St Valentine's Day, a customs officer reported finding an unusually large number of dead rats around Huddart, Parker and Co's facility on the eastern side of Darling Harbour. Seven rats were seized there and found to be infected. The following day Dr WG Armstrong, one of Thompson's colleagues, inspected the wharves and told the owners to start cleaning them up and destroying the vermin. Nearly a month later, when Thompson himself toured the area, he found that little or nothing had been done. The wharf owners were told to get their shit together or they'd be quarantined. In fact the medical men wanted to evacuate the whole area, but it was the focal point of colonial trade and closing it would have been like shutting down all of Sydney's docks and airports for a couple of months today.

While the city's commercial, political and medical interests con-tended over their response to Payne's infection, the plague spread; nine cases in the first three weeks, then twenty-two in the next fortnight. By the sixth week the epidemic was established and would rage until August. Two thirds of the 303 victims went down in those last two months. The disease struck quickly, the infected falling from good health to severe illness within an hour. Chills, shivering and acute headaches announced the arrival, sometimes

The Virgin's Lie

in company with intense pain in the back and lower abdomen, sometimes followed by them. Victims first vomited up all the contents of their stomachs, then continued heaving a green or blue bile. Their faces flushed, their eyes suffused, they often began to feel an aching or pricking in the lymph glands. Constipation set in, if they were lucky. If diarrhoea ensued it was almost always a very bad sign. Sometimes the most moderate onset was rapidly fatal. One man simply lost his appetite for a day or so. He went to the office where he worked as a clerk, left for home at midday with a fit of colic and had turned up his toes by ten that night. Another man rose at six, had breakfast, washed, dressed, sat by his kitchen fire and was found dead at 9.30 a.m.

If they made it into the second day, the patient's symptoms became manifest and gradually more intense. More often than not, unlike Payne, they couldn't raise themselves from their beds. Their eyes closed over, their complexions grew pallid or livid or, in a few severe cases, sallow or yellowish, while they emitted a peculiar smell. A thick white coating covered the tongue. The skin grew hot and dry or, in the worst cases, cold and damp. Their temperature rocketed, pulse quickened, speech blurred, some passed into coma while 'in others, more commonly, delirium commenced' with a furious excitement and they had to be restrained as they struggled to flee their beds, tortured by delusions and sleeplessness. By this stage, for many, their beds consisted of a cot on the hot, bleak shores of North Head, where the government had established a quarantine station. There victims and their contacts were strictly isolated from each other. Contacts bathed and changed their clothes and were detained for five days. Convalescents were discharged when they'd had a normal temperature for ten days, provided they had no unhealed sores.

LEVIATHAN

The plague reached its maximum, intimate intensity for those it touched during the third day. Complete prostration and muttering delirium ensued; frequently stupor or coma intervened, and if bad diarrhoea set in at this point it meant the deep-six for you. The tongue turned brown and dry. The exhausted heart beat with a weaker, more rapid pulse. For many it simply stopped beating and never restarted. In those cases, as Thompson explained in a passage of sombre beauty, the bodies of patients at North Head were consigned to a specially engaged undertaker. The joints of the coffin were rendered watertight. The bodies were wrapped in a sheet soaked with disinfectant. The lid was screwed down, the coffin itself was enveloped in a coarse, wet, disinfected cloth and delivered to the quarantine depot. 'It was ... there buried without further precaution in sandy soil, on a steep slope falling to cliffs above the Pacific, and at a part of the grounds far removed from common use.'

A hundred and three succumbed to this first attack of the plague. That the toll wasn't greater is a tribute to the work of John Ashburton Thompson and his staff. They marshalled what forces they could and swept through the plague zone, scouring and cleansing it of a century's accumulated filth. On 1 March a poster was released by the Department of Public Health, in both English and Chinese, which warned: 'Plague is present in Sydney. It has been introduced by diseased rats, and there is great danger of it spreading still further.' It warned everyone to be on the lookout for rats, because as soon as they started to die off in one place, or realised they were being trapped and killed there, they quickly moved on. It warned householders to take care that their doors were not broken, to close them at night and to make sure that rats couldn't wriggle past sewer traps into the home. Readers were told to

The Virgin's Lie

gather all scraps of food, bones and vegetable matter and either burn them or secure them in a strong box, to leave no water where rats could get at it and to kill any rats that entered their premises. 'Dead rats found about premises should not be touched until they have first been scalded with boiling water where they lie,' the poster cautioned. 'They should not be taken up in the hands but with tongs; they should be burnt.' Panic ensued, of course, with the health department besieged by thousands of frightened people demanding a shot of the city's scarce antiplague serum. They invaded the department, 'packing the staircases beyond the possibility of movement and at imminent risk of a disastrous accident'. The building itself, complained Thompson, was unapproachable because of the large crowd which gathered outside and 'desperately resisted displacement'.

By 23 March the government had finally been convinced that whole blocks of the city had to be closed and given over to work gangs who would clean the streets, lanes, yards and houses. Thousands of men – sanitation inspectors, rat killers, cleaning staff – were sent into the plague-struck areas. Hordes of people were evacuated as the teams burned off piles of lumber and dragged away tonnes of garbage, ashes, dung and stable bedding. Well-kept houses were limewashed from cellar to attic. Woodwork was scrubbed with carbolic water. Carpets were torn up, floorboards removed and replaced with 'good floors, properly closed jointed and caulked . . .'. Stone, brick and earth floors were thoroughly scoured. Drains, gullies, sinks and toilets were flushed with hot water, then flushed with carbolic water, then dressed with chloride of lime. The ramshackle, makeshift buildings and sheds which housed so many of Sydney's workers were simply pulled down and removed. Nearly 4000 houses were thus inspected and cleansed, to the great annoyance of the displaced occupants. The local member of parliament, Billy Hughes, faced the wrath of his suddenly unemployed, homeless constituents when he visited a quarantined area. A crowd gathered at the barricades and screeched and howled at him, one man threatening to tear his limbs off and throw the dismembered carcass into a plague ship. Hughes, who later disparaged the cleaners as a pack of drunken desperadoes 'hired by a tyrannical Government to carry out the bowelless edicts of the Health Department', wrote that one woman tearfully informed him they had whitewashed her piano.

The plague and its side effects fell heavily on these people. Their rage at being tipped out of their hovels, compounded by the loss of waterfront work, is understandable, even if a little shortsighted. Although the plague spread beyond the slums, killing a handful of people in Manly for instance, its blow landed hardest in that wedge of the city which had been doomed from the moment Arthur Phillip consigned the convicts to its barren slopes. The demolitions which saved the greater part of Sydney amplified the process of squeezing the poor into smaller, denser and dirtier ghettos. When the plague flared up again the following year, it killed another thirty-nine people, largely from the same area. In 1907, after minor outbreaks in every year since the first, Thompson's last report stressed once again that the only way of controlling the plague was to keep man and rat separate and the best way of doing that was not by killing the rats but by 'improving the construction of buildings'. And for the first time in well over 100 years the authorities seemed to be listening.

As is so often the case with transplanted *arriviste* societies, the opinions of foreign worthies were important. London, Paris and

The Virgin's Lie

to a lesser extent New York were all emerging from the dark chrysalis of the nineteenth century as strikingly transfigured urban showpieces. Paris had spent fantastic sums on reconstruction in the decades since the turmoil of 1848. Following municipal reforms London was increasingly coming to look like the capital of the world's preeminent power rather than some Hogarthian waking nightmare. And even in the home town of hyperautonomy and extortionate greed, New York City's Art Commission had an absolute right of veto over any planned public development. In contrast Sydney was home to a number of widely travelled and well-informed public figures who were only too aware that her creaking frame simply could not support her destiny as the second city of the British Empire.

Private interests had so effectively usurped control of the city that the twentieth century dawned on a bustling port which seemed to be an experiment in the civic utility of true anarchy. Part of the blame for the plague lay in the hopelessly decayed infrastructure of the waterfront, itself the result of 100 years of unplanned development by competing self-interested private businesses. Also at fault was an uncontrolled building industry which rested on a rock-solid foundation of riotous land speculation. All was not darkness however. As the plague boats beat their melancholy passage up the harbour to the quarantine station, the same reformist energies which lit up Paris and London were sparking to life in Sydney. The Sydney Harbour Trust was created in February of 1901 to administer the port and launch a massive public rebuilding program. Municipal councils became active in slum clearance and waste management while conducting a wider debate about forming one overarching body to run the whole city. The urgency of these issues found expression in a Royal Commission established in 1908 to report on the city's transport system and built environment.

Robert Gibbons neatly summarises the contemporary deficiencies of the metropolis in *Twentieth Century Sydney*. The city and the North Shore were still cut off from each other. The harbour was badly congested and polluted. The suburban railway system stopped at Redfern until 1906, and then Central, leaving the city's streets congested by tram traffic. Train lines didn't even run through most of the eastern and western suburbs. Atmospheric pollution was uncontrollable. The streets were ugly, narrow, dusty and followed no logical pattern. Slum clearance mostly just moved the problem elsewhere and new suburbs were as unplanned as the old ones. It was widely recognised that all of these problems were due to weak regulations and a lack of cohesion amongst under-resourced public bodies. There was, says Gibbons, consensus about what needed fixing. The disagreement was in the details.

The 1908 Royal Commission was tasked with providing a grand plan under which these sorts of problems could be tackled. Aesthetic considerations were also to play an important role in its deliberations. Thomas Hughes, the city's lord mayor, was named president of an eleven-man panel which included aldermen, engineers, a former inspector-general of police, reps from the Institute of Architects, the Master Builders Association and the real-estate lobby. According to Gibbons they were nominally representative, reasonably expert, well travelled and well informed. They conducted the country's first true planning enquiry, producing a report of exceptional quality which recommended major changes to the road system, the construction of a bridge linking the city with the North Shore and an underground electric railway loop in the CBD, linked to expanded suburban services. The contrast with the reports of the previous generation could not be starker. Where the observers of the city's slums in the late nineteenth century could do little but reel at the problems they encountered, Tom Hughes' men stuck squarely to the task of grappling with them. Their report didn't unleash an avalanche of public funds to sweep away the city's ills. Years would pass before the first train rumbled under George Street or across the Harbour Bridge. But many of their recommendations did eventually move from the realm of wishes into the world of concrete and steel, raising a modern metropolis in the process.

The grand scale and refinement of this future city could already be discerned in Walter Liberty Vernon's neoclassical Art Gallery and State Library, which both sent their massive Greek columns skywards in the decade after Federation. Vernon was also responsible for Central Station, which displaced thousands of corpses from their not-so-final resting place in the Sandhills Cemetery, and which Tom Hughes' commissioners envisaged as the western anchor of a monumental avenue running from Circular Quay up a widened Macquarie Street and into a majestic amphitheatre of buildings at Belmore Park. Before the Bridge and the Opera House were conjured up as the symbolic talismans of Sydney, the city suffered a want of epic, man-made iconography and the commissioners were attending to its beauty as well as its utility. (In those days the two were not exclusive.) In their final report they wrote that while public works designed to alleviate the city's traffic problems should take precedence, 'the importance of Sydney as the chief metropolitan city of Australia demands that improvements designed to add to its beauty and attractiveness shall have the fullest consideration'.

They quoted DH Burnham, a respected American architect, who enthused about the 'delightfulness of a city' as an 'element of the first importance to its prosperity'. The Harbour Trust's mammoth waterfront redevelopment between 1907 and 1922 was very much a project in this mould. In Graham Jahn's *Sydney Architecture*, Trevor Howells places the Woolloomooloo Deep Sea Wharf and the Walsh Bay Finger Wharves at the extremes of marine building technology and on the edge of a design revolution which saw the state's obsession with neoclassical forms eroded by the quaintly named Arts and Crafts movement. A reaction to 'the aesthetic, social and political crises' of the Industrial Revolution, the movement 'railed against the architectural sterility or outright stupidity of thoughtless historicism . . . where a railway hotel such as George Gilbert Scott's St Pancras Hotel impersonated a Gothic cathedral, or a hallway heater masqueraded as a mediaeval suit of armour'. The city's new wharves reflected this turn to utilitarian simplicity, as did the woolstores which grew like topsy nearby. The largest structures in Sydney at that time, their 'ironbark post and beam internal structures wrapped in muscular load-bearing and unpainted face brickwork expressed the nobility, simplicity and genius of functional architecture'. Out in the 'burbs these changes found expression in the Federation cottages and later the Californian bungalows which spread over the former pastoral estates of the colonial elite.

Alexander Stewart Jolly's Belvedere in Cremorne drew direct inspiration from the work of prominent Los Angeles architects Greene and Greene, in whose work 'timber was used with an almost Japanese expressiveness, together with "earthy" materials such as rough clinker bricks and smooth river stones'. Low, spreading roofs with deep, overhanging eaves and the use of dark varnished or oil-stained internal joinery inside and out embodied the Arts and Crafts idea of honest and truthful expression of materials ... Such flash trimmings were largely conceits of the upper and middle classes of course. The great unwashed either crowded into the contracting slums or, increasingly, were dispersed to the city's dusty fringes where they had a surfeit of fresh air but no shops, schools, churches, pubs, jobs or, frequently, running water. Their homes' use of earthy materials had less to do with Japanese expressiveness than it did with the usual suspects of material shortages and profiteering. Their dispersal, which accelerated in the 1920s, was partly the result of a strange coincidence of interest between Sydney's ever-rapacious land developers and the workers' own representatives. Testifying before the 1908 Royal Commission, Catherine Dwyer, a delegate from Trades Hall, took pains to rebut suggestions that the working classes could be housed in blocks of flats, saying that 'the flat system' destroyed family life and was 'not conducive to morality'. The infant death rate in English tenements was very high, she said, a result of their dark, poorly ventilated design. The unions would prefer to see those workers who did not have to live in the city housed in the suburbs with 'one family under one roof'.

The rich, on the other hand, found themselves increasingly drawn to apartment life as the demands of maintaining large estates and mansions became prohibitive. Herbert Millingchamp Vaughan, an English travel writer who stayed a few months in Sydney just before the Great War, professed himself astonished at the conspicuous absence of 'household life' there. He found that large numbers of the well-to-do no longer lived in their own homes, having decamped like a bunch of damned continentals for pensions and hotels. The reason, wrote Vaughan, was not hard to find. 'It is the universal lack of competent domestic service, which renders housekeeping a trial, and even a torture of which the

Englishwoman ... can have no conception.' Unprotected by the certainties and comforts of the English class system, Vaughan was horrified by the high wages and 'appalling insolence' of these antipodean harpies, who were 'a real source of terror to the unhappy householder'. The better class of apartments at least had the pick of capable and well-behaved servant girls and thus the better-off found themselves abandoning thirty-room villas for three and four bedroom flats in serviced establishments like the Astor in Macquarie Street and the Macleay Regis in Potts Point, the last of the great apartments built before the Second World War.

The Astor, overlooking the Botanic Gardens, was built as a speculative venture by a former grazier turned property magnate. Described by Jahn as the 'grande dame of elegant high rise apartment living in Sydney', the Astor's apartments sprawled over huge areas of the building's thirteen floors. They were connected by dumb waiter to a restaurant in the basement. Its classical elements muted by *moderne* restraint, the Astor was a favoured haunt of early feminists like Ruby Rich and the Geach sisters who were often to be seen tooling off up Macquarie Street, in 'their Buick driven by a uniformed chauffeuse', to do battle with government ministers, journalists and the captains of industry on behalf of the city's women.

The Astor and the Regis were the glamorous bookends of Sydney's first serious fling with apartment living. The twenty-year hiatus between the two world wars was characterised by a cosmopolitan shift all through the city's heart and along its eastern sea front. While the rich gathered in sumptuous hotel-like accommodation, tens of thousands of middle-class couples also opted out of the first flickers of the Australian dream, choosing to live in flats rather than houses. There existed just under 2000 flats when

The Virgin's Lie

Vaughan arrived in the city with his notebook. In 1921 they numbered 13000, and in 1933, 36000, an explosive rate of growth. At first most of the action was up on the ridge in Kings Cross, where the early colonists' mansions were either chopped up into units or simply knocked over and replaced by high-rise apartments. With the returns from this sort of development being much more attractive than those available for detached housing, the rugged scenery and expansive estates of the coastal suburbs soon drew the attention of builders. After Manly, Bondi and the other beach-side locales had been weighed down under a new layer of Art Deco, Spanish Mission and simple modernist blocks, the inner western suburbs, starting with Ashfield, were next in line. So thorough was the colonisation of Bondi that no trees shaded any of its thousands of little homes and apartment blocks well into the 1960s when Gavin Souter wrote that every glazed tile roof between Bondi Junction and Dover Heights glistened on a bright day as though painted with an oily suntan cream.

When the census takers totted their figures from the count of 1911 they found a third of Sydney's population still squeezed into the centre of the city and its old inner ring of terraced suburbs. Twenty years on this had fallen back to a sixth of the total. The plains of the west and south-west were increasingly covered in red tile roofs which spread along the train lines and then filled in the spaces in between. In 1920 most of the settlements within thirteen miles of the city 'still had the appearance of villages'. At night lonesome lights from isolated villas twinkled on the dark plains surrounding them. By day farmers and market gardeners went about the business of feeding the half million souls who lived between their allotments and the sea. But as the arches of the Harbour Bridge drew closer together those lonely properties were becoming 'less and less isolated'; the gardeners were 'pushed towards the urban fringe and the once separate villages were being joined in an octopus-like suburban conurbation'.

Naturally, in linking the city's sundered halves, the Bridge played its own role in the early growth spurt, although not exactly as expected. It destroyed the North Shore community of Milsons Point and impoverished the small businesses of North Sydney who had hoped to profit from it. It was a big plus, however, for those wealthy North Shore types who could meet the stratospheric price of private motor transport, and not surprisingly it lined the pockets of more than a few developers. The opening on 19 March 1932 was attended by both irony and farce; the former provided by Premier Jack Lang's decision to freeze the Royals and their representative out of the ceremony in favour of his own good self, the latter by a muddle-headed fascist called Francis de Groot who took deep offence at Lang's impertinence. At least three quarters of a million people jammed into the CBD for the ceremony, leaving the rest of Sydney bare of life. A journalist who chartered a flight for the spectacle saw just a single human being outside the city centre, a lone golfer revelling in the chance to get a round in on a bright hot Sunday. He was not the only fanatic at large that day. A pack of right-wing yahoos calling themselves the New Guard had decided to disrupt the ribbon-cutting in the name of King and Country after Premier Lang so ungraciously nudged the King out of the deal. De Groot, an Irish antique dealer living in Rushcutters Bay and a former captain of the Hussars, had donned his old uniform and ridden his horse onto the Bridge behind an official mounted escort. He nearly didn't make it, his horse having slipped and fallen behind. A police officer noticed his distress, however, and held up traffic while de Groot caught up with the troopers.

The Virgin's Lie

Nobody seemed to notice his presence near the official dais and the Governor even returned his salute as he passed by.

Lang had just finished speaking and the Minister for Works had just started when de Groot spurred his horse forward, slashed at the ribbon twice with a sword and yelled, 'On behalf of the decent and loyal citizens of New South Wales, I declare this bridge open!' The Premier, who had been under close guard since word of a bizarre plot to throw him off the Bridge had been received from the Agent-General in London, jerked around momentarily before settling back to watch a couple of burly coppers pull the nutter from his horse and give him something to go on with. So much for the farce. The irony was that the New Guard should have been driven to its prank by the 'communist lover' Lang at all. For it was Lang's supporters, the working class of the hitherto divided points of Sydney's opposite shores, who suffered most from the Bridge's construction while the wealthy and the bourgeoisie who formed the Guard's cheer squad benefited by it.

The Bridge project had been encouraged by North Sydney Council and its small business backers, whose assets were protected from resumption and seizure. But there was no protection for the 500 homes demolished to make way for the Bradfield Highway. Letters of protest were pointless in the face of forced evictions. The government did not look favourably on any suggestion that the dispossessed should be compensated, and in fact only five people were. Unsurprisingly with the local market destroyed, local businesses soon fell into crisis as well. Commuters could now bypass North Sydney and other commercial centres began to develop further up the line, leaving the area around the Bridge to stagnate until the latter half of the twentieth century.

One sector of the economy which did take off with the laying of additional railway tracks was land speculation. When thousands of British migrants arrived after the Great War needing to be housed and put to work, frenzied speculation and boom psychology took hold in the city's real-estate offices. As Peter Spearritt points out, land subdivision could be fantastically lucrative when developers were not required to provide fully made roads and had no responsibility for the provision of any services. All they really had to do was write the ad copy and bank the cheques. One shameless self-promoter who banked a lot of cheques before the Depression closed him down was Sir Arthur Rickard, 'the outstanding land developer of his era' and the foundation president of the Millions Club, a high-tone cabal of business barons and political figures who gathered over port and cigars to thump the tub about immigration, socialism and the economy. It later evolved into the Sydney Club. A natural salesman, Rickard was one of the first developers to latch onto the awesome possibilities of modern advertising, packaging raw, untouched bushland as 'fine residential and weekend property'. Guileless investors were ferried out to swampy river frontages in the city's remote fringes and plied with free cups of tea and a lot of high pressure guff about living rent free in healthy surrounds. Others who wished to escape the urban life altogether were pitched 'farmlets' in areas like Bankstown where they could raise pigs which were guaranteed to return 'enormous prices'. There was no need to worry about taking your pigs to market, according to Rickard. The market would come to you, with buyers constantly scouring the countryside desperate for porkers to purchase.

Sometimes the same area could be pitched to completely different marks, as in Rickard's *Realty Review* of February 1924, an attractively packaged magazine with a buxom, bare-legged flapper on the cover, smiling seductively at potential buyers from her river punt. 'Arthur Rickard and Fair Dealing are Synonymous,' boasted the mag, 'to think of one suggests the other'. In February of 1924 Fair Dealing Arthur was trying to flog the same patch of turf in Bankstown to both young home buyers looking for 'a peerless situation' on the Georges River, and any would-be pig farmers seeking a couple of acres of well-drained farm land for their noxious pursuits. Rickard was not the most unscrupulous of the land boomers, merely the most successful. Others such as Greater Sydney Estates took his advertising techniques into the twilight zone. For instance they pushed their Narrabeen holdings on the basis of proximity to the city. Only ten miles away, screamed the adverts. Which was true, if you could fly. If you had to drive it was sixteen miles. And if you didn't have a car, like most people at that time, the trip to Narrabeen was an epic journey indeed.

The Depression did for Rickard and a lot of his buddies in the Millions Club. It also squeezed off the growth of Sydney until after the Second World War. The actual shape of the city had not changed much, even with the influx of new settlers after 1918. Use of the urbanised core had greatly intensified though and the fingers of growth which had splayed out along the train lines had thickened, especially around the 'knuckles' of the train stations. There, writes Spearritt, were all the amenities: draper, mercer, estate agent, hairdresser, banks, tea rooms, butcher, laundry, garage (with petrol pump on the pavement), newsagent, fruiterer, bootmaker, chemist, grocer, florist, fish and chip shop, dentist, doctor, school and pub. Even the fastest growing suburb of the period, however, could still turn a primitive face to the world. In 1927 Lane Cove, which more than doubled its population in the 1920s, was mostly still rocky and precipitous bushland when journalist

Charles Whitham wrote, 'There are spots around Tambourine Bay where one can stand at night, and see no friendly house or street lamps. If it were not for the reflection in the sky, there is nothing to indicate proximity to a great city.'

It wasn't until 1938 that the building industry recovered and then only briefly, before the Second World War shut everything down again. Military installations and hospitals for the wounded were the focus of building activity in the early 1940s and when hundreds of thousands of servicemen returned from the conflict there was literally nowhere to house them or their families. The Depression and the war had left Sydney short of maybe 90 000 houses. The situation was so serious that the RSL, never a hotbed of radical activity, threw its support behind hundreds of members who illegally occupied large, deserted buildings in Kings Cross and Bondi Beach, demanding the right to stay.

The decade after the war saw countless numbers of these people transfer their dreams of home life from the older established inner city suburbs to the vast plains on the city's edge, where the Housing Commission threw up thousands of simple dwellings along river flats and over the last untrammelled estates of the nine-teenth-century land barons. Golf courses were given over to rough, uncurbed streets flanked by seemingly endless tracts of identical fibro houses. The care and aesthetic refinement which had gone into the Federation cottages and Californian bungalows of the century's early decades were abandoned for the exigencies of mass production. Even so it was not enough to meet demand. Tens of thousands of young couples simply bought their own block of land somewhere out beyond the horizon and spent the next ten years raising a home on it. Just as many could not afford even that and were forced deeper into the bush, beyond even the most remote

The Virgin's Lie

planned settlements, where they carved their futures out of brute nature. Poet and novelist Gwen Kelly found herself in such a community at Mt Colah, penning a portrait of the city's frontier which remains a beautifully realised piece of early New Journalism, published many years before the genre developed in America.

Kelly lived amongst suburban settlers who were as hardy in their own way as their forebears of the nineteenth century. They turned their skills and stamina on the Australian bush with as much determination as any of Caroline Chisholm's people. Indeed they lived amongst the more comfortable descendants of those hardy travellers; long-settled rural families whose homes 'were usually wooden with wide verandahs and plenty of ground, or ivy-covered brick with slate roofs. Some had overgrown ancient gardens running along the edge of the creek, some were backed by the beauty of half-decayed orchards.' The houses of the soldier settlers were often no more than tents to begin with, run up on blocks of bush without a path, 'let alone a road, to penetrate the scrub'. Husbands and wives hacked at the gum trees and lantana during months of ground clearing, in scenes which recalled the labours of the First Fleet convicts raising their own wattle and daub huts in the primordial forests of Sydney Cove. With the ground clear the pioneers of the 1940s and 1950s would often spend a few more months pushing a track through to the nearest road, up which they would then haul expensive lengths of timber, plywood and asbestos board, much of it purchased on the black market at a ridiculous mark-up. Kelly thought the homes they built unpretentious, even humble, avoiding

the consciously contrived variation of the best housing settlement, or the wearying monotony of the worst ... They were unique, individual homes shaped from the owner's own design limited only by the restricting demands of money. Quite often the patterns were commonplace, lacking the structural magic of the creative architect, sometimes curious where the quirks of unorthodox human nature had been given full rein ...

They became mixed communities, independent and proud. Many of the new citizens were skilled tradesmen, ex-soldiers who used their gratuities as a deposit, bought their block of land, ran up a temporary shack or garage and set to work in their spare time to make a home. While the newspapers ran articles on the iniquity of the forty-hour week, and the comfortably housed from the North Shore gave hurt little radio talks on the destruction of our green belts, they rose at five to travel the twenty-odd miles to work, arriving home again well after five in the evening to spend the hours between dinner and bed labouring on their own building. Nights and weekends were alive with the constant beat of the hammer, the whirr of the saw, the odorous skid of the plane. When they ran out of money they built cupboards and laid bricks for their wealthier neighbours, or their wives took jobs in the stores of the nearest suburb. Their babies were conceived in garages or unfinished back rooms, against the grand day when the whole family would move in. Sometimes two or even three children had appeared before this happened, and new bedrooms or sleep-outs were carefully tacked on to the original design. If they were bricklayers, they built in brick, the brown-red walls rising as a mark of their conscious superiority as tradesmen and by inference, as citizens.

Here Kelly catches a glimpse of a none too subtle ideological

The Virgin's Lie

agenda behind government support for this housing boom. As an Anglican canon had said in the Depression, 'A man does not fight for his boarding house, but he will fight for his home.' Even the *Sydney Morning Herald* had understood this 100 years earlier when it questioned why the city's slum-dwelling underclasses should owe any allegiance to a society which allowed them to wallow in such squalor and misery. The massive increase in home ownership after the Second World War was, in part, explicitly encouraged by governments to guarantee the loyalty of their working masses. Unlike earlier growth, however, it was not tied as tightly to the railway lines. Cheap mass-produced cars liberated Sydney's workers and sent them hurtling across the basin like a blast wave which swept all before it.

Mass transport, an efficient power grid and the telephone also liberated business and industry from the spatial demands of a horse-powered economy. As millions of settlers swarmed over the western plains and along the coast to the north and south, commerce and capital followed them for the first time, establishing a feedback loop of fantastic growth. The kinetic energy of a growing city no longer travelled solely along the railway lines which radiated out from Central Station. Everything flowed everywhere and micro-cities such as Parramatta and, later, Chatswood grew like dwarf stars within a metrogalaxy. The simple, easily sketched structure of the city had been left behind forever. It had become a leviathan, evolved from a few small cells, those lonely canvas tents which Ralph Clark thought looked so 'pretty amongst the trees' in 1788.

The explosive change did not just spread outwards. It shot skywards as well. The same commercial forces which had devoured the town's mudbrick core after the arrival of Macquarie were still at work a century and a half later. State cabinet had temporarily crimped the Manhattanisation of Sydney's skyline in 1912 when they restricted building heights to forty-five metres after civic horror at the spectacle of Culwulla Chambers soaring fifty-one metres above Castlereagh Street. Culwulla, a speculative venture which utilised the latest American high-rise technology, would remain the tallest building in Sydney until 1956, when the irresistible pressure of money blew the cap off any height restrictions. In that year American technology and style returned to Sydney in the form of the MLC Building, a long rectangular box of thin cement wafers, heat-resistant glass and aluminium panels, all hung on a steel skeleton arranged around a 'wind-resisting service core'. It was not simply the height, the design or the engineering wizardry which marked this building as a departure from the old sandstone elephants of yesteryear. Its location on the North Shore signalled the renewal of a part of the city pretty much obliterated by the Harbour Bridge. The north's neglected streets, lined with small struggling businesses, drew the attention of giant companies like Ampol and British Petroleum who were looking for headquarters sites without the hassles of heritage restrictions and competition for space which they encountered in the established CBD. Their towers climbed over the bones of the old working-class suburb, raising a sister city across the water. Lacking the original city centre's many layers of history, however, North Sydney became something of a doppelgänger; a soulless facsimile from which life quickly drained when the office workers who peopled it during the day switched off their lights and departed for the night.

The developers and insurance companies which funded this boom looked like achieving similar success in the CBD as their skyscrapers crushed great swathes of the old masonry and wrought-iron city under foot. The giants' footprints destroyed multiple blocks run through with the secretive alleys and wynds of the nineteenth century. Sometimes sweatshops and other remnant industries disappeared beneath their massive concrete footing. Sometimes much more valuable swatches of the older town's fabric were torn apart and discarded. The old Theatre Royal was buried under Harry Seidler's sixty-five storey MLC Centre, while thirty small sites and a quiet world of back lanes disappeared when he sent the stunning circular tower of Australia Square soaring fifty storeys over George and Pitt Streets. The Royal Exchange and both the Royal and Imperial Arcades were levelled and excavated. Wrecking balls crashed through the elegant Italianate facade of the Hotel Australia, atomising polished marble and sculpted plaster and silencing a few ghosts of the city's cafe society which had been drawn to the specialist booksellers and tea rooms gathered around the hotel in Rowe Street along with a collection of high-class jewellers, florists and quality restaurants.

Rowe Street, which these days is little more than a litter-strewn access lane for the MLC Centre – and, somewhat piquantly, for Arthur Rickard's old haunt the Millions Club – was formerly the infamous Brougham Place, described in the 1870s as 'the nightly resort of itinerating musicians, knife-grinders and other out-of-doors businessmen'. The opening in 1891 of the Hotel Australia, the self-appointed premier hotel of the Southern Hemisphere, changed all that. It was said that if you wanted to meet anyone in Sydney (or at least anyone who was someone) you need only sit in the Australia, perhaps to sip on your Chateau Mouton Rothschild for an hour, and all of society would eventually pass you by. At the entrance on Castlereagh Street two giant bronze figures held aloft magical electric lights in front of imposing red granite columns and stained-glass doors. Those who passed through left the dusty, foul-smelling chaos of nineteenth-century Sydney behind, gliding into the cool of the vestibule with its polished stone columns and intricately tiled floor. Wandering through to the Grand Central Court, the relieved visitors could easily imagine themselves in one of the finest establishments of London or New York. It was a magnificent chamber, washed in bright light which streamed in through an ornamental roof of wrought iron and glass. Here clicked the buttoned-up boots of Sydney's most important women on their way in gloves and hats to the Ladies' Writing and Reading Room, an oasis of privacy with 'all the necessary paraphernalia for correspondence and literary pursuits'; or perhaps to Herr Ohensschlager's excellent hairdressing saloon which boasted 'every accessory' demanded by refined modernity, 'including medicated and electric baths'. And over there, by the aquarium, in their dark woollen suits, gathered the city's most powerful men; traders, industrialists, the sons of the squattocracy, perhaps to lunch in the Australia's fine dining room, or perhaps to scheme in the deep Moroccan leather armchairs of Mr F Thrower's much admired billiards room. The Australia, wrote Arnold Haskell, was Sydney's Casino, and Sydney itself, to the leisured visitor, a bright, sunbaked Riviera resort, an English Nice or Cannes.

It was this leisured, naive and parochial outpost which was consumed by the jackhammers of the 1960s and 70s; the smaller, more intimate world of Harold Cazneaux's photographs which captured so well his achingly sad, almost haunted study of the old Royal Exchange on the corner of Pitt and Bridge Streets. Taken around 1934 the scene could have been shot in the Old World, so soft is the light into which the hansom-cab driver is leading his horse, and out of which rides the future in the form of a slightly menacing

The Virgin's Lie

motorcar. The few scattered pedestrians, although dwarfed by the Exchange's elegant Corinthian mass, still own the scene, their minute forms integral to the moment. A favourite haunt of ships' captains and shipping agents, a centre of commercial and social life, the building was much loved by the city, but this was not enough to save it from the wreckers in 1965.

This once-upon-a-time city of Harold Cazneaux was a world of 'quiet alluring poetry'; where Mark Foy's department store set up a circus on their roof at Christmas, with swings, carousels and slippery dips; where a cannon fired to mark one o'clock each afternoon, ten minutes before the single mail plane to Brisbane droned over the city; where a lunchtime crowd would gather with sandwiches in paper bags at Swains, the stationers, who daily cranked up a gramophone to play 'the best music to be heard in Sydney'. Draught horses and trams still vied with the automobile for supremacy in that vanished city. The quirky, the odd and the defiantly individual could all still stand out. The city's landscape cheerfully accommodated harmless oddities like Arthur Stace and Bea Miles, micro-celebrities whose fame came from their daily travels in eccentric freedom across the face of the metropolis. Arthur chalked the word *Eternity* a million times on the footpaths and in doorways. Bea recited Shakespeare, terrorising cab drivers and hunting for sharks off Bondi with a knife clamped between her teeth. (She normally wore it strapped to her thigh.)

Hyperdevelopment and the acceleration of life seemed to press these endearingly wonky fragments of humanity out of the city's frame of reference. The hundred mile city, as Deyan Sudjic termed it, admits of no place for the sincerely offbeat. Its grotesqueries are Herculean and Kafkaesque rather than intimate and personal. Its buildings are often little more than 'aesthetically worthless rent slabs' for stacking human capital, which is itself to be consumed or discarded at the whim of the market. In such a place it sometimes feels as though the city is eating itself. Architects and developers with little or no sympathy for the nuances of history and the needs of the human beings who must actually live inside their nightmares have reworked the wedge of land which forms the city's heart with a series of profoundly antihuman, brutal and vaguely Orwellian schemes such as the Masonic Centre (of course), the knitted concrete face of the Hilton Hotel, and the giant brooding militarised bunker of the Sydney Police Centre in Surry Hills.

All is not darkness however. A dress circle of interesting and, God help us, sensitive skyscrapers is emerging around the juncture of Macquarie and Pitt Street where megaspiv Alan Bond's elegant Chifley Tower is engaged in a conversation, as architects love to say, with the darker and more aggressive twin towers named after Governors Macquarie and Phillip, and where Renzo Piano's altogether more refined spires promise to hide their environmentally friendly charms behind long skirts of floating glass. And these skirts are, apparently, to have a bit of a chat with the sails of the Utzon's Opera House down the hill a-ways. The block which the Chifley dominates presents as a series of architectural time capsules, all laid open for the curious passerby. Four buildings share the block, each representative of a quantum leap in the sophistication of city's built environment; from the simple Georgian austerity of the 1842 Angus and Coote building, through the optimistic post-Victorian bombast of John Burcham Clamp's 1911 Wyoming, the unfortunate functional cracker box of Hambros House (which is not even striking enough to be impressively ugly), and the digital-era opulence of the Chifley. This latter structure, the city's first billion-dollar building, is a cathedral of global

The Virgin's Lie

capital. Between the intimidating millionaire's trinket shop Tiffany's on the ground floor and the fantastic luxury of restaurant Forty One way above in the clouds, are stacked thousands of knowledge workers, layer upon layer of them: lawyers, bankers, management gurus, consultants, insiders, promoters, ten-percenters, pretenders and players. Very few of them will ever make anything as concrete as the builders and tradesmen who raised the tower in which they work but, by manipulating intricate systems of symbol and meaning, they daily create, assign and distribute insane amounts of wealth amongst those corporations which can afford to bid for their services.

The only redistribution of wealth which takes place here is amongst those corporations and their ilk. Very little leaks out of the cool marble atrium and onto the streets below, and that which does, does not stray far. It is doubtful if one dollar of each billion at play within this building ever makes its way out to the far horizon, to the badlands, which thankfully dissolve into a convenient haze on most days. Out there live the figurative descendants of those slum-dwelling wretches whose revolutionary potential so worried the *Herald* 150 years ago. You can gaze benignly down on them, or at least in their general direction, from Forty One's Krug Room, where a marvellous tartare of yellow-fin tuna with beetroot oil and oscietre caviar, accompanied by a chilled glass of Krug's excellent '85 Clos Du Mesnil will leave you at peace with the world below, no matter how poor a state it is in. For to venture out there is to leave behind the genteel world of Tiffany's and Forty One and to travel amongst savages. Out there, in places like Macquarie Fields, you will find 'slums of the most abject kind'. Out there, where the poor and abandoned prey on each other for lack of more rewarding targets, you will find dozens of discrete, ugly little worlds which almost perfectly mirror Henry Parkes's description of nineteenth-century Ultimo as a region of 'human slaughter houses'. For nowadays the poor, like the Iora, have been dispersed. No longer concentrated in the inner city, they are encamped on the western and south-western fringes of the metropolis, up to half a million of them, uneducated, unemployable and with little future beyond daytime TV, junk food, bad drugs and madness.

Some years ago, researching an article for *Rolling Stone*, I spent a couple of weeks living on the streets amongst the lowest members of this urban tribe, the ones who could not even make it into Department of Housing accommodation. They spent their nights in warehouses and toolsheds, under old buses and in the smashed graffiti-scarred bodies of trains, in humpies, squats and refuges, in halfway houses, crisis centres, on the doorsteps of shops, in parks, toilets and even in graveyards, sleeping on cardboard and using heroin rather than hot milk to lull themselves to the land of nod. I stayed a few days in Penrith with a couple of teenaged break-and-enter specialists named Snake and Heather who haunted a shooting gallery above a fish and chip shop. Two stinking foam mattresses, one of them half burned, were the only items of furniture. Decorations consisted of about six or seven months' worth of heroin detritus, fast food refuse, some rags and a couple of oily organic-looking smears on the wall which I declined to investigate. When the ambience of the gallery became too much even for them, they could take short-term refuge at a nearby drug rehab centre. It was an old stone place which would now fetch a cool half million in the former slum suburbs of Glebe or Darlinghurst had its clients not set about systematically destroying it for want of anything more interesting to do.

One of the rehab coordinators told me there had been so much

The Virgin's Lie

damage done the previous year that they had stopped bothering with repairs, except for reinforced steel doors and bars. The week before I arrived the centre's windows had been broken, its screen doors slashed, fence palings kicked out, toilets demolished and walls graffitied. A bare concrete slab lay where the laundry had once stood. It had been torn down after being damaged in territorial fighting between rival groups who were sleeping in it and the garage a few metres away. It wasn't much of a garage, just an L-shaped humpy of rotting timber and rusted corrugated iron. Both ends of the L were open but in winter it was home to a dozen or more. The dirt floor was still littered with the refuse of their smackpacks: condoms, wrappers, swabs and discarded ampules of sterile water. A train line ran past less than thirty metres away. These were the disorganised poor, without sufficient intelligence or skill to manoeuvre themselves into state-sponsored housing. However, looking at places like Macquarie Fields, Claymore and Airds, the question would have to be asked whether they were that much worse off. And in the long run I would suggest maybe not.

A weird sort of spatial mythology seems to inform our thinking about slums just as it did a hundred or more years ago. Then, middle-class moralists called for slum clearance without actually specifying what would happen to those who were cleared. It was just sort of assumed that the viciousness and degradation of the poor was somehow caused by their proximity to vicious and degraded surroundings. The idea that poverty and its ills were actually a function of the market never occurred to them. There are strong echoes of this today. A few years ago the government spent a couple of million dollars correcting some of the design faults of the Macquarie Fields housing estate, which had originally been laid out on what was thought to be an attractive open plan, with lots of winding cul de sacs and esplanades, walking tracks and shared recreation spaces. In fact, seen from the air, the estate resembles a giant clenched fist, trapping its reluctant residents within a painfully tangled knot of broken fingers. The shared spaces were free-fire zones contested by the young and the hopeless. The walking tracks became getaway routes. And the whole intensely inward-looking layout, which sat at the very edge of urban development, and was physically cut off from nearby suburbs by a wide stretch of road, encouraged the inhabitants, so it was said, to think of themselves as cut off from society. Just as the poor of Durands Alley once felt that the city had 'cast them from its bosom to perish in dirt and dishonour'. Street alterations sought to address some these problems but while blocking off rear-lane access may deny housebreakers a simple entry and escape route, it does not fundamentally realign the structure of wealth and power. And it does not address the stone-hard economic reality that these people, as a class, are doomed. Unemployment on the estate is universal. The majority of residents are second or third generation welfare recipients. The Salvation Army set up a soup kitchen there after discovering malnutrition amongst the young. For some of those children it is not just a matter of being poorly educated but not being educated at all. Local police recently found a nine-year-old boy who had never once been to school because his mother had forgotten to send him.

Should there come a day when somebody with more political savvy than Pauline Hanson is able to tap into the deep well-spring of malice she exposed, perhaps the *Herald*'s revolutionary fears of the nineteenth century may well come to pass in the twenty-first. It will, I guess, come as a shock to most of us. For

The Virgin's Lie

like our upper-class forebears in Georgian London, the lives of the poor – the real poor – are still as remote from our everyday concerns as life in the Forbidden City of 200 years ago. Those lives *are* increasingly solitary, nasty, brutish and short. Sir John Fielding and old Freddy Engels were right. Their sufferings are less observed than their misdeeds, and the well-fed are a race 'wholly apart' from the hungry. The lucky occupants of the Chifley Tower have much more in common with the emerging global class of well-educated, highly paid knowledge workers than they do with any sexually abused, uneducated, drug-addicted housebreaker from their own city's outer suburbs. Some will find it ironic that the space between their lives, a yawning, rapidly growing chasm, has been cleared by the same forces – money and power – which light up such fantastic post-industrial beacons as the Chifley. But I don't.

3
Only the Strong

Titles are tinsel, power a corrupter, glory a bubble, and
excessive wealth a libel on its possessor.

PERCY BYSSHE SHELLEY, *Declaration of Rights*, 1812

The English bayonet of the early nineteenth century was a work of evil beauty; up to forty-three centimetres in length, a tapered steel spike, with blood vents for easier withdrawal from the quivering bodies of its victims. It had first proved itself in the 1740s against the Jacobite rebels of Scotland, whose awesomely savage Highland charges had previously swept aside redcoat armies like gossamer veils. At the battle of Culloden Moor in 1746, however, poor old Bonnie Prince Charlie's mad red-headed countrymen were chewed over by English artillery before being skewered like 5000 cocktail sausages on the Duke of Cumberland's well-drilled ranks of bayonets. It was a signal victory for the men with the long knives, even if it was achieved against an exhausted, starving and heavily outnumbered enemy whose attack was torn to shreds by cannon shot long before it reached the shimmering steel points of the English line. This mattered not. The Highland charge had been broken for the first time and most observers put it down to the steadfast employment by the English troops of their bayonets.

All the armies of Europe had adopted the bayonet as a standard infantry weapon by the 1800s, but no army in the world embraced the myth and utility of cold steel like the British. Under Major

Only the Strong

General James Woolfe and, somewhat later, the Duke of Wellington, the British combined the bayonet's defensive capabilities with the extremely aggressive charges of the conquered Highlanders to sweep away challenges to their imperial power in Canada, India and most of continental Europe. Wellington, who had driven off an attacking force of 60 000 men with the fixed bayonets of only 5000 on the subcontinent in 1803, was to destroy countless Napoleonic advances all over Europe. He seemingly achieved this through the simple expedient of placing in front of the French a thin red line of British infantrymen with their Brown Bess muskets and tempered steel. The bayonet, as much as the gunboat, came to symbolise British power and more: the innate mightiness of the British race. The image of a resolute red-coated line of British fighting men with bayonets fixed positively hummed in the national consciousness. So we can only guess at the effect on the incandescent temper of Captain William Bligh when His Majesty's representative in the colony of New South Wales looked out of his window just after dinner on the evening of 26 January 1808 to see about 400 bayonets glinting in the setting sun as the 102nd regiment advanced on his house in the second great mutiny of his career.

Bligh had been mulling over his second glass of wine with a small clutch of supporters when one them, William Gore, glanced out of a window at the western end of Government House to see the Governor's personal guard behaving rather oddly. Lieutenant Bell, who commanded the detachment, seemed to order them to prime and load their muskets. The small garrison then turned and advanced up the hill at speed. Gore, the colony's provost marshal – a sort of sheriff – hurried back to tell Bligh, who was still enjoying a drink with his secretary Edmund Griffin, a merchant named Robert Campbell, John Palmer the Commissary of the government stores, his deputy James Williamson, and the acting chaplain, Reverend Fulton. The Governor calmed his excited marshal, telling him to keep an eye on the soldiers. Gore left the drawing room, intending to return to his own house nearby. But at the back door of Government House he blundered into magistrate Doctor Thomas Arndell and the two men fell into animated conversation.

The power players of the town – the military and civil officers, the merchants, traders and large landowners – had been in turmoil for a number of days. Not that the town itself was aflame with riot and confusion, for the elite were but a handful of men amongst about 3000 inhabitants. But in the drawing rooms of the rich and powerful and in the officers' mess of the New South Wales Corps, hard-hearted, desperate, and occasionally drunken men contemplated violence, treason and revolt. Some of them were good, wise men, some were stupid, and some were simply possessed of rat-bastard cunning, insatiable appetites and knives in their eyes. The disorder of the previous few days was manifest in the commotion which suddenly broke out at Captain Bligh's dinner party. His guests could see a small party of armed redcoats charging up through the Governor's landscaped gardens. The artillery pieces of the New South Wales Corps, some 400 metres away, seemed to have been moved to allow them to fire on Government House. And a long line of soldiers, two or three abreast, attended by a small number of wealthy civilians and watched over by a much larger number of alarmed common people, was snaking its way down from the massive barracks parade ground high on a hill above the western reaches of town, with colours flying, bayonets fixed and the regimental band playing the grenadiers' march. Figures appeared in the doorways of the rude brick huts on the

Only the Strong

slopes of the Rocks, craning to make out the cause of the distur-
bance. The half-wild dogs which haunted the town charged about,
barking in excitement. Dust lifted from the tramping of hundreds
of pairs of marching boots. And twenty years to the day, almost
to the hour, after the founding of the settlement, the man who
claimed to be the first to set foot in Sydney Cove, the then Major
George Johnston, commander of the regiment in Sydney, drew his
sword and led his troops across the stone bridge over the Tank
Stream to topple the colonial government. If the irony struck Johnston at all, he seems to have kept it to himself. But chances are it
didn't. He was suffering the aftermath of a monstrous alcoholic
binge as he launched his coup d'etat; one arm was in a sling and
his face was all bashed up and horribly bruised from an unfortunate drunk-driving incident two nights before.

Back at Government House Bligh had called for his dress
uniform and sword and had hustled upstairs to retrieve a few
papers. His orderly was sent on a futile mission to saddle his horse
for a quick getaway. Bligh was convinced that if he could make it
to the Hawkesbury region, the settlers there, small farmers who
had done well under his administration, would flock to his side
against the combination of powerful business interests behind the
coup. That was never going to happen though. Even if he could
have made the two-storey leap onto the back of a fast nag, his
own guard under Lieutenant Bell had already surrounded the
house and the rest of the regiment was but minutes away. Bligh
was standing at the top of the stairwell with Palmer, Campbell and
the others when the lower levels of the house suddenly filled with
soldiers. Gore, Arndell and the good Reverend Fulton were the
first to encounter the mutineers. They were not, however, the first
to offer resistance. That honour fell to Bligh's daughter, Mary,

who charged down to the gates of Government House to give Lieutenant Bell a piece of her mind. She had apparently inherited her old man's sharp tongue and her screeching assault was alarming enough to bring Robert Campbell running down through the grounds. He found the Governor's daughter trying to bar the soldiers' way, but she was pushed aside and they swept on. Campbell raced back ahead of them, reaching the house a minute or so before Bell and getting in through the front door before Reverend Fulton locked it.

Palmer, who had left Bligh stuffing papers into his jacket, came down the stairs to be confronted by the strange sight of Fulton still barring the front door, even though other soldiers had barged in through the back. A couple of officers were yelling at Fulton, demanding entrance and getting a lot of backchat and attitude in reply. Fulton cried out that they could drive their bayonets into him if they chose. A few metres away to his rear, Gore was pushed aside by the bayonet of a Lieutenant Draffin (who was completely mad, his brother officers later testified). A private quickly followed up with his rifle butt. As soldiers rushed past him on the stairs, Palmer went over to Fulton and advised the Reverend to let them in. Troops were already pouring through the back door anyway and Palmer was fearful they might take the good father up on his challenge and drive a bayonet through the glass. The chaplain yielded and even more soldiers thundered in to search for the Governor.

It would be at least another hour and a half before they found him. Bligh had retreated to a servant's room upstairs, where he continued destroying some papers and hiding others. His supporters were led away under arrest and most of the hundreds of troops who had marched on Government House were sent out to search

Only the Strong

the gardens and surrounding land, just in case he had made that leap to freedom. Others scoured the house, becoming increasingly frustrated by their inability to lay hands on the old sea dog. A lieutenant did open the door of the servant's room while Bligh was hiding there, but in the excitement he hardly even glanced about, telling his men they need not search the place, the Governor wasn't there. He pulled the door closed and Bligh heard the search party rumble off down the stairs, rummaging through other parts of the house and damning his eyes. He stood a long time in that spartan room. Outside, the sunset died and darkness fell; the absolute darkness of prehistory, feebly held back by a few candles and lamps. Scouts rode out into the gloom, whilst others beat the bushes and ransacked the outhouses. Bligh knew by now there would be no escape to the Hawkesbury, no resistance from his loyal supporters, no avoiding capture and humiliation.

After standing in silence, for what seemed an eternity, the Governor heard the coarse voice of Sergeant Whittle yell out to his men to help him in another search of the upstairs rooms. Their boots pounded up as Bligh tried to stuff a couple more papers into his shirt. Then they burst in, about ten of them, furious drunken men with bayonets fixed. Someone cried out that the Governor was found and Bligh heard a cheer go up. Confused and enraged, he tried to jam his hidden papers further inside his waistcoat, causing the troopers to think he was going for a gun. One of the soldiers cried out a warning and another lunged forward with his bayonet, growling, 'Damn your eyes, if you don't take your hand out of there, I will whip this into you ...' Bligh called out to Whittle to keep his man off and at this moment Lieutenant Minchin pushed through the crowd shouting, 'Sergeant, keep the men off, the Governor is not armed; I will answer for it, the

Governor is not armed!' Minchin took Bligh by the arm and led the furious, dishevelled and now former Governor down the stairs.

Or that was Bligh's story anyway. Whittle, who was keenly interested to see the Governor's demise after Bligh had ordered his house demolished, claimed that he was found hiding under the bed with feathers stuck to his uniform. Minchin, defending the uprising at Johnston's court martial a number of years later, said a corporal told him they had found Bligh under the bed and testified that his coat was full of dust and feathers. 'He appeared to be very much agitated,' said Minchin. 'Indeed, I never saw a man so much frightened in my life, in appearance. When I went into the room, he reached his hand to me, and asked me if I would protect his life. I assured him his life was not in danger and I would pledge my own safety for his. I then told him that Colonel Johnston was in the room below, and that I would see him safely to him if he would allow me . . .'

Historians have been getting all hot and bothered over this scene for nearly 200 years. Now, as then, there doesn't seem to be any conciliation. Either he was pulled out from under that bed, covered in dust and feathers and pleading for his life, a scene which 'would make the real heroes of the British Navy blush with shame and boil with indignation' according to Johnston at his own court martial; or he was bundled up at knife point and frogmarched downstairs in high dudgeon, probably spluttering in purple, spit-flecked rage. Myself? I prefer the latter version. Whittle was a scoundrel, a forty-two year veteran of armed service who avoided a lot of uncomfortable questioning by fainting dead away like a grand dame with the vapours while under cross examination back in England. He was also flatly contradicted by the evidence of Private William Hutton who testified that he was one of the first to enter the room and he found Bligh *atop* the bed, reaching into his coat.

Only the Strong

Minchin, who would also stand condemned by any conviction of Johnston, his commander, was caught out a number of times on the witness stand, perhaps most importantly over the issue of whether a twenty-one gun salute was fired by the rebels to celebrate their uprising. Minchin, who had charge of the colony's artillery, denied ever lining the guns up on Government House and further denied any allegations of a salute being fired the following day. Bligh's counsel then trapped him by producing the entry of the colony's deputy store keeper, a Mr Gowan, in the day book for 27 January 1808: 'Government use – Eighty-four pounds gun powder. Royal salute on account of maj. Johnston taking the government of the colony.'

Minchin and Whittle, like most of the Rum Corps, were a couple of lying hounds whose first thought was always for their own interest. And the rebels' interest was naturally to paint as black a picture as possible of the man they deposed. When they could find nothing incriminating in the papers they seized at his residence, they did as villains have always done and dipped their brushes into the poison pot anyway. All of the officers maintained that when Minchin led Bligh downstairs he meekly, almost thankfully handed over power. Johnston himself said:

At length he was found and brought to the room where I was. When he was introduced I gently informed him of the step which, by the requisition of the people, I had been obliged to take. He answered, he was very sorry he had incurred public displeasure; had he been aware that such had been the effect of his conduct, he would have acted otherwise; and he resigned all authority into my hands, publicly thanking me for the handsome manner in which I had carried the wishes of the people into execution . . .

LEVIATHAN

All Johnston's supporters testified along these lines but anyone who actually knew Bligh and his incendiary temper could only have reacted by slapping their thighs and wiping tears of mirth from their eyes. Whatever the real story – and Bligh *never* accepted the rebels' authority – the brute fact was that when the sun rose over the harbour next morning, power had been transferred by bayonet rather than law, and a new government was settling into place. The strange confluence of forces which combined to destroy Bligh's administration have long since dissipated and their protagonists turned to dust in the ground. But the protean nature of power in Sydney and the fierce, uncertain currents of creation and destruction which were exposed by the coup, remain as potent in the digital city as in the mud-brick village. To understand the origin of these forces is to see the modern city anew, with a sort of x-ray vision which reveals the underlying structure not to be concrete and steel but rather lust, greed, hubris and a ceaselessly shifting but morally inert and insatiable will to power. To peer deeply into this ghost city, the one lying beneath the surface of things, is to understand that Sydney has a soul and that it is a very dark place indeed.

Where lies power in the city? With the mayor? In the office of the premier? In the boardrooms of the high towers? With the mandarins of the state? The courts? The wealthiest, most ruthless criminals? The people? At first it may seem simpler to answer in the context of a small transplanted prison colony, but even in the Sydney of canvas tents and mud-daub huts, the governor's supposedly supreme authority was illusory. Long before William Bligh was deposed at gun point, other governors, less troublesome and more reflective than he, had seen their will thwarted and their rule

Only the Strong

covertly undermined or even brazenly defied. The stomach pains of which Governor Phillip complained in his first despatch were exacerbated for years by his deputy, Major Ross. A quarrelsome, bad-tempered whiner, Ross was deeply unpopular and constantly looking to pick fights and sew discord. Judge-Advocate David Collins wrote of his 'inexpressible hatred' for the man; whilst Ralph Clark said he was, without doubt, the most disagreeable commander he had ever served under. For Phillip the personality clash was more serious, with Ross seeming to take grim delight in frustrating the Governor's rule at every opportunity. He encouraged his officers to disobey Phillip's commands, stirred up trouble between the marines and the convict guards, complained bitterly of his men sleeping under canvas and then hindered Phillip's efforts to build a barracks for them. Phillip must have danced a quiet jig when Ross returned to England in December of 1791.

Unfortunately his replacement, the friendly, easy-going Francis Grose, proved a lot more malleable but infinitely more destructive. Grose had distinguished himself in the American War of Independence, getting shot to pieces in handsome fashion on two separate occasions. Invalided home, he passed a couple of years as a recruiting officer, eventually being offered Ross's position in Sydney as the head of the proposed New South Wales Corps. The British army then was not the professional force of today and you have to grasp the differences to understand why things went so horribly wrong in 1808. When Grose was offered the chance to raise the regiment, it was as much a speculative venture as a military one. He was, in Ross Fitzgerald's phrase, the proprietor of the corps. He promised to set up the companies without expense to government, put out his shingle and waited for the right sort of chaps to buy their commissions. British officers of that era were not full-time professional warriors.

Most were paid for specific periods of service, often for specific missions. Many bought their way into a regiment with a keen eye for the plunder it might bring. A posting in Sydney, on the edge of a continent ripe for the plucking and with a guaranteed supply of virtual slave labourers, appealed to these struggling middle class types whose advancement at home was severely curtailed by their want of filthy rich ancestors. Thus they often arrived in Sydney deeply in debt and on the lookout for a piece of the action.

And action they found, due to a woeful lack of foresight in setting up the convict outpost. The problem, as SJ Butlin so succinctly put it, was that the equipment of the First Fleet did not include money. Nobody thought to fold a bit of cash in amongst the thousands of tonnes of gear crammed into those groaning wooden tubs. Or, as Phillip himself wrote, 'this country has no treasury'. He had been given authority to buy livestock and supplies en route, with bills drawn on the British Treasury, but these were gross and unwieldy implements for dealing with smaller transactions. The architects of the settlement had not considered what would happen when it evolved into something other than a prison farm with a small, strictly controlled command economy. Money wasn't needed in prison, went the reasoning, therefore it had no place in Sydney.

In reality, of course, prisons are thriving Petri dishes of economic activity, with all manner of goods and services bartered between inmates and captors. Tea, tobacco, dry socks and blowjobs all had value in convict Sydney and could be traded for something as coarse as a mug of home-brewed rotgut or as refined as a love letter. The multiskilled felon, Thomas Barrett, who minted those near perfect replica coins out of melted-down belt buckles and pewter spoons during the fleet's stopover in Rio, knew more about

Only the Strong

the human condition than the high ministers who consigned him to exile. He understood that people have needs and desires, which they will pay to have satisfied, no matter how far from home they are or how low they have fallen. Trade is inevitable. But Phillip was not equipped for it and so substitutes for a local currency had to be found.

Some small sums were dug out of the pockets of convicts and marines – forgotten pennies and shillings, the sort of low-grade travel shrapnel anyone who's been overseas would be familiar with. Butlin also argues that a few of the craftier transportees probably managed to smuggle some of their ill-gotten booty into the settlement. Traders, explorers and military expeditions also called into the harbour from time to time, leaving deposits of coinage and small banknotes. So much global small change had accumulated by 1800 that Governor King was moved to assign purely local values to the town's stockpile of guineas, gold mohurs, ducats, pagodas, rupees, Spanish dollars and Dutch guilders. Large batches of foreign *geld* tended to leak out of the colony quickly, however, spent on supplies purchased from visiting ships. Four and a half thousand Spanish dollars, sent to Sydney after Phillip complained to London of his cash shortage in November 1788, were soon dissipated. As colourful and varied as the colony's supply of early coinage was, it remained hopelessly inadequate, forcing the settlers to rely on more primitive, makeshift arrangements.

The first of these – promissory notes – were a simple, if occasionally problematic alternative. Lacking banknotes, convicts, soldiers and free settlers merely shrugged and wrote their own. These notes, which were nothing more than promises to pay for a product or service, passed from hand to hand as often as a modern banknote. They were transferable, negotiable IOUs, written by everyone from the meanest lag to the governors themselves, for debts of three pence up to hundreds of pounds. But in a society of forgers, con men and thieves of course, they often changed hands at a heavy discount. Written on any scrap of paper, often torn, smudged and glued back together, they were a highly dubious system of exchange, because anyone with a quill could literally print their own money. Some printed their notes in very fine ink on very flimsy paper, hoping never to have to make good on their promise. Many were forged over the names of the colony's leading lights. In 1799 Chapman Morris was sentenced to death for erasing a letter from James Williamson and writing in a promise to pay £23 above the signature. Butlin writes that the ready acceptance of torn notes, pasted back together, led a number of rogues to rip up notes from the same person and tack them together to create bills of greater value than those originally issued. 'Even when individuals had printed forms stamped with their initials to ensure forgery of at least no other name, notes with these initials cut away were accepted in spite of the note itself advertising forgery.' Vexed by the number of worthless, grubby, fading notes which constantly reeled through the nano-economy of early Sydney, Governor King repeatedly tried and failed to remove them from circulation. But even the courts ignored his orders to pay the private notes no heed, and they were still circulating when Macquarie sailed for England nearly twenty years later.

Many of the notes promised to pay a certain amount of money, but just as many promised to pay in wheat or other goods, indicating another important form of exchange in this rickety, jury-rigged marketplace – barter. And foremost amongst the many items which might be bartered was rum, a catch-all name which meant any sort of spirituous liquor, from fine French brandies to

Only the Strong

mouldy bladders of toxic moonshine. Rum's narcotic embrace offered the surest escape from the burdens of a life lived so hard that tea and sugar were considered a luxurious indulgence, and it remained a preferred method of payment to labourers for up to forty years. It was not the only method of payment of course. Sometimes, if only rarely, money itself was used. More often employers combined several modes of remuneration, with tea, sugar, wheat, meat, clothing and rum all being common. When Captain Anthony Fenn Kemp was paymaster of the New South Wales Corps, he refused to pay his men in cash, setting up a store in town and fobbing them off with whatever useless crud he had managed to lay in since last payday. If some insolent private demurred, perhaps not understanding the advantages of being paid a month's wages in the form of a grossly overpriced coil of rope or some old hessian sacks, the good captain would scream abuse at him until he saw the error of his ways. In one recorded instance he turned on one upstart in a furious rage, yelling that he was 'a damned saucy, mutinous rogue' and threatening 'to have him flogged for his impertinence. Against this bullying the soldier had no redress; he was forced to take his pay and dispose of the goods as best he could.' Most workers were only too happy to take their wages in kind, however, creating a serious problem for the governors, a business opportunity for the officers, and a fault line in the power structure of the town which would crack wide open in 1808.

Every governor from Phillip to Macquarie railed against the rum trade and its attendant evils, and all failed to suppress it. When Phillip sailed from Sydney for the last time he made a gift of two ewes belonging to the Crown to every settler, on the condition that they be retained and used to increase the colony's flock. No sooner was he out of the heads than his former subjects were rushing to trade in their windfall for grog. Every settler, bar one, was said to have sold their ewes 'at five gallons of spirit a head' to the officers of the corps. Governor Hunter, whose complaints about the spirit trade and widespread drunkenness were as impotent as they were frequent, nonetheless recognised the value of a tipple in motivating an otherwise dozy workforce. Much work which cold hard cash itself could not purchase would be done by labourers for a small tot of rum, he advised London. Behind the success of so many officers' farms lay a large body of convicts or emancipists who worked in their spare time simply to procure such delicacies as tea, sugar or rum, and Hunter believed that the public accounts would benefit greatly and more satisfaction be 'given to the workmen were we in possession of those little luxuries so much sought after'.

The unfortunate episode with Phillip's ewes however, shows that the central role of rum in the economy worked to benefit some more than others. In *British Imperialism and Australia*, Brian Fitzpatrick describes the system of paying farmers and labourers in grog as being 'highly profitable to perhaps one in two hundred of the colonial population and oppressive or ruinous to the one hundred and ninety-nine'. In June 1796 Hunter, who had tried to regulate the spirit trade, found it necessary to alter his previous order licensing a small number of operators to run retail liquor stores, proclaiming that far from solving the problem he found 'nothing but drunkenness and idleness among every part of the settlement'. He banned the payment of spirits for grain and reinforced his ban on unlicensed grog merchants.

The practice of purchasing the crops of settlers for spirits has too long prevailed in this settlement. It is high time that a trade

Only the Strong

so pernicious to individuals and so ruinous to the prosperity of his Majesty's colony should be put an end to. It is not possible that a farmer who shall be idle enough to throw away his labour for twelve months for the gratification of a few gallons of a poisonous spirit, and by which he is to be deprived of his senses for several days, can ever expect to thrive or enjoy those comforts which are only to be procured by sobriety and industry.

Governor Bligh, who cared little for alcohol himself, was in no doubt about its evils.

A sawyer will cut one hundred timber for a bottle of spirits – value two shillings and sixpence – which he drinks in a few hours; when for the same labour he would charge two bushels of wheat, which would furnish Bread for him for two months.

As was the case when Government House tried to regulate the physical growth of the city, proclamations and orders designed to suppress the growth in spirit trading failed in large part because the people charged with enforcing the rules – the officer class – were the same ones who profited from undermining them. Bligh for one was quick to sort out the villains and victims of the trade.

The farmers are involved in Debt, and either ruined by the high price of Spirits, or the high price of Labour, while the unprincipled holder of spirits gets his work done at a cheap rate and amasses considerable property.

In a sense the conflict was inevitable. Marooned on the far side of the planet, with no way of knowing whether London had remembered to send out desperately needed supplies – and, if it had, whether those vessels had survived the hazardous voyage – the colony was forced to turn to private initiative to survive. If the state was unable to guarantee the delivery of supplies, individuals would have to take its place. Those individuals, as Butlin points out, would have to be free, with access to capital, worthy of credit and with some education and organising ability. They would need to combine to defeat the monopoly of ships' captains who called into the starving settlement to dangle tantalising cargoes of food and drink before famished customers. There was only one group who fulfilled all of these requirements – the officers of the corps. They had access to reserves of foreign exchange through bills drawn on the Treasury in London for their salaries. They controlled the court system. Under Grose they effectively administered land grants and the supply of labour. And of course not to be forgotten, in the background, marching and drilling and raising clouds of red dust on the parade ground which looked down over the town, were the hundreds of well-armed men they commanded.

The solidarity of the corps in the face of outside challenges should not be underestimated. They sent a clear message to everyone that crossing one member of the corps meant crossing all of them. In their willingness to stand by their rough-headed troops and see off all comers the gentlemen of the New South Wales Corps at times resembled nothing so much as a latter-day chapter of drunken Hell's Angels. In the first week of February 1796, for instance, the civilian populace of the town were given reason to fear for their lives and property after a master carpenter named John Baughan had a set-to with the military. Baughan and some private were nursing a feud from having previously worked together. Whilst he was supposed to be guarding a storehouse, the

Only the Strong

soldier, who knew Baughan to be working in a building nearby, lay down his rifle and wandered over to chat with a friend standing outside. The subject was Baughan, the conversation was loud and the language would have made an old sailor blush. Baughan, too smart to be drawn into an open confrontation, crept out the back of the house, saw the soldier without his weapon and quietly snuck away to retrieve it himself. He carried the musket off to the sergeant of the guard who had no choice but to put the private on report.

The next morning, 5 February, Baughan and his wife were roused by a drunken mob apparently consisting of every member of the corps who was not then on duty. They broke open the gate to the Baughans' residence, a neat little house the couple had worked hard to furnish in some style and comfort. They smashed the windows, entered the dwelling and took to the corner posts with an axe. They broke Baughan's bed, tore the bedding and smashed chairs, window frames, drawers, chests and in short, according to Governor Hunter's report, 'demolished everything within his possession'.

Baughan had tried to defend his home, having had a few minutes warning of the mob's approach. He'd armed himself with a gun and threatened to use it on the uniformed rabble who gathered at his front gate. That held them back for a short time but they had the numbers, surrounding his property and trampling the fence on the far side, which he could not defend. A number of soldiers rushed up behind the terrified carpenter, tackled him and wrestled him to the ground, grinding his face into the dust and placing an axe on his neck, swearing that if he so much as stirred they'd chop off his head. Keeping him subdued like this, wrote Hunter, they completed the ruin of his property, 'to the very great terror of the man's wife, after which they went off cheering', and marched in a body across the parade ground in front their commanding officer's house.

Hunter was under no illusions about the seriousness of the incident. He wrote to Captain Paterson of the corps complaining that the conduct of some of its members had been, in his opinion, 'the most violent and outrageous that was ever heard of by any British regiment whatever'. He warned that he would regard any further aggravation as open rebellion, for which the ringleaders would answer, 'most probably with their lives'. He had no idea of how prophetic his words were when he told Paterson that

> they must not – they shall not – dictate laws and rules for the government of this settlement; they were sent here by his Majesty to support the civil power in the execution of its functions, but they seemed disposed to take all law into their own hands, and to direct it in whatever way best may suit their own views.

John Macarthur, who would later pull corps commander George Johnston's strings during the Rum Rebellion, was then a captain in charge of the company from which the rioters were drawn. He wrote to Hunter seeking to have the charges against his men dropped, after they had expressed 'their contrition' and 'sincere concern'. They promised not to act up again, said Macarthur, and to cover the Baughans against any loss they may have suffered. Hunter backed down and the men were admonished by their commanders. However, the severity of that jolly good talking-to was called into question by Macarthur's threats to Dr William Balmain over the matter.

Only the Strong

Balmain, a civilian magistrate, had made his way to Baughan's wrecked house to interview him about the attack. Baughan and his wife were so fearful of an another reprisal raid, however, that they refused to cooperate. Balmain played the heavy, threatening to charge them for obstructing his investigation, but they wouldn't be moved. Mrs Baughan in particular was convinced the soldiers would murder her husband at the slightest provocation. Word of Balmain's investigation soon made it up the hill to the barracks and the surgeon found himself in receipt of a letter from Macarthur demanding details of his inquiry. Messengers hurried back and forth across the village with a series of increasingly angry notes as the entire officer corps protested their indignation at the magistrate's 'shamefully malevolent interference' in their affairs. Balmain, who knew only too well that Macarthur lay behind all this, challenged him to a duel, calling him a 'base rascal and an atrocious liar and villain'.

In reply Balmain received a lesson in solidarity from Macarthur's brother officers. They wrote collectively, rejecting his claim that his quarrel was only with Macarthur. The abuse previously heaped on him was in fact the opinion of the *whole* corps. They regarded his conduct with the 'highest degree of contempt and indignation'. And if he had a problem with that and wanted satisfaction, he had only to ask and the corps would appoint 'an officer for that purpose, and if he should fail in giving Mr Balmain the satisfaction required, another and another will be fixed until there is not one left to explain'. They assured the surgeon that this was no empty threat, that they were all 'earnest for an opportunity of punishing' him. Balmain, for his part, very wisely chose not to fight a rolling series of pistol duels with every officer of the regiment.

This dispute was not just a lot of pompous boofheads standing on a ridiculous code of personal honour. It was a forewarning of the deep rift developing between the town's two most important power centres: the civil administration centred on Government House, and the military–commercial complex nominally centred on the officers' barracks but essentially directed by one man, Macarthur. He was not the only officer to engage in trade and farming of course. The strength of the officers came from their acting in concert. But none acted with more audacity or ruthlessness than John Macarthur. He had organised one of the combine's first trading forays in October of 1792, when the officers chartered the *Britannia* to buy supplies at the Cape. As inspector of public works in 1799, he virtually ran the colony on behalf of the military. But he was only able to play that role because the acting governor, Francis Grose, had largely abandoned his post and its powers.

Grose was not what you would call a dynamic sort of guy. No sooner had he settled his wounded butt into Phillip's chair than he was disposing of as many of his responsibilities as good manners would allow. He devolved responsibility for Parramatta to Captain Foveaux, the corpulent, asthmatic military commander of that expanding satellite town. Similar arrangements took effect in Sydney. Civilian control of the colony evaporated with the quick removal from office of the magistrates and their replacement by army officers. For the first time in the history of the colony, rations for the military were increased above those of the convicts. Grose had little taste for discomfort, according to Judge Advocate Collins, and he certainly had no intention of following Phillip's example of vigorous personal leadership. He retired to his predecessor's farm where, he wrote, 'I live in as good a home as I desire ... [with] a sufficiency of everything for my family. The

Only the Strong

climate, though very hot, is not unwholesome; we have plenty of fish, and there is good shooting.' It was, all things considered, a spiffing way for a chap to see out his autumn years.

Power abhors a vacuum, however, and others rushed in to assume the prerogatives of his office, if not the trappings. Left to their own devices, says Ross Fitzgerald, the military began to arrange colonial affairs to their own benefit. Grose decided that private farms, especially the large holdings of the officers, would be the colony's salvation, granting to his fellow officers thousands of acres and convicts to work them. The man in charge of this process was Macarthur, whom Grose increasingly relied on as an advisor and administrator. Appointed inspector of public works for the Parramatta and Toongabbie areas, Macarthur, whom Grose called 'the old head on young shoulders', was virtually handed the keys to the colony. He was also the regimental paymaster between 1792 and 1799, an appointment which doubled his own salary and placed him in control of the funds which financed the officers' mercantile ventures.

In Macarthur we find a nemesis for Bligh's Greek tragedy. The sources of power are many: economic, military, religious, social and political institutions are all imbued with their own forms of authority. The activation of such power, however, requires an act of human will. Grose arrived in Sydney with almost unlimited power *on paper*, but he seemed happy to disperse his authority, first ceding it to men like Foveaux and Macarthur, then watching it leach away as they applied it to their own ends. Other governors, Hunter, King and Bligh foremost amongst them, struggled to retain their authority in the face of daily challenges from competing power centres. In John Macarthur greed, treachery, cunning and a monomaniacal gift for self-promotion combined with undeniable business acumen, a razor-sharp mind, and dreams of glory way above his station, to forge the strength of will needed to build an empire from nothing and lay waste to its challengers. He was also fortunate in having married well. His wife Elizabeth was an astute farmer and businesswoman and arguably contributed more to the establishment of Australia's pastoral industry than her trouble-making partner. Indeed, had Elizabeth's wise head been on John's shoulders, the family fortune would probably have been many times greater and the Macarthur name would never have been inextricably linked with infamy and rebellion. Her dial should have been on the old two-dollar note instead of her scheming husband's.

Almost every governor who encountered Macarthur had trouble with him. Reprimanded by Phillip, he withdrew from all social contact with Government House, this while still a mere lieutenant. Grose, who gave him as much land and autonomy as he could deal with, had an easier time of it. But Hunter, the next naval officer to try to rule the colony, quickly fell out with the now Captain Macarthur after attempting to reverse some of the policies by which Grose had entrenched the military autocracy. Macarthur then 'sent serious criticisms of Hunter's administration directly to the secretary of state and military commander in chief', precipitating Hunter's recall to England. Hunter's official caution that 'scarcely anything short of the full power of the Governor would be considered' by Macarthur as sufficient was echoed by the next governor he tormented, King. Governor King sent the 'perturbator' back to London for a court martial after Macarthur had shot his own commanding officer in a very dodgy duel, King writing: 'Experience has convinced every man in this colony that there are no resources which art, cunning, impudence and a pair of basilisk eyes can afford that he does not put in practice to obtain any point he undertakes . . .' and 'that if Captain Macarthur returns here in any official character it should be that of Governor, as one half of the colony already belongs to him, and it will not be long before he gets the other half'.

Relentless pressure, confrontation, subterfuge and violence were all well within Macarthur's tactical range. Besides the duel with his commander which led to his initial exile from Australia, he also drew his pistol on the master of the convict transport which carried him to Sydney, shooting a hole in his greatcoat on the Old Gun Wharf at Plymouth Dock. He would boast later to Governor Ralph Darling that he had 'never yet failed in ruining a man who had become obnoxious to him'; and his long-running feud with Judge-Advocate Richard Atkins, himself a rogue of the first order, stands as a near-perfect example of how to wage a savage campaign of personal vituperation. Atkins, a 'tall, fine-looking, over-rosy and middle-aged gentleman, prepossessing in appearance, engaging and easy in manner' vied with Bligh for the honour of being Macarthur's most hated adversary, although this didn't redeem him much in the judgmental governor's eyes. In 1807 Bligh described Atkins to the Home Office as 'the ridicule of the community'. He said that Atkins had passed sentences of death 'in moments of intoxication'.

> His determination is weak, his opinion floating and infirm; his knowledge of the law insignificant and subservient to private inclination and confidential cases of the crown, where due secrecy is required, he is not to be trusted with.

To Atkins, the high born legal officer who was finally humiliated during the rebellion, must go the honour of one of the most withering attacks on Macarthur's character after the latter, a mere draper's son, charged him with a catalogue of crimes in an early feud:

LEVIATHAN

What must your sense of shame be when you, a Goliah [sic] of honour and veracity, should resort to a subtifuge at which the meanest convict might blush, by skulking from substantial meaning and screening yourself by a jingle of words from the manly perseverance which should mark the character of a man professing as you do. The quibble between charges and assertions is of too flimsy a texture to require a comment. It is only worthy of a dastardly coward like yourself. Your original meanness and despicable littleness pervades your every action. It shows the cloven foot. Return to your original nothing; we know what you have been, and what you now are; and believe me an honest and industrious staymaker is a more honourable and more useful member of society than such a man as I hold you to be. Let me ask who has been the incendiary – who has been the promoter of all the feuds and animosities between individuals in this colony? You sir. You are likewise the man who has had the audacity to accuse me with having acted officially and individually with injustice, oppression and peculation [embezzlement] – nay even highway robbery. You, who four years ago, was only a lieutenant, pennyless but by his pay, and now is reputed worth £8,000. Let this colony hear witness where lies the strongest presumption, you or me being the oppressor, peculator or robber. On this subject, viper, you bite a file; the day of retribution will come, and believe me it is not far off . . .

Atkins was wrong as it turned out. The day of retribution was a long way off for Macarthur, who returned from his banishment to London in triumph, having convinced the authorities that far from being punished for shooting up a superior officer, he should

Only the Strong

instead be given five thousand acres of prime grazing land and thirty convicts to work it so that he might establish a colonial wool industry.

While he deftly turned to his own advantage an episode which would have ended in ruin for anyone else, Macarthur's enforced absence between November 1801 and June 1805 coincided with a further atomisation of Sydney's power structure which he could not control or even respond to. Although a succession of governors had been unable to check the rising commercial influence of the officers' cartel, a couple of former convicts and one free settler proved themselves more than capable.

Margaret Stevens has observed that, apart from Macarthur, the officers' business activities remained 'rudimentary and unenterprising, based mainly on the permanent demand for spirits. They made no attempt to anticipate a more sophisticated demand, or to carry the risk this would entail.' Others were not so lethargic. It was considered more than a little *déclassé* for the officers to openly engage in trade, being gentlemen and all, so they had to retain the services of frontmen or women. Some of these cutouts, such as the convicted thieves Simeon Lord and Henry Kable, took to commerce with infinitely more zest and guile than their uniformed masters. Lord, who acted as a retail agent for Lieutenant Thomas Rowley, used his experience to set up as an auctioneer and wholesaler after 1800, providing visiting ships with an alternative outlet to the officers' syndicate which had long skimmed the cream off the high prices of imported goods. About the same time Kable, who had kept shop for a number of officers, went into business with James Underwood, a boat builder who had arrived on the *Admiral Barrington* in 1791. Kable and Underwood launched themselves into the sealing industry, using vessels built in Underwood's yard on the Tank Stream, and by 1804 they were employing sixty men and gathering up to thirty thousand skins a year from Tasmania.

The most important economic development of that period, however, was the arrival of a free man, a merchant and trader by the name of Robert Campbell, the same Campbell who rushed from Government House on the night of the rebellion, responding to the screams of Bligh's daughter Mary as she attempted to block the charge of the main guard. Campbell was an honest Scotsman, fair-minded, brave and charitable. He was the youngest surviving son of the laird of Ashfield and at the age of twenty-seven took sail for India to join his brother in the family's colonial business. He passed through Sydney in 1798, scouting for opportunities, and returned with a speculative cargo in February 1800. Campbell must have been a far-sighted man to see the commercial promise of a poor, remote village surrounded by dry, dull-looking forest and serviced by one rickety wooden wharf. The month he arrived to establish a new branch of his company, the total white population of Australia was less than 5000 and Sydney's share of that but a fraction. The people who made up this potential market were a deeply unimpressive crew, many of them near permanently drunk on the 50 000 gallons of hard liquor which had arrived in just the previous four months. Campbell had chosen to hazard the family silver on a prison town which could not afford to build a new jail. As the summer southerlies pushed his ship up the side of the continent, Governor Hunter worried about the lax arrangement for storing the colony's gunpowder, given all of the Irish troublemakers who had been arriving recently. The Reverend Marsden was grumbling to the Duke of Portland that 'Satan's Kingdom seems to be so fully established and his power and influence so universal among us that nothing but an uncommon display of Almighty power can shake his throne'.

Only the Strong

The less than impressive state of Campbell's local market was mirrored in the chaotic regulatory structure within which he would have to operate. The legal system of the hybrid prison society was arbitrary, untrustworthy and run by some truly underwhelming judicial minds. For instance, as Campbell prepared to sell his cargo from the *Hunter*, Joseph Holt, a recently arrived Irish rebel, tried to sue Captain Salkeld of the *Minerva* for sixty guineas which had been paid for the passage of Holt's son. Instead of allowing the boy to stay with his parents, Salkeld had insisted on quartering him with the sailors and had then made him work through the voyage. Holt sued for a refund of the fare and for the wages his son should have been paid. However, having been warned about the town's judge, Richard Dore, Holt kept watch late one night and spied Dore receiving a bribe of 'a ferkin of butter, a cheese and five gallons of spirits' from Salkeld. Unsurprisingly, the judge trashed Holt's case, saying he and his family were just convicts. Holt, who had not actually come to Sydney as a convict, protested and the judge ordered him to shut up. Holt tried again and Dore had him thrown out of court, saying his conduct was a perversion of justice and if he said another word he'd be committed to jail. In explanation of Dore's behaviour (assuming the free cheese wasn't to blame), he'd probably drunk more than his fair share of those 50 000 gallons of rum which were sloshing around town and he was in the middle of slowly and painfully carking it. At any rate, this was not the sort of predictable, rule-based environment in which your average businessman prefers to operate.

Campbell had entered an economy which had no money and no certainty, where the courts, such as they were, had been thoroughly contaminated and abused by the town's contending power players. The workforce, drawn largely from Britain's urban centres, was demoralised and unsuited to agrarian pursuits. A military cartel controlled much of the primitive trade and financial markets. And tens of thousands of nautical miles, haunted by privateers and hostile foreign warships, lay between Campbell's Sydney outpost, the family's Indian operations and their metropolitan headquarters back in the UK. In the face of all this, Campbell prospered. The wharf and warehouses he raised were the finest in the harbour and by 1804 held £50 000 worth of merchandise, which was 'worth more than all the paymaster's bills drawn during the seven or eight years of the officers monopoly'. Campbell amassed this fortune through the revolutionary practice of paying a fair price to his suppliers and taking only a small margin from his customers. He offered credit at generous rates and took payment in grain. It was a complete departure from the methods adopted by his competitors in the corps who gouged margins of up to 1200 per cent from their captive market, and Campbell proved very popular with both the small settlers and the governors. Two hundred farmers signed a memorial for him in 1804 which stated, 'But for you, we had still been a prey to the mercenary unsparing hand of avarice and extortion.' He was too powerful for his competitors to destroy, although he was probably lucky that Macarthur had been banished from Sydney for the first years of his company's life. Nobody else had Macarthur's malign genius for destruction and by the time he returned, Campbell's empire had expanded beyond his reach and had, with the help of men like Lord, Kable and Underwood, undermined the hegemony of the corps. Fitzgerald and Hearn summarise the shift neatly:

By 1801 fundamental changes were moving the colony's economic structure away from the arbitrary regulation and

Only the Strong

simplicity of the prison camp. Yet the colony's government still firmly reflected the interests of the gaolers, and the governor retained widespread powers over gaoled and free alike. At times, when the governor had been inclined to relieve himself of his responsibilities, the military had been ready to accumulate that power to itself.

And the officers, notwithstanding the rise of Campbell and Company, were not quite finished yet.

One early meeting between Bligh and Macarthur was a scorcher. The most detailed description comes from Macarthur's testimony at George Johnston's court martial, although we should probably recalibrate this version in light of Macarthur's well-known penchant for lying his arse off. He portrayed himself as something of an innocent little lamb wandering into the mad governor's slaughtering pen; but if you ignore the self-portrait of a delicate petal, bruised by the violence of Bligh's temper, and instead imagine two ferocious egomaniacs turning purple with rage and gobbing poison phlegm into each other's eyes, chances are you'd be right on the money.

Macarthur had approached Bligh about the extravagant promises of land and servants he had been given in London. King had managed to fudge the issue long enough for it to become his successor's problem. About a month after Bligh had taken control of the government, Macarthur rode out to the Governor's residence at Parramatta to front him on the issue. He found Bligh walking in the gardens alone and, seizing the chance, smarmed up to ask whether Bligh 'had been informed of the wishes of the Government' respecting Macarthur's affairs. He was particularly anxious that Bligh understand the advantages which would accrue to the colony from Macarthur's own ascent to the ranks of the grotesquely rich. The impression created by Macarthur at this point is of a hand-wringing Uriah Heep, desperately trying not to upset the infamous Bounty Bligh's volcanic temper. Upset it he did, however, Bligh exploding in his face, 'What have I to do with your sheep sir? What have I to do with your cattle? Are you to have such flocks of sheep and such herds of cattle as no man ever heard of before? No Sir!' Macarthur then told the court martial:

> 'I endeavoured to appease him, by stating that I had understood the Government at home had particularly recommended me to his notice. He replied, "I have heard of your concerns sir; you have got five thousand acres of land in the finest situation in the country; but, by God, you shan't keep it!" I told him that as I had received this land at the recommendation of the Privy Council and by order of the Secretary of State, I presumed that my right to it was indisputable. "Damn the Privy Council! And damn the Secretary of State too!" he says.'

Later in the day, with Macarthur still tugging at the Governor's elbow, seeking his indulgence, Bligh burst into another rage, again damning the Secretary of State and screaming violently, 'He commands at home. I command here'. In the meantime Bligh had upbraided poor old ex-Governor King who was lingering a short while in the colony, abusing his long-suffering, emotionally fractured predecessor so vehemently for indulging Macarthur that he actually burst into tears. In William Bligh, it seemed, Macarthur's unyielding Olympian will had finally met its match. Bligh had arrived in the colony unsure of the extent of his powers but with no doubts about the mission he had been assigned. He was to bend Macarthur and his ilk to the imperial will, and if they would not bend, he was to break them.

The wild energy generated by the clash of these two men and the interests they represented was constrained and intensified by the cramped political structures in which they were forced to make war. Twenty years of ill-considered policies and neglect had created a polity every bit as primitive, crude and harsh as the physical environment in which their battle unfolded. Civil society in convict-era Sydney was to London's political mores and practices as the rough, meandering huts of Soldiers' Row were to the Houses of Parliament. In conception, the governor stood as a facsimile of the king before the Civil War. He was almost an absolute monarch, with the power of life and death over his subjects. Rivalry, folly and indolence, however, soon drained authority from the governor's office, and when Bligh was approached to take the position in 1805 he confessed to his patron Sir Joseph Banks that he had no idea of the limits to his power in the colony. Soon after arriving he seems to have decided there were none, other than the desire of Macarthur and his allies to thwart him. Richard Atkins told Johnston's court martial that Bligh had once fumed at him, 'The law sir! Damn the law. My will is the law, and woe unto the man who dares disobey it'.

Bligh, in one sense, was right, so flimsy was the legal foundation of British rule. Jeremy Bentham, the legal philosopher and neophyte criminologist, obsessed about the tyranny which he insisted had been unlawfully established within the folds of Sydney Harbour. Bentham described the penal settlement as a system of misgovernment and a nursery of martial law and, examining the laws passed to establish the colony, professed himself astonished.

'Compared with the immensity of the superstructure,' he wrote, 'the scantiness of the basis exhibited a Colossus mounted upon a straw.' For the most part, what passed for justice in New South Wales was, to Bentham, 'so much lawless violence' and the criminality of the convicts was but a trifling matter compared with that of the ruling class. He was less concerned with the outrages of the corps than with the lack of anything approaching liberty or democracy within the remote society. The governor had full legal power over the convicts, he agreed, and considerable authority over the naval and military officers and other ranks. He likewise had some power over the masters and crews of British vessels in the port, and arguably some limited power over foreign vessels which called in. But over the civil officers and the convicts who had served their time, and over free settlers and their families, said Bentham, he had none. The problem was that, as free British subjects, they could not be ruled by the King or his governor without their consent, given through an elected parliament.

Over British subjects, the Agents of the Crown have exercised legislative power without authority from Parliament: they have legislated not in this or that case only, but in all cases: they have exercised an authority as completely autocratical as was ever exercised in Russia: they have maintained a tyranny ... a too real tyranny of fourteen years: they have exercised it not only over this or that degraded class alone, whose ignominy may seem to have separated their lot from the common lot of the fellow subjects, but over multitudes as free from blemish as themselves: they have exercised it for the purpose of exercising the most glaring of oppressions: for the purpose of inflicting punishment without cause on those whom the whole fund of

The point of Ben Buckler before the big rock washed up. *(Courtesy of Sydney City Council Archives)*

The big rock at Bondi, with author for scale.

Sitting lightly on the sandstone, a fine example of the first class housing available to the working classes. *(Courtesy of Sydney City Council Archives)*

The city eats its own. A council truck investigates a small to medium-sized pot hole. *(Courtesy of Sydney City Council Archives)*

The price to be paid for living at the edge. Lincoln Crescent after the conflagration.
(Courtesy of Fairfax Photo Library)

A bumper crop for Sydney's rat catchers. *(Courtesy of Sydney City Council Archives)*

White supremacists defend mainstream Australia from undesirable elements. *(Courtesy of Fairfax Photo Library)*

Nattily dressed detective and colourful Sydney identity, Fred Krahe. *(Courtesy of Fairfax Photo Library)*

Property developer and colourful Sydney identity, Frank Theeman. *(Courtesy of Fairfax Photo Library)*

Gordon and Wendy Gallagher before cancer and the police service took their toll.
(Courtesy of Wendy Gallagher)

Gordon as a young cop, terrified that someone might ask him for directions or something.
(Courtesy of Wendy Gallagher)

Only the Strong

just and legal punishment had already been exhausted.

Bentham said it was totally repugnant to the constitution and Magna Carta that the King or his representatives should exercise legislative power 'over English subjects in England, or anywhere else' without the concurrence of Parliament. For whom or what was the protection afforded by Magna Carta intended, he asked? For the inhabitants of the land, or for the soil only; for the flesh and blood, or only for the stocks and stones? 'Limited as the power of an English King is over Englishmen in England, in what book will he find that it is absolute over them everywhere else?'

This would not have been a problem had Sydney remained a prison camp as intended. But Bentham was right. As soon as the first free citizen set foot there, or simply materialised once their term of punishment expired, neither the officers of the corps nor the governor had any more legitimate claim to control their lives than Bentham himself. Of course this was a legal philosopher's problem. From the first days the governors were less concerned about legal niceties than ensuring that the colony didn't starve. Legitimacy was assumed and power – or, at the very least, submission – was guaranteed not simply by the law but more immediately by the bayonet, the whip and the musket. Sydney was almost a laboratory experiment for political scientists wishing to examine the evolution of a polity, although in this case it seemed to evolve backwards, from Hobbes's *Leviathan* to a state where all were ceaselessly at war with each other.

So, returning to an earlier question, where lay power in the Sydney of Bligh and Macarthur? In the knotted leather teeth of the cat-o'-nine-tails? In the barrels of the corps' artillery pieces? In the officers' mess? Government House? The courts? Unfortunately rock-solid answers, when grasped at, reveal themselves to be chimeras. To begin with, as Hannah Arendt wisely counsels us, power should not be confused with violence. Governmental power arises from people acting in unison. It rests on opinion and consent. Violence, on the other hand, is instrumental. It requires tools, be they clenched fists or loaded guns, and in its pure form it can sweep away the most powerful institution in a twinkling. Sergeant Whittle, with one thrust of his bayonet, could have terminated Bligh's command no matter how many settlers supported him, and no matter how great the power conferred on Bligh by their sovereign. Such force, writes Arendt, does not depend on numbers but on implements; those who oppose violence with mere power will soon discover that they are confronted not with men but with men's artifacts. 'Out of the barrel of a gun grows the most effective command ... What can never grow out of it is power.'

But didn't the penal settlement of Sydney rest on a foundation of ferocious violence? On the scaffold and the sword? On whippings which flayed the victim's meat from their bodies so that bones and spinal cords and jellied flesh were exposed to the air and the shocking impact of the next blow? The precautions of the First Fleet marines, training cannon loaded with grapeshot into the holds where the prisoners lay, do not convey an impression of much confidence in the 'consent' of their cargo to the journey ahead. The constant alarms raised by early governors over the revolutionary potential of the Irish prisoners betray a dread of increasing numbers of inhabitants with no respect for their authority.

Here was the crux of the problem which so vexed Bentham. The whole structure of governance in New South Wales rested on the consent of the governed, who far outnumbered their captors. But there was no formal means, such as through an elected council, by which this consent could be given. The citizens, settlers and transportees might well support the administration, but other than by signing memorials there was no formal channel for this support. More importantly, for those who did not support the administration, there was no forum in which to oppose it. Inevitably, they sought other forms of resistance. This often took place in the courts, a natural outlet for conflict in a society lacking a parliament, a free press or civil rights. As Bruce Kercher explains in his history of the civil law in New South Wales, the courts provided more than just a location of these political conflicts, and the law itself was more than an expression of ruling-class power.

> It was also the means of resolving disputes about the extent of that power and, sometimes, a restraint on it. In early NSW there was more than one group which claimed to rule, and the debate between them was heard within the law, with references to legitimacy, fairness and adherence to legal forms. In short the law was both the weapon in the struggle for dominance and a constraint on power.

As the town slouched through the fierce summer daze of 1807–8 and John Macarthur manoeuvred to frustrate a governor he had long perceived as a threat to his economic interests, he resorted to the rhetoric of English liberty and, unknowingly, with some po-faced, unintentional humour, to the arguments of Jeremy Bentham. Chronically restless and testy, tortured by painful dyspepsia, Macarthur was afflicted by the fear of losing status and wealth which gnaws at all members of the bourgeoisie lucky enough to scratch and claw and cheat their way to prominence. There is some evidence he had already set a collision course with Bligh. Charles Walker, commander of a ship belonging to Macarthur, recalled talking to his boss after a minor disagreement with the Governor, Macarthur supposedly threatening that if Bligh did not look after his interests and those of 'some of the other respectable gentlemen of the colony ... he [would] perhaps get another voyage in his launch again'. (Referring to the small boat he was set adrift in by the crew of the *Bounty*.) Walker also claimed that when he returned from sea in November 1807, Macarthur told him 'that the colony had suffered Governor Bligh to reign long enough, [and] there would soon be an alteration'. As you might expect, Macarthur flatly denied these allegations at the court martial. Were they true, he could have swung for treason.

It was another of Macarthur's ships which proved the catalyst for rebellion. On 15 November 1807 his 102 tonne schooner *Parramatta* eased up the harbour, returning from the Society Islands with over 75 000 pounds of pork in her belly. Macarthur was not able to land the cargo, however, because Robert Campbell, acting as naval officer (a sort of customs inspector), impounded the ship for having carried a stowaway convict out of Sydney in June. Macarthur and his partner Garnham Blaxcell lost both the ship and an £800 bond. An incensed Macarthur claimed Campbell had 'virtually dispossessed' him of his vessel. He refused to take any responsibility for the crew, who were trapped on board without pay or provisions as port regulations banned them from disembarking. The captain and crew ignored this, of course, and on 14 December they landed and sought out Judge-Advocate Atkins, who had been ordered to investigate the matter by Bligh. Atkins listened to their story then wrote to Macarthur, saying that his abandoning the men was the cause of their breaking regulations by coming

Only the Strong

ashore without permission. The judge requested Macarthur's presence in town at ten the next morning 'to show cause for your conduct'. Macarthur simply flicked aside his old enemy's sword thrust, denying any responsibility and directing Atkins's enquiries to Campbell. Atkins's counterstrike was a warrant for Macarthur's arrest, delivered to the family's property at midnight on 15 December by the chief constable of Parramatta, Francis Oakes. Oakes had ridden out to the farm and, finding the homestead in darkness, tapped on a window. A sleepy, crumpled Macarthur appeared in his bedclothes to let the constable in. On reading the warrant he flew into a rage, finally calming down enough to write Oakes a note to take back to his masters.

> Mr Oakes, – You will inform the persons who sent you here with the warrant you have now shewn me, and given me a copy of, that I never will submit to the horrid tyranny that is attempted until I am forced; that I consider it with scorn and contempt, as I do the persons who have directed it to be executed.

For good measure Macarthur told the Oakes that if he came back, 'to come well armed' because he would not submit 'till blood was shed'. He was fibbing, as it turned out. Atkins quickly, probably drunkenly, and no doubt gleefully, fired off another warrant and Macarthur was arrested and hauled before the magistrates a day later, without spilling a drop of his increasingly blue blood. The bench, which included George Johnston, committed him for trial in the next criminal court in January 1808.

John Macarthur celebrated Christmas 1807 by laying plans to counterattack on a number of fronts. The criminal court consisted almost entirely of officers from his former regiment, whom he knew he could rely on. Unfortunately the presiding judge was Richard Atkins, who could also be relied on, but not in a good way. Macarthur had to neutralise his old foe, rally the troops and somehow craft a defence with a semblance of credibility to a possible charge of high treason. Atkins was easily dealt with. The rum-sodden old joke had run up a mountain of bad debts in the colony, circulating worthless promissory notes and creating a legion of enemies besides Macarthur. One of these creditors sold Macarthur a fifteen year old note for £82, including interest, which Macarthur then took around to the judge's house on Bridge Street. There, banging on the door and dancing around the garden, noisily but fruitlessly demanding satisfaction of this debt, he established grounds for challenging Atkins's place on the bench due to his bias. (Of course everyone already knew Atkins was biased against him – this was a guy who had once said Macarthur was 'a Toad in a Hole feeding on his own Poison' and accused him of stalking around 'like Sin and Death seeking whom he may devour' – but it's the form of these things that is important.)

Knowing only too well that the trial was to be as much a political struggle as a legal dispute, Macarthur tended to his allies as well his enemies. This meant not only the officers who were to sit in judgment on his case, but also the members of the mercantile class who felt themselves hard done by under Bligh's administration. The Governor made no secret of his preference for the small landholders; 'plain sensible farming men' he called them, 'of moderate expectation'. Just as he made no secret of his disdain for the wealthy traders and merchants who sought unfair advantage over these landholders, telling Sir Joseph Banks that, given a chance, 'those who consider themselves of the superior class' would have made the modest settlers their vassals in no time. In this he was correct. Macarthur had written to the Duke of Portland as far back as 1796, complaining that the only reason colonial farming was not well advanced was because most small holders were idle drunkards who should be 'obliged to employ themselves in the service of an industrious and vigilant master'. His alleged remarks to Captain Walker that the small farmers were all rascals, and that Bligh would be much better off servicing the needs of the principal landholders, sit comfortably alongside this opinion.

Of course Bligh, inherently paternalistic, had not simply favoured the small landholders over the big end of the village with his opinions. More importantly, he had advantaged them through policy. For someone like Robert Campbell, who had been raised to competition and risk, this was not such a problem. For the officers who had built their fortunes on lazy, monopolistic indulgences, it was intolerable. Unfortunately for the Governor, he was also his own worst enemy, uniting his foes and dividing his friends. The emancipist traders, those convicts made good, were not natural allies of the officers. In fact when you got down to it, they were implacable class enemies. No former hoodlums were ever going to make it onto a gentleman's Christmas list. But Bligh, unreflective, bombastic and reckless as ever, put no effort into securing the loyalty of men like Lord, Kable and Underwood. Far from it. He had them arrested in August 1807 and banged up in the town gaol 'for having written to the governor in improper terms'. So when Macarthur was skulking around town during the ten days of Christmas in 1807, claiming Bligh was close to establishing a tyranny, who were they to disagree? They, like the officers, had done very well out of Sydney. They had all risen far above their stations and they were all terrified of suffering any reverse. Bligh's actions, such as gaoling the traders and ordering the demolition of houses in the government domain, raised the prospect of greatly diminishing or even destroying what many had built up.

An operator like Macarthur knew the main chance when he saw it. Bligh's determination to return the anarchic sprawl of Sydney to its virgin state as government turf was a gift. Many of the soldiers who would soon march on Bligh did not bunk in the regimental barracks, preferring to live with their convict mistresses in cottages about the town. These were some of the same cottages which so enraged Bligh when he stared across his gardens at grounds which should have been his reserve but which were instead run through with muddy tracks and blighted by illegally built huts and shanties with their unkempt gardens, stray dogs and itinerant, rutting pigs. Shortly before his trial, with many of the soldiers deeply worried about their leases and homes, Macarthur, who also had a lease on the ground claimed by Bligh, arrived with a large body of troops to fence in his land. It was a stunt, but Bligh couldn't help himself. He took one look at that glistening steel bear trap and jumped in with both feet, dispatching the superintendent of public works, Nicholas Divine, and a party of convicts to tear down the fence a few days later. They arrived to be confronted by Macarthur, flanked by Captains Edward Abbott and the odious Anthony Fenn Kemp. Macarthur ignored the superintendent and, taking one of the heavy fence posts himself, defiantly fixed it in a hole. Divine swung down from his horse and wrenched the post out of the ground, declaring that he did so on the order of the Governor and adding a little melodramatically, 'When the axe is laid to the root, the tree must fall'. If Macarthur was hoping for a demonstration of the soldiers' precarious hold on their homes and property, he could not have scripted the moment better

Only the Strong

himself. The soldiers, witnessing or hearing of this encounter, could have been in no doubt about where their interests lay in the conflict which was fast drawing near. Sydney, wrote surveyor Charles Grimes to Captain John Piper at Norfolk Island, was a hell.

And through this vale of fears and uncertainty strode Macarthur, whispering, beguiling, insinuating. Sowing a vintage crop of malice. Plying his former troops with lashings of cheap grog. Stalking about the parade ground of the barracks the night before his trial, while inside his son and nephew lavishly entertained the corps' officers, his judges, at the riotous debauch which occasioned George Johnston's drunken road accident. This was their last supper, whether they knew it or not. History lay in front of them, their best days behind. Their domination of Sydney was drawing to a close, a domination which was not necessarily 'a question of rum monopoly or gangsterism', as Fitzgerald and Hearn put it. 'It was the milieu of military influence over all aspects of colonial life and administration, for it was the corps, not the Governors, who represented the continuous and familiar form of authority in New South Wales.' And by their actions on the morrow they would lay waste to that authority even as it reached its zenith.

Violence is the last resort of the impotent. When influence has faded and power 'vanished like a dream', we stand naked before fate. Hundreds of armed soldiers marching on a dinner party at Government House and dragging the King's own representative into custody at bayonet point may present, at first blush, an image of absolute power. But in fact it was a manifestation of growing impotence. The officers displayed their unchallenged power when they acted in concert to first drive down the price a visiting ship's captain could demand for his cargo, and then ramped up the price their monopoly charged for the same goods sold into a captive market. The officers demonstrated their lack of power when, unable to manipulate the court system on 25 January, they launched a military revolt the following day. Every decrease of power is an open invitation to violence, as Arendt observes, if only because those who once held power and feel it slithering out of their grasp have always found it difficult to resist the temptation of substituting brute force in its place. Violence however, unlike the exercise of power, needs a justification, and thus the men who launched the coup had to cast about for a reason to explain themselves to London, whose authority they had effectively usurped. They found one. Without so much as a smirk they pleaded that without their armed rebellion there would have been ... an armed rebellion.

On 26 January 1808, the town, according to the rebels, trembled on the threshold of a mass revolt which would have been much uglier than their considered actions. At Johnston's court martial his witnesses lined up to paint a picture of an unholy, disorganised bloodswarm rising from the hovels of the common people and sweeping away all in its path as they exploded against William Bligh's frightful tyranny. So inflamed was the population that the corps was merely performing its duty of protecting the Governor by removing him from office. Unfortunately for Johnston, Bligh produced just as many witnesses, of somewhat greater credibility, who described the town as being in a peaceful state, except for some understandable tension amongst those few leading citizens actively involved in the Macarthur crisis. Chief constable Oakes described Sydney on the evening before and the morning of trial as being 'in peace and quietness; a few people met about the court house door when the officers assembled'. He disagreed violently that the uprising was necessary to restore the peace. 'Public peace restored!' he choked. 'I don't know that it was ever broke, unless they were the military who broke it; I never saw anybody else break it and I was a witness to every transaction that took place ...' Asked whether there was a 'a great concourse of people' at the barracks as Johnston was driven towards it, he replied:

> No; I was standing just at the end of what they call Soldiers' Row, and immediately after he arrived I saw the soldiers and officers repairing towards the barracks. I don't believe there was a single person more than common on the parade when I saw Major Johnston driven there. Directly after his arrival I saw some of the soldiers going towards their little huts, without their regimentals, and I saw them immediately afterwards in their regimentals repairing towards the barracks.

Far from rising and demanding the corps overthrow the Governor, Oakes testified that most of the townsfolk were greatly alarmed when the drums and fife beat the order to arms. James Harris, a shipwright working in the cove, swore that, 'No person, that I could hear, knew the cause of their marching up, nor for an hour after they had been in front of Government House; upwards of two hundred persons were round me, and not one of them knew the cause of it.'

The immediate cause was John Macarthur's inability to lever his inebriated adversary, Judge-Advocate Atkins, from the bench. Macarthur had arrived at the large red-brick courthouse with a quiver full of poison arrows to fire at Atkins, who only just managed to convene the hot, crowded courtroom before the accused leapt to the fore, demanding the judge remove himself from the bench. Atkins tried to shout him down, ruling him out of order, but Captain Kemp, one of six officers arrayed around the bench, told him to 'shut up and let Macarthur speak'. Pandemonium broke out, with the judge, the accused, the officers and the crowd of onlookers all bursting into argument. Atkins slipped out of his seat, keen to remove himself to a safe distance from his fellow judges while Macarthur lit into him with a stream of abuse from a prepared statement, ending with a rhetorical flourish directed to the six officers.

You have the eyes of an anxious public upon you, trembling for the safety of their property, their liberty, and their lives. To you has fallen the lot of deciding a point which perhaps involves the happiness or misery of millions.

Atkins suddenly yelled out from across the room that he would have Macarthur committed for contempt, at which Kemp raged, 'You commit! No Sir! I will commit you to gaol!' Atkins lit off through the mob, forgetting to take his papers with him in his panic. Seizing the indictment, the officers were able for the first time to see the case against Macarthur. Atkins, with the assistance of a convict attorney, George Crossley, had reached into a lucky dip of charges, including seditious libel of the Governor. The indictment read in part:

That the said John McArthur [sic] being a malicious and seditious man, and of a depraved mind and wicked and diabolical disposition, had been deceitfully, wickedly, and maliciously contriving and abetting against William Bligh, Esq., His Majesty's Governor-in-Chief of this territory.

Only the Strong

As Ross Fitzgerald and Mark Hearn point out, one irony was that in compiling the charges, Crossley and Atkins referred to an edition of *Blackstone's Commentaries on the Laws of England* edited by Professor Edward Christian, brother to Fletcher who had sent Bligh over the side of the *Bounty* so many years earlier.

Anthony Fenn Kemp, having seen off Atkins, called the court to order and, with his brother officers, ruled that the defendant's objections to the judge were 'good and lawful'. A series of notes passed up and down Bridge Street over the next few hours as the officers demanded Bligh replace Atkins and Bligh refused, demanding the return of the judge's papers. At three-thirty in the afternoon the officers wrote again, informing Bligh that Macarthur would not be spending any time in the lock-up, as they had it on good authority that the 'infamous' George Crossley was conspiring with some other ne'er-do-wells to murder him there. (Admittedly, Crossley was pretty infamous. One story had him placing a fly in the mouth of a corpse so as to claim there was life in the body as he held the corpse's hand to forge a signature to a dodgy will.) Bligh signed an arrest warrant for Macarthur and requested the corps' commander, Major Johnston, crawl out from under his hangover and restore some order to his men. Johnston begged off, citing serious injuries from his little accident following the mess dinner. Bligh spent the evening before the coup hunkered down at Government House. Macarthur attended to his designs for the trial, which went a little awry at nine the next morning when Provost Marshal William Gore caught up with him and executed Bligh's arrest warrant.

The Governor meanwhile, wrote again to Johnston, informing him that his officers seemed to be guilty of treason and thus would have to appear before a panel of magistrates. When Johnston read this letter, he said it 'occasioned temporary forgetfulness of my bruises, and I immediately set off in a Carriage to the Town' where, at five o'clock in the afternoon, he ordered the gaolkeeper to release John Macarthur. Macarthur returned the favour by writing out a letter imploring Johnston to remove the Governor, 'as every man's property, liberty and life were ... endangered by the alarming state of the colony'. It was signed by about 100 people, mostly well after the rebellion, undermining Johnston's defence that a huge congregation of the leading colonists had been desperately urging him on. Indeed, even his supporters had trouble naming more than a handful of civilians who gathered at the barracks late that afternoon, and all of them were Bligh's implacable enemies.

However, to seize power and then to wield it successfully, without retribution, the rebels needed at least the facade of legitimacy, a fig leaf, however small, behind which to hide their naked ambitions. Nobody really bought it of course. Macquarie was right on the money when he damned the corps on behalf of the King and packed the whole mutinous lot of them back to England. It was a fatal move for many of them. Having been twenty years in the mild climate of Sydney, the first northern winter killed off scores of the soldiers, their wives and children.

Johnston, who had been skilfully inveigled into leading the mutiny, was cashiered by his court martial. He was lucky to escape with his life. Allowed to return to New South Wales, he saw out his few remaining days with an ex-convict wife and a mountain of liquor and died from alcoholic excess. Bligh, the man he deposed, was never really vindicated. Of all the players in the drama of 1808, however, Macarthur himself perhaps best reveals the protean nature of power in Sydney, the way its form constantly

Only the Strong

shifts and changes. He remained in virtual exile in England for nearly seven years after Johnston's trial, beset by despair, physical pain and encroaching madness, and fearful of being arrested and tried for treason by Macquarie. In September 1817 he was finally reunited with his family in Australia. But he, like his arch-nemesis Bligh, could not surmount his own nature and it was not long before he was dabbling in politics and squabbling with governors once more. By 1821, even as he consolidated financial and political power again, fate schemed to ruin him. As his most generous biographer MH Ellis wrote:

> Those who dealt with Macarthur no longer dealt with a reasonable man. They dealt with a pain-racked fanatic, though few yet realised it. His ethical foundation was eroding. The curbs were off a nature distorted by suffering and a sense of grievance. He now had no mercy for those who stood in his way or did not follow him to the limit in his enterprises and obsessions.

As his plans for the Australian wool industry came to fruition and his long influence of colonial affairs was recognised with a seat on the Legislative Council, his once keen Machiavellian mind began to fail. Madness and paranoia stalked him through the halls of his Camden Park home. Plots, enemies and danger lurked everywhere. He accused his loyal wife, the loving and long-suffering Elizabeth, of adultery, and in 1832 he was finally declared insane. He died on 11 April 1834.

David Finney, a freed convict, was bashed to death on a cold day in June 1843. Rain, or the threat of it, lay hard on the city, as it had for most of that month. Thunderheads lumbered like sleepy elephants around a horizon which faded in and out of view as thick smudges of rain scudded low over the plains. A fierce southerly which had been blowing on and off for days moaned through the rigging and snapped the waterlogged canvas of more than seventy ships then resting in port.

Scores of Finney's former colleagues scuttled over the waterfront at the Cove that winter, cutting and laying stone for the new Circular Quay. The ringing of the convicts' picks and hammers was the only significant activity in Sydney at that point, however, as the town slouched through the worst depression in its history. Each day new bankruptcy notices appeared in the *Herald* as the colony's opulent merchants went belly-up with sixty, seventy and eighty thousand pounds worth of debt to their names. The newspapers all carried long reams of adverts for auctions where the canny shopper could pick up boatloads of luxury goods at crippling mark-downs. Shareholders and directors met constantly, fretting on omens and storm warnings which seemed to promise that worse was on the way. The week Finney was killed, the shareholders of the Sydney Banking Company fought through the rain to meet at the banking house on George Street to consider winding up the business.

The bank, which had problems with sticky-fingered staff, had been drawn into the crazed speculative boom of the late 1830s, only to spear-dive into the crash of the early 1840s. This was the same catastrophe which gave Caroline Chisholm her start in migration and charity relief, as thousands of poor British workers arrived in a port where the economy had flatlined. The tangled roots of the crisis ran deep. An insanely successful wool industry had sucked in millions of pounds of British capital during the

Only the Strong

1830s. The colonial government spent a million pounds of its own money importing poor families on bounty ships as labour for the pastoral industry. These gross tidal flows of capital through the entrepot of Sydney excited fantastic growth in what we now call the service sector, with enormous fortunes made by auctioneers and banks and the soft-handed professional classes who serviced them. They in turn poured their wealth into luxurious new town-houses and estates, while the men they employed – hundreds of carpenters, stonemasons, blacksmiths and coopers, painters, brick-layers and engineers – all spent their generous wages in new shops and taverns, filling the pockets of publicans and waiters, cooks and coach drivers, tailors, barbers, shoemakers and brewers. These men and their families also needed houses, and hundreds of rough two bedroom humpies mushroomed out of the mud around the city fringes. The streets roared with life and madness and greed and the gritty red dust thrown up by carts and horses racing to the waterfront to deliver teetering mountains of wool and wheat and load up with even larger piles of furniture and fine goods for the interior. Speculators gambled their newly found fortunes buying land and cargo which they simply sold on to the next greedy fool, who again sold it on and on and on. And when the game had spiralled out of everyone's reach it kept spiralling still. Away into the immense, timeless antipodean sky, fuelled by credit which was advanced by banks, controlled by the very same mer-chants who'd grown so wealthy in a giddy round of commercial poker where the stakes kept soaring long after everyone had run out of chips. The rocket soared up and up until, of course, it burst. A depression in Britain wiped out demand for Australian wool. El Niño's hot breath ruined the harvest for two years. Convict trans-portation to New South Wales ended after local agitation, taking with it all of the home government's associated spending and, just as importantly, the settlers' supply of cheap labour. The money from land sales which the colonial government had held in local banks was siphoned off, spent on shipping over thousands of migrants, most of whom turned out to be completely unsuited to rural employment. The banks called in their own markers. And the giant, confused, untenable, creaking mountain of debt on which everything rested suddenly slipped and crashed.

Sydney in that bleak wet June had a sombre, somewhat bucolic appearance. The great surge of development which would be fuelled by the gold rush lay another decade in the future. The city, while much progressed from the simple, handsome township Macquarie had left, was still largely contained within the valley of the Tank Stream. Cows, goats and sheep wandered and grazed at its fringes. The principal streets were still impassable in bad weather. Some factories, tanneries and breweries had been established around the swamps to the west, but the economy had not diversified or matured into the massively complex structure it would later become. One big hit was enough to stop it dead. The fusillade of blows which rained down in the first years of the 1840s simply made the rubble jump. By the winter of 1843 hundreds of building workers were out of jobs. Dozens of half-finished cottages – in one of which the broken, bloodied figure of Finney would shortly be found – were scattered amongst the rotting timbers of others which had collapsed and been abandoned by bankrupt developers. The homes of working men were stripped bare as landlords, unable to extract any cash for their rent, took furniture and even clothing in lieu.

Ben Sutherland, an unemployed upholsterer retained by the government to survey the working class districts, encountered destitute families where nobody had eaten in days. He described the

Only the Strong

house of a silversmith in Castlereagh Street where just a few broken sticks of furniture remained scattered about the floor. The man's children were all crying from hunger and his wife was dressed in miserable tattered rags which had been patched so many times they were beyond any further mending. In the house of a labourer named McLeod he found a number of children with the distended bellies and dull eyes of starvation, chewing at dirty potato parings they had scavenged from the street. At another address Sutherland talked to an immigrant named Turton who was unable to leave his hovel. Having given all his clothes to the landlord and shopkeepers in trying to maintain his family, he had been left naked.

There were, perhaps, two shafts of light to penetrate this gloom. In the *Colonial Observer* of 14 June, Edward Campbell advised the hungry, shivering inhabitants of Sydney that new equipment for 'roasting, cooling and grinding' coffee was available at his family's George Street premises. It produced a rich, heady brew, far superior to anything then available in the colony, and was so popular that Campbell roasted twice daily. 'A luxury the public had not the benefit of before,' he said, and very much appreciated by the continentals then resident in Sydney, 'particularly those who have had the advantage of Parisian residence, where coffee is brought to the very acme of perfection . . .' The same paper carried extensive reports of another innovation which was sure to raise the town's depleted spirits: the colony's first election. The long struggle between Government House and the town's rival power centres – a replay at high speed and in miniature of hundreds of years of European political development – was inevitably heading from the autocratic to the democratic. The despotic executive powers of Phillip and his successors had been crimped, if only a little, by the creation of a Legislative Council and some legal reform in 1823. It wasn't much of a democratic revolution though. The council consisted of about half a dozen of the Governor's best buddies. They were appointed by him and had the privilege of offering advice which he would then ignore. The number of good old boys who got to take vice-regal tea and crumpets while being ignored increased over the years, as did the range of stuff they got to be ignored over. In 1843, however, all that changed with the first *sort of* democratic elections to a council which *sort of* had some power of its own.

It wasn't a smooth transition, however, as David Finney discovered around eleven o'clock on polling day when a fearsome mob of drunken partisans, disenfranchised Irishmen, hungry labourers and opportunistic criminals fell on him at Brickfield Hill and clubbed and kicked him to death. A man named Mooney, a wheelwright, was arrested and tried for the murder, but so confused was the attack that despite a large number of witnesses, the court was unable to discover who struck the fatal blow, or indeed who struck any of the blows. Finney's injuries were massive, and yet all confined to the skull, indicating a frenzied but well-directed assault. His right eye was jellied, the temple on that side of his head obscenely pulped. A long ragged wound had been torn open over his left ear, exposing the gristle and bone beneath and affording the doctors who performed the post-mortem a good view of the massive eggshell fracturing which ran from left to right across the orbits, even before they peeled back the skin and opened the skull to discover a large pool of dark, thickly coagulated blood on the surface and at the base of the brain. Bashed unconscious and left for dead in the mud, he was dragged into the unfinished shell of a nearby house and left there, sightlessly staring up into the day's

Only the Strong

bleak drizzle. Five hours later, with just a weak flicker of life in his undamaged eye, he was picked up and carried to the Benevolent Asylum where Dr Cuthill, assessing the damage, decided 'no medical skill could have saved the poor man's life'. He died shortly after.

The mob which did for Finney was one of many which roamed at will through the town on election day, forming, splitting, clashing and merging like frenzied amoeba of political violence. Most of the fury seems to have been directed at the supporters of William Wentworth, the eventual victor. Although a fiery liberal in his younger days, Wentworth increasingly found himself snuggled up with the champions of landed wealth. He was a fascinating character, the product of a bit of raunchy business below decks between the disgraced surgeon D'Arcy Wentworth, one of the builders of the Rum Hospital, and convicted clothes thief Catherine Crowley. D'Arcy made a pile in the colony, where he worked as a merchant, surgeon and police chief, despite allegations that he had ridden as a highwayman in the old country and been forced to Sydney by the subsequent scandal. His wealth purchased a classical education for his son and fuelled William's acute desire to be accepted into Sydney finest salons and drawing rooms, a desire which foundered on the town's rigid segregation of former convicts and the freeborn pastoral elite. William never forgave those ignorant snobs, seizing at any chance to avenge the insults they heaped upon his parents. Arrogant, obstinate, mischievous and contemptible, the pastoralists – with their wagons circled tightly around their mad leader John Macarthur – often winced under the lash of Wentworth's caustic rhetoric.

The pastoral elite, of course, were themselves mostly one generation removed from embarrassment and owed their high station to land stolen from the black natives and worked by white slaves or the poorest indentured migrants. What they lacked in breeding, however, they more than made up for in self-delusion and hypocrisy. An aristocratic junta, Wentworth called them, 'who monopolised all situations of power, dignity and emolument'. When the enlightened Macquarie broke their oligarchy and promoted the interests of the emancipated convicts, he 'instantly drew on himself their unrelenting and systematic hostility'. But, as Wentworth explained, with Macquarie initially enjoying the support of London, the wily curs in Sydney eased their public protest against his liberal policy 'although it was still as repugnant as ever to their feelings'. Instead they shifted ground and, while praising the soundness of the principle, leapt on every chance to condemn its application.

> Accordingly, every emancipist who was fortunate enough to become the object of the Governor's countenance and protection, was instantly beset by this pack in full cry. Not content with hunting up and giving false colour to every little blemish, which they could discover in the individual's history, they scrupled not to circulate as facts every species of calumny to which an unbridled and vituperate ingenuity could give birth.

D'Arcy had suffered at the hands of this 'vituperate ingenuity', when JT Bigge, whose commission of inquiry put a bullet into Macquarie's administration, repeated the slander that Wentworth the elder had been packed off to Sydney in chains rather than as a free man (even if under a dark cloud). In reply, Wentworth Jnr savaged Bigge the 'booby Commissioner', challenged anyone repeating the lie to back their words up with a duelling pistol and

Only the Strong

set out to destroy the power and privileges of those high-born dogs who had cocked their mangy legs on his beloved father's name. Ironically, while his unrelenting assault on ruling-class interests laid the foundations of Australian democracy, he grew to mistrust and oppose that democracy as his own fortune and power waxed fat. The legacy of his opposition, and of the hostility of the pastoral lobby to those rude popular forces which reached their highest pitch in the metropolis of Sydney, was 150 years of laissez-faire chaos within the cauldron of the city.

Legal study in England prepared Wentworth for his assault on the citadels of power in Sydney, but the polish of elite schooling could not disguise the roughness of his personality. A shambling, raw-boned man, a commanding orator, he inherited his old man's good looks and powerful physique. He presents in a later-life portrait which now hangs in Parliament as a barrel-chested elder statesman, a sad-eyed prophet with a mass of white leonine hair and a truly Roman sense of his own importance. The artist was kind, or perhaps Wentworth's wife scolded him into dressing properly for the sitting, which shows him in a dark, natty-looking jacket and a handsome if slightly excessive bow tie. His daily appearance was more eccentric, especially for one so wealthy. Shabby old corduroys and an unfortunate, ill-fitting morning coat were his preferred ensemble in Parliament. A generous entry in the *Australian Dictionary of Biography* describes him as a 'Gulliver in Lilliput', Elizabethan in spirit, 'splendid and defiant'. A deep sense of history, an enduring faith in the classical values and a love of Burke's splendid oratory, with its 'evocation of the greatness of Augustan Rome and England' were his guiding intellectual lights. But his passions were more Byronic and violent and warred within him his whole life. Manning Clark, who seems to have been unable to forgive him for abandoning the lower classes, wrote that 'it was as though the gods had planted in him great talents and fatal flaws for their sport'. Clark opened up on him with both barrels in the second volume of his history, describing the first member for Sydney as being possessed of a 'rancour and malevolence in his heart towards all who stood in his way'. Honourable members of the British Parliament, learned judges and that other mighty ego-maniac John Macarthur all felt the hot blast of his wild temper when they dared slight him or his family name. Macarthur made himself a target when, having agreed to allow young Wentworth the honour of his daughter's hand, he withdrew the offer. 'I will pay him off in his own coin,' growled a wounded, incensed William to his father.

Manning Clark thought the slovenly and disrespectful younger Wentworth had largely squandered his great gifts in vulgar vendettas by the time he took his seat in the Legislative Council.

His air of faded grandeur seemed to have had its root in no common soul. At times he looked like a tamed tiger about to sidle from one end of his cage to the other for a chance to claw those who teased or enraged him. On such occasions his face became quite florid and was marked by a look of wildness which often comes over the face of a man for whom destroying enemies is the great sport of life.

Wentworth could have sat in the Council many years before but had refused to be appointed to the position, arguing that the early, unelected form of the Council was a 'wretched mongrel substitute' for an elected assembly. He called it an 'anomalous and unnatural creation', before setting out to obtain its destruction. His early

Only the Strong

adult life was devoted to curtailing the autocratic powers of Government House, and his public career was marked by decades of bruising and sometimes savage confrontation with a succession of governors as he sought to claw away the armoured authority of that office. His feud with Ralph Darling, governor from 1825–31, was an epic confrontation unrivalled since the clash of Bligh and Macarthur twenty years before.

During the reign of Darling's predecessor, Governor Brisbane, Wentworth and his partner Dr Robert Wardell had grasped the nettle of press censorship and set up a newspaper, without reference or deference to Government House. Sydney had never known a free press where those violent shifts and fault lines of opinion which constantly cleaved its small, incestuous society could find expression, and the Colonial Office in London was none too keen on the idea. Brisbane, however, was all for the experiment and thus audacity triumphed, much to the chagrin of Darling, the cold, hard-hearted militarist who quickly crossed swords with Wentworth and Wardell and the crop of rambunctious newspapers which sprang up in the space they cleared. Darling, who had wondered back in London 'whether he would have the power to silence' this 'vulgar ill-bred' demagogue, discovered that he did not. When Wentworth and his fellow editors attacked the Governor, stirring up trouble and agitating for trial by jury and an elected assembly, Darling attempted to destroy them by imposing a tax on the papers and empowering the courts to banish any recalcitrant press men from the colony. He went after Wardell and Wentworth's publication, the *Australian*, for seditious libel, but his hapless, ill-prepared legal counsel were demolished in court by the 'effrontery and talent' of the defendants.

It was an exemplary victory. Macquarie would have banged

them away in irons. Bligh, at a guess, would have hung them by their thumbs and screamed incomprehensibly at them. For Darling, whose whole career was a testament to unswerving military obedience, the challenge to his authority was anathema. But there was little he could do. It was a long time since Government House had been the seat of all power in Sydney. Even though the weak, faux liberal institution of the unelected Legislative Council was more a symbolic curb on Darling's will, it was a potent sign of the accelerating drift of power away from his office. As JJ Auchmuty puts it, since neither a ship nor a prison makes any pretence at democracy, the personalities of the governors were of dominating importance for the first fifty years of the colony's existence. For all their problems and the constant, niggling challenges to their rule, the governors' decisions determined how the inhabitants of Sydney would live their lives. When Ralph Darling was sent packing in 1831 that was no longer the case. Wentworth celebrated his recall to London with an awesomely debauched open house at his Vaucluse property. Over 4000 Sydneysiders trekked out along the rough path of the South Head road to launch themselves on a mountain of free food and grog. Gin, beer and thousands of loaves of bread were laid on while a whole bullock and twelve sheep were slowly roasted, rotating over the coals on an enormous spit. The party kicked on until dawn the next day, cementing Wentworth's place in the hearts of the common folk.

The Wentworth of 1843, however, while still a firebrand, was not the much-loved people's tribune of his youth. His increasing wealth had fostered a commonality of interest with the same freeborn gentry he had made a career of tormenting. And his contest with Captain O'Connell, a favourite of the Catholic working class, inflamed sectarian feeling amongst those very same starving,

Only the Strong

unemployed artisans who were denied a chance to vent their frustrations by the restrictive nature of early voting laws. Only wealthy white adult males were entitled to vote in 1843, excluding two-thirds of the colony's men and all the women from any say in the first parliament. Desperation denied one form of expression will usually find another and the murder of Finney was but one outburst of political fury that week. The wonder is that the authorities, who had long harboured fears of mob uprising amongst the poor – and specifically the Irish poor – didn't foresee the trouble and prepare.

The nomination ceremony for the city electorates, held on Tuesday 13 June, had spun out of control when a crowd of seven or eight thousand (more than double the number of eligible voters) had swarmed into Macquarie Place where the hustings had been erected. The huge, raucous crowd, which seems to have included most of the town's adult population, jammed the nearby streets, causing terrible confusion. They spilled over the balconies and out of the windows of surrounding buildings and blocked all access to the platform where the candidates were to be nominated. In the days before traffic, machinery and high-rise buildings, the roar of the masses must have reached to the outskirts of town. In the immediate vicinity the noise was so great as to drown out all else, especially as fist fights and vicious brawls erupted within sections of the crowd, transmitting their violent energy through the close-packed unwashed hordes.

Unaware of the scenes which awaited them, William Wills, the Lord Mayor's secretary, who had exhausted himself preparing for this day, recorded his weary pleasure at seeing the official procession to Macquarie Place, where his boss was supposedly in charge of proceedings. 'The mayor was in his carriage drawn by four beautiful greys,' he wrote in his journal, 'accompanied by two of the aldermen, the Town Clerk and his secretary – the turnout altogether would not have disgraced the Lord Mayor of London.' The scene at the hustings, unfortunately, was a disgrace to Sydney. Hundreds of supporters of each candidate had marched on the scene with bands playing and flags flying. Wills had thought to control access to the small wooden hustings platform by issuing tickets to the candidates and a few supporters; but, spying each other across the sea of top hats, cloth caps, suit jackets and workmen's bibs, the contenders charged the steps instead. The loud, constant rumble cycled up into a thunderous roar as they met and fought for possession of the platform. Newspaper reports of the wild melee vary according to the sympathies and biases of the proprietors, but it seems O'Connell's men gained the ascendancy and repelled the attacks of Wentworth's crew with all the savage, bloodthirsty glee of any well-entrenched defenders seeing off a disorganised, inflamed rabble. Wentworth's running mate Dr Bland was nearly choked to death by one assailant and thrown bodily from the decking into the nineteenth century mosh pit. About two to three hundred brawlers were engaged at one time, with random bursts of ugliness flaring elsewhere in the huge assembly, especially around the omnibus where brewing baron Robert Cooper's low-rent supporters fell on any opposition with muddied hobnailed boots while Cooper harangued them from above.

Cooper, whom Wills described as 'a huge tall man of most repulsive visage and dress', provided the campaign with both comic relief and a frisson of Victorian horror. He was transported for receiving stolen goods and Wills described him as 'a most illiterate fellow [who] has not two ideas beyond distilling gin, at which he is so successful as to be one of the richest men in NSW'. Cooper

Only the Strong

drew his support from the lowest reaches of the city, from the poorest workers and the hardest drinking, most unruly criminals. When his legions marched they did so behind loaves of bread spitted on pikes to demonstrate their champion's concern for the everyday struggles of the underfed. To the city's burghers and merchants, those soggy loaves must have looked uncomfortably like the severed heads of the French aristos during the republican uprising of the previous century. However, while the underfed could march and parade to their hearts' content, they could not vote. The softening of their woes would have to rely on the tender mercies of the propertied few, represented by Wentworth and Bland, and as these fine chaps were apparently in favour of importing Asian protoslaves to drive down the price of labour, it's perhaps not surprising the lower orders jacked up when, at about one in the afternoon on polling day, it became obvious that neither Cooper nor their other favourite, the dashing populist officer O'Connell, were likely to get a guernsey in the first elective assembly.

The worst trouble broke out, as might be expected, in the slum district of the Rocks. Polling booths had been erected there, high above the harbour, on the boggy, windswept crest on which the colony's flag staff stood. Kent Street runs at the foot of this hill, past the Lord Nelson Hotel, now one of the oldest pubs in Sydney, then one of the biggest buildings at Millers Point. A clutch of cottages, a windmill, some shipbuilding yards, wharves and a couple of more substantial terraces complete the picture in JS Prout's 1843 sketch of the area. Voters making the hard climb up the hill passed long-horned goats grazing amongst massive sandstone boulders. The whole area had been 'a waste howling wilderness' until recently. As the count progressed a large, ill-tempered group who had gathered on the heights turned nasty. Sneers and threatening stares directed at opposing campaign workers turned into snarls and insults, which quickly escalated into an uglier, two-fisted debate. The mob, who were allegedly fired up with lashings of Robert Cooper's gin, turned on Wentworth and Bland's supporters. They attacked the booths and workers, demolishing everything and scattering the terrified staffers. John Jones, a ship owner and Council alderman, was besieged, his sister screaming, 'Murder! Murder!' as someone (reports vary as to whom) ran down the steep, slippery banks of the hill to Jones's own wharf to alert a band of whalers and seamen to their boss's distress. They armed themselves with whale lances, blubber spades, axes and harpoons before charging up the slopes to do battle. Jones meanwhile had run through one of the attackers, John Holohan, with a spring blade concealed in a walking stick, jabbing the man in the elbow and driving the spike home till it emerged from his upper arm. Holohan later claimed he had been standing quietly with his hands in his pockets when the agitated ship owner had knifed him. Jones in reply said that Holohan had come at him with a club. The whole convulsive, hysterical circus was smashed by a charge of the mounted police who thundered into the riot and let fly on all sides. No sooner had they broken up this mob when the heavily armed whalers from Jones's ships arrived and the police had to wheel around and sail into them as well. Again, reports of the panic differ according to the prejudices of the journal or paper reporting the scene, but they all agree that around about this point, Jones himself fled the area, either to escape his attackers or the police. Either way, he legged it successfully, flying down the slopes and leaping into a small boat which carried him to safety on the other side of the harbour.

Only the Strong

The angry, frustrated mob streamed down the slopes of Flag Staff Hill and dispersed through the muddy streets of the town, quickly meeting up with other friends and allies in a rolling series of riots which surged around the city all day, killing David Finney and laying waste to dozens of houses and buildings whose owners had the audacity to display the colours of Wentworth's victorious ticket. One reporter suggested that 'a delusion had got into the heads of some Irishmen' that rioting on election day was not a punishable offence, possibly because their preferred candidate was the son of the colony's military commander, Sir Maurice O'Connell. Chances are, though, things would have got out of hand even without this piece of muddle-headed sophistry. Politics involves a lot of symbolic action in democracies, even unformed neophyte democracies. The ballot on which so many rest their hopes is as much a device for channelling and defusing the wild spirits of a population as it is a means of apportioning power. Locked out of the process at a time when the hard earned comforts and certainties of their lives were under violent assault from the depression, it's not surprising the proles and the *untermenschen* reacted so aggressively.

Nor were the punches coming solely from one direction. Early in the day a rambling crew of Wentworth's supporters were only too happy to rub up hard against anybody they found wearing the green ribbons of their enemy. Isolated fist fights and head kickings flared all over the central city area as agents of the two groups met. Hyde Park, then a vast expanse of open ground known as the Race Course, was the scene of a massive brawl which saw the end of any effective presence by the Wentworth contingent. 'After this,' reported the *Australasian Chronicle*, 'the partisans of O'Connell and Cooper mustered in such strength that their opponents were unable to keep the field.' They then turned on the nearby homes of Wentworth supporters such as Sam Lyons, the auctioneer. Ripping palings from fences and wrenching stones from the ground, the rabble launched a fusillade of improvised missiles at the auctioneer's handsome villa, smashing up to 100 plate-glass windows. They attacked Dr Whittle as he rode his carriage down Pitt Street; devastated the Australian Hotel in Lower George Street; and fought their way into the house of Isaac Moss, driving his wife and children from their bedrooms. Here and there leaders on horseback charged ahead to keep an eye out for the mounted police. The inflamed mob howled and made for the polling booths at the Race Course, destroying Wentworth and Bland's little camp as they had done on Flag Staff Hill. At this point, according to the *Herald*'s man, the mounted police arrived and were joined by Captain Innes who asked their sergeant to help him capture the ringleader. Putting their spurs to the flanks they charged, but one of the rioters swung at Innes's horse with a club, catching it with a heavy blow to the jaw at which the animal reared up and took off. Before Innes could regain control, he had run down a woman wearing a green ribbon, further enraging the mob. The captain steadied his horse and returned to the unconscious woman, crying out for someone to get her a doctor. But he was soon surrounded by angry men, all bearing clubs and sticks, yelling that they would kill him. He managed to break through the press and crush, galloping off to the protection of the mounted police and asking them to join him in a charge to disperse the crowd. Volleys of rocks and fence palings followed him and the sergeant begged him to flee, fearing the mob would finish him off. Innes demurred as the rioters charged the police, turning his mount and making for the edge of the park as more stones and clubs sailed through the air, thudding into his back and his horse. He put the charger to the fence rails and cleared them in one regal bound, 'wooden leg and all'. As night fell, it was feared the depredations would worsen and hundreds of troops from the 80th Regiment marched down from the barracks. Retracing some of the Rum Corps' steps, they fanned out through the town to secure the peace. However, while armed troops, bad weather and alcoholic stupor helped return a semblance of order to the streets of Sydney, the creation of an elected government was to bring chaos.

It may be important that Sydney was, in effect, a *tabula rasa*. Unlike the cities of the Old World, no slow sedimentation of history lay beneath its streets. It had no long-established power structure. It was what JW McCarty would call a commercial city, a pure product of capitalism's global expansion in the nineteenth century. Old World centres founded in Roman or mediaeval times grew organically, their modern forms still influenced by a patch-work of buildings and streets, canals and bridges, and political, economic, military and religious institutions established hundreds or even thousands of years in the past. In contrast, the cities of the New World sprang into being, often at a single, identifiable moment in time, to find themselves according to McCarty 'fully exposed to the levelling effects of the expanding world capitalist economy'. Sydney shares in this a common heritage with the metropolitan centres of other recently settled areas in America, Canada and New Zealand. No gradual, millennium-long transfer of power from rural hinterland to urban core marked their evolution. Nor did industrialisation prompt their emergence on the world scene, as it had in Manchester with its cotton mills, or Pittsburgh with its steel foundries. Rather, the fantastic growth of the commercial city was fuelled by economic globalisation, hundreds of years before the term's currently fashionable incarnation. Sydney has always been a global city, subject to the ebb and flow of the world's capital, even when it was little more than a semirural village and a couple of rickety wooden wharves.

It was those wharves that were important. They were the point at which the city's inhabitants touched the vast, roaring river of world trade and were either dragged under and drowned or came away clutching ingots of silver snatched from the current. Manufacturing, in contrast, was not important in the early days of the commercial city. It followed rather than inspired urbanisation. In 1843 Sydney's factories were still an inconsequential part of its economy. Isolation made it necessary to produce locally simple goods like shoes and hats, and industry, such as it was, first arose to meet these needs, only diversifying with the growth of the rural sector. Milling, brewing, glass and pottery making, spinning and boatbuilding all played early roles but no matter how large or sophisticated the town's factories became, the primary role of the city was as a base 'for the opening up of new lands'; an assessment which was passionately embraced by the colony's leading citizens, that aristocratic junta of wool-growing princes which Wentworth alternately attacked, envied or defended, depending on his own situation at the time. They believed Sydney existed simply to provide the means of moving their wool into the overseas market as cheaply and efficiently as possible, and they had the money and power to ensure this vision was not challenged.

All through the last century and up until the Second World War, the rich of Sydney and indeed of all New South Wales, were drawn overwhelmingly from the ranks of these pastoralists and, to a lesser extent, from the merchants who serviced them. Bill Rubinstein,

Only the Strong

writing in the *Australian Economic History Review*, undertook the substantial task of ranking the State's top fifty wealth holders in each five-year period between 1817 and 1939. Graziers and land-owners topped the survey at every stage, followed by their commercial brethren in exporting, warehousing and somewhat less often in retailing. It was only in the 1920s and 1930s, with the rise of large-scale manufacturing and mass consumer society, that other sources of significant wealth really established themselves. Before then agriculture had no rivals as the big rock candy mountain of the antipodes. That's not really surprising. What is surprising in Rubinstein's analysis was how *poor* the rich were. Perhaps the single most important statement which can be made about the very wealthy in Australia, he wrote, was their very low level of wealth, at least comparatively speaking.

By 1845 New York was home to 113 millionaires. By 1892, while Australia was belly-crawling through another of its culture-defining economic catastrophes, over 4000 American millionaires were sitting on their treasure chests, cackling with avaricious glee. However, in the entire period between 1788 and 1939 Rubinstein could find only eight bona-fide millionaire estates in New South Wales, two of which were probated largely in England. Until the gold rush and the long boom of the late nineteenth century, any man who could lay his paws on £10 000 would rank amongst the wealthiest on the continent. John Macarthur, for instance, left an estate of only £40 000. This in a country with one of the highest per capita levels of income in the world.

Rubinstein posits a couple of obvious explanations such as the minuscule size of the local market, limited local capital, state-owned railways and intercolonial trade barriers. A more intriguing possibility, however, lies in cultural factors. Many of the wealthy came from the 'shabby genteel' class of England and Scotland, who were not big risk takers but rather innate conservatives, a group Wakefield disparaged as being of the twentieth rank in society. They came in the 1820s, as had the men of the Rum Corps, seeking opportunities denied them at home. James Henty, one of the more substantial early migrants, set forth the rationale in a letter to his brothers.

What can we do in England with £10,000 amongst all of us ... brought up as we all have been unless we chose to descend many steps in the scale of Society and which our feelings could ill stand, having at the same time an opportunity of doing as well and perhaps considerably better in New South Wales, under British Dominion and a fine climate ... How many thousands are there who go to India for twenty years certain of a pestilential climate under a burning sun and for what? Why, to secure themselves (if they live) £400 or £500 a year for the remainder of their lives in England. At the expiration of ten years in New South Wales I shall be much disappointed if we individually are not worth double that sum ... and immediately we get there we shall be placed in the First Rank in Society, a circumstance which must not be overlooked as it will tend most materially to our comfort and future advantage?

The free settlers of means in the 1820s and 1830s were practical and robust but not necessarily gifted or innovative. They tended to ferret out a niche and settle into it, seeking as much indulgence and help from the government as they could. The conservatism of these leading figures is difficult to comprehend across the arc of 200 years. It was a conservatism not so much monolithic as simply

Only the Strong

ubiquitous. There were many divisions within their closed little world but the fracture lines ran over shared ground, part of which was 'a loathing of taxation too absolute for the twentieth century mind readily to comprehend', and of course an intense fear of the mob rule of democracy. What state would you be in, asked Governor Denison, were you to throw political power into the hands of such an ignorant and vicious population as existed in New South Wales?

The image which entranced the colonial elite was of the landed gentry of England, whose style of life they sought to impose on New South Wales, in spite of the drastic dissimilarity between English and Australian rural conditions, and to the great detriment of those who lived as blue and white collar workers in the rapidly growing metropolis on Sydney Harbour. The dozen or so noble villas which appeared atop the ridge at Woolloomooloo in the 1830s were material expression of the new elite's affinity for old-money expressions of style and dominance; the titles, the veneration of landed estates, the hierarchical attitudes, the myth of gracious living, as GC Bolton put it. So powerful was this vision of arcadian splendour to the tatty yeomen who chased it that *any* change was perceived as a threat. On New Year's Day in 1850 for instance, the *Herald* reflected smugly on the steady progress for which the town and colony could thank the settled and somnolent pastoral industry. Not for New South Wales the explosion of California's gold rush. When the precious metal was subsequently discovered the paper was aghast. The colony was about to be 'cursed with a gold-digging mania'. James Macarthur, John's son, an otherwise considerate and intelligent conservative, was so freaked out by the menace of gold that he wrote to the Colonial Secretary urging 'the government [to] temporarily prohibit all mining' and halt 'the deranging & upsetting of our social system to its very foundation'.

This social system would have warmed the heart of his crazy old man. James's brother Edward once explained the naked workings of this 'social pyramid' as being determined by 'an all pervading law – they who possess Capital will be always proportionately few in relation to the numbers to be employed'. Any undue departure from this happy circumstance – happy for James and Edward that is – could only be destructive. 'The Capital and substance of the Community will be squandered and the elements of its prosperity dissipated.' The proper role of those drunken, rioting, unemployed Irishmen who tore up the town on election day was not to sit around in their grimy hovels waiting for an improvement in the building industry. Their role was to chase sheep around the Macarthurs' paddocks, to harness themselves to a plough, to fell trees or engage in some other worthy rustic pursuit. They were to think of themselves as the solid foundation on which a kind of wonderful plantation economy would erect a civilized superstructure. They weren't to aspire to anything more than this. It would be 'destructive'. And they were certainly never, ever to contemplate taking power themselves. The very idea was an affront to the natural order.

James developed this line of thinking with reference to rival owners of capital – and competing centres of power – when he published an extended treatise on the constitution of the colony in London in 1837. His book argued that in a convict colony mere riches did not necessarily qualify the wealth holder to sit amongst the first rank of society and guide its development. Convict innkeepers might have as much money as a respectable landholder, perhaps more, but that did not make them better or even equal

Only the Strong

men. A sense of honour and virtue was lacking. Unfortunately some of these disreputable characters and their bastard offspring were beginning to think 'that the colony was *theirs by right*, and that the emigrant settlers were interlopers upon the soil'. These presumptuous chaps needed to be excluded from power. The destiny of the colony had to be left in the capable hands of the gentry, those two or three hundred families whose great estates marched 'south and west from the capital' and were centred around Camden, Campbelltown, Goulburn and Bathurst and in the river valleys of the Macquarie and the Hunter.

Michael Roe characterises the men who headed these families as the lords of Australia. Distinguished lineages were uncommon, but many had gleaned some idea of leadership in the army or navy. Their elegant mansions were filled with fine crystal and china. The walls were adorned with original oil paintings of British heroes like the Duke of Wellington, the first Earl Grey and Sir Walter Scott. London's merchants provided French-polished mahogany dining chairs, rolls of the finest quality Brussels carpet and 'rich crimson silk and worsted bell ropes with tassels and rosettes'. They rode together in hunt clubs; masters, servants and twenty hounds tearing through the fields of Pennant Hills. They dined and played billiards at the Australian Club, where 'election was by ballot, and one black ball in ten would exclude a candidate'. They read the latest English journals at the Australian Library, which was just as exclusive. They built churches and chapels for the Anglican cause and established private schools where their sons might not be trained simply in Latin and mathematics but also in leadership and 'that gentlemanly tone and bearing which are difficult of acquirement in a Colony so peculiarly situated as this'.

The *tone* of their lives, the style with which they comported themselves, was almost as important to the *nouveau riche* as the practical business of amassing and protecting their fortunes and influence, not surprising given the sort of low-rent villains like Robert Cooper who shared or even exceeded the landed barons' wealth, if not their sense of decorum and pretensions to breeding. In a new, wide-open society where everything was up for grabs, these members of the bourgeosie cast around for ways to express their superiority over the less worthy and settled on the concept of respectability. Cooper and even Wentworth might be commercially successful, but one was thought a pirate and the other the son of a damn'd whore and a highwayman. The great mass of the populace, it goes without saying, were not even worthy of the consideration given to these parvenu. In reply Wentworth, who could be a real trouserman and party animal when the mood took him, mocked society's obsession with respectability in his book of 1824. 'Scandal appears to be the favourite amusement to which idlers resort to kill time and prevent *ennui*,' he wrote 'and, consequently, the same families are eternally changing from friendship to hostility, and from hostility back to friendship again.'

Nonetheless, those who took it seriously took it very seriously indeed. During the 1830s the *Herald* could work itself into an apoplectic spasm at the prospect of former convicts throwing back gin slings and cucumber sandwiches at Governor Bourke's garden soirees. Government House was the focal point of society with Lady Denison recording that 'Being, or not being, admitted here is, in this place, considered as the great criterion of a person's social position.' Good breeding and high station guaranteed access, indeed demanded it. Colonel Mundy, deputy commander of the forces under Sir Maurice O'Connell, had hardly unpacked his bags on arriving in Sydney before awaking to discover 'a mound of

Only the Strong

visiting cards, interlaid with numerous invitations to dinners and evening parties'. For others, gaining that entry was more problematic, as the merchant GF Davidson discovered.

> To obtain admission to good society in Sydney when my family first arrived there was no easy matter. Not that there was any lack of it in the place, but the residents were, very properly, shy of strangers, unless provided with testimonials as to their respectability.

The testimonial, a letter of introduction, could be a passport to the city's self-serving oligarchy, but naturally one had to be very careful from whom one sought testimonials, as a correspondent for Charles Dickens's journal, *Household Words*, discovered.

> Every man who emigrates has a large packet of letters of introduction ... I had about thirty ... Selecting one addressed to the manager of a joint-stock bank, I set out with the rest in my pocket. The gentleman received me graciously, read my letter deliberately, asked me every conceivable question about my birth, parentage, education, expectations, relatives, pursuits and intentions, amount of capital in hand and in prospects, and ended by observing that no doubt I should find something to suit me; in the mean time, the best thing I could do was to lay out my money in shares in his bank; luckily, I did *not* take his advice. Having answered all his questions, I put my packet of letters into his hands and inquired their value.
>
> 'Oh,' he said, 'mere sham bank notes I suspect; however, let us sort them. In the first place, understand, young gentleman, we are divided into at least three sets, but you have only to do

with two, the Free Colonists and the Emancipists. Many of the latter are wealthy, educated, and personally respectable; but if you mean to associate with the other party, you must avoid the Emancipists, except in mere trade transactions, in the same way as you would a black bear in New York. If you visit one, you cannot visit the other. There are half a dozen of your letters good . . . and as to these, which are addressed to wealthy people, but quite out of the pale of society, I should recommend you to burn them.'

The gentry did not merely perceive themselves to be at the social pinnacle of Sydney, they 'sought to impress this principle on the legal and political institutions of their adopted country'. Of course their preferred model for society was a sort of vaguely despotic rural theme park, while the centre of their world was a rapidly modernising commercial sea port which was about to endure fifty years of fantastic, unrestrained growth. The gentry themselves, however, did not fare so well. Many were wiped out by the depression of the 1840s. Many more, unable to compete with the squatters who simply seized land, were forced to abandon their expensive estates and strike out beyond the boundaries of settlement as squatters themselves. Here they entered a much more primitive, hostile world, coarsened by the violence of an undeclared war between natives and invaders. Here says Roe, were men acting without grace or restraint or care for the public good, their struggle with the Aborigines – exemplified by the massacre at Myall Creek – reflecting not only contempt for the law but crude ugliness of thought and deed. The wool they grew still underpinned the entire economy, however, giving the squatters the same power and interests as their refined prototypes and leaving the tension between city and country unresolved. With time of course, and a steady accumulation of money, the squatters began to take on the cultured characteristics of the gentry they displaced until, by the end of the century, they were almost indistinguishable. They maintained the same gracious villas in town. They sent their children to the same exclusive schools. And they sat in the billiards rooms of the same clubs, drinking the same brandies and laying the same plots against the same enemies. One of the principal enemies, then as now, was the city and its insatiable appetite for scarce resources which should have been directed to making the grazier's lot that much more comfortable and secure.

This tension had been exposed before the depression of the 1840s by the resistance of large rural interests to the establishment of a city council in Sydney. That fear of mob rule, coupled with the wealthy's intense loathing of even minimal taxation, was electrified by the spectre of an elected council. They had squealed like stuck pigs when Governor Bourke first floated the idea in the 1830s. His successor, Gipps, who had already alienated the pastoralists by executing the Myall Creek killers, needed two tries to get his legislation up with Wentworth leading the counterattack. When it became obvious a city government would be created, Wentworth and crew tried to exclude the great unwashed with a high property franchise, up to £100, if that was what it took to keep the riffraff from the corridors of power. They failed and the first elections, which preceded the ballot for the Legislative Council by eight months, were held on a £25 franchise. The city's aristocrats were flogged by a pack of butchers, publicans, tanners and builders, as well as a miller, a draper, a cabinetmaker, a tailor, a druggist, one 'esquire' and some merchants; half of them native born and several, to the exquisite horror of the *Herald*, the sons of convicts.

LEVIATHAN

Ten years of sniping and trench warfare commenced, with some early close-quarter work between Wentworth and the council over the role of the police during the election of 1843. Wentworth accused them of incompetence and bias, claiming to have seen the Superintendent of Police himself destroy one of his banners. Policing functions, where the state authorises its agents to mete out whatever violence it deems reasonable to maintain whatever order it thinks necessary, were just one set of powers the agri-business complex in the colonial Parliament was loath to see handed over to a lot of unwashed, lower-class yahoos. City council historian Shirley Fitzgerald characterises the relationship between these levels of government as a contest between colonial or State authorities 'often ready to allocate administrative tasks but reluctant to hand over real power' and civic officials forever 'going cap in hand to the legislature for more control, more manoeuvrability and more money'.

The act which established the council, or corporation as it was then known, gave it responsibility for controlling development and suppressing 'disorderly houses, roads and pavements'. However, as Paul Ashton notes, while a city surveyor was charged with enforcing regularity and good order in the town, the colonial government, concerned not to impinge on the interests of private property, drew up an act which lacked any legal weight. Part of the problem, Fitzgerald explains, was that the city corporation could not create legislation, but only administer the act, which was altered at the bidding of Parliament. Successive corporation acts were more 'administrative codes' than enabling legislation for a separate sphere of government. Vague wording further undermined their utility. Some of the council's so-called powers were not even laid out in its own legislation but salted throughout the Police Act, the Road Act, the Streets Alignment Act and the Building Act, themselves all fairly wobbly pieces of legal drafting. Thus any deficiencies which confronted council officers could not be remedied by their own aldermen, but only by appealing to 'a conservative and dilatory legislature'. The subservient role of Sydney in this legislature – and incidentally a measure of the threat it was seen to pose to rural interests – was manifest in the rigged electoral boundaries which gave 'an overwhelming preponderance' to wealthy rural voters.

Ashton cites the crumbling, awesomely potholed streets of the capital as a focal point of strained relations between these competing stakeholders. These weren't potholes as we understand them. One which opened up in Liverpool Street in April 1855 was four metres deep, while another which appeared in Crown Street a month later was about seven metres long and three metres deep. Later clashes over road works would erupt between the council and 'the gas company, the government works department ... the Water and Sewerage Board and the Hydraulic Power Company'. In December of 1844, however, Alderman Edward Flood complained that the colonial government had simply ignored the council's role altogether. The *Herald* had just that morning carried 'a long notice of streets being opened by the Government at the north end of the town, of which the Corporation and their Surveyor had no knowledge whatever'. Flood, fined £50 after punching out a conservative lawyer who'd called the city's aldermen idiots, railed against Macquarie Street for refusing to hand over 'all sums which had been raised by direct taxation on the citizens of Sydney'. He complained that Sydney's men in the Legislative Council, Bland and Wentworth, 'did not perform their duty to the City'. Instead they simply represented the interests of certain wealthy individuals. Ashton cites this as a telling analysis of the State's view of Sydney, which existed only to channel 'raw produce to the imperial power'.

The City's growth was not to be hampered by an interfering civic authority nor were unhealthy democratic tendencies, evident in a good many of the councillors, to curb economic development and the process of capital accumulation. Urban growth was to be left to that invisible hand in which liberal political economists were to invest so much faith and capital during the nineteenth century, and to the individual and corporate interests of the urban bourgeois.

Should the city fathers – there being no mothers, as Ashton quips – ever demonstrate 'significant reluctance to facilitate the changing demands of manufacturing, industrial or finance capital', the representatives and beneficiaries of that capital stood ready to blade them. Dismissal was a 'civic cornerstone', with the State or colonial cabinet putting a bullet into the city council on four separate occasions. Each sacking was ostensibly a result of incompetence or corruption, but beneath the camouflage lay the glinting steel of raw politics.

When cabinet first removed the aldermen in October 1853, it cited their failed attempts to engineer a permanent water supply and sewerage system for the town. Connections to the main line had increased; however, supply from the swamps had not been augmented. Hence summers were increasingly marked by rationing of the sludgy brown trickle which emerged from the city's taps and pumps. The council blamed the restrictions of its enabling act which denied it any power to raise adequate funds without 'virtually forcing the Corporation into an act of fraudulent insolvency'. The city's income from rates was never going to cover the cost of its responsibilities, with a report by Councillor Thurlow concluding that 'at present the Council has to contend against such gigantic ends, with such trifling means, that the contest is hopeless if not ridiculous'.

Macquarie Street hit back with its own investigation, which accused the council of incompetence and corruption. Its machinery was cumbrous, its controls inefficient, the mayor's allowance excessive, and the councillors acted 'not with the desire faithfully to discharge the duties of the office, but to raise themselves to a false position in society'. They 'used their position to improve their own property at public expense', and some 'sought election chiefly to gratify their wives' ambition to attend a Queen's Birthday Ball at Government House'. Fitzgerald describes this ferocious report as lacking in any detailed proof, a credibility deficit the legislators simply made up for with bucketloads of innuendo. When the battle climaxed with the council's abolition, the state authorities effectively acknowledged the truth of Thurlow's earlier claims by empowering three administrators to borrow £400 000 for sewerage and water works, an amount nearly seven times greater than had been available to their predecessors.

This seething antagonism, an endless struggle for control of the city which continues today, was largely responsible for the decades of neglect which culminated in the plague outbreaks of the early 1900s. The council, reinstated in 1857, was well aware of conditions within the poorest quarters of the city. Its own health officers and building inspectors continually reported on the abysmal state of the slums and the pressing need to do something about them. Legally, however, they were virtually powerless. With awareness increasing through press reports and the work of investigators with the Sewerage Board, the council leveraged a City Improvement Bill into Parliament in 1877. It would have given the council power to condemn and demolish a lot of the buildings where the plague erupted later. However, a select committee in the Legislative Council – which was by that time the upper house of Parliament – cut the legs out from under the reformers. A chorus line of developers, slum lords and architects had danced through the hearings singing an old favourite of the MLCs – the bill gave 'arbitrary and excessive' powers to the city and was an unconscionable imposition on the rights of property owners. The solution, for want of a better word, was to divide and conquer. The council's surveyor was given authority to identify dangerous buildings which should be demolished, but he then had to refer the cases to the separate and often hostile Improvement Board which was supposed to order demolition or repair. The board, consisting of a lot of self-interested 'professional gentlemen', refused to order the demolition of slums for health reasons. Only if the actual buildings were in imminent danger of collapse would they allow the council to move.

The council twisted and turned, trying to get its way through work-arounds of the legislation, at one stage evicting the tenants of the worst slums while still charging the owners rates. A good deal of demolition was carried out in this way, but as it took place in the middle of a decades-long building boom, it is likely that commercial pressures would have seen those buildings come down anyway. The tactic of hiving off the council's powers and investing them in contrary, antagonistic bodies like the Improvement Board was a constant of the last century with, for instance, the Board of Transit Commissioners usurping council power over road traffic in 1873 and the Metropolitan Water and Sewerage Board taking over one of the city's most important and prestigious roles in 1880. In 1897, a dispute between the council and the telegraph department escalated to the point of the mayor threatening to deputise 500 special constables from the ranks of his staff to forcibly prevent the colonial authorities from digging dangerous tunnels in the city centre.

This divisive strategy continues today through a multiplicity of nonrepresentative boards and authorities such as the Roads and Traffic Authority, the Waste Management Authority, the Central Sydney Planning Committee and the dozens of bodies with conflicting responsibilities for the management of Sydney Harbour. All of these have in common their genesis in the corridors of Parliament House rather than Town Hall and all represent the ad hoc, unaccountable and occasionally desperate decisions of a long line of State governments which knew that to cede any real power to the city would enfeeble their own position. More importantly it would expose the lords of capital, be they pastoral, commercial, financial or digital, to the rude claims of the commons, the descendants of those unruly, disenfranchised drunks who tore up the town when they realised the city's powerful elite had walked all over them in the elections of 1843.

None of this is to suggest a hegemonistic structure to power in the city. Quite the contrary in fact. The defining image of power in Sydney is not of some exclusive cabal, manoeuvring in secret to realise its venal designs. Nor of a few discrete elites, playing remote Olympian games with their subjects. Rather, power is atomised and the field on which the powerful contend is a confused, contrary realm of fractured lines, uncertain alliances and shifting schemes. The Parliament which continually neutered municipal authority was itself constrained by the precarious and short-lived majorities commanded by successive governments. Party discipline as we know it did not exist, largely because the Labor Party did not then exist. Governments were led by more or less charismatic individuals such as Henry Parkes around whom formed shaky coalitions whose members often shifted allegiance according to their interests of the day. With no organised party to represent the interests of labour, a rough, laissez-faire liberalism prevailed. The great battles were not fought over State intervention in what were seen as private 'social' affairs – such as poverty or health problems in slum districts – but over State intervention in commercial affairs through the promotion of either free trade or protectionism.

Members of Parliament were not paid until 1889, meaning only men of some wealth could afford to sit. Politicians such as Sydney Burdekin, a pastoralist with extensive interests in city real estate, including much slum housing, were not about to 'tamper with market forces or the rights of property'. And with the day to day survival of their ministries being so uncertain, the premiers, who would later evolve into the de facto governors of the twentieth-century metropolis, were neither inclined to, nor capable of, wielding executive power for the good of the whole city. It should not be surprising that in such a place and time the battles went not to the just, only the strong.

One cold night in the middle of the Great Depression an unemployed bricklayer named Jack Acland realised that he could not feed his child. It was his first child, six months old, and there was no food in the house. In saying that, Jack was not exaggerating or being figurative. There simply was *no food*. Nothing. Not for Jack, his child or his wife Phyllis. He had just started on relief work, a primitive, infinitely more savage version of modern work-for-the-dole schemes. It was heavy, unrelenting physical labour which hollowed out already hollow men and left them moaning or weeping or simply shuddering in their beds in the morning. Jack had walked

Only the Strong

the five miles home from his first day with his mind in turmoil because payday, contrary to his expectations, was not until Thursday week.

Phyllis, he recalled, was 'a bit desperate because there was no baby food left in the tin'. There was nothing for it but the street. He tidied himself and searched out the old violin which he had nearly pawned to pay for their wedding. Another lodger, who sometimes sold flowers, or tried to, offered to join him and 'rattle the box'. Unfortunately it was a late shopping night, as he remembered, and every 100 yards or so down Parramatta Road some desperate bastard like him was already scratching away on a violin. The police had tired of moving them on. Jack wasn't unique, his plight was no more serious than anyone else's and there was simply nowhere to stop. They walked and walked, legs and back already protesting after the exertions of the day, and finally finished up at Marrickville. Jack's companion said, 'Listen, mate, if you're going to play, you'd better hurry up. You've only got half an hour!'

Jack's knees started to shake. Then his whole body. He was standing by the gutter and all he could think of was one piece, 'Play, Fiddle, Play', a recent hit. Jack Acland placed the cool, familiar form of the violin beneath his thin cheek and nervously drew the bow. Then he played and played and played. The same tune. Over and over again. Time dragged by. Traffic passed. Pedestrians ignored him. Nobody placed as much as a slug in their box until, at last, a little girl took a ha'penny from her father, 'and two young girls come along and put in threepence each'.

I thought, 'How terrible this is, taking ha'pennies off kids.' My mate got demoralised and he put the box down at my feet and stood on the corner. I was still on 'Play, Fiddle, Play'. I couldn't get off it. I said, 'How much is in that box?' He said, 'Eleven-pence ha'penny.' A small tin of Lactogen was one and six! I had only a few minutes to go until nine o'clock and my knees were still shaking. A young fellow come out of a barber's shop. He'd just had a shave and a haircut. He looked at me, put his hand in his pocket and dropped two bob in the box. I stopped playing, got into the tram, paid my tuppence fare, and I got out at Newtown Bridge as the chemist was about to close. I said, 'A small tin of Lactogen, please,' and, of course, he was only too pleased to sell me something. So I come home, the big hero with a tin of Lactogen, and some change! And after we'd fed the baby we had some ourselves.

Jack and Phyllis Acland's story, which opens *Weevils in the Flour*, Wendy Lowenstein's great oral history of the Depression, is stark yet unremarkable; a trail of tears which millions walked through a decade of hunger and fear. Economists said the worst was over by 1933, but for countless victims, including the Aclands, desti-tution persisted until the Second World War when their services were suddenly needed again. Riggers and welders who had raised the arc of the Habour Bridge were laid off in '32 and did not see another pay packet until they set to building warships or the massive Garden Island graving dock ten years later. The Sixth Divi-sion which was to fight in North Africa and Greece, was home to thousands of hoboes and swaggies whose first regular feed in years was the salty, fat-soaked chow ladled out by army cooks at boot camp. The Aclands had no security until at least twelve months after the war started when Jack joined the air force. Nearly every day of the 1930s had been a grim scrabble for survival. Their children were born malnourished. An auntie died of starvation.

Only the Strong

Clothing often consisted of nothing more than flour sacks or corn bags cut up and sewn back together. Food was often begged for, or simply imagined. 'We'd lie in bed and say, "We'll get up and cook bacon and eggs,"' said Phyllis, 'and all the time we knew there was nothing to eat in the house.' She told Lowenstein about the shame of asking the butcher for meat on credit.

'He'd been giving some meat to this bloke for his greyhound dog, and he knocked me back. I used to get so embarrassed, to have to ask for anything I wasn't paying for. People would share clothes, but not food very often. I borrowed an egg off a girl friend one day, and we parted bad friends because I couldn't give it back to her. You had to beat it up and mix water in it. The milkman had already thinned the milk and we had to thin it again ... You'd get sick and you'd just have to suffer it. Get fish heads from the market and make soup.'

The most demoralising thing, according to her husband, was that 'you couldn't see the outcome. You seemed so powerless ... I cracked up. I couldn't see any point.' Jack spent most of his time trawling the city, looking for work, tramping through the streets with his shoes falling apart, flapping with each step. He'd cut himself cardboard soles, but it would get so there'd be no sole left, just the uppers. It was nothing to walk thirty or forty kilometres in a fruitless search for work. 'You'd be out all day, had to keep on the move,' he said. 'The *Herald* would only give you an indication. You mostly got your jobs on the hoof, [you'd] walk around everywhere. Take a bit of lunch. Frightened to take a tram because you might pass a street where there was a job. It used to wear you out.'

'He came home this day and cried,' said Phyllis. 'Put his head down and cried like a big baby'.

Tens of thousands of men like Jack, proud men – the heroes of Gallipoli and Villers Bretonneux – were similarly chewed up in the free-fire zone of the market. War correspondent Charles Bean had looked on their war as a trial of national character, with the decisions of generals and governments worked out through the 'machinery of men's nerves and muscles at the fighting edge, where nation grated against nation'. Now the same generation faced a new trial, in which the decisions of bankers and finance ministers caused desolation and poverty in a thousand bleak little streets and factories where the brute contradictions of capitalism ground up hard against each other.

The waterfront provided a daily spectacle eerily reminiscent of Henry Mayhew's descriptions of life at the bottom of the heap in nineteenth-century London. The constant arrival and departure of ships, even during the lowest ebb of the Depression, held the faint prospect of minimal pay for painfully harsh toil, and thousands of desperate men were drawn to it. Five or six hundred would gather at the gates of a wharf where there might be work for a handful, appearing well before dawn and waiting until late in the night on the off-chance they might just scramble over their mates to earn a few shillings hauling tonnes of wool bales or chalk over the sides of the steamers. The Hungry Mile, they called it. A mournful stretch of waterfront starting at number three wharf Darling Harbour and extending to Bathurst Street.

'I've seen them there in Sydney,' [an old wharfie named Albert told Lowenstein]. 'Picking up labour on the Hungry Mile. The foreman would pick up all his pink-eyes, all his plums. And he

Only the Strong

might have ten or twelve job tickets over. He'd scramble them amongst the lot. Throw them up in the air. You'd be like dogs. Your mate would become your worst enemy. You might get one on the ground and go to pick it up and somebody would stand on your hand. The foremen held you in contempt.'

Jim, a contemporary who ranged from Leichhardt as far south as Wollongong in the search for work, described, without knowing it, a modern facsimile of the scenes recounted by Mayhew in *London Labour and the London Poor*.

You line up outside the steel works at Port Kembla from about six o'clock in the morning. There was a little bit of an office and there might be a hundred, three hundred, four hundred men. Some days you might be lucky and there's only sixty. You'd be listening all the time, waiting. All of a sudden a chair would shift inside the office. Everyone would turn around, waiting, see! And then no one would come to the door. You'd settle back a bit and look around again. Somebody would shift the chair again and you'd all look up. Then the door opened and the bloke would stand up there. 'You!' 'No, you! Behind!' And there'd be forty or fifty blokes behind you. You'd watch them going up . . . Just like an auctioneer in a sale yard. Looking for a decent sort of beast . . . That went on for a long, long time. Once you got up to nine o'clock you'd say, 'Well, the only hope of getting a job today is if some bloke gets killed.' Then you'd either stay there till lunch time or you'd get on your bike and ride to Metal Manufacturers. You had to be at Metal Manufacturers at nine. Then round about nine o'clock, the industrial officer, you'd see him walking around, only he'd walk straight to the gate and he'd say, 'No!', then you'd get on your bike and ride to the Fertiliser, then back to the steel works again. Then you'd go for the half past three, and you'd be there all night perhaps.

Modernity and the past were intimately threaded through the fabric of the city at that time. Early model cars and lorries jostled with horse-drawn transport. The roads themselves were a diverse combination of gravel and mud, asphalt, tar, concrete cubes and wooden blocks. The tarred wood blocks were greatly appreciated by the poor in the Depression as they could be stolen and burned for warmth. Describing such a scene outside her office near the Rocks, Lydia Gill incidentally revealed the solidarity by which the lower classes tried to lighten their load.

Once a gang of workmen were lifting the hard jarrah blocks just in front of our office. These blocks had a little tar on them and so made excellent burning for the home fire, but the workmen told the children they must not touch the blocks until the workmen had gone home. There was a pile of blocks outside our window, about seven feet high and about four feet at the base. My junior by a few years called my attention to these blocks at 4.30 p.m.; it seemed that every child in the neighbourhood was there with something to carry them home. They had billycarts, bags, buckets, boxes pulled by bits of rope and old school cases. When we looked again at five to five, just before we left we wondered if we had seen a mirage. There was not a child in sight, nor were there containers of any sort, no workmen and not even a broken piece of tarred timber to show what had been there.

Phyllis Acland also commented on the difficulty of heating

Only the Strong

whatever hovel she and her family found themselves in, admitting that they would burn almost anything to keep warm, the palings off a fence, furniture, rags and lumps of dried manure from the grocer's horse. But everybody, she agreed, was on to those wooden paving blocks. While their parents swallowed any lingering pride to beg for stale bread from the baker or a discarded pig's head from the butcher, the barefoot, lice-ridden children of the city's poor swarmed through back lanes and building sites scavenging for rubbish, for rough hessian sacks which might be turned into blankets, for old fragments of leather or pieces of twine which a father might use to repair his shoes. The massive demolitions by which the State and local authorities had cleared swathes of the inner city after the plague offered up scraps of wood and kindling. (Like the cavernous voids left by the property crash of the 1980s, many of these earlier forsaken holes remained empty for decades after the factories and warehouses which were meant to fill them failed to eventuate. The fabulously Orwellian Sydney Police Centre in Surry Hills sits on such a plot.) When all initiative and ingenuity failed, when the house stood empty without a stick of furniture to be sold or a morsel of food to be eaten, the destitute made their way through the city to wharf number seven at Darling Harbour. There they joined thousands of others, lined up for a ticket to take to the Benevolent Society at the other end of the city near Central Station. A small parcel of food, 'a tin of plum jam, a tin of condensed milk, a tin of syrup, three or four loaves of bread and a big hunk of meat cut just any way' went into a sugar bag which they then hauled home to the family. This could take all day and burn up more energy than the relief parcel itself contained. No wonder that people died of starvation in suburbs like Paddington.

Jocka Burns, a radical with the Unemployed Workers Movement

remembered one fellow traveller, a 'great seller of the workers' press', staggering into a church hall at the Five Ways. 'He used to have cardboard in his boots,' said Burns. 'He came up to the rooms in Paddington one time and he just collapsed, dropped dead through hunger ...' While the burden fell most heavily on the lower classes, none but the very wealthy were entirely spared. Tom Galvin, who was forced into the shantytown just inside the heads at Botany Bay, which was sardonically known as Happy Valley, recalled one former scion of the eastern surburbs who tumbled headlong down the social register. For such people the landing was much harder. They couldn't take the rebound, said Galvin.

'The ordinary wage plug, he'd perhaps weather the storm, he was more hardened. [This] one chap ... he and his wife wheeled a pram from Paddington. He had a double-barrelled name, but he was a dill. They had nothing. People got together, gave them something to eat, tried to find them a blanket. We built a hut for them. He wouldn't have known how to do anything.'

Galvin remembered there being about 120 shacks, with sand floors and old bags hung up to keep out the wind. Maybe 300 people lived there at the end of the tramline, in the most famous of the shantytowns which mushroomed around the city. Labourers, shop assistants, clerks, anyone who couldn't get a job or pay their rent bunked down in clouds of fleas and mosquitoes. It was at least a little more civilized than sleeping rough in the caves or under the trees in the Domain or the city's other parks as many thousands of single men did. The outcasts elected their own management committee which lobbied the nearby golf course to put on water for the camp. Local fishermen let them have some of their catch

Only the Strong

and Chinese market gardeners donated the cheaper produce they could not sell. An Aboriginal man entertained them with a snake dance. Galvin said it was a perversely healthy lifestyle, all that fresh air and simple food, but self-loathing still gnawed quietly at the souls of men who thought themselves failures. And for women the arrival of a child, once a joy and a blessing, could now be the darkest of moments as the close margins of survival were shaved that much thinner. When Lowenstein asked Galvin if the prospect of a new child was a disaster, he remarked frankly, 'There was no pill. They used a crochet hook or something. There were a lot of miscarriages.'

This was life in the raw. The trappings and pretensions of late millennial Sydney were unknown. Survival was the only consideration for most. This brought out both the better angels and the crueller demons of human nature. Lydia Gill writes of middle-class girls quietly leaving little food packages around the city for the poor to find, while Jack Acland spoke bitterly of bosses who would take on a family man with a wife and a gaggle of children to feed, knowing they could drive him so much harder – so hard in Acland's case that his employer could then sack a whole crew of less frantic workers. At the very apex of society, however, it seems this economic holocaust was not as catastrophic as the depression of 1843 which all but decapitated Sydney's ruling class. Rich men did lose fortunes of course, especially with the collapse of the stock market. But the structure of the city's economy was much more complex by the 1930s, the roots of wealth much deeper. A newspaper baron like Robert Clyde Packer might have seen the worth of his shares in Associated Newspapers tumble from £200 000 (about $4 million today) to about half that, but he still had a big wad of the folding stuff in his pocket. And those who did manage to hang onto their wealth often found their purchasing power increased anyway as prices went into free-fall. Hence, as Paul Barry mischievously points out, RC, as Kerry's grandfather was known, could happily use his newspapers to demand savage cuts to wages and welfare spending 'even as he laid out several thousand pounds to buy a new racing yacht'.

The disconnection between the fates of the emerging megarich and the masses whose consumption created their wealth was paralleled by another development, one less comfortable for the wealthy. One of the surprising things about the election riots of 1843 was not that they flared and died away so quickly but that they happened at all. Edward Macarthur had not been alone in holding dear to a view of society with a very wide base and a very pointy apex and a very long distance fixed immutably by God between the two. The lower classes themselves had been gulled into accepting their degraded position and the riots were in one sense an aberration. The common man was not meant to think or yearn for higher things. He was to accept his lot, no matter how diminished. The intervening century had wrought great changes however, even if, on the face of it, Sydney's poor fared little better in the Great Depression than they had in the crash of 1843 or the depression of the 1890s. For one thing the labour movement had materialised and held out the promise of a brighter future, if not for the workers themselves then at least for their children. Organised agitation for better wages and conditions was only part of this deal. Through the Labor Party the lower orders had a shot at the brass ring, control of the state itself, a prospect which would have reduced the early Macarthurs to apoplectic derangement.

The coming of socialism and its apparent realisation in the Russian Revolution were 'for the rest of the world as if an enormous explosion had gone off, followed by a succession of sporadic fireworks of different sizes, some of them very beautiful and unlike anything ever seen before'. (Granted, it does seem a little weird now, but you have to bear in mind that after the bitter experience of the First World War millions of people were looking for a secular creed to replace their decaying faith in institutions such as the Church and the Crown. And the decades of the gulags, mass murder and totally bogus architecture *were* still in the future.) Revolutionary socialism, despite its subsequent disgrace, was as momentous a development as the rise of organised labour because, unlike the union movement or the parliamentary labour parties, it attacked the very basis of modern industrial society. It said that wealth and power were not, as once supposed, God-given. In fact they were not even legitimate, having been stolen or extorted from the working stiff who in turn was morally justified – indeed historically impelled – to violently seize what was rightfully his. That they were capable of such action had been demonstrated to millions of working-class men and women by their service in the Great War, where they had been schooled in organisation, discipline and violent mass action. Just as importantly they had also learned that they were brave and could survive a titanic struggle with the machinery of a hostile state. These lessons – that the system did not love them and that it could be successfully attacked – were crucial to those who led the most militant and radical struggles for the oppressed during the Great Depression. Of course the lessons were not lost on their enemies either.

Reactionary paramilitary groups grew just as quickly as the Communist Party and other, less hard-core outfits on the left. Francis de Groot, the nutjob on horseback who had nearly botched his mission of upstaging Premier Jack Lang at the ribbon-cutting ceremony for the new Harbour Bridge, owed his allegiance to one of the largest and nuttiest of these right-wing private armies, the New Guard. Founded over a few snifters at the Imperial Service Club by Colonel Eric Campbell and half a dozen or so ticked-off former army officers, the Guard was to be a semi-secret force of North Shore dentists, Woollahra shopkeepers and really committed orchardists who would give their all to resist 'Langism, Bolshevism and Jewish corruption'. Nearly 50 000 strong at their height, they represented a spontaneous expression of fear and loathing amongst the precariously positioned bourgeoisie. The same anxiety for position and relative privilege which had induced the officers of the Rum Corps to launch their coup in 1808 lay beneath persistent, if faintly ridiculous, murmurs of a possible New Guard putsch in 1932.

Campbell, a decorated war veteran and successful solicitor, ran a lucrative practice representing 'pastoralists, merchants, professional men and financial institutions'. Some of these men would be destroyed by the Depression but those who hung on were much more fearful of the threat to their livelihoods posed by Moscow and Marxist theory than Wall Street and chaos theory. While de Groot's ride on the Bridge will doubtless constitute their slash mark on history, the Guard's campaign of constant low-level harassment of the left was arguably more significant, even if ultimately futile. While hundreds of New Guard yahoos drilled and trained to seize and protect country railway crossings and bridges in the event of an uprising, many more were actively involved in a violent spoiling campaign against left-wing activists in the city.

To the true ruling elite they were useful idiots. To the *Herald*, according to Souter's corporate history, they were less a threat to the State's democratically elected government than a reassuring

Only the Strong

fallback position should Lang's much despised Labor government itself 'exceed legal bounds'. Should any attempt be made 'to upset the constitutional order and establish some system that would please the Friends of the Soviet Union, they will oppose it by open and downright means,' explained the *Herald* on 24 July 1931, before asking, 'Is there anything discreditable in a policy such as that?' Obviously not as far as the Fairfax press was concerned.

To the likes of relief worker Jim McNeill, however, the New Guard were simply fascists, his experience with them prompting him to join the International Brigade in the Spanish Civil War. 'I could see what vicious types they were and what they would do in power,' he told Lowenstein. 'I understood then what fascism meant and that they had to be defeated'. McNeill saw them arrive to break up Communist Party or Unemployed Workers Movement rallies time and again, in their expensive cars 'from Vaucluse and Potts Point and other silvertail suburbs'. Hattie Cameron, who lived in a street at Bankstown in which only three men had jobs, witnessed one such assault on a small market near the local railway station. 'The local unemployed organisation collected donations of vegetables, used clothing and other odds and ends, and they had permission to run stalls in the park,' she said. The New Guard drove out from Sydney one night to attack the market. 'It was a bloody business,' recalled Cameron. McNeill had an even fiercer encounter on the North Shore.

A New Guard shot at me at a meeting in Drummoyne. The Council elections were on and we had a meeting, and the New Guard started holding a meeting on the opposite corner. After about five minutes their leader hopped down and led them over to our platform and the crowd parted, all except the solid core around the speaker, the stalwarts who always stayed to defend the platform. When they got within hitting distance they launched out with their fists. Steve Purdy, who was chairing the meeting, beat one of them to the punch and the bloke fell to the ground. One of the New Guard pulled a pistol and as he did I went over to Steve to be alongside of him, and the bloke said, 'Stand back!' I hesitated – he was only a few feet away – and then I ducked and went towards him. One New Guard had grabbed Purdy by the chest, and the other was raining rabbit killers on the back of his neck. I pulled this bloke away. And I felt a bullet whistle just past my ear. I was hit once or twice in Spain, in the International Brigade, but I never felt one come closer than this without actually hitting me! Later the story got around that it was a dummy, but it was a real bullet all right!

The passion for biff was by no means one-sided as a Labor Party man explained to Lowenstein.

The ALA (Australian Labor Army) was formed to protect Labor's speakers from attack by the New Guard and it did this. It's impossible to recreate the atmosphere of that time. It was electric. Walking about the streets, you could feel it in the air. Everybody was talking about it – what's going to happen! We were drilling. Because on the North Shore we had the New Guard, all two bob toffs. It was a fascist organisation. We were drilling to oppose them. We were carrying loaded sticks to meetings with the centres drilled out and filled with lead. We wore a red badge with ALA on it, Australian Labor Army. We had to have protection for our speakers. There were thousands of members of the New Guard ... '

Only the Strong

We had white tape sewn round our coats under our collars and coat lapels so in a fight we could fold them up and we'd see the white tape – so we wouldn't be hitting one another. We weren't playing. The rank and file of the Labor Party was in it, and trade unionists too. Our local branch of the Labor Army would probably have had about two hundred members. We were dinkum! For instance, we were running a meeting at Flemington in the Auburn electorate and Billy Lamb who was subsequently the Speaker in the State Parliament was on the platform. The New Guard members came rushing in and started pushing us around. We resisted and it was on for young and old for a while. As soon as they saw we weren't going to run away, they did! But Lamb himself pulled a revolver to keep them at bay.

It is tempting to see such eruptions of violence as an aberrant jolt to a more refined narrative of liberal political development, to view them as 'un-Australian', that unctuous cliche so beloved of tabloids and politicians. But of course political violence is inherently conventional, even banal, and those describing it as unpatriotic or anathema to some presupposed national culture are either deceiving themselves or, more likely, trying to hoodwink a wider audience as their own interests come under attack. It is not enough, however, to simply ascribe such eruptions to anger, frustration or some other inflamed passion. This, as Murray Edelman points out in *Politics as Symbolic Action*, is tautological. Adopting for a moment Edelman's own framework, which has the appeal of being both breathtakingly cynical *and* enlightening, the clash of left and right in the 1930s, of Anglo and Asian in the 1870s, of 'Irish' mobs and Wentworth's 'respectable' citizens in 1843 can all be profitably examined within the richer context of contending myth and symbol. So too with Bligh and the Rum Corps in 1808 and the neo-Nazi attacks on National Action's exposed, peripheral victims of the 1980s. This is not merely to render abstract an otherwise functional and bloody process, but to try and understand some of the brute forces which have shaped and continue to shape life in the city. It is about the most basic elements of power, about recognising the inherently coarse process of who does the fucking and who gets fucked.

In this scheme politics is relevant to everyday life to the extent that it addresses immediate concerns for wealth, status and autonomy, the last being a matter of individual freedom; freedom to act in pursuit of one's goals and its corollary, freedom from constraints whether concrete – such as early legislative attempts to suppress the rum trade – or abstract, such as cultural norms which kept Catholics or women under the thumb until well into this century. Edelman's contribution is to fashion a study of politics in terms of mass psychology rather than simple 'outputs' such as legislative programs. He assumes, in the language of a policy geek circa 1968, that people's beliefs and positions 'are mobilisable rather than fixed' and that the significant outcomes of political activity 'are not particular public policies labelled as political goals, but rather the creation of political followings and supports: i.e., the evocation of arousal or quiescence in mass publics'. From this point of view, political manoeuvring itself becomes the endgame, 'for in the process (rather than in the content of statutes, court decisions, and administrative rules) leaders gain or lose followings, followers achieve a role and a political identity, and money and status are reallocated'.

What this means is that an understanding of the power structure

Only the Strong

of Sydney at any time in its history becomes as much a matter of penetrating the mind of the city as cataloguing the most significant players and the resources at their disposal. It segues neatly with Hannah Arendt's contrasting of violence and power. Deciding where power lies is not simply a case of totting up who commands the big battalions, but must also take into account issues of consent, allegiance and belief. The instruments of the Rum Corps – four hundred bayonets and a couple of field guns – were always going to overwhelm Bligh and his dinner guests. But the traditional submission of the military to lawful authority, the coup leaders' apprehension about their own legitimacy and their concerns about the continuing loyalty of small landholders to the King's representative were all problems of individual or mass psychology rather than logistics and firepower. The rebels had to place their story within an acceptable context and this required them to fashion the myth of an impending revolt amongst the wider populace.

Such a myth, explains Edelman, is an unquestioned belief held in common by a large group of people which gives complex and bewildering events a particular meaning. Political events, which are frequently tangled and ambiguous, and which often relate to such intimate and powerful concerns as one's actual survival, are among those most likely to engender anxiety. The political universe thus 'needs to be ordered and given meaning'.

For those who do feel threatened because of a gap between what they are taught to believe they deserve and what they are getting, attachment to a myth replaces gnawing uncertainty and root-lessness with a vivid account of who are friends, who are enemies, and what course of action must be pursued to protect the self and significant others.

LEVIATHAN

The belief that William Bligh or Jack Lang is about to impose a dictatorship; that a police SWOS team murdered David Gundy in cold blood; that the poor are simply part of God's design for society; that protests in favour of welfare payments are controlled by communists acting on behalf of Moscow; or that hordes of Chinese are steaming towards Sydney to smoke dope, build disgracefully cheap polished furniture and copulate with all the white women they can get their hands on are all examples of myths, widely subscribed to, which have at different times channelled Sydney's 'anxieties and impulses' into shared expectations, freeing thousands of people from responsibility for their own fates or actions. Each evoked 'a specific political role and self-conception' for those who accepted the myth in question; the Rum Corps rebels, the New Guard, anti-Chinese protesters and so on. That each myth touched, however fleetingly, on some aspect of political reality made them all that much more vivid and tenable.

It explains why the riot which erupted in the depression of the 1840s simply died away in a fog of alcohol, exhaustion and bad weather; while protest and reaction in the Great Depression of the 1930s was sustained at much more intense levels for much longer. The city had changed its mind. Whereas Edward Macarthur's mythology of a divinely ordained if deeply unfair social order was almost universally accepted in the nineteenth century, by the twentieth, as we have seen, it had been violently rejected by those at the bottom of the heap and was even out of fashion with those at the top, who no longer held their property and privilege on the basis of divine right, but because of worthiness, by dint of hard work, intelligence, thrift or whatever. 'In a caste system assumed by all its participants to be divinely sanctioned,' writes Edelman, 'subordination and unequal benefits mean that the world is as it

Only the Strong

should be; in a polity with a norm of social equality the same facts come to mean deprivation and an incentive to resistance.'

That resistance would not go unanswered of course. Nor was it restricted to low-level clashes between the cutouts and agents of much greater forces. At the highest stations of the city the passions were just as intense as those aroused in the gritty, street-level combat between the New Guard and the left. Such extreme times called forth an extreme man, State Premier Jack Lang, a working-class hero or Satan incarnate, depending on which side of the battlelines you stood. Like Bligh, Macarthur and Wentworth before him, Lang's character encompassed a Shakespearean maelstrom of great potential and mortal frailty. His private contest with the demons of a spiteful, paranoid, overweening ego and a wildly aggressive will to power translated to the wider world because of the crucial position he held in both the city's and the nation's power structure during the Depression. Within Sydney the battle for dominance between State and municipal authority had long ago been decided in favour of Macquarie Street. Ninety years of resource starvation and countless defeats in the war for autonomy had pretty much rendered the city council an irrelevancy for all but the most basic purposes. One of its last great missions, the provision of electricity, was slowly clawed from Town Hall's grasp in the 1920s and finally removed altogether in 1935. The vaunted concept of a government for Greater Sydney had been destroyed by an alliance of State politicians and suburban aldermen, none of whom were willing to cede the smallest measure of their own power. Federal government was still in its infancy and had not yet even seized from the States the right to levy income tax. The primary site of government power thus lay not in the eerily quiet and desolate sheep paddock of Canberra, but in the various State capitals and especially, given their population and economic dominance, in Sydney and Melbourne.

The nineteenth-century idea of the minimal government, which did little more than build and protect infrastructure, had been beset by the political rise of the working class and the constant carping of those middle-class do-gooders who argued that private charity could not alleviate the suffering of the urban poor – and indeed that their suffering deserved relief, a truly radical position. Lang himself had an early schooling in the bitter gospels of deprivation when his father's illness reduced the family to Dickensian poverty during the boom of the 1880s. You can draw a straight line between this experience and Lang's pioneering of government welfare in the 1920s, including child endowment, widow's pensions and worker's compensation. These were State-wide measures of course, but they were appreciated most keenly where the poor were most numerous and this meant in those densely populated inner-city slums which had escaped demolition after the plague, and further out in the threadbare industrial suburbs which were growing in the south around Botany Bay and in the west at places like Auburn, which Lang represented in Parliament. It was not appreciated by the rich, as you'd imagine, who did not see why they should be forced to pay for such dangerous socialist experiments. And just as power had progressively shifted from Government House to Parliament House, so too had it leaked from the public into the private sphere.

The commercial interests of the city, which Lang snarled at and berated as 'the Money Power', had grown explosively in importance and influence from the days when the Rum Corps turned official status to private gain. The crude nature of that primeval economy stood in relation to the complexities of the modern

Only the Strong

metropolis as a bark canoe to an aircraft carrier. Heavy and light manufacturing, telecoms, power and transport systems, media, finance, construction and service industries – all the elements of advanced civilization – had been raised over Sydney's pastoral–commercial foundations with remarkable speed. And just like that earlier combine, the new potentates were not averse to deploying superior firepower to protect or advance their own interests. Unremitting attacks on the Labor Party, and in particular on Jack Lang by the Fairfaxes' *Sydney Morning Herald* were a good example. Despite once being described as 'one of the best treasurers' by Sir John French of the Bank of New South Wales (now Westpac), Lang was portrayed in the press as a sort of violent, troglodytic berserker who would unleash an orgy of Marxist butchery on the State the moment he thought he could get away with it. Lang unfortunately was often his own worst enemy in this confrontation, drinking from the bottomless well of his many hatreds and lashing out at his enemies with blasts of vicious, unthinking rhetoric which would have left even William Bligh grasping for an answer.

He was an exceptional guy, Lang, a real stand-out character, for good reasons and bad. Like Wentworth a large powerful-looking man, he was uncouth yet yearned for respectability. The *Australian Dictionary of Biography* records that he seldom laughed. He suffered from insecurity and had many followers but few intimates. Like his admiring protégé Paul Keating he aroused extreme feelings of loathing and loyalty amongst both peers and the general public. He was a real-estate auctioneer, not a traditional trade for a Labor man, but the auction block fashioned his crude, effective speaking style: 'rasping voice, snarling mouth, flailing hands, sentences and phrases punctuated by long pauses'. With a bald, high-domed

347

head, a thick moustache and garbed in 'the uniform of the successful Edwardian man – the three-piece suit, watch and chain, stiff collar, sober tie, polished boots, and obtrusive felt hat', he should have been more at home in the billiards room of the Millions Club. But he was a hater, a brawler and a true believer and he turned his evangelical skills against the big-money families such as the Fairfax clan and their small-change champions on the North Shore and in the east, in those stiff-necked, respectable middle-class suburbs where the word of the *Herald* was holy writ and the New Guard's recruiters did such good business. The anarchists of high finance played with the lives of common folk for 'sheer personal gain', growled Lang, 'putting them to work under the whips of hunger, throwing them into idleness to keep them in discipline, manning them for war, dividing them in peace' and drawing a toll in gold, 'counted over in human tears and blood' from every activity into which they were thrown. 'Are we to be driven to desperation ... before the Governor dismisses him?' pleaded the *Herald* in 1931.

Not all of the fire which zeroed in on the Premier during the Depression came from his right flank, however. The left maintained a guerilla campaign of sniping and harassment, partly on general principles because the Labor Party was regarded by communists as a 'social fascist' organisation, or as one anarchist put it 'socialiste de café latte', and partly because Lang's position at the head of the State's repressive machinery made him a natural if unwilling ally of the very same 'Money Power' with which he was locked in mortal combat. The issue, as so often in Sydney's history, was real estate.

The speculative land boom of the 1920s had thrown up thousands of new houses and apartment blocks, but by the early

Only the Strong

1930s many of these, as well many thousands more in the older, established suburbs, lay empty whilst an army of the homeless unemployed, like Tom Galvin, drifted about the city seeking shelter in parks, drains and shanty towns. In *Twentieth Century Sydney* Nadia Wheatley cites a figure of nearly 11 000 empty dwellings in the metro area in 1935, two years after the worst of the Depression had supposedly passed. Widespread home-ownership was a phenomenon of the 1950s, with most people renting before the Second World War. As unemployment rocketed towards thirty per cent, the big real estate companies which owned or managed swathes of rental housing found their cash drawers bare as tenants fell behind in their payments. Without the dole or rental subsidies of a modern welfare system, the outcome was inevitable – mass evictions.

In April 1930 the Unemployed Workers Movement, a 'fraternal organisation' of the Communist Party, resolved to oppose the evictions. Their pragmatic campaign, organised around 'a series of small scale demands' seemed to galvanise the unemployed. Membership grew rapidly, with UWM branches expanding in number from about thirty at the end of that year, to seventy by July of 1931. Each branch boasted approximately 200 members and the reach of the movement stretched from the inner city out to Bankstown, right into the personal fiefdom of Premier Lang himself. Wheatley explains that Lang's 1930 changes to the Landlord and Tenant Act, which he had promised would end the daily spectacle of families being strong-armed into the street, had done no such thing. Nor had he increased the dole as promised, although he had appointed nearly 100 inspectors, known as 'dole pimps' to generally menace and aggravate welfare recipients.

To be fair, Lang did have his own problems at this point. All Australian governments had borrowed heavily during the 1920s and were now being gouged by interest repayments. Having embarked on a massive re-engineering of the State capital with projects like the Harbour Bridge, the underground rail system and the electrification of the city and suburbs, New South Wales found itself insolvent in February 1931. Adding to this tide of woe, the Government Savings Bank, in which forty per cent of the State's population held their money, had been undermined by an awesomely reckless election campaign in which Lang's conservative opponents repeatedly asserted that he would steal depositors' savings to pay for his election promises. Lang did not help matters by refusing to pay the State's debts to London, saying that English bond holders could wait until he had fed the unemployed before they received any money. The politics of the time were confused, brutal and terrifying. Lang's Labor followers went to war with the federal Labor Government while simultaneously fending off attacks by radical left-wingers in the Communist Party and right-wingers in the New Guard. The Government Savings Bank went belly-up in April 1931, with thousands of desperate depositors packing Martin Place to withdraw their savings during a cyclonic storm which saw mountainous seas bursting way up the sheer cliff faces at South Head, while blinding cataracts of rain scourged city streets. Governor Phillip Game faced intense pressure to sack the Premier, with the first rank of Sydney society cutting him dead as long as he refused.

Lang's problems were of no concern to the homeless, however. The same rain squalls roared over them as they herded their children under trees or bridges while their few remaining sticks of furniture were washed away or simply fell to pieces in the deluge. The Unemployed Workers Movement established local committees to fight the evictions. When a family approached the movement a

Only the Strong

delegation would head off to confront the landlord and argue their case, more or less menacingly, depending on the response they received. If no joy came from negotiation, pickets soon appeared outside the real estate office responsible and, if necessary, outside the property itself. Particularly odious real estate agents soon found themselves with large glazier's bills for window repair. When the bailiffs arrived to seize or remove any furniture, large threatening crowds would block their access or simply pick up the family's belongings and take them back inside. Should all this fail, an occupation of the house commenced, with up to two dozen UWM activists remaining in place, around the clock, for weeks at a time. It should be noted that these tactics were only ever employed to protect family homes. Single men who found their way to the movement through forced or threatened eviction often finished up in hostels, dossing down with Communist Party organisers. These young, tough 'political bushrangers', as one activist called them, provided the hard core of a sort of militant flying squad which could be despatched on short notice; if a bit of boot and fist work was needed to see off a posse of New Guards for example.

The final tactic, occupation and armed resistance, seems to have evolved naturally from the preceding manoeuvres some time in May 1931. The Surry Hills committee had heard at the end of February that a worker was about to be evicted but, having foiled the bailiffs the next day, found the agents refusing to give in. The police, the bailiffs and the agents all returned twice more in quick succession. The protestors reached the fairly pragmatic conclusion that they would have stay in place until the workers had gained a complete victory. This aim was not entirely preposterous.

The UWM were completely committed to their fight and viewed

any eviction 'not merely as a personal tragedy for the family involved, but as a setback to the whole struggle against evictions'. It was this perseverance, argues Wheatley, as well as a 100 per cent success rate, that so alarmed the property-owning establishment. The undivided and often threatening support of hundreds and even thousands of local residents lent a great deal of street cred and leverage to the UWM. However, recalling Hannah Arendt's caution about the nexus between a failure of state power and the subsequent inevitability of state violence, the response of the government, whether Labor or conservative, was predestined. There would be bloodshed.

The first of that winter's anti-eviction battles took place on 30 May 1931, a Saturday, and was an easy victory for the police, their last. The house in Douglas Street, Redfern, had been home to the McNamara family since 1920. They had been good tenants for a decade, never missing a rent payment until a year after McNamara lost his job. The Redfern branch of the UWM had placed a picket on the house at the start of the month when the landlord had taken out an ejectment order. But having been assured by the Colonial Secretary that no police would be used to enforce the order, only a handful of activists were in place on Saturday when half a dozen cops sledgehammered the front door and sailed into them with their batons. The surprise and the violence had the intended effect. The skeleton crew were hustled out of the house and quickly scattered.

Just over an hour or so later they returned in a red truck with about thirty reinforcements. A couple of labourers who were still moving out the family's possessions were overwhelmed while their two police guards were set upon by club-wielding activists. A large crowd of locals who gathered to support the evicted family were

Only the Strong

'completely and actively hostile' to the police, who drew revolvers to hold them back while their own reinforcements rushed from Redfern station. The extra officers quickly cleared the street, arresting a couple of people for bad language and riotous behaviour. The UWM had flown a red flag from the balcony beside a placard which demanded an end to evictions. The flag was torn down and the placard broken into pieces. The Communist Party's *Worker's Weekly* newspaper almost cheered, for now the unemployed would truly know on whose side Jack Lang stood. For too long, it crowed, the unemployed had been conned into the belief that Lang was with them.

> Too long have they looked to the leprous Labor Government for salvation! Too long have they been kept quiet by the giddy vapourings of Lang's demoralising demagogues! Enough! They have bitterly bought their knowledge! The bill remains to be paid!

A week later in Starling Street, Leichhardt, that bill was presented to about twenty police who confronted a much larger, angrier crowd who refused to disperse. This time the UWM had prepared their weapons, with a number of improvised batons later discovered inside the house they were guarding. One was made from a solid plug of lead, reported the *Herald*, which was soldered to a flexible wire ending in a number of coils to form a grip. The pickets and police laid into each other with abandon this time and both sides suffered casualties. Outside a crowd, 200 strong, howled abuse at the officers and had to be driven back down the street by a baton charge. The threat detectors of the establishment press were quick to pick up on this worrying escalation. The *Sun* claimed Moscow was behind the whole business.

LEVIATHAN

It is a common assumption among those who are content with existing status and power relationships, says Edelman, that when those with less status finally get their shit together they represent a threat to the established order, and that so long as they are not organised they are either impotent or loyal. We can see in the first weeks of June 1931 the flux and flow of these relationships, the way that Edelman's 'mass publics' were becoming aroused and mobile, growing, dividing and fusing like so many amoebae suddenly excited from quiescence into action. Such movement, promising disruption and even radical change, is always an anxious affair. For the truly ascendant – like the Fairfaxes – for those middle-class types who dream of ascendancy and for those who are simply aligned with them – like police officers, for instance – a whole world of ordered privilege and rewards is at risk. Meanwhile, those fighting for change must deal with the consequences of their actions, withstanding attacks both physical and semantic, calculated and ad hoc. Whether a communist with a fundamentally radical agenda or an unemployed man with a simple but urgent need for a minor redistribution of wealth, the advocate of change stands before an onslaught of the powerful. Both sides will inevitably frame their stories, their myths, in an exculpatory, heroic fashion; the UWM resisting fascist enslavement; the brave, outnumbered police constable confronting hateful and fanatic Marxists. These myths give meaning to otherwise confused and furious encounters. They justify violence, encourage endurance, stiffen the sinews and summon up the blood. Escalation is almost unavoidable. It came a week and a half after the clash at Leichhardt, heralded by the crackle of gunfire on the outer fringes of the city at Brancourt Avenue, Bankstown.

The field of battle was far removed from the usual rats' nest of constricted and gloomy inner-city streets. Brancourt Avenue at that time was described as a wide, open thoroughfare bordered by grassy verges. It lay at the edge of development, where 'paddocks and scrub stood between the scattered fibro and weatherboard cottages'. One of these squat, grey little boxes was home to John Parsons, a thirty-nine-year-old returned serviceman. He had fallen behind in his rent and prevailed upon the local UWM branch when the landlord came calling. They had been in attendance for three weeks and having learned some of the lessons of Redfern and Leichhardt had prepared quite elaborate defences. More than half the picketers were former soldiers and had drawn on their military experience to run up barbed wire and build sandbag revetments. To the same improvised batons they had used at Starling Street, they added a grab bag of axe and pick handles, iron bars, garden forks, stones and bricks. The police were just as ready for action. They commenced their attack twenty minutes before they were legally permitted, turning off power to the area after hearing the protestors may have electrified the barbed wire. Most importantly they came in overwhelming numbers. At least forty police stormed the house itself, with another hundred or so held in reserve nearby. It is uncertain who threw the first stone, and largely irrelevant. The air was soon thick with them, the sound of the fight carrying across the quiet suburb. The police, who had to cut their way through the wire entanglements under a constant barrage of stones, replied with gunfire and volleys of rocks. An inspector leading a squad around the side of the cottage in a flanking movement was struck on the temple and dropped like a sack of shit, the base of his skull shattered by the blow. A Constable Dennis, forcing his way through a window, was hit by a brick and then an iron bar. He fired into the house, shooting the leg out from under Richard Entock. It took half an hour for the police to subdue the sixteen defenders after a savage round of hand-to-hand combat. A convoy of ambulances ferried the wounded to hospital where doctors were faced with an amazing array of bullet wounds, gaping cuts, broken skulls and sprained, fractured and bruised limbs. The house was virtually demolished. Not a window was left intact, reported the *Herald*.

> Inside there was devastation. Scarcely a piece of furniture remained. The floors of what had once been bedrooms and living rooms were littered with dirt, blue metal, broken glass and the crude weapons which the occupants had used. Blood-stains marked the floor and the sandbags on the front verandah.

The *Worker's Weekly* ran an article by one of the picketers who laid the blame for most of the property destruction at the feet of the police. After bashing their defenceless prisoners

> they then began an orgy of destruction, ripping and finally burning the small belongings of the tenant and the pickets. A violin and music, the pickets' overcoats, the tenant's child's clothes, bedding, blankets, even a few loaves of bread and tins of jam were thrown into the bonfire.

Here was fascist barbarism indeed. Destroying food, clothing and culture (in the form of the violin). Was nothing beneath these brutes? The *Weekly*'s correspondent also denied claims in the mainstream press that the tenant was not even at the house. Parsons, he wrote, was in the thick of the fight, and 'only saved from being killed by the actions of another worker' who threw himself on top of the old soldier as a gang of cops laid into him with their batons. According to the *Herald*, it was 'one of the most serious disturbances ever dealt with by the police in New South Wales'. But it paled beside Black Friday, in Newtown, two days later.

Like the Rum Rebellion, the anti-eviction riot in Union Street, Newtown, on 19 June was a highly plastic event which morphed from a shocking example of state-sponsored brutality into a stirring triumph of the city's finest over the spectre of violent anarchy – depending on who was perjuring themselves at the time. Union Street was then, and still is, a narrow, claustrophobic passageway into a dense maze of roads, alleys and lanes in the wedge between King Street and Erskineville Road. Led by fearless lesbians, the renovating class has been gentrifying the area for years now, but in 1931 the new elites were a long way from this grim patch of turf. The only ferals were cats and dogs, turned loose by families unable to feed themselves, let alone any pets. You could still live and die in a place like Newtown without setting foot outside its boundaries; and although the war and the Great Depression had plucked and torn at the suburb's intricately woven fabric, the ties of neighbourhood were still much stronger than they are today. This would help explain the large crowds, hundreds strong, which constantly milled about in front of 143 Union Street during that bitterly cold wet week in June when the UWM moved into the little two-up two-down terrace in response to yet another eviction order. It would also explain the way the crowd swelled to many thousands when the police arrived, and the vehemence with which they screamed and hurled defiance at the government's hired muscle when they attacked the picketers.

LEVIATHAN

There is little point trying to reconcile the alternate versions of what happened on Black Friday. It is as though the day itself split into competing time lines, humming through the same space, involving the same men, but somehow existing in completely different worlds. Inspector Jim Farley, who commanded the force of forty to sixty police officers, described a routine operation gone wrong when his cool-handed squad arrived with a warrant and were instantly bombarded with stones, bricks and foul-mouthed communist abuse. Several police, including Farley, were struck and one constable was knocked down. Farley braved the rain of missiles to wave his piece of paper and shout, to no effect, 'Be sensible men. Stop throwing. I have a warrant to enter here'. The crazed UWM men continued to rain half bricks and pieces of concrete into the street, one of them shouting, 'Come on, boys, into the fucking bastards.' Even civilians were taking hits from the poorly directed fusillade. Finally, after much forbearance, some police drew their revolvers and fired on the house, driving the men on the balcony inside. Farley, who by his own evidence did not seem to have maintained much tactical command, noticed a number of police disappearing down the narrow passageway at the side of the property. As a handful of his men scaled the balcony he made his own way down the side. After a brief moment he entered the rear of the house.

'The whole place was in a state of confusion,' he later stated at the UWM men's trial. 'A large number of bags of soil were lying about both rooms on the ground floor. I then directed the police to take the defendants out into the back, which was done. They remained there for a few minutes. I kept them under observation. The police patrol arrived and the defendants were brought to Newtown Police Station.' A challenging task, expertly handled, by

Only the Strong

hard-nosed professionals. Inside, Farley counted sixty-eight bags
of soil and took note of 'a number of stones, pieces of bricks,
concrete and a banner', along with other crude improvised
weapons such as iron bars, knives, sticks and home-made clubs.
He had been on the job thirty-one years when he led his men into
action against the UWM and it was his considered opinion that
they were facing 'very grave danger'. All of the defendants were
armed and none stopped fighting until the last man went down,
at least thirty or forty minutes after the first rock bounced off the
scone of one of his officers.

The evidence of Farley's officers was a little more dramatic, a
little more confused, and a little more disconnected from reality.
Constable Ray Kelly, who led the assault on the rear door of the
house, described the harrowing experience of trying to force his
way through an entrance which had been blocked with a sheet of
iron and a massive pile of sandbags. Rocks and bricks pounded
into his chest and head as he tried to squeeze through, while ranks
of heavily armed communists waited eagerly on the other side with
sticks and iron bars. One of these men, Joseph Garbett, had even
fashioned a spear out of a length of gas pipe. He thrust it at Kelly,
piercing his tunic and puncturing his left arm. Garbett then ran
into the front room while Kelly fought with a young picketer
named Reg Hawkins, who smashed him in the head with a steel
bar. Sergeant George Phillips, who followed Kelly inside, said he
was hit on the arm by a brick, thrown as he scrambled over the
collapsed mound of sandbags. Someone swung a chair leg at him,
injuring his thumb as he tried to fend off the blow. He never drew
his revolver, not once, he said. He couldn't name *one* officer who
did. In fact, although he heard something that may have sounded
like a gunshot in the wild melee, he couldn't swear that's what it

was. Constable William Resolute Gibbons, from Hurstville station, the third man through the door, was struck in the right eye and collapsed to the ground as soon as he made it inside. He clambered to his feet, only to be hit with a chair on the back of the head by a man called John Murphy, a thirty-nine-year-old hellcat swinging this chair with one hand and an iron bar with other, laying into policemen all round him. 'I arrested Murphy,' said Resolute Gibbons somewhat matter-of-factly, 'and later he was removed to the back yard'.

The *Herald*, which characterised the 'desperate fighting' as a battle between the police force and communists, reported that the police fired steadily at the walls behind which the reds cowered. The paper ran Inspector Farley's line that this was justified by 'the terrible shower of stones' which rained down on the officers; however, it contradicted his testimony that the shooting just sort of broke out, instead depicting it as a deliberate act. 'At an order from the officers in charge', wrote the *Herald*'s man, 'the police retired, many of them bleeding profusely from jagged wounds ... After a short consultation, the police drew their revolvers. At a word of command they commenced firing . . .' Only one protester was hit, according to the report, and it was not known how. Perchance, the journalist offered helpfully, 'the wounded man was struck by a bullet deflected from its path'.

Having driven the rock throwers inside, the majority of the police made for the small path by the side of the house. At the same time half a dozen plain-clothes men and uniforms who had gained access to the house next door started to force their way past the partition dividing the upstairs balconies. The house was 'fantastically barricaded' at that point, with loops of barbed wire around the iron railing and sheets of galvanised iron fixed to block

Only the Strong

any approach. While these police fought with frantic communists who wielded bludgeons, lead piping, fence palings and wooden batons ripped from the furniture, dozens of their colleagues leaned with all of their weight against the fence at the side of the house which 'collapsed with a crash of rending timbers'.

They leapt across the wreckage and reached the back door of their objective without serious casualties. Using a heavy hammer the vanguard of the attacking force smashed the back door to pieces. Entry was still barred however by a thick wall of sandbags. Wrenching out the broken fragments of the door, the police, after terrific effort, succeeded in making a breach in the sandbag defences. By this time, summoned by the frantic calls for help from the guards on the ground floor, most of the men on the top floor rushed down the staircase to a small room at the back. It was here that the terrible hand to hand combat occurred. Diving one by one through the narrow breach in the sandbags, the police steadily met the terrific onslaught of the besieged men ... The room was absolutely bathed in blood. Practically every man in the room was bleeding from one or more wounds. Insensible men lay on the floor while comrades and foes alike trampled on them. The walls were spattered and daubed with bloodstained hands.

The *Herald* couldn't really explain how the police managed to pass, one by one, through the narrow opening at the rear without being bashed unconscious by the gang of well-armed thugs inside. It was as though the commies were actors in a really bad martial arts movie, only attacking one at a time, at the protagonist's convenience. In fact, the police cleared their passage by firing through the aperture at such a rate that those inside thought they were under attack from a machine gun. Nadia Wheatley points to the *Sun* newspaper's unwitting corroboration of the pickets' claims by its description 'of bullets striking below policemen coming downstairs'. The squad which had broken through on the upstairs balcony were almost shot by their own colleagues firing blindly into the back of the house.

While the picketers admitted to throwing rocks at the police, they said it was in self-defence, after the first shots were fired. And rather than a heavy, unremitting bombardment of the street below, their volleys were sporadic, poorly aimed and futile. In contrast with the conflicting evidence of the police, every single picket who was in a position to witness their arrival described the same scene. About half a dozen patrol cars and a large red bus, unmentioned by the *Herald*, slewed into Union Street and drew up a short distance from the house. The police jumped out with their guns already drawn and 'stampeded' towards 143, firing into the air and then at the balcony. This account was supported by numerous witnesses outside the house, some of them independent, in the large crowd which had been listening to speeches all morning.

There were eighteen men inside the little terrace when someone yelled out, 'Here they come!' Upstairs on the verandah stood Percy Joshua, twenty-nine, from Redfern. He would end the day with a fractured skull, a busted, cut-up shoulder, contusions to his left ear and cerebral concussion. Next to him stood Joseph Garbett, the man Ray Kelly accused of trying to run him through with a barbed length of gas piping; Robert Clark, who had been speaking to the crowd below; a feisty young dude named James Miller; the even younger and feistier Reg Hawkins; and a returned soldier named Leslie Goldberg, a married man with four kids who wouldn't make

Only the Strong

it home to Darlington that day on account of a fractured skull, a fractured jaw and a badly pulped face. Clark was standing next to Garbett as a bullet tore through his arm and sent him staggering back into the room. 'Bullets were thudding into the walls, scattering dust and pieces of plaster everywhere,' said Clark. They crouched down and started heaving bricks in retaliation, but the gunfire continued, with hot rounds pinging off the rails, slamming into the iron sheeting with a loud metallic clang, biting huge chunks of plaster from the walls, filling the air with choking dust and debris. The men gave up, dropped to the floor and crawled for the exit. Constable Hughes from Newtown testified that when he and his colleagues fought their way into this balcony room an ugly brawl erupted with a large group of communists who were waiting for them with clubs and pipes. In contrast, the pickets said that they had fled into the rear bedroom to avoid being shot and had just noticed a couple of cops sneaking across the kitchen roof when about five plain-clothes men appeared at the door and charged into them. Young James Miller had heard the glass breaking on the balcony doors and wanted to smash the back windows, perhaps as an escape route, but his mates said, 'Don't! There are coppers out there, they'll shoot you!'

'I picked up an iron bar and said they'll shoot us all the same', said Miller. 'So we might as well die fighting'.

Suddenly a cop yelled, 'Here's the bastards!' and Miller had his chance.

Garbett, with his useless, dangling arm, dropped to the floor and crawled through the ruck of flailing men, heaving himself over the banister of the staircase and landing with a crash down below where Constables Kelly and Hollier were making heavy work of the armour-plated back door. A brace of pistol shots roared through the hole they had battered. Hiding under the stairs, where he had scuttled as the bullets began zipping past, Len Emmerton, one of the older men, saw the police break through at the back and come down from above. A couple of his comrades had tried to shore up the sandbags at the rear but they had been driven away by the gunfire. Raymond Dare had heard the banging at the back door.

I could see the police trying to hack their way in. As I was looking through the opening I saw a policeman deliberately shoot into the room, the bullet just buzzing past my ear. I could hear a lot of shots being fired but was under the impression that they were blanks being fired to frighten us, but when I heard the bullets hit the wall I knew that I was very much mistaken and that the police were bent on getting us even if some of us were killed in the process. I got out of range of the door and told Garbett that they were firing into the room and he said that he knew that as he had just been hit in the arm with a bullet ...

Dare ran through to the front room where most of the men were now waiting. Some fearful. Some furious. Some calm and some crazed. Norman Mailer once wrote that fighting aroused two of the deepest anxieties men contain; not just the fear of getting hurt, 'which is profound in more men than will admit to it', but the contrary fear, equally unadmitted, of hurting others. Those men in the front room, caught in the confluence of these two types of panic, were at a mortal disadvantage as the cops piled in and the numbers of combatants swarming through the narrow halls and tiny rooms soared towards fifty. Unlike the police they did not live their lives immersed in random and banal violence. Many had seen combat in the war, but for some that simply meant shellshock rendered them unfit for this sort of action. As the riot-beast kicked and gouged, pushed and shoved, screamed, shouted, cursed, punched and batoned its way towards them, it must have robbed many of their courage. All those straining bodies so closely confined, all smashing into each other and running at white heat. All those hearts racing, eyes darting. The room would have been warm, maybe even hot, with their closeness. It stank. It reeked of human funk and fear. The police did not hesitate when they breached that last sanctuary. They charged in 'and started to baton us unmercifully', said Dare.

> Three police came at me with their batons raised to strike and I tried to defend myself as best I could. I warded off one blow but the other two gave me some curry and batoned me till I was nearly unconscious. As I lay on the floor I saw some of the police pull Murphy to his feet off the floor and batoned him something awful, not letting off until he was a bloody mess …

Patrick Storen, who had played cards in the front room until the patrol cars arrived, was one of the hardy crew who ran to throw themselves against the sandbags when the sledgehammer first pounded against the back door. He had never believed the police would move against them, placing his faith in Jack Lang's Labor government. But when someone yelled out that the cops were there he grabbed his overcoat for fear of losing it 'in the fight which I knew was in front of us' and hurried out. Something struck him over the eye in the back room and he missed most of the fighting there, coming to on the floor of the front room again, where a scene of bestial intensity was playing itself out.

There seemed to be a fierce fight taking place. As I attempted to straighten up (I was lying face down over a table at the time) I was dealt several blows over the head with a baton and knocked to the floor. I glanced around and could see men lying on the floor, some covered with blood. The room was then full of police and they were using their batons and boots in all directions. There were a couple of men still engaged in the tussle with police in the centre of the room while numerous other police were bashing those who were already on the floor and some who had been forced into the corner of the room. Several times I attempted to raise myself from the floor only to be beaten down again. After a while I was pulled back up onto my feet and placed against the wall. Men were being handcuffed and taken outside. I staggered out into the back room and was making towards the broken down back door when I was grabbed ... given another bashing and pushed backwards out the door over some bags of sand.

Up to this point the police and protesters' stories diverge significantly, sometimes on major facts, sometimes on questions of nuance and understanding. From the moment the UWM was finally 'beaten down', however, the divergence was total. Inspector Farley's dry recital of the facts as he knew them had the activists taken into the arms of blind justice and delivered to the holding cells at Newtown. The prisoners themselves described an hour or so of unceasing brutality, starting in the back yard of 143 where they were thrown in a heap on the remains of the broken fence and flogged without mercy. Most of the men were unconscious said John Stace, but still the coppers stood on their necks and flayed them with batons which were already sticky with congealed

Only the Strong

blood and shreds of human scalp. Frogmarched down the side of the house, John Murphy had his head rammed into the rough brickwork by a jack who said, 'We'll kill you, you red bastard'. Raymond Dare had earlier seen Murphy fetched out of the house by a cop who said, 'You look pretty red now, you red bastard', and 'punched him on the face a few times'. They were all dragged into the street where the crowd was howling in impotent rage. The *Herald* described the UWM's men as 'almost insensible' when dragged to the patrol cars. The crowd, it reported, was definitely antagonistic to the police. Numbering many thousands, and stretching for half a kilometre on each side of the house, they hooted at the appearance of each bloodied constable and cheered their heroes from the UWM. They grabbed rocks and chunks of concrete from a nearby road excavation, hurling them at the receding patrol cars.

At Newtown station, said the protesters, they walked a gauntlet from the car doors to the charge room. Said Dare, 'As we were going into the charge room each one in his turn was given a horrid time. The police were lined up all the way inside and as one of us went past they either punched or kicked us. I was kicked on the knee and nearly knocked over'. He saw Murphy knocked out again and pummelled all the way out of the room on his way to hospital. Patrick Storen watched five or six cops bashing one of his mates. In James Miller's car every prisoner who alighted was given one massive punch to the jaw by a bizarrely efficient policeman, almost as though he was ticking them off his sheet for the day.

Garbett, nursing his gunshot wound, saw Les Goldberg smashed on the jaw and knocked out by a plain-clothes officer. It was a 'brutal blow', according to Robert Clark, which sent him 'crashing to the floor like a pole axed steer'. Goldberg was perversely fortunate though. He remembered alighting from the patrol and starting to walk across the station yard, then 'nothing more till I woke up in the hospital having my ear stitched'. Garbett heard a cry for help, turned around and saw Hawkins who was handcuffed to Emmerton. Emmerton was unconscious and Hawkins was desperately trying to drag him away from the blows of the police, their arms a blur as they worked him over like threshing machines. 'Hawkins got a hold of my hands with his free hand and we dragged Emmerton into the corner of the charge room', said Goldberg. Clark, standing nearby, peering through the red haze of his own pain, could not even recognise Emmerton, so gross were his wounds. Hawkins, who had broken two police batons with his thick skull that day, described the assault.

When I reached the door of the charge room one policeman hit me in the face, blackened my eyes and cut my lip. They then set about Emmerton. They knocked him down and kicked him. I called to Garbett to help me pull him into the charge room. We dragged him into a corner of the room. As the policeman took the handcuffs off another policeman hit me as soon as I stood up. When I got to the counter to give my name, the policeman behind the counter hit me on the hands with a ruler and said, *Don't stain this counter with blood, you Russian bastard.*

Many of the activists mentioned the police calling them Russian, or in one case German, despite their mostly Anglo names and thick Australian accents. More than one protester lying broken and bleeding on the pile of fence palings behind 143 heard the police say, 'We'll give you Red Russia, you bastards', before hopping into

Only the Strong

someone with their boots and nightsticks. It raises the interesting question of just how strongly the police held to this myth. Rationally, of course, they knew that their enemies were simply working-class men from Redfern, Leichhardt, Surry Hills and so on. They may even have surmised, had they cared to, that most of the older men, those aged in their early thirties and above, probably served in the army during the Great War. Looking at Black Friday now, we don't have to work too hard to tease out any number of strands running through our Anzac mythology, such as courage under fire or persistence in the face of futility. But of course the Anzac legend was long ago appropriated by the national establishment, and the fact that many of the Anzacs turned 'red' in response to economic chaos and violent repression simply does not compute. It is dissonant information which, if accepted, would threaten the significance of a national legend. It would, as Edelman said, 'destroy meaning'. Meaning imposes order on chaos, which allows us to see patterns in confusing events, to anticipate the future and negate any ugly surprises. The belief that some shadowy Marxist conspiracy is behind violent anti-eviction protests 'gives meaning to the riots and precludes surprise when they recur'. On the other hand information, the truth of what happened that day, as opposed to meaning 'involves complexity or lack of order' and an inability to foresee the outcome of such violence. Unlike meaning, says Edelman, information is transmitted, and what is transmitted is complicating premises; for instance, that protesters are not agents of Moscow but simply hungry and pissed off.

It doesn't really matter that the police 'knew' the protesters were not actually Russians or Germans. Because beyond the level of mere abuse, down in their brain stems and in their meat, they also *knew* these men represented a threat to the order they were paid to preserve. Lang knew it too. The thousands of people who cheered the staggering protesters to the patrol cars told him so. On the day, the police were always going to prevail. As Hannah Arendt noted, 'in a contest of violence against violence the superiority of the government has always been absolute'. But that superiority evaporates as the consent of the governed fades. Nadia Wheatley makes the point that to have advanced any further the UWM would have needed guns and the will to use them, and the crowd in Union Street would have had to overrun and destroy the police lines. Nor could the violence have stopped there. They would have had to challenge the State in exactly the way the police, the media and the establishment feared.

Who can say whether the spectacle of the police beating on his own people forced Lang's hand? Or whether it was the surge of the crowds outside these eviction protests that lit up his radar. With each new eviction, support for militant and radical action seemed to increase exponentially. Whatever the cause, within a week the Attorney-General had tabled legislation purporting to guarantee fair rents and curtail the evictions. This deflated the UWM's campaign which died away after Black Friday. It was to be some time before the activists realised they had been sold a dud and that the new laws did not really empower them at all. By then it was too late. For Lang, too, the end was nigh. His clash with the commonwealth government and his old enemy the 'money power' was more purely a political struggle than the street battle over evictions. Within a year Governor Phillip Game would demonstrate that not all the power of his office had been eroded when he dismissed the Premier and finally snuffed out the hopes of any of the working classes who still retained faith in their hero, 'the Big Fella'.

Only the Strong

This perhaps is the dirty little secret of violence; not that it is ugly and unjust, but that it promises so much and delivers so little. This promise, that by a strong arm and valiant heart a man may bend the world to his will, is a recurring dream. Sometimes, on waking, it might even seem that this dream lies within reach, that with one mighty lunge the oppressed might take what is rightfully theirs. Of course, peering at the wreckage of their lives through blackened eyes, the hungry, battered men of Union Street must have known that such dreams almost never come true.

But then, within a generation, for one brief shining moment, they did.

Property development, as the refreshingly cynical Deyan Sudjic tells us, is an edgy, maverick industry where successful practitioners constantly morph from street-corner hucksterism to pinstriped respectability and 'the naked realities of guile, bravado, aggression and ego' are always close to the surface – if not actually free to tear all over the landscape, devouring everything in their path. Even by these high standards, however, Frank Theeman was one of the city's more colourful identities. He came on like nothing so much as a Swingin' Sixties James Bond supervillain, with his Strangelove accent, his Coke bottle glasses and a supporting cast of thugs and weirdos. But unlike Ernst Stavro Blofeld, on whom he seemed to model himself, Theeman didn't want to destroy the whole world, just a little bit of it. By 1973 he had quietly bought up a long string of elegant but decaying Victorian terraces on the high sandstone ridge overlooking Woolloomooloo; the same pleasant heights where the town's A-list of the 1830s had run up their Georgian villas and retired from the fug and bustle of horse-drawn

Sydney. Old Tom Shephard had once laid into them for destroying the scarp's natural beauties with 'the murderous hoe and grubbing axe'. Now Theeman planned to emulate them with a massive development anchored by three awesomely hideous skyscrapers which would bury the neighbourhood's antique charms under immense tonnages of concrete and ugliness. Embodying all of the bestial, breathtaking horror of what was then world's worst architectural practice, Theeman's plans evoked the sort of profoundly antihuman environment you could expect to create if you cross-pollinated the grossest excesses of triumphant capitalism with the aesthetic sensibilities of whatever engineering department the Romanian secret police tasked with fitting out the torture chambers in their blank-faced, ferroconcrete punishment palaces.

Theeman of course was not a lone rider on this awful crusade. For nearly twenty years developers had laid siege to the city, destroying great swathes of graceful sandstone buildings, scattering the serfs before their onslaught and riding away with fistfuls of loot. The fat times of the 1960s were wild enough to blow away any lingering ghosts of the 30s as everyone cashed in on the boom, although of course some profited more than others. Property developers and the wizards of finance who stood behind them were the white-hot internet stocks of the era as their profits and market value rocketed far beyond the gravitational pull of economic reality. The eventual outcome was as inevitable in 1974 as it had been in 1929, 1891 and 1842. The physical legacy of this modern crash was more striking, however, with the mutation of a previously charming if sleepy city centre into a dense labyrinth of unleaseable high-rise office space which was often stylistically repugnant and technically flawed, recasting nineteenth century problems of overshadowing and air circulation on an epic scale.

Only the Strong

Like all the previous booms the speculative tornado which ripped through Sydney's property market between 1968 and 1972 spun up out of a confluence of fantastic greed and wilful, bone-headed stupidity, supercharged by a frightening credit binge. The capitalist system, as Schumpeter observes, does not grow slowly and steadily, like a tree, but jerkily, in fits and starts, often linked to technical advances like steam engines or computer chips. Revolutions in business systems, such as mass production lines or radical developments in financial processes, can also act as catalysts to rapid growth. In the early 1960s Sydney, that 'pure product of capitalism', which had always been wide open to the chaotic jolts of global finance, was the focus of a number of such developments. The city's population had ballooned as a result of massive immigration and the natural increase of the postwar baby boom. Low unemployment and rising wages ensured this emerging metropolis was also a hot market, with demand for housing and services creating a natural boom in construction and consumer goods. The city fringes rushed away from the site of first settlement, although development accelerated around the old core as well, with hundreds of small building companies responding to the demands of millions wanting easy access to the city centre. Their demand increased the density of life in the inner suburbs which began to lose terraces and detached dwellings to larger unit blocks where fifty people could be crammed into the space previously occupied by four or five. The construction giants poured billions of tonnes of concrete into shopping centres, schools and community facilities for the increased population.

This natural boom underlay another explosion of investment in office construction. During the 1950s and 1960s American multi-national firms had built up enormous reserves of US dollars in

European, especially British, banks. This money, the germinal form of today's global capital markets, was hot, liquid and promiscuous, not caring where it went or what it did as long as there was a pay-off on the deal. MT Daly writes of millions of dollars surging from London to Sydney and into the accounts of Australian mining companies such as MIM, Comalco and Hammersly Iron to fund their expansion during the sixties. And just as the city's growth spurt of the 1830s occasioned a diversification of the primitive agrarian economy into slightly more sophisticated manufacturing and services, so the minerals boom of the 1960s helped transform a provincial capital into a true global city. The pastoral–commercial combine which still dominated the local economy before the Second World War was rendered subordinate, if not totally irrelevant by the shift. Daly outlines the change in *Sydney Boom, Sydney Bust*, tracing the rise in power of merchant banks, life assurance companies and foreign lenders as local developers gorged themselves on bloated lines of credit while they annihilated block after block of old warehouses, hotels and shopping arcades to raise homogenised stacks of offices to meet the needs of newly wealthy mining companies and the banks, lawyers and accountancy firms which served them. The perennial clash of municipal and State authorities distorted an already unbalanced system when cabinet sacked the elected city council for a third time, replacing them with commissioners. During the twenty-two months that planning authority rested with these three appointees, development applications went orbital, as the building industry dived through the window of opportunity. Throughout 1969 and 1970, urban planning in Sydney 'entered the realms of absurdity'. Paul Ashton describes meetings of the City Planning and Improvement Committee, which assessed hundreds of millions of dollars worth of

Only the Strong

projects, taking an average of two to three minutes. Every application was passed.

As before, the system formed a sort of synergistic feedback loop, the process consuming itself while simultaneously growing fatter and hungrier. At first, land in Sydney was cheap compared with New York and London. The yield on office space in Sydney was twice that in London, and with interest rate differentials the potential returns were stratospheric. The market behaved like a magic slot machine, showering the players in gold doubloons as they desperately tried to feed in more coins. The frenetic pace of development quickly ate up all the easily exploitable land so that the few blocks left to develop 'acquired a scarcity value and were bid up strongly'. It was madness of course. Like the crazed speculation of 1841 and the blind rush for nonperforming internet stocks of the 1990s. When the hysteria of the crash receded and the survivors looked about them in 1976, they found a city where thirty per cent of its new high-rise offices sat waiting for tenants in empty, ticking stillness.

A glutted market and spiralling interest bills played as important a role in this crash as they had in previous crashes. But there was a significant difference between this disaster and those that preceded it: the role played by the city's lower orders. Of course by 1974, people didn't use the phrase lower orders any more, at least not in public. Edward Macarthur's simplistic division of society into the owners of capital and everyone else, with the riding boots of the former wedged firmly on the throats of the latter, was losing its validity. Class divisions were still important – vitally so as it turned out for the city's property magnates – but other lines of division were also cracking open. Postwar prosperity had enriched the working class and enlarged the middle class. The struggle for survival, which had still been such a close-run thing for the poor during the Great Depression, was much less acute for white Australia after 1945, allowing it the luxury of gradually fracturing along those stress lines which would permanently alter society's contours in the last quarter of the twentieth century; lines which included race, gender, sexuality and educational privilege. This process of splintering the formerly rigid tungsten axis around which the city's power structure had coalesced can be placed within the context of Sydney's natural tendency towards shifting patterns of dominance and conflict. The difference, for a few short years at least, was that whereas the poor and the workers had once been irrelevant to the process – or victims of it – in the 1960s and 70s they emerged for the first time as players and winners. The vehicle by which they took this trip down the glory road was a strange and wonderful collection of hard-knuckled, unskilled labourers; figurative descendants of all those other labourers who had been bundled into the stinking holds of England's convict transports.

One of the first business empires to take a blow from these shovel-toting bandits was AV Jennings, that 'very proud old builder' who had survived a traumatic birth during the Depression to thrive in the postwar years. In 1968 they found themselves in possession of 4.9 hectares of rare, pristine bushland at Hunters Hill. The scenic riverside locale had remained largely undisturbed throughout white settlement and now presented a remnant wilderness of banksias, sheoaks, grevilleas and kunzeas in which thrived colonies of ringtailed possums and native birds. Development-minded local councillors referred to the area as 'a tick-infested rubbish dump', although the dump they described was in fact 'an Aboriginal midden dating back to 1200 AD'. Having

Only the Strong

shelled out four hundred grand for the midden and surrounds, these very proud old builders were in no mood to listen to a bunch of housewives who were a little ticked off at their plan to run up a couple of high-rise apartment towers on the graves of the poor old ringtailed possums.

The bushland had been preserved since the 1890s by its long-time owners the Kelly family as an informal nature reserve for the local community. In the can-do civic spirit of Menzies-era stay-at-home mums, Monica Sheehan, Chris Dawson, Betty James and Kath Laheny worked the appropriate political channels for all they were worth to keep it that way; writing to local aldermen, to State and federal members, to responsible ministers, to the Premier and getting exactly nowhere and nothing in return. Jennings were prevailed upon by the State Planning Authority to finesse their design from a high-rise concept to a low-rise village of luxury houses, and Premier Robert Askin did send the lobbyists an unctuously deceptive telegram on the eve of a tight election, saying: 'Very hopeful of a helpful decision on your problems and will advise within 24 hours'. But after winning the ballot he never did get around to calling them back and of course Jennings' new plans still ended with those possums buried in concrete. Betty James explained how their accepted reality began to dissolve and that ghost city which lay beneath the surface of things was revealed.

We were inexperienced in the ways of business and politics but we learned week by week as one step led to another. We found out quickly that politicians had a language of their own; that decisions were made behind closed doors; that power and money came first and that people's wishes came second, if considered at all.

LEVIATHAN

In June of 1971 therefore, the Battlers for Kelly's Bush, as they had become known, turned to an unlikely ally, a rowdy, two-fisted band of actual, swear-to-God communists and industrial brawlers known as the Builders' Labourers Federation. Or BLF for short. The startling, unprecedented quality of this manoeuvre is difficult to appreciate in a post-Cold War world. For the class these women represented, communists had crawled out from under the same rock as Nazis and paedophiles. Communists were killing their sons in Vietnam. Communists hated the Church. Communists ran gulags and death camps. They liked brainwashing and espionage and cheating at the Olympics. They were probably mixed up in drugs and lesbianism. They had definitely taken over the universities. They had enslaved half of Europe, all of China and were no doubt plotting their advance on Hunters Hill at that very moment. Communists in the union movement leapt out of their bug infested beds every morning to wolf down a bowl of cold borscht and plot the destruction of the sort of decent, God-fearing small to medium sized businesses owned by the husbands of women like Monica Sheehan, Chris Dawson, Betty James and Kath Laheny. Communists were not to be trusted.

But the communists of the BLF, as it turned out, were the last hope of the ringtailed possum. After the minister for local government, Pat 'the Mortician' Morton, signed a rezoning order which cleared the way for Jennings' bulldozers, the Battlers approached the labour movement. The Federated Engine Drivers and Firemans Association (FEDFA), whose members would drive those dozers, tabled the women's request for assistance at the Labor Council on 3 June. The unionists agreed to not to carry out any 'bulldozing, grading and land clearing work', delighting the women and encouraging them to seek further help from the BLF, whose members would ultimately build the planned luxury homes. The BLF was then a weird, exotic form of life which could probably only have existed in the atmosphere of the sixties and early seventies. Described by Meredith and Verity Burgmann as 'a corrupt and conservative' gangster regime in the 1950s, the New South Wales chapter of the BLF was remade into something entirely different by a group of reforming idealists during the following decade. The Burgmanns' history of the BLF, *Green Bans, Red Union*, exhaustively details this struggle, describing a union which at the height of its powers was as much of a threat to the mummified dinosaurs of the labour movement as it was to the insatiable greedheads of the private sector. Under the leadership troika of Joe Owens, Bob Pringle and Jack Mundey the BLF grew into the most militant, radical and successful union the city or indeed the country had ever seen.

What separated it from other traditionally combative unions was the BLF's commitment to radical democracy inside their organisation and a novel coalition of social movements outside. The BLF of that time was not like other unions. Its office-bearers were paid no more than the members. They could not stay in office indefinitely, being required to return to their tools after a couple of years. Consulting and involving the membership was not just an empty phrase but something of an obsession. The union leaders would not make a move without the say-so of their membership, and once that sanction was given they could not be moved from it by threat or inducement. (Mundey was once offered a twenty million dollar bribe 'to allow half of a proposed development to take place', according to the Burgmann history, an approach which was flatly rejected.) Their power sprang from a militant solidarity and technical changes within the building industry itself. The gargantuan nature of the projects underway in the city concentrated thousands of builders' labourers in a relative handful of sites, and the significance of their role in high-rise construction was amplified by the new production techniques such buildings entailed. As the Burgmanns point out, 'the developers' need for speedy completion of speculative projects, financed by venture capital loans at high interest rates, gave a tactical advantage to the building industry unions, which they were loath not to exploit'. Refusing overtime or 'a strategic sick day became an industrial weapon of great potential'. Interrupting concrete pours could have disastrous consequences and the 'ability of builders' labourers to walk off, or threaten to, before completing a pour was an important bargaining point'.

The BLF would use any weapon in its armoury to prosecute the cause of its members who, it must be said, worked in one of the most uncivilized and fractious industries of modern times. The management ethos which had replaced a whole work crew with a starving, desperate Jack Acland in the Depression – because the boss knew a family man could be whipped that much harder – was alive and kicking forty years later. Builders' labourers died on construction sites every year because the development companies would not spend money on safety until forced to. The seething hostility which existed between boss and worker is probably incomprehensible to anyone without first-hand experience. They were, quite simply, enemies. The success of the BLF in confronting this enemy welded the largely uneducated membership of working-class white males, newly arrived migrants and, most surprising of all, women labourers, to the union leadership. Encouraged by their success in battles for the more traditional objectives of improved wages, safety and working conditions, the

Only the Strong

supposedly conservative working-class BLF members fought campaigns for women's rights, homosexuals, students, prisoners and of course the environment.

Kelly's Bush, the first green ban, was put in place after union president Bob Pringle met with the Battlers' full committee of thirteen women. (According to the Burgmanns the women were a little intimidated by the prospect of meeting this mad leftie who had recently been photographed by the *Herald* 'sawing down the goal posts at the Sydney Cricket Ground to prevent the South African rugby team playing'.) Pringle suggested the union could place a ban on the site, but only if the membership agreed and only if the local community demonstrated that opposition to Jennings' proposal was widespread. A neighbourhood meeting of 600 residents confirmed their support for the ban after which the BLs put their hands up for it. The significance of this action should not be underestimated. By declaring the site black, the workers were denying themselves employment in an industry where job security was more a matter of wish fulfilment than reality. The residents seeking their help were scions of the upper and middle classes, the sort of people who'd signed on with the fascist New Guard to take pot shots at starving workers in the 1930s. And, when you got down to it, no builders' labourer was ever going to be welcomed into their neighbourhood, even if they could afford to move in, which of course they couldn't. However, the labourers' antipathy for businesses like AV Jennings, the incredibly buoyant conditions across the rest of the industry, and the leadership's evolving concern with New Left issues such as the environment and urban planning overrode these objections. The ban came down on 17 June 1971. When Jennings shrugged and said they'd simply go ahead with nonunion labour, they received a swift, brutal lesson in the altered state of their relationship with residents of Hunters Hill. A telegram arrived from a Jennings building site at North Sydney. It threatened that if the company tried it on, if even one tree was lost, 'this half-completed building will remain so forever, as a monument to Kelly's Bush'. The Hunter's Hill site remains virgin bushland to this day.

The success of this alliance led to an awakening of communities across the city. Residents' action groups sprang up by the dozen to fight unwanted, unrestrained development. A second green ban was placed on a development at Eastlakes in November 1971 after Parkes Development broke a promise not to build on land set aside as a recreation area. Plans to annex vast areas of Centennial Park and Moore Park for a State sports centre, including an 80 000 seat stadium, 10 000 seat entertainment centre and 'a gigantic parking lot', were hyped as a massive boost to commerce and industry; although the main beneficiaries would be the developers who poured elephant bucks into the coffers of Askin's conservative coalition, walking off with fantastic profits – and eleven knighthoods – in return. A residents' action group, which included Nobel prize winner Patrick White, twitched about in futile opposition until the BLF put a bullet into the whole concept in June 1972.

The confrontation over the sports centre was not the first direct challenge to the State. In 1968 the government had established the Sydney Cove Redevelopment Authority to convert its ownership of what remained of the Rocks into a geyser of cash. Even after extensive demolitions for plague clearance and bridge-building, a large population of waterfront workers, seafarers and their families remained as tenants of the Maritime Services Board in the clutch of terraces and boarding houses which survived.

Only the Strong

Gaping at the berserk inflation of land and building prices a short distance away in the CBD, Cabinet decided to realise its asset in one spectacular orgy of exploitation. After ramping up rents for their low-income tenants by 200 and 300 per cent, the State government popped the champagne corks to reveal their blueprint for a 21 hectare, $500 million profanity, featuring high-rise office blocks, apartments, luxury hotels and department stores. Working-class families who had paid rent to the State for generations would be evicted, while private consortiums of multi-national investors were blessed with the certainty of ninety-nine year leases over this 'public land'.

As with all previous planned developments in the Rocks, no provision was made for the accommodation of the residents. A few token historic buildings would be preserved as curious trinkets but the social fabric of the area would be shredded. In January 1972 bulldozers moved in to begin demolition but a confrontation between residents and drivers led to the FEDFA and the Amalgamated Metal Workers Union joining the ban placed on the project by the BLF in November of the previous year. Askin's government had amended provisions of the Landlord and Tenant Act, which the Union Street protesters had taken such a beating for in 1931, leaving the Rocks' residents with no protection against their landlord; i.e., the very government which had just stripped them of their rights. As the Burgmanns explain:

Previously, the landlord had an obligation to the tenant to pay compensation or to adequately rehouse people being displaced; since the amendments, the landlord had no responsibility to the tenant and the tenant had no legal claim on the landlord. Pringle and Owens [from the union executive] objected to these changes in a statement defending the ban: 'we believe that these amendments are contrary to the rights and needs of the people. Progress should be for all the people and not be detrimental to some for the benefit of others'. Having lived in the area for decades, paying rent to different state authorities over the years, probably paying for their homes several times over, Pringle and Owens insisted these people had 'a right to dignified consideration'.

What the Sydney Cove Redevelopment Authority figured was that these people had the right to get the hell outta Dodge. When contractors pushed the issue by trying to demolish some garages and workshops in Playfair Street a squall of protest, violence and industrial mayhem erupted in a two-week-long battle with thousands of unionists walking off sites around the city, five hundred of them storming the disputed building site. Hundreds of police arrested dozens of workers and residents. As with every other clash in this period, however, the initiative lay with the coalition of protesters. As long as the bans remained in place, the developers and their backers, in this case the state, were effectively powerless. While work on SCRA's grand design was paralysed the residents formulated a 'people's plan' for the area which stressed a continuing presence for low-income housing along with cultural, civic and small business uses in the renovated historic buildings. Restoration work on these properties had not been banned and by 1974 the government found itself in the humiliating position of having to accept the residents' vision. The restored properties were returning handsome rents while Treasury was haemorrhaging money over the interest bill on loans for the stalled high-rise projects.

The Rocks were spared but sirens were shrieking in boardrooms

TAX INVOICE
ABN - 39 234 516 816
Original
Receipt - 28/10/2005 - 10:19:51
Node No - 7
Receipt No - 29012

2 X Promo-City Rail Day Tripper Adult	$16.00

Total Sales	$16.00
Total GST	$0.00
Total Due	$16.00
Cash	$16.00
Tender Amount	$20.00
Change Due	$4.00

Post Code : 0001
Served By : Staff

Node Number :7   Ver 7.2.1.0

Only the Strong

all over the city. By the mid-1970s BLF green bans had thrown a choke-hold on projects worth at least $3000 million (in 1974 dollars). When told he was taking bread from his members' mouths, union secretary Jack Mundey replied that they would rather build 'urgently required hospitals, schools, other public utilities, high quality flats, units and houses, provided they are designed with adequate concern for the environment, rather than to build ugly, unimaginative, architecturally bankrupt blocks of concrete and glass offices'. Fine words, but you don't snatch three billion big ones from a gang of land sharks and walk away unscathed. A short distance from the Rocks, the scene of the union's greatest triumph, the hammerheads bared their teeth.

Mick Fowler was a big, bull-necked seaman with a slightly scary Dennis Lillee moustache, sideburns like Texas and a hint of Elvis in his hairstyle. He was fond of playing jazz, spinning yarns and – just quietly – smoking dope. But if you didn't know him, his ham-hock fists, tightly stretched body shirts and drooping cigarettes lent an air of physical menace which your average bohemian would be incapable of synthesising. He had gone down to the sea as a young man and the life there had hardened him some. He'd worked some tough ships, walked some mean streets and was more likely to be roused to anger than fear by the likes of 'Karate' Joe Meissner. Like Mick Fowler, Karate Joe presented a fairly intimidating front. With Fowler, a generous, ukelele-playing hepcat, it was just a matter of appearances. With Karate Joe it was business. Meissner (aka Machine Gun Joe, aka Ivan the Hoon) had been hired by Frank Theeman to facilitate the rapid transit of a lot of inconvenient pensioners, battlers and boho spongers who were standing between Mr Theeman and a pile of money. A Very Big Pile Of Money.

Meissner, who would later win fame in the lowbrow derangement of the 1980s Love Boat scandal, was then learning the ropes as a minor villain, looming in the Victoria Street doorways of recalcitrant tenants, carrying an iron bar and speculating on their domestic arrangements and/or travel plans. Most took the hint and fled but some proved disagreeably contrary, Mick Fowler amongst them. Returning home from a long voyage on a bulk carrier, Fowler had been looking forward to stowing his kit in the small room he rented in an old boarding house at 115 Victoria Street. His mother had digs in the same building and there are a couple of versions of what happened next. In a video interview held at the Mitchell Library Fowler himself says he was surprised to find his mother sitting on the front step, surrounded by their belongings, terribly upset, dazed and hopeless, clutching fifty dollars which she'd been given by Theeman to cover the cost of moving and storage. Contemporary press reports said Fowler had received an eviction notice by telegram while still at sea and his mother was missing when he arrived home. The *Seamen's Journal* later claimed Theeman's enforcers had broken into the little apartment, terrorised his mother and stolen his musical instruments and stereo equipment while he was away.

The fine details aren't that important. Just take it as read there had been some first-class villainy. What was important was Mick Fowler's decision to contest the eviction. Borrowing some pliers and scratching up a posse of five or six friends, he fronted Joe Meissner and a couple of uniformed cops at the front gate of his home. Ignoring Karate Joe, Fowler addressed the nearest cop with rising anger.

Only the Strong

'Look, I'm Mick Fowler,' he said. 'I'm the legal tenant. I live here. My gear's been put out, the joint's been broken into, I'm very upset. I've come 2000 fucking miles to find this and you're pushing me aside!'

Meissner pushed in, insisting that Mick was no longer a tenant. 'I represent the owner and I want him arrested,' he said.

'And with that I was fucking well arrested and handcuffed and taken up to Darlinghurst Police Station!' spat a disgusted Fowler on the video.

A heavy vibe lay over the largely deserted street. Of the three or four hundred tenants living there at the start of the month, only a dozen or so remained. They had formed the Victoria Street Residents' Action Group to resist both the eviction campaign and Theeman's overall scheme; but a few days before Fowler arrived, one of the group's principals, a short, tough, nugget of a bloke named Arthur King, was grabbed up from his home and spirited off into the night. He had gone to bed at eleven after chatting with friends for a couple of hours. Waking with a start when the light came on, he saw a man standing by the switch, silently staring at him. The man turned and left as King struggled up to give chase. Hurrying into the hallway he was jumped by another two intruders. They hustled him out of the flat, dumped him in a car and drove to a motel room south of the city. Tied, gagged and blindfolded, he was held until Monday when Theeman's quiet persuaders bundled him back into the boot of the car and drove to Kings Cross. The boot had a small hole through which King could catch glimpses of the outside world. His abductors pulled up in front of a brothel called the Venus Room, a cheesy dive which formed part of Abe Saffron's empire. While King was missing, panicky friends searched anxiously as carloads of blocky-looking young men tore through the street yelling, 'We're going to get you and you'll be gone'. When King reappeared on Monday he spoke briefly to friends, collected his possessions and left forever.

Prowlers broke into the houses of the few remaining tenants, smashing windows, removing locks, kicking down doors and wrenching off taps so that the properties flooded. Then, three days after his first set-to with Karate Joe, Mick Fowler returned with reinforcements. Mick, some locals and about fifty or sixty hefty comrades from the BLF and Fowler's own Seamen's Union converged on 115 and fought their way through a thin line of Theeman's hired muscle. Surrounded by this formidable crew and puffing contentedly on a cigarette, Fowler told journalists that they expected violence from the 'karate experts' when his furniture arrived. But, already reeling from a storm of insinuation and bad PR after the King kidnapping, Theeman had his men withdraw.

Like his allies in Macquarie Street, Frank Theeman was taking a bath on interest repayments. As Trevor Sykes noted, the fat days were over. By mid-1973 the long bond rate had blown out by a point while debentures leapt to nine per cent. 'By September of that year long bonds had reached 8.5 percent and debentures were out to eleven, the highest they had been in two generations'. Theeman was pissing away maybe fourteen to sixteen grand every week; bad karma in a highly geared racket like property development.

It was no coincidence that around this time arsonists seemed to discover a particular affinity for the surviving buildings of Victoria Street. Squatters had taken heart from Mick Fowler's stand, gradually appearing by the dozen to take over the abandoned and rapidly decaying terraces. The campaign, which was originally concerned with the bankrupt aesthetics of Theeman's plan, shifted to

Only the Strong

encompass expressly political demands for the retention of low-income housing. Dozens of squatters flocked to the street on the heels of a few hardy pioneers. Some were just footloose activists looking for action. Some were awakened environmentalists rallying to the cause. But most were poor workers and students, among them a large number of women, who were attracted by the cheap accommodation and communal atmosphere which blossomed as everyone set to work cleaning and restoring the decaying properties.

A pack of mad libertarian drinkers and fornicators, known as the Sydney Push, were drawn into the battle on the side of the residents and BLF. They helped organise street patrols to ward off arson attacks – although a young black woman was still killed by one deliberately lit blaze. Theeman, too, had his own patrols out. At any one time at least twenty or thirty goons could be found lounging against the street's wrought-iron fences, having a smoke, glaring at any nearby protesters. These were 70s goons of course, so they tended to turn out in hipster flares, Adidas sneakers, nylon Gloweave shirts and long greasy hair. But what they lacked in sartorial impact they made up for by toting pick handles everywhere.

The improvised weapons proved themselves more than mere ornaments in January of 1974 when Theeman, having beaten the squatters in the Supreme Court, was able to deploy fifty or sixty hipster goons with the active support of the police force to clear out his investments. The protesters knew a confrontation was coming after the State's Justice Minister green-lighted the use of police to turn them out of their new homes. They took to the barricades with the ghosts of 1931 at their side. Most boarded themselves up behind their dilapidated Victorian facades, some receiving help from striking labourers to erect more substantial defences with scaffolding taken from city building sites. Theeman's 'controllers' – as he styled his outlaw band of karate experts, nightclub bouncers and standover men – launched their assault watched over by two hundred police at seven o'clock in the morning. Unlike the riot of '31, this was extensively covered by print and broadcast media so the scenes, although pretty wild on the black and white news footage, were not as savage as they might have been. The controllers ordered the occupants of each house to leave and when they didn't, set to demolishing the front door with crowbars, pickaxes and sledgehammers. The video looks almost comical now, like a bunch of roadies and bass players from Slayer and Spinal Tap trying to smash their way into a concert venue or something. But the screaming women and children, the swirling punch-ups and crashing glass convey an intense sensation of madness and fury. Val Hodgson, one of the action group organisers, said she felt secure in the opening moments, while her house was still full of old friends. 'But it was just the banging and the thumping', she said excitedly, urgently, 'and knowing of the imminent destruction and seeing the ceiling fall down and the lightbulbs flicker ... and they tipped caustic soda on Eric ... it was really quite terrifying. They were menacing, through the holes they made in the window, snarling and snapping and saying, "We're gonna get you." It was so frightening I was pleased when the police rushed in to prevent them doing us any damage'.

'Well I'm sorry', said Theeman in his spooky Blofeld voice sometime later. 'But I didn't think to call the Salvation Army to get these people out would be the right thing'.

With squatters forced out, Fowler was once again left as the sole

Only the Strong

tenant. He was talking with BLF secretary Joe Owens when Theeman suddenly appeared with a couple of bodyguards, ex-cops. Owens joked that Theeman didn't have the numbers for negotiations and suggested he go grab a couple more heavies, but Fowler invited his arch nemesis inside.

'He opened up straightaway', said Mick, pointing out that the squatters were all gone and that he was 'the only fly in the ointment now'. '"We'll move you into a nice place across the road," offered Theeman. I said, Frank, you're missing it baby, don't you understand what it's all about? This struggle hasn't been for you Frank Theeman to sit down with me Mick Fowler and offer me the fuckin' world. You know. There's been 399 other people come into this. There's been men out of work and people arrested and beaten and handcuffed and Christ knows what. *There's been death*. There's been *kidnapping*. Don't you understand? I don't want any money'.

What he wanted was the past made new again. He wanted wharfies and working mums and old men and young students to be able to live quietly in the shabby but pleasant tree-lined street he had shared with his own mother and friends for so long. They may have owned no property, had no connections, amounted to nothing, but they did have 'a right to dignified consideration'. The alliance of residents and building unions achieved this unlikely goal in the Rocks and down the hill from Victoria Street in Woolloomooloo, but success in Potts Point was not as absolute. The bans and squatters delayed Theeman for so long that when construction did commence, his initial design – described by even the Visigoths of the State Planning Authority as one of the worst pieces of visual pollution they had ever encountered – was much compromised. The ugly stubs of apartment blocks which blot the northern end

391

of Victoria Street today are one-third the size Theeman first planned. But they did get built.

The crash of 1974 destroyed a legion of developers but as they went down they took the BLF with them, removing the main agent of their frustration. An alliance of developers and corrupt officials from the federal BLF connived to destroy the New South Wales branch during an intervention which the Burgmanns describe as 'a brutal standover'. The odious Norm Gallagher rode in over the wishes of the local membership and purged the branch of its progressive leadership. On the day he lifted the green ban on Victoria Street, Gallagher motored past the scene of January's battle in Frank Theeman's car. According to Theeman, Gallagher just looked at the empty desolated structures and said he should have torn the fucking lot down. If true, it's a moment worthy of a Hubert Selby Jnr story; a fitting denouement to a darkly compelling fable, elegantly sculpted, rich with metaphor and finely calibrated to emotional nuance, character and the victors' amoral detachment from their sins and ethical conceits. A powerful stream of contempt runs through the story, contempt for the past, and contempt for any measure of value which cannot be gauged with a pocket calculator or an eye to the main chance. Pressing the question of where power lies in such a city as this, you eventually penetrate a place with a cold vacuum for a moral core.

In October 1998, in a week-long series attempting to answer the very same question, Rupert Murdoch's flagship broadsheet, the *Australian*, limped to the conclusion that in Sydney, a 'city of a thousand networks', power was protean and constantly shifting between separate cells of influence in finance, government, construction, law, the media and primary industry. After two decades of retreat from civic society in favour of rule by market forces, the

Only the Strong

commercial city was ascendant again. The planning powers assumed by government in reaction to the chaos of the green bans had been eroded, or quietly abandoned, so that when the redevelopment of East Circular Quay provoked similar outrage to SCRA's original proposals for the Rocks, or Theeman's for Potts Point, the responsible authorities simply turned up their open, honest palms and declined to accept any responsibility at all. Decisions affecting the lives of the city's four million people are now as likely to be taken at a meeting of fund managers for AMP or Bankers Trust as on the floor of Parliament, although the cynical might say, so what? The new decision makers are no more remote than the old.

Perhaps the difference is a matter of form. Public power must at least maintain the facade of responsibility, while private power is beholden only to itself. The point at which they intersect, however, is contested and the outcome is politics, that process by which 'wealth, status and autonomy' are lost or gained. In politics we can see the sparks thrown off as the powerful contend for turf and leverage, even if the battle itself is too complex to comprehend. More revealing than anything the *Australian*'s contributors wrote was what they did not write. Their own employer, the eerily powerful Rupert was missing in action. The *Australian*'s in-house media analyst, the endearingly feral Errol Simper, scratched out a few notes explaining how the *Telegraph* had usurped the *Herald*'s influence over the city's daily political agenda, but of Rupert's influence over the highest offices of the land, there was no mention, nor of Kerry Packer, playing Gog to his Magog. Perhaps a series on the power structure of Sydney may have benefited from an investigation of the deals cut to alienate public space within the Sydney Show Ground for the private benefit of Murdoch's Fox

Studios; a deal sold as providing Sydney with the facilities to cash in on the digital entertainment revolution, facilities which quietly mutated into a hokey old theme park. Or perhaps not.

The *Australian*'s series, which opened by admitting that it may be better to ask if anyone is actually in control, confirmed the proposition that power is not a unitary concept or force in this city. Developers like Theeman, who thought themselves the masters of a little universe while government abrogated its responsibilities to manage the city (or connived in its despoilation), awoke after Kelly's Bush to discover that the power vacuum had been filled. From that moment, their previous freedom to act lay open to challenge. The swift resort to physical intimidation and force revealed another truth, one transmitted earlier in 1808, 1843 and 1931; that violence is not power, that in fact it betrays the absence of power and remains the last resort of the impotent. If Frank Theeman had been a truly powerful man, he would not have needed the likes of Joe Meissner to enforce his will. In a sense, had Theeman been powerful enough he would have simply *willed* his monstrous creation into being. Culture has always been subservient to capital in Sydney, the will of Edward Macarthur's chosen few determining the fate of the rest. A truly powerful Theeman would have willed the tenants of Victoria Street away and the city would have disposed of them. I guess it did, in the end, but only after their fierce resistance undid his ambitions.

These truths then are self-evident: that power in the city is not unitary; that violence is not power; and that human will is primary. But having peeled back these layers of meaning there is something more in here, another shape beneath the surface. Something dangerous. It was there in the dawn of 3 January 1974 when dozens of Theeman's bandit 'controllers' wielding crowbars and pick

Only the Strong

handles first stepped into the expectant quiet of Victoria Street protected by 200 police officers. At that moment the ghost city, that shadow state of government, big money and the underworld, was exposed for a moment, blinking in the sun. It was an alliance Wendy Bacon called 'legal and illegal violence working together', the most frightening thing there is, and it is the last of Sydney's stories.

4
Pig City

Who was the bagman, who was the hitman,
Who were the front men, who were the bit men

Pig City, THE PARAMETERS

On a winter's night some ten years ago I sat on the step in front of the old Woolworths store at Kings Cross. I huddled deep inside a borrowed army jacket as the rain came down in a cold, oily film, working its way through three layers of clothing. It had been that way all year, a taxi driver told me. All the squats were filling up and flooding out, and it was cold enough some nights to snap-freeze the occasional wino. My step outside Woolworths was in the middle of things and not a bad place for sitting around, checking shit out. A bit frantic sometimes. I watched a girl get speared through a window once. She lurched around with her head flapping open, blood gushing everywhere. ('I'm all right, I'm all right, just fucking leave me alone!') But at least I was out of the rain, and I could doze off occasionally without having to worry too much about getting rolled. I was working. I'd had this crazed idea to shame Bob Hawke for not following through on his promise that by 1990 no child would live in poverty. His spin doctors were going to work on the problem as the date approached, recasting his ill-considered promise into a claim no child *need* live in poverty. Or something like that.

I didn't live in Sydney at that point. I was still moving from couch to couch in Brisbane, pulling down about three or four

Pig City

hundred dollars a year working for student magazines. So homelessness and poverty were issues I felt qualified to comment on when I pitched the idea to *Rolling Stone* of my living on the street for a couple of weeks, sleeping in parks and eating McRefuse from dumpsters until I'd worked my way deep inside the story. *Stone*'s editor lent me the army jacket and pointed me up William Street where I soon became part of the furniture. My twitchy, angry loner routine, lack of personal hygiene and round-the-clock presence quickly marked me out as someone special even within the incredibly weird matrix of King Cross neighbourhood dynamics. Before long it seemed everybody was trying to score drugs from me, except the drunks, who just wanted to share their battered paper cups of cheap port and backwash with a brother who was so obviously down on his luck.

Two or three nights into my first week on the step at Woolworths I was chewing joylessly on a toasted chicken sandwich, working on my thousand-yard stare. It was early, but a few drunken fist fights had already flared up and died at the train station. I planned to wander over there later, for a drink and a smoke with a dreadlocked hobo named Graham, an ex-Navy man who'd done all his dough on some ruinous investment scam before taking a long hard slide into the gutter. The warm air which rushed up from the station was a godsend to us outdoor types, and when Graham wasn't suffering from some sort of psychotic episode he was quite good company. He asked once what I was doing on the streets and I told him, truthfully, that I was a writer. He looked at me for a second before saying, 'Yeah, I'm outta work meself at the moment too.'

This time of night, even with the rain and the cold, the footpath was thronged with hookers and buskers, some Japanese tourists, bikers, freaks, businessmen, one or two sailors and wandering packs of losers from the burbs. It was still quiet though, with none of that speedy, kind of trippy sensation that comes down later on. A couple of stolen-watch dealers and a lightning-sketch expert set up nearby. Next to them was a thin family man with wet hair and a fat blonde wife. She nursed an infant and shivered on a wet hessian sack while he murdered Dylan on a three-string guitar. They had no shoes and he made just three dollars, one for each string. They had another child who came over once. But she was crying so much the man yelled at her and she took off again.

I finished my sandwich and shifted around, trying to work some warm blood into my cold, numb backside. I decided what I really needed was some new cardboard because the old box I was sitting on was wet and starting to disintegrate. But to go looking for more would mean losing my A-list seat, so I stayed put in the pulpy mess and before long a girl staggered over. She was young, maybe thirteen or so, and soaked through to the skin. Violent chills swept over her every few seconds. Her torn grey miniskirt and pink Minnie Mouse top were no protection against the weather. One dirty white slipper flapped off in the wet crap on the pavement and I moved over as she slid down beside me, holding her head and whimpering. Her legs were chubby and turning blue from the cold. I wondered how long she'd sit there invading my personal space. I wondered what her trouble was, and then he came rolling over. An unhappy pimp. He looked a bit older. About fifteen, maybe seventeen, I figured, but in much better shape. He wore a new pair of boots with acid-wash jeans and a good leather jacket. He crouched down and punched her, a blow which would have sent her head back into the glass door with a crack had she not seen it coming and flinched into a tight defensive ball.

Pig City

'I'm getting jack of this, Helen!' he hissed. 'This is the third time this week. You're really giving me the shits, you know.'

He hit her again. He was only half my size and I suppose I could have given him something to go on with, but what was the use of it? Helen would be back every night until she died. And anyway, I told myself, who needs the attention? I stared past them to the road as a minibus full of public servants and drunken bank clerks inched through the traffic crush. Someone had tied balloons inside the vehicle and out. Confetti and streamers swirled around in the back and every now and then a beer can flew out. I asked myself whether their disgusting yet candid voyeurism was any worse than my paid subterfuge. A young woman in a Tarago hurled a bottle of wine cooler from the window, laughing as it smashed on the ground. I muttered, 'Bitch,' but it meant nothing to either of us and then my focus came back in a rush as the pimp yelled again.

'Come on, Helen!' he shouted, digging his fingers into her arms and shaking her so hard I thought her head might jiggle right off. 'You can't keep doing this, can you?' *Slap!* 'You gotta go back to work, dontcha?' *Shake!* 'You can't fuckin sit 'ere all night feelin' sorry for y'self, can you?' *Slap!* 'You can't go home. You gotta get out an' earn a dollar, eh? Gotta go back to work? Eh?' *Slap!* 'Ah come on, wake up! I gotta get back to work too you know.' *Smack!*

But the girl could only go with the blows, lifting her head an inch or so to ask for another shot of heroin before a backhander whipped in and cut her off.

'Look, you can't have another! You've already had one tonight. You have another one an' you'll die wontcha, hey? You know that.'

'*Wannanutha,*' she blubbered as the boy ground his teeth. He stood up and walked a few metres away before turning with his hands on his hips. It looked like he was lining up to punt kick her out of the world. I shivered and leaned away from the girl as the wind picked up. The stolen-watch dealers asked him to move out of their way.

'Look, are you goin' back?' he asked the girl softly, doing a slow burn. 'You can't have another hit and you have to go back to work.'

Helen bunched her fists in the shock of greasy brown hair which hid her face and whimpered. He waded in and hit her twice, hard enough this time to send her head into the glass with a couple of thuds.

'You're not getting another fuckin shot, Helen!' he yelled. 'That's all there is to it. Now straighten out and get back to work or we're gonna have a fight. You don't wanna have another fight now, do you, Helen?'

No. Helen just wanted another shot. I thought then that he might smash her clear through the window. But instead he knelt down to search in his bag until he came up with a packet of cashews.

'Here,' he said softly. 'These are your favourites, eh? Cashews?' He moved the hair out of her face and pushed some nuts between her lips. 'Eat up, Helen. They're good for you. You like nuts, doncha, mate?'

But the nuts wouldn't stay in. They fell from her slack lips, unheeded as she moaned for a shot. The young pimp kept trying to push them back in but she shook her head slowly and rocked from side to side. Finally she pushed her chin down onto her chest and he muttered, 'Shit,' and threw the packet away. 'Look,' he sighed heavily. 'You're buggering up me schedule, Helen. I gotta go see a bloke up the Wall in a minute and I still gotta do Michelle round the corner. So you gonna go to work or what?'

'*Wannanutha ...* '

He tapped her lightly with the back of a finger to drag her attention back to him. 'Listen,' he said, 'if you go to work now and come up the Wall in an hour or so, we'll see about getting you another shot, eh? How's that sound?'

It must have sounded okay because she looked up at him for the first time. Then she slowly gathered together whatever it takes for thirteen-year-old junkies to push themselves off the tiles and back onto the footpath to ask strange men to fuck them for money.

I never saw her again, but that's not unusual. Faces come and go all the time up the Cross. After I had lived in Darlinghurst for a couple of years I realised there were some stayers, perennial hookers and doormen and local crims who never seemed to leave or change or even breathe in some cases. But they were all old hands who had cut some sort of Faustian deal to survive on the edge of the abyss. The younger faces almost never lasted. They just disappeared or grew so old so fast it was like watching a special effects movie. In that way heroin was almost occult in its power, a magic dust which could suck the life right out of your face. This was ten years back of course – a long time before the Wood Royal Commission, before the 5T or heroin chic – and Sydney did not dominate the national heroin market as it does now. In those days interstate syndicates tended to run their own shows, importing, wholesaling and distributing independently, whereas now Sydney's control of the trade is nearly absolute. Even Melbourne's massive appetite for China white is largely fed by hundreds of kilos of Number 4 arriving in shipping containers at Darling Harbour every year.

LEVIATHAN

Helen was very much a bottom feeder in this food chain and most likely her nattily dressed pimp was not that far above her. She was just a user. He was probably a user-dealer and above him were another three or four levels of ounce dealers, brokers, wholesalers and importers. The ounce dealers were visible, still having to get down and dirty in the marketplace, but the more rarefied levels were, and remain, virtually invisible. At that point, in the late 1980s, the cops would have fingered the Chinese and the Lebs as the most likely candidates to head up the biggest and best organised import networks, but beyond that speculative leap it all became a little pear-shaped and confusing, with distribution from the warehouse via hundreds of networks of local players, mostly Anglos, some of whom, it turned out, carried badges and guns. While a lot of disorganised criminal activity saw weights of up to one or two kilos come in strapped to the body of courier 'mules', or simply sent through the mail to a series of post office boxes, the really heavy hitters might never even lay eyes on the stuff they imported in job lots of ten, twenty or thirty kilos. They would arrange the finance and logistics of a payload, most likely from Burma, through Thailand and into Sydney via shipping containers or air freight. That purchase through a broker in Hong Kong or Bangkok at twelve to fifteen grand per kilo would then arrive to be broken down into one or two kilo packets for distribution to any number of wholesalers, all buying in at up to a quarter of a million dollars a kilo. The wholesalers would step on the product for the first time, diluting it with glucose, icing sugar, caffeine, chalk, soap powder or even plaster of Paris for sale in five and ten gram lots to their ounce dealers at two or three hundred dollars a gram. The ounce dealers, most often profit takers rather than users, would dilute their buy again before dealing to one or two dozen regulars, at which point the likes of Helen's pimp became involved.

While the machinations of the drug industry's royal families remain mysterious, the activities of the soldiers and serfs are not. The fix which Helen's pimp had allowed her earlier in the evening had probably come from a five gram score, either bought in a dealer's car while on the move or paid for and retrieved from a nearby stash. When I lived near the Cross a coffee shop owner in Roslyn Gardens grew so tired of junkies and user-dealers plucking their purchases from where they had been pinned to the tree outside his cafe that he took to rushing out with a baseball bat and threatening violence every time he noticed someone moving towards the spot. The original importers and wholesalers of the batch from which Helen scored would have been almost one hundred per cent certain of never being detected or arrested. Those hassles were a hazard which she, her pimp and his supplier were much more likely to face, although the risk could have been minimised by a judicious alliance with whichever syndicate was at that point running the local drug and sex rackets with the active connivance of the local police.

Also unlikely to face arrest and prosecution were the thousands of casual users living in the inner city, the joy-riders who held down normal jobs and might score once a month or a fortnight or a week, depending on their level of income and addiction. These were the ones who really surprised me when I first arrived in the city; lawyers, journalists and advertising execs with a nagging habit worth maybe a hundred or two hundred dollars a week. They could maintain a facade of detachment from the low-rent, scabbed-over aesthetics of the street-level smack trade, but every now and then one of them would take a hot shot from a batch that maybe hadn't been stepped on as often as usual and then a couple of dozen of their numb, bewildered friends and relatives would make the long trip out to the crematorium to pay their respects and wonder what the fuck went wrong.

What went wrong in Kings Cross was exhaustively and painfully documented by Commissioner James Wood who tried to hunt down and slay what Queensland academic Dan O'Neill used to call the Beast. O'Neill was referring to the tropical mutation of that same strange confluence of feral capital, the State and the underworld which was a motivating force behind the violence of the green ban backlash. Wood was less directly concerned with the debauching of civil society than his colleague Tony Fitzgerald had been, but the evil possibilities of any partnership between 'legal and illegal violence' informed his investigation, as it had the Royal Commissions of Justices Costigan, Stewart, Williams and Moffitt before him. Moffitt directly compared the subversion of the State by organised crime to attacks by fascist or communist enemies, writing in 1985 that the corruption of public institutions was so advanced that 'we are dangerously close to ... ruination'.

For me, however, the image of ruin was closer and more intimate. I did not have to contemplate the corruption of public officials or the systemic subversion of liberal institutions to appreciate what lay in wait for a city which seemed to embrace its most dangerous and charismatic criminals so fondly. I had been to enough funerals. And on my last night in the Cross for *Rolling Stone* I got to look the Beast in the eye. I had been on the street for about a week or so and was starting to be accepted by all as a hopeless derelict. Late one night I was standing at the corner of Elizabeth Bay Road having a sandwich and a cup of tea when this fucked-up, ratty-looking guy suddenly beamed down beside me to ask if I wanted to buy some coke. His nose was all smashed in, and dark dried smears of blood caked his unwashed face and clotted his thin, struggling beard.

'It's good shit, man,' he babbled. 'Peruvian flake.'

I figured he had been into his own wares, it being considered very poor form amongst your professional dope pedlars to front complete strangers in the middle of the street and commence retailing. He assured me in his weird warp-speed babble that he would not rip me off, I could ask anyone on the strip. He was a good bloke, a great bloke, and his shit was the best. 'So whattaya reckon?' he said. 'You wanna buy some a this?' I tried to walk away but he followed me, spruiking his stuff the whole time, his frying eyeballs darting about randomly, not really looking for anything, just lost. It was getting sort of tiresome when some other dealers I had met in a pub across the road came by. The bigger one, whom I knew as Ian, asked what I was doing. When I told him about my ratty little friend he laughed a big generous laugh and told me, somewhat redundantly, that I was on the point of being ripped off. 'Don't buy it off this useless little prick,' he said. 'Buy it off me.'

Ian couldn't understand that I didn't really want his coke, icing sugar or baby powder either, and we fell into an argument there on the street. Who was buying what, from whom, for how much. We all had very different ideas on the matter, and our full and frank exchange of views might have gone on for hours if a young Aboriginal boy had not staggered into our magic circle. I recognised him. He was a standout piece of human wreckage in a place where the debris piled up very quickly. I had given him fifty cents a little earlier and he had somehow gathered enough money for a small cap of heroin which he held out to us along with his fit and a ruined arm. He wobbled about on thin scabrous legs which should have folded ten times or more but which always managed to stay locked underneath him. His speech was thick but the insistent arm he pushed forward made his words unnecessary. 'Do my arm,' he mumbled. Ian and his friend simply ignored him. The psychotic coke dealer wasn't taking any messages on that frequency and so after a while everyone looked at me. I could say I refused because I didn't want to help the boy kill himself, but that would be bullshit. I just didn't want to go near his suppurating wounds or dirty needle.

'Go and see the girls across the road,' I said. He didn't want to but none of us would stick him and he eventually left. The broken-nose guy quickly returned to the business at hand, but Ian was giving me his stone face. Drug paranoia had locked in and he was away. 'You're a narc. You're a fucking cop, aren't you? I can't believe I done this. Shit, I made a real mistake talking to you. I can't fucking believe it.'

Well, something had to be said, and I finally settled for 'Get fucked,' and took off. Things were a bit confused but I remember tearing along for a minute before looking back to find Ian and his mate following me. Then the other idiot popped up again and grabbed my arm. 'They think you're a cop,' he muttered frantically. I told him it was bullshit, I didn't need it and I was going.

'Yeah, yeah,' he gibbered, 'I know you're not a cop, you're the grouse, mate. So . . . what d'you reckon, you wanna buy some coke off me?'

I blessed his drug-addled greed and told him I would buy his coke if he went back and set the others straight, which he did and got into a fight, while I took off in the opposite direction. I did not return to the Cross for a long time after that. I moved on to Penrith, hanging out with a couple of street kids who were so pleased that someone was taking an interest in their story they offered to pull a few break and enters for me. When they discovered I didn't drive they suggested stealing a car so I could learn. And when a fence accused me of being a narc in the beer garden of their local hotel, they jumped all over him with some fairly credible death threats. This sense of solidarity was one of few positive memories I took away from that story. I was continually meeting winos who would share their last spit-flecked cup of McWilliams port, hookers who were always ready with a spare cigarette or a bite of their Mars Bar, and feral kids who would roll a suit for a couple of hunded dollars and shout all of their friends to a massive blow-out at McDonalds. I was surprised to find such depth of fellow feeling amongst such miserable castaways, but I was not surprised that it never extended to the well-fed, and of course it evaporated at the precise moment you added smack to the equation.

The black kid who needed help to stick himself probably found it. But chances are he was ripped off on the deal. If another junkie volunteered to shoot him up, it would have likely been on the basis of a taste for the shooter, and if they were hanging out as badly as he was, they would have sucked up as much shit from the spoon as they could get away with. I never saw the kid again, unlike Ian who was still spooking around two years later, although he looked cadaverous and used up. I doubt the kid made it through another two weeks, let alone two years. His story, like Helen's, was only ever going to end in one place and on a bright morning in November I followed them there.

The main autopsy room of the Glebe morgue runs to sixteen tables but the observation studio where this woman lay contained only one, behind glass, through which the procedure could be observed from viewing tiers. The autopsy room had a blue floor, greyish walls and was dominated by the large stainless steel table around the edge of which ran a moat. A trolley with gloves, towels, brushes, a squeegee and a soup ladle stood ready, near two wheelie bins, one red and one black. The woman, who was aged about fifty according to the staff, caused some initial confusion. It transpired that she had once been a man and had taken the chop. The surgeons had done their jobs well and the unexpected discovery had led to a short delay while the forensic assistants stood around scratching their heads.

A few hurried inquiries established that the woman may have been an IV drug user and possibly a sex worker, which opened up the possibility of Hep C or HIV-AIDS infection. The most likely cause of death, at that point, was an overdose. The doctor decided not to take off the top of her head, as is normal at the start of an autopsy, commencing instead with a long, vertical incision in the abdomen. A few of the other observers – law students on a supervised visit – groaned at this point. One of them, a young woman, eventually apologised and hurried from the room. She was quickly joined by a pale-faced lecturer. The students had not been exposed cold to the obscene intimacy of the cutting room, having had four hours of lectures accompanied by an increasingly bloody and grotesque slide show. The systematic desensitisation was not effective in all cases unfortunately, and the corridor outside the viewing room was soon populated by the more tender or imaginative of the group. I had seen enough dead junkies lying around Darlinghurst over the years to cope with the spectre of the waxy, somewhat unreal figure being progressively dismantled in front of us, but it required an effort of will not to make the intuitive leap to images of dead friends on the same table. A colleague from a magazine had recently overdosed and while the sight

Pig City

of a forensic assistant using a giant pair of pliers to cut through the ribs of Jane Doe was moderately confronting, it was much less disturbing than the unbidden visions which suddenly assailed me of my friend being similarly violated.

I had been shocked by her death, not realising she had been on the gear and never really understanding the attraction in the first place. One friend, another writer, had sneered at my naivety, saying I couldn't possibly take a position unless, like him, I had slipped the spike into my own arm. Others, who had fought and won their own wars with the dragon, still spoke affectionately of its warming balm, its sweet, soft passage through their veins. And of course it was hip. The coolest magazines in the world had conspired with the hottest photographers and models to foist the pornographic charade of heroin chic upon the clueless masses. Sadly though, its incredible Zen cool never did make it off the pages of *Juice* or *The Face* to comfort the dying Aboriginal stick insect who offered me his bruised, ulcerated arm. And search as I might I could find no chic in the green tinge which lay over the skin of Jane Doe, or the rigor mortis which bunched and pointed her toes to the ceiling like the tip of a rhino's horn. It was nowhere to be seen in the heavy, glistening organ block which the morgue staff wrestled from the vast wound in her stomach. It was absent from the hairless, wrinkled slit of her counterfeit vagina which, slightly open, gaped at a roomful of gawking strangers. And the soup ladle with which a nurse scooped the last pools of contaminated blood from her abdominal cavity did not emerge with even the smallest measure of savoir faire dripping from its plastic cup.

This was the terminal point of the city's heroin trade, the unavoidable denouement of institutional corruption and personal debasement. It was, to borrow from Eugene O'Neill, a long day's

411

journey into night. That it should end here, on the stainless steel tabletop, was fitting in a way, as though the city had one last sick joke to play. For this was the morgue where it was revealed in 1996 that nine of the ten forensic assistants had been routinely stealing from the dead. The theft, known to the morgue workers as ratting the corpses, was a long established practice, possibly originating in the 1970s. Cashing in on the reluctance of police to search badly decomposing remains, the morgue attendants developed techniques for searching a body in front of the cops which would alert them to the presence of money hidden, for example, in the deceased's underwear. Concealing the discovery from their squeamish observers, they would return later to claim the plunder. An investigation by ICAC detailed instances of some workers virtually racing to the freezers to ransack bodies which had been checked in by honest colleagues on previous shifts. And while one senior staffer boasted for many years of nabbing a particularly large rat, worth over $1000 dollars, the small change which jingled from the pockets of the dead onto the mortuary floor was not beneath their attention either, often being scooped up and spent on a beer and a burger at the local pub for lunch. Besides the corpse ratting, ICAC exposed a system of kickbacks from a local funeral parlour, whose director palmed the staffers $150 for each grieving family referred. For a city which considered itself inured to the corrupt excesses of its public officers, the ghoulish behaviour of the morgue staff was an unforeseen and even a perversely refreshing experience. In the end there was, it seemed, no outrage so profane it could not come to pass in Sydney.

Laissez-faire liberalism constrained government action in many areas when the minimal city was born in 1842. But crime was not one of them. Established as a sinkhole of criminality, the city provided for a defence against its own populace with a nightwatch as early as August 1789. The camp had suffered many months of poultry theft and vegetable larceny, prompting Phillip to appoint twelve well-behaved convicts to a nightwatch which would roam over four districts: the huts and public farm to the east of the Cove, around the brick kilns up the future path of George Street, on the western side of the Cove up to the female convicts' quarters, and beyond them to the Observatory. As Judge Advocate Collins wrote, it would have been better had the first police force been composed of free citizens rather than 'a body of men in whose eyes, it could not be denied, the property of individuals had never before been sacred. But there was not any choice'. Phillip was happy with the innovation, reporting to London 'that for three months not a single robbery was committed in the night'. As so often in early Sydney though, trouble arose when the military objected to civilian authority. The power of the nightwatch to stop and detain wandering soldiers was an insult according to the marines' commandant Major Ross; one they would not stand for 'while they had bayonets in their hands'. Phillip was obliged to stop his little police force interfering with the late night ramblings of the military, despite the fact they were often the very thieves the nightwatch was supposed to suppress. Six marines had been executed in March that year for systematically robbing the public stores.

The systemic nature of the conflict was confirmed during the administrations of Hunter and King, with Lieutenant Colonel Paterson playing the role of spoiler in place of Ross. Hunter had augmented the nightwatch by grafting the ancient English office of constable onto the local scheme, with the towns' neighbourhoods being allowed to vote for their police officers from 1796. These police were to be controlled by magistrates, but Paterson objected to his officers serving in such positions, causing a headache for both Governors, who did not have many suitable candidates to call on. The inevitable feud ensued, with King removing the corps' officers from the bench after Paterson had written a snakey little missive saying no men under his command would be allowed to do anything which detached them from their military duties. King also replaced his military bodyguard with a mounted troop of 'provisionally emancipated' convicts, commanded by a disgraced officer, transported from India for killing a man in a duel. The bodyguards wore military uniforms, and were referred to as troopers by King, infuriating Paterson. His anger at this slight on the honour of the corps was further aggravated when his complaints were dismissed with a smirk by King, who pointed out that many members of Paterson's honourable regiment were themselves former convicts.

The problems of staffing the police with criminals which Collins had alluded to were acknowledged by Hunter in July 1799 when he mused that the recently increased number of robberies gave him reason to suspect that many of his constables were either 'extremely negligent' or had been 'prevailed on' by the town's housebreakers to be 'less vigilant than they ought to be'. Any further slackness would 'give room for strong suspicion of their honesty, and dispose the more respectable inhabitants to suppose them partakers with the thieves'. A fusion of these issues – the inherent corruptibility of Sydney's police force, and the shifting, unstable power structure of the town – can be seen in the Rum Rebellion, with Macarthur's concerns, whether real or contrived, that he would be murdered while in custody at the town gaol.

Before handing over to Macquarie after the coup, the corps's Lieutenant Colonel Foveaux scratched out an exculpatory letter, attempting to defend the rebellion while simultaneously condemning it. He also wrote of his many worthy administrative efforts including reform of the police, which he made 'the object of my very particular and constant attention'. So unremitting was the vigilance he demanded 'from every person connected with it, that scarcely any offence escaped detection', ensuring 'a degree of tranquillity, security and subordination which would be entitled to some praise'.

Not so, according to the dour Scot. 'At the time of My first taking charge of this Government,' he wrote, 'I found the Police of the Town of Sydney very defective and totally inadequate to the preserving of Peace and good Order ...' Macquarie turned his earliest thoughts to formulating a Code of Police Regulations with the aim of preserving the peace and '... protecting the Persons and Property of the inhabitants from the Attacks and Plunder of the Midnight Ruffian and Thief.' Needless to say his reforms were, he thought, much better than Foveaux's. Indeed his system was not to be surpassed by that 'of any City in Europe'.

Previous to this Police Establishment, our Streets frequently exhibited the most disgraceful Scenes of Rioting, Drunkenness, and Excesses of every kind, and each Morning brought to light the History of Thefts, Burglaries, and Depredations which had been Committed the Night before. Happily such Occurrences are now almost totally suppressed ...

Not so according to the dour Scot's own inquisitor, JT Bigge, who thought the police very inefficient and who railed against the town's love affair with liquor, purchased from a battalion of licensed and unlicensed dealers. In criticising one magistrate who was himself involved in the spirit trade, Bigge forewarned of a conflict between public duty and private benefit which would plague the city for more than two hundred years. Although it did not seem to affect the manner in which the magistrate had carried out his duties, wrote Bigge,

> In a community, wherein it was of the utmost importance that the exercise of magisterial authority should be placed above the suspicion of being actuated by personal motives, it was certainly unfortunate, and it is still to be regretted, that any foundation for such suspicion should ever have existed; and that any of the magistrates should have had, or should now possess an interest in the extended use of a commodity, which they knew to be the cause of mischief to the colony, in proportion as it was the cause of profit to themselves.

Even a sympathetic historian such as Thomas O'Callaghan, who wrote in the *Journal of the Royal Australian Historical Society* in 1923 that Macquarie's reforms led to the dawn of a new era for the colony's police, could find grounds for criticism. He thought the nightwatch system, where constables patrolled with a cutlass and rattle, calling the time every half-hour, was of benefit to nobody but thieves, housebreakers and other such villains. 'They certainly benefited by the custom,' he wrote, 'as it enabled them to know when and from which direction the police were approaching'.

The early police suffered from many obvious shortcomings.

Pig City

Between May 1825 and October 1826, according to Hazel King, fifty-seven officers were dismissed and twenty-five resigned from a force which barely exceeded fifty in total. Many of the men were inveterate drunks, simply because the community from which they were drawn was itself full of alcoholics. Before 1833 quite a few of the higher ranking officers were also illiterate, with the Assistant Chief Constable for one being unable to read his own warrants. Most of the early commanders were forced to resign through scandal; one of them, Colonel HC Wilson, claiming that the constables he had ordered to work in his home as carpenters, shoemakers and liveried servants, were in fact his bodyguards, and that their fine livery was a disguise. Deeper strains, however, were occasioned by the city's fundamental schism between 'the felonry and the free'. Macquarie, who in his darker moments thought the entire colony consisted only of those who had been transported and those who *should* have been, excited open hostility by appointing two freed convicts, Simeon Lord and Andrew Thompson, to the magistracy. The Reverend Marsden quickly refused to share a bench with them and Judge JH Bent closed the Supreme Court rather than have its sacred halls befouled by ex-convict attorneys.

The clash of these forces, which later found expression in the endless proxy war between Macquarie Street and Town Hall, flared over control of the police in the 1840s. The mid-forties in particular were haunted by the angst of the propertied classes over increasingly violent crime as the city's starving unemployed grew more desperate. Wentworth, who had accused the police of bias against him during the elections of 1843, was amongst those agitating for a parliamentary inquiry into the supposed crime wave. The disorganised, uncoordinated structure of the colony's numerous police forces doubtlessly contributed to the problems, although another reason for the Legislative Council's inquiry lay in their ambition to wrest total control of the police from the city council. The council shared responsibility for funding the police at that time and the police themselves had responsibility for a number of matters within the ambit of local government such as 'nuisance inspection', or waste management as it is now called. The aldermen complained of having to pay for a body over which they had no control, frequently demanding that they be given such authority, as was the case in England. Those sorts of disputes were only ever resolved in one way, however, and in 1862 the colonial government established the New South Wales Police Force under its exclusive control.

This early and intense politicisation of crime and policing created a template which still shapes the eruptions of neostupidity which pass for a criminal justice debate in the city today. Two centuries on, with rationalist policies forcing a retreat of government from the civic sphere, the freedom of movement available to political actors is limited, while demands for intervention are not. Crime control, through the agency of the police, remains one of the few areas in which political rhetoric is not constrained by neoliberal philosophy, hence the recurrent spectacle of 'law and order' elections in which the major parties spend millions of dollars outbidding each other for the punishment-freak vote.

The job, as the police service is known to its members, reeks of politics. Station politics. Service politics. State and city politics. All caught up with media politics, drug war politics and good-cop-bad-cop, ICAC, PIC and union politics. It's politics which decides how a cop will do his job. Politics which says what that job is. And politics which destroys any cop fool enough to disagree or misunderstand. The Macquarie Fields command, for instance, is

Pig City

one of the most politically sensitive in the State. Over a hundred nationalities live there, but unlike the pleasant cosmopolitan theme parks of the east and north, the Mac Fields story is not a narrative of cultural success.

The command takes in huge housing commission estates at Claymore, Minto, Ingleburn and, of course, Macquarie Fields itself. They sprawl over the dry hills of Sydney's time-worn basin. Some of the oldest neighbourhoods, pioneer settlements founded by returned servicemen in the late 1940s and 50s, retain a quirky appeal, their well-tended gardens and asbestos-board bungalows testifying to four or five decades of loving attention. But they rest uneasily within vast tracts of poorly designed faux townhouses. Burnt-out car bodies lie abandoned in the worst streets where two of the guarantors of modern urban civilization, the ambulance service and firefighters, fear to tread. So far removed from the commonwealth of the city do some here feel themselves, they are famed for attacking firefighters who respond to blazes in the neighbourhood. Some families on these estates can tell of three or four generations who have never known employment – although the generations do cycle through a little quicker in these parts. The command is thought to be home to the country's youngest grandmother, a twenty-seven-year-old woman. With clusters of tightly packed private housing often sitting like enemy camps behind a natural line of defence such as a freeway, a creek or in one case a golf course, outbreaks of class friction are inevitable. In July 1999 400 residents of Woodbine, an almost exclusively private suburb, protested the building of a footbridge linking them to Claymore. The Woodbiners, reported the *Daily Telegraph*, believed public housing tenants from the Claymore estate would 'break into their homes, steal their cars and vandalise their property'.

LEVIATHAN

Politics can be a strangely empty concern out here. But while the constituents of Sydney's millennial slums count for little in the hard calculations of the ruling elites, they are an important symbolic presence in the endless guerilla war between those elites. An alliance of convenience between the mass media and the city's various political competitors has defined crime as a hot-button issue, and the Mac Fields police command, with its dense concentrations of the doomed, the insane and the abandoned, provides an arena in which these actors can perform their version of a Japanese Noh play, a form of theatre in which little actually happens but the actors in their masks and vivid costumes suggest the essence of a story, or a myth. In the theatre of the city's southwest Murray Edelman's thesis takes on immediate significance; for those made anxious by a gap between their expectations and bleak reality, a myth can replace gnawing uncertainty and rootlessness with a dramatic account of who are friends and who are enemies. The identification of the enemy does not have to be accurate.

The seed of an especially powerful myth, that of Asian youth crime gangs, germinated shortly after Geoffrey Blainey prepared the ground in the mid-1980s. By July 1986 the city's media were transfixed by the spectre of 'race war' in the western suburbs. Huge gangs of Lebanese and Vietnamese youths were reported to be battling for turf with knives, swords, clubs, billiard cues, fence palings, machetes, broken bottles and martial arts weapons such as *nanchaku* (two short lengths of wood joined by a chain, made famous by Bruce Lee and called 'numb-chuckers' by the *Sun-Herald*). On 7 July, at the 'Battle of Bankstown', up to sixty street fighters were said to have flayed each other in the Bankstown Mall as shoppers 'fled in terror'. The fight, described as 'World War

Pig City

Three', 'running gang warfare', 'a vicious fracas', and a 'replay of the Vietnam War', was followed on 16 July by another in the suburb of Marrickville where a young Lebanese man, Tony Maala, was stabbed and seriously wounded. The *Sun Herald* opened its account of the second encounter with these lines of cool-handed prose:

> The tension was sharp as the sheath-knife plunged into the stomach of the Lebanese teenager, now lying in a pool of blood. His Vietnamese attacker had fled. Friends comforted the bloodied victim. Lebanese women cried, while their men shook their heads in disbelief.

The *Sydney Morning Herald* asked, 'Youth gang brawls: is it adults next?', declaring the city's ethnic communities 'faced the very real danger that youth gang violence could escalate into serious adult conflict'. The Police Minister called for 'action' the next day. While Maala was seriously injured, and some fighting actually did break out on both occasions, the media's response – citing such impeccable sources as 'the whisper around the old town plaza' and 'the word out on the streets' – was only vaguely connected to reality. The Battle of Bankstown for instance, the initial engagement of the city's putative race-hate war, was revealed on investigation by the Ethnic Affairs Commission to have involved only half a dozen or so actual protagonists. And the reports of the Maala stabbing at Marrickville were so incoherent and wildly contradictory as to be useless for any purpose other than indicting the journalists concerned. On 18 July the *Herald*, for instance, reported the Marrickville fight was a result of a dispute between a Vietnamese and Lebanese youth 'who were in the same class in the Canterbury area'. When the knife was drawn, 'the alarm went out to the Bankstown gangs, who arrived on the scene in carloads to take up the battle'. Exactly how the alarm got out, or how carloads of Bankstown hoodlums made it to Marrickville in the short time it took the police to respond, was not explained. The *Daily Telegraph* provided a possible solution: the *Herald*'s version of events never happened. According to the *Telegraph*'s man the two sides 'sprang apart' as Tony Maala dropped to the ground, and police were on the scene 'in minutes'. Too late, however. The youths had already 'split up' and run off 'in all directions'.

The gross inconsistencies of the city's two major newspapers' accounts were never resolved but that did not matter. The Asian youth crime story developed its own momentum anyway. As they charged after it, into the suburban badlands, most reporters cut their ties to the world of real things and passed like tongueless blind men through the night, decoding any dimly perceived movement on the Asian youth crime front by reference to third-rate Ninja movies and a dopey sort of free-floating Aryan anxiety. The accuracy of the suburban race war fable was less important than its potency as a myth which gave meaning to ominous and perplexing events. Although the early dispatches from the front made token gestures towards the role of unemployment and a lack of resources in fomenting unrest, the wider national debate about the 'Asianisation' of Australia ensured that the media's focus was pulled in hard on Asian, and particularly Vietnamese, 'youth gangs' above all else, irrespective of confounding information. For instance, an Institute of Criminology study by Patricia Easteal analysed criminal records through the mid to late 1980s for both Vietnamese and non-Vietnamese youth in New South Wales and found that the Vietnamese had a significantly *lower* crime rate. Thus, suggested Easteal, 'sensational media reports are not indicative of the level of criminal activities within the Vietnamese community'. Easteal found that Vietnamese youths were generally two times less likely to commit a violent crime, four times less likely to drink drive, and fifteen times less likely to use illegal drugs. Most of the Vietnamese offenders came from four Sydney suburbs, as do most Vietnamese. Three of these areas had higher crime rates in 1976, prior to the arrival of the Vietnamese community. Easteal compared the media images of Asian gangs as 'Mafioso-like, complete with godfathers who induct parentless refugee minors into their "families" and force them to commit extortion, robbery, car theft and gambling/drug offences' with the evidence of youth workers and community leaders speaking of small groups of bored and lonely teenagers with nothing to do. More recently, researchers from the National Drug and Alcohol Research Centre spent two years in Cabramatta burrowing into the area's heroin culture, and finding in 1998 that

Cabramatta has been demonised as the 'crime capital of Sydney'. The evidence suggests that this perception is incorrect. Rates of serious crime in the suburb are unexceptional and the image of bloody streets controlled by 'Asian gangs' is simply inaccurate. Data from the NSW Bureau of Crime Statistics and Research indicate that Cabramatta is 'safer' than many areas in the inner city of Sydney.

Rates of assault, robbery without a weapon, robbery with a weapon other than a firearm, domestic burglary, motor vehicle theft and shop theft 'were all substantially greater in inner Sydney than in Cabramatta'. What Cabramatta did have, however, was 'a disproportionate share of offences related to the possession and sale of narcotics'. And, of course, the 5T gang.

The 5T are a long-time favourite of desperate news editors with space to fill and deadlines to meet. Their name, redolent of the 3 Lions and the 14K Triad, derives from the five Ts tattooed on the gang members' forearms. The Ts have been translated as meaning murder, money, sex, drugs, violence, prison, lack of respect, bad attitude and an unhealthy love of machetes, billiard cues and, naturally, 'numb-chuckers'. But as both youth workers and streetkids told me some years ago when I was researching the first heady moments of the 5T's rise to fame for *Juice* magazine, the meaning was, originally at least, infinitely more saccharine. *Tuoi Tre Thieu Tinh Thuong*: Young people lack love and care. But such maudlin ooze has never sold newspapers, unless it is poured over cancer babies and beached whales. Nor is it much use for amplifying and channelling mass anxieties about spiralling crime rates, racial conflict and socioeconomic decay. To magnify and direct such fears creates a setting in which the beliefs and positions of millions are mobilisable and 'the creation of political followings' becomes more feasible. The arousal of those feelings is often of more political consequence than the outcomes generated. Manoeuvre around such issues as 'Asian youth gang violence' and the ensuing ebb and flow of mass support are the life force of politics and more important to the actors concerned than outcomes such as the Carr Government's 'knife legislation'.

For the legions of the city's poor, unemployed and even middle-class people whose experience of the 1980s and 1990s was not of white shoes and Cointreau balls, intense economic change nurtured corrosive fear and a sense of powerlessness. There is no solace in blaming impersonal developments like 'globalisation' in such circumstances. So the anxious parties look for explanations in myths of failed or guilty leaders, dangerous outsiders or simple conspiracy. A related consequence is the appeal of Edelman's 'hero-leader', often riding in from outside the system to deal with the threat. It is no accident that someone like Pauline Hanson appeals powerfully to the victims and losers of fifteen years of economic and cultural revolution. In such situations neither the 'enemy' – be they Asian youth gangs or the World Bank – nor the hero-leader – say, a maverick politician or talkback radio demagogue – can be viewed as a complex, ambivalent human being with a potential for empathy. 'They are perceived as embodiments of a particular role,' writes Edelman. Their mythic role.

By the early 1990s the 5T were getting regular press as a large, organised, mafialike outfit, maybe 100 strong, with a formal structure of rank and rules and with links to other unspecified 'Asian crime gangs'. New members were said to go through an initiation (involving some criminal or violent act), were sworn to secrecy and devoted Total Loyalty to the gang. They were 'known' to sit at the hub of Cabramatta's huge open air heroin market, putting them in control of the city's drug trade, and have since been fingered for extortion rackets, home invasions and the murder of John Newman, the local member of parliament. About the only thing not known about the 5T gang is how a bunch of dozy, beer-loving tabloid journalists continually scored the hot gear on such a violent, secretive, fanatically devoted crime ring. But of course there is no fashionable cachet in telling the readers that you wheezed up to the clippings library with a sticky bun and a cup of coffee to crib your notes from whichever poor, po-faced hack got the job of breathing life into the Asian crime gang caper before you.

While facts (such as the calibre of the bullets which blew away John Newman) are as hard and tactile as a pebble in the mouth, their meaning is always negotiable. Before the MP's murder was exposed as a possible end game of a power struggle within the local branch of the Labor Party, it was widely *known* to be a payback killing for Newman's stand against the 5T. The murder was a perfect fit for the myth that the 5T were what was wrong with Sydney. Their insidious connections to 'adult' Asian crime gangs were flooding the city with heroin and causing the social chaos which the anxious and the displaced seemed to perceive all around them. So resource deprivation and the massive collateral damage of economic restructuring were suddenly transformed into a story of race war, and the common interests of people from poorer suburbs in the city's south-west were fractured along ethnic lines. Rather than youth centres, education, job training and infra-structural investment, politicians mobilised support on the promise of more police and harsher laws, driving a wedge into communities already riven by multiple stress lines. Occasionally this lack of a sense of proportion and irony would backfire amusingly, as with the ALP's mooted 'crackdown' on youths who wore their baseball caps backwards. A ghastly fashion mistake yes, but hardly a crime. At other times, however, the comic gave way to the tragic. In 1993 for instance, while the *Herald* cranked up early warnings of 'child gangsters' and 'Asian terror gangs' on page three, the *Sun Herald* buried a short report that in the previous twelve months, thirty thousand migrant children had missed out on places in English language courses. Despite the media's increasing interest in ethnic crime, nobody seems to have bothered to note a possible relation-ship between the emergence of the 'child gangsters' and the federal government's decision to consider retrenching another forty per cent of staff from the English language program after an initial cut of twenty teaching positions.

None of this is to deny that the 5T exist. They do and this is the saddest element of all, for their creation was avoidable. When the first stories of the 5T were being laid out at the *Telegraph* and the *Herald*, the gangs were little more than groups of unemployed Vietnamese teens who had slipped through the net of the secondary school system and often had no close family to rely on. Coming from refugee camps in Hong Kong where 2000 children were kept under armed guard for months without seeing daylight, they may never have been in school. Some had seen their families killed. They arrived in Sydney, were given a few months English training if they were very lucky, then set loose to fend for themselves. April Pham, a youth worker in Cabramatta, told me that they didn't think of themselves as having 'low self-esteem'. They just thought of their lives as shit. They could not even cope with welfare. In March 1991, during a deep recession, the Bankstown, Cabramatta, Fairfield, Marrickville and Campsie social security offices combined had only two Indochinese aged between sixteen and eighteen receiving job search allowance. 'Half the kids don't have any income,' said April. 'The dole is a huge hassle. We virtually have to drag them in there. They live off and with their friends, a dozen in a one-bedroom flat. They share expenses. If one has fifty dollars, everyone gets it.'

This was the 5T in its earliest days. But even bullshit has a critical mass and past that point it becomes self-generating. Cut off from any other source of identity, the loudest message those young Vietnamese had beamed at them was 'street gangs'. If they ever sat on the floor of their dismal unfurnished flats and wondered what this strange new country expected of them, they need only attend to their media image. Unfortunately that particular fantasy was powered by an alternating current. Just as the symbol of a powerful underground teen-mafia explained the suburban catastrophe of drug-fuelled crime – and offered salvation through the symbol of an unshackled police force waging their War on Drugs with a nuclear armoury of supercharged drug laws – so too did it provide a reassuring myth for their notional enemy. Cast adrift in an alien world which obviously distrusted and feared them, the rootless beta-version outlaws were presented with an expertly crafted narrative of their own power and significance. They weren't sloughed off failures. They weren't pathetic. They were not doomed. *They were the 5T.* And though they might walk in the valley of the shadow of death they would fear no evil because they were the *baddest motherfuckers* in the valley. I mean, really, what did everyone expect them to do? Get a haircut and a job flipping patties at McDonalds?

Barbara Tuchman once described the behaviour of governments which pursue policies plainly contrary to their own self-interest as the march of folly. Wilful blindness, self-deception or, as Tuchman calls it, woodenheadedness, has played an important role in governance since the Trojans decided to place within their possession that big, suspicious-looking horse their implacable enemies the Greeks had mysteriously left outside the gates of Troy. It was epitomised, she writes, by Phillip II of Spain, 'the surpassing woodenhead of all sovereigns', of whom it was once said, 'no experience of the failure of his policy could shake his belief in its essential excellence'. The policy-makers who responded to the 5T as a cause of urban decay rather than a symptom had only to contemplate the city's criminal history of a century before to understand the end point of their woodenheaded policies – just as the politicians of the nineteenth century

Pig City

had been informed, at length, time and again, of the grim consequences of allowing slums to arise in their midst.

In the 1880s and 1890s the city's gangs were composed of poor Australian, Irish and English slum dwellers. Known as larrikins, they were the offspring of those benighted creatures described by WS Jevons and a series of Royal Commissions and reports into the conditions of the city's working classes. Like New York hoodlums or the *gamin* of Paris, they were as much a product of the slums as the plague rats of 1900. And just as the slums are still with us today in different form, so are the larrikins, except now they are called the 5T, the 108 Gang, Sing Ma or the Bankstown Boys. If that seems to oversentimentalise the modern city's social bandits, it shouldn't. We see the larrikin through the soft focus lens of time's passage. When he actually roamed the street he was perhaps even more of a terror to the respectable and the well fed than your average Asian youth gang today. In January 1884 *Sydney Quarterly Magazine* said the city at night was haunted by what they called a 'formidable evil'. Of the Victorian youth gangs, it was no exaggeration

to say that they are surcharged with every species of abomination; now ready to murder, in the fierce abandonment of their lust, a defenceless woman; now seizing with gusto the opportunity of stabbing a decent lad, the contemplation of whose respectability has lashed them into unquellable fury.

And just as Bankstown Mall was supposedly turned into a free-fire zone by gang warfare, so were the parks and alleys of Sydney rendered impassable by turf wars between the likes of the Blues Point Mob, the Livers and the Rocks Push as bands of larrikins 'swollen with insolence and wine' formed opposing parties to contend 'with infinite spirit by means of stones and fists'. The larrikins, like the 5T, followed a classic evolutionary path from low-level street offences to organised criminal enterprise. By the 1880s they had gathered into 'pushes' which more or less controlled areas like the Rocks, Woolloomooloo, Surry Hills or Glebe. Said the *Quarterly*,

> So uniformly dangerous and pestilent is this element becoming in some quarters of this city, and so uniformly insufficient is our august police force to act on their flagitiousness, that – unless a speedy reformation is effected – respectable citizens will have nothing left but to provide themselves with weapons of defence.

In 1897 the State's enlightened and forward-thinking comptroller-general of prisons, Frederick Neitenstein, reported to Parliament on 'the causes and prevention of larrikinism', remarking on the way 'certain phases of crime' seemed to periodically bloom, mature and eventually pass away. He commented favourably upon British programs to alleviate the shocking conditions of the slums, which Neitenstein was convinced were the cause of this 'undisciplined animalism'. He also tagged another culprit, blaming sensational media coverage for inflaming the situation and giving a lead to the easily led.

James Murray, who in 1973 analysed the phenomenon of the larrikin pushes, was struck by the parallels with his own era and wrote, 'it may be that the last thirty years of the twentieth century in Australia will see migrant pushes as troubled and dangerous as the pushes of the nineteenth'. He was mistakenly prescient. Murray predicted the possibility of gangs arising in Sydney and Melbourne's Italian and Greek communities. However, political consensus on migration and a relatively strong economy had seen those arrivals integrated quite comfortably. During the 1980s and 1990s, economic restructuring and the erosion of that consensus by a cultural dread of non-European migration denied many migrants from the Middle East and Indochina the same advantages. The picture was not unrelentingly dark of course. Tens of thousands of overachieving Asian-Australian university students suggested another story beyond the Battle of Bankstown. But they stood in apparent contradicton to evidence of 'gang violence, drugs and related crime among young Indochinese' noted by even the most sympathic observers, such as Nancy Viviani in 1996.

Viviani reviewed Patricia Easteal's work on conviction rates for young Vietnamese in the 1980s when the media's 'Asian youth crime' monster had just slipped the leash. She came to the depressing conclusion that Easteal's positive assumptions were no longer justified. By the mid-1990s young Indochinese were increasingly being jailed for serious offences, taking up ten per cent of the beds in the State's detention centres even though their parent community comprised only two per cent of the State's population. Describing the increased conviction rates as alarming, Viviani said the 1990s had also seen a shift towards organised criminality, with Chinese triads, Yugoslavs and Romanians all becoming involved. Even so, she cautioned, the young street bandits were not the kings of the drug trade, only its pawns. Like their larrikin forebears, however, they had evolved from ordinary street crime to more sophisticated forms of business. The larrikins graduated from mugging and random predation to organised joint ventures with Chinese opium dealers and the illegal gambling trade, just as the 5T progressed from shoplifting and minor assault to increasingly violent robberies and, of course, retailing heroin.

LEVIATHAN

The larrikins were just as politically sensitive as the 5T (or whichever felafel-eating posse the *Telegraph*'s editor anoints as the *gamin du jour*). Ambrose Pratt, who claimed to have acted as a lawyer for one of the pushes in the 1890s, said that at their height they had cowed both the police force and the judiciary. The small wooden truncheons carried by police were of no consequence to men who were inured to violence of much greater savagery than anything one or two constables might deal out. And no witness would lightly testify against criminals 'whose hearts were strangers to remorse, and whose vengeance was known to be implacable'. Pratt alleged that by voting en bloc in the city's minuscule electorates, and by terrorising candidates who stood without their approval, the pushes even built up a reservoir of tacit support on the floor of Parliament itself. This influence was supposedly brought to bear against legislation which armed the police with guns in 1894. Cabinet pushed a number of legal reforms through with 'the greatest difficulty', wrote Pratt. 'The pushes bestirred themselves, and it was soon made manifest that they possessed astonishing political influence, for the Bill was bitterly contested.'

Pratt claimed that the police were first armed after a pitched battle between a number of pushes at Leichhardt. Like some of the clashes of the 1980s 'race war' this showdown was supposed to have been prearranged and the police, on gaining knowledge of the fight, set out to disrupt it. The former push lawyer described the ensuing humiliation as the police arrived late. They rushed the brawlers and took eleven prisoners in the first moments. The larrikins, however, then combined against the common foe and a desperate struggle followed with three constables being seriously wounded. The rest, wrote Pratt, finding themselves outmatched, fled for their lives, taking two prisoners with them.

Pig City

There ensued the extraordinary spectacle of two score blue coats running like hares before a mob of yelling lads, not one of whom could have been more than twenty-two years of age. After a hard chase they reached and entered a steam tram, the driver of which immediately sent his engine full speed city-wards. The pushes, eager to rescue their comrades, followed for half a mile, battering the cars with showers of stones, but were then distanced.

In contrast, Peter Grabosky's *Sydney in Ferment*, the definitive survey of the city's criminal history, cites the Bridge Street sensation in February 1894 as the catalyst for the decision to arm the city's police. Grabosky, who is sceptical of the wilder claims about the pushes' influence and power, puts parliamentary opposition to harsher laws down to the simple mechanism of the newly elected Labor Party representing the interests of its working-class constituents. Grabosky argues that the Labor men did not share the property-owning classes' hysterical fear of the larrikins and simply resisted repressive legislation which would have fallen most heavily against their own people. Parliament did allow the police to go armed, however, after three burglars suspected of turning over the Union Steamship Company's offices were nabbed by the police in Bridge Street. The burglars defended themselves with iron bars and took down five unarmed police in the melee. The cops strapped on their sidearms shortly after, although the idea had been mooted much earlier.

Just over 100 years later, constables saddle up for patrol with equipment remarkably similar to that of their turn of the century peers. Most refinements have been a matter of increasing, rather than radically altering, the potential force an officer can call on. The modern baton, for instance, is much longer and heavier and could easily shatter a man's arm if swung with sufficient intent. Handcuffs are still made of steel, but the old service revolver has been replaced by a fifteen-shot semi-automatic Glock. The only two items of kit a nineteenth-century constable might not recognise immediately are the can of capsicum spray and the rubber gloves. A quick squirt in the eyes of a rambunctious larrikin would quickly demonstrate the effectiveness of the former. It might take some time, however, to explain why contact with the bodily fluids of a modern offender can be as fatal as a knife slash or pistol shot; hence the need to carry gloves.

It is a moot point whether Sydney is more violent now than in 1900. Technical advances have certainly improved the weaponry available on both sides of the thin blue line. At the same time there isn't a cop alive who won't tell you that drugs, especially heroin, have introduced a level of viciousness to the criminal milieu that was unthinkable a generation ago. Before smack, one Mac Fields detective complained, there was a healthy respect for law enforcement. But not now. A junkie might kill a cop just to avoid arrest on a minor possession charge. Almost on a whim. 'The junkies, they don't care about themselves,' said the detective. 'They don't care about each other or their friends or their family and certainly not the police.' Another detective, fourteen years on the job, said simply, 'They're not scared of us now. We really have lost control of the streets.'

What is beyond dispute is the significance of the city's treacherous and ambivalent politics in shaping the perceptions of crime and the cops' response, especially to the drug trade. Few of the artefacts of postmodern life have the capacity to inspire the new deadly sins of fear, loathing and cluelessness – as well as the older ones of envy, gluttony, lust, anger and sloth – as do drugs. Their ubiquity, their omnipotence, their amorality make them symbolically powerful and thus objects of fierce political contention. As P. Manning wrote in 1980,

> Most persons have learned, as a result of socialization to the conventional meanings attached to government, policing and the law, to view policing and especially drug policing as a series of dramatic confrontations between good and evil, in which the police possess the preponderance of resources, skills, and virtue. We expect that they will emerge victorious, given adequate resources, if they display sufficient courage and determination. We focus attention, therefore, upon successes, are given little information on failures, and naively view police action as exclusively creating solutions to the drug problem.

When you punch through the static of PR and bullshit surrounding the war on drugs, however, 'it is quite clear that they rarely achieve success, even defined in their own terms, that they often produce unanticipated negative effects', and that much of what is achieved happens through the ad hoc efforts of poorly resourced and over-extended men and women whose working reality is almost completely disconnected from the rhetorical fantasies of their political masters. The extent of that gulf came home to me when I sat in on the morning briefing at Macquarie Fields where I was spending a few days trying to understand the workaday concerns of a suburban police station.

At least a dozen or more of the station's senior officers wandered into the briefing room just before nine a.m. Apart from the mug shots and records of sixty-two repeat offenders Blu-tacked to the rear wall, there was very little to distinguish the room from a small lecture theatre in a suburban TAFE college. Cheap plastic chairs were scattered around an overhead projector which had eaten a big slice of the station's annual budget for capital works. Everyone looked washed out under the fluorescent lighting and nobody rushed to claim the seats at the front. One of the sergeants sitting down the back deadpanned, 'At least the boss can't kick my arse from here.'

The station boss, Superintendent Les Wales, arrived looking slightly incongruous, more like the old accountant he used to be than the area commander he is. Wales's professional background had equipped him for the demands of the new police service, however, which runs on business plans, mission statements and corporate strategies, unlike the old force which got along famously on meat pies and Toohey's Old. Wales had spent the previous day at a meeting of regional commanders which had endlessly repeated the Gregorian chant of modern management: do more with less.

'This is the message from yesterday,' said Wales as he placed a transparency of a simple hand-drawn dollar sign on the overhead projector. The command had been praised at the meeting, he said, but he had also been told they could do better. Wales ticked off a number of cost-saving measures before revealing that another region was under-strength by eighty officers. 'So,' he said somewhat apologetically to Jude, his human resources chief, 'we're being ordered to give up eighty because we're apparently over-strength.' Jude, a civilian not constrained by the chains of rank and discipline, left nobody in any doubt as to her opinion of this audacious raid, demanding to know why they should put up with it. Les Wales smiled a gentle knowing smile. 'Don't ask the hard questions, Jude.'

Having swallowed the medicine from Regional, discussion moved onto crime levels and station management. A local hardware supplier had been spoken to by the Chamber of Commerce about selling cans of spray paint to teenagers with mischief on their minds. Assaults at automatic teller machines were up. The coroner was about to tear strips off another command for allowing untrained officers to supervise prisoners in custody, and consequently all relevant Mac Fields personnel were going to be put through a training course. The new raincoats had arrived, as had some new computers, although they could not be installed because of millennium bug problems. Finally, said Wales, it was possible all of the chooks in the State were about to be slaughtered because of Newcastle disease, so they'd have to work up a plan for dealing with a possible truck crash involving thousands of contaminated poultry corpses. A groan escaped the lips of a sergeant sitting next to me. 'There goes me Thai cooking,' he said softly.

As the conference wrapped up and middle management, sergeants and senior constables filed out, Wales hung back with his two lieutenants, Dave Shorrocks, the crime manager, and Mick Donovan, the station's duty officer and Wales's second-in-command. Shorrocks was a small, tightly wrapped sort of guy who would be played by Lee Van Cleef with hawkish intensity in the made-for-TV movie of *Mac Fields*. He'd started his working life as a bank clerk and had always wanted to join the old force but failed on his first attempt. He was too small. After a couple of years of pumping iron and scarfing up banana milkshakes they let him in and he set his course for the drug squad. He still had something of an evangelical air about him when discussing drugs, an intensity which went way beyond the average cop's standard issue blank, humourless stare, and it made me wonder if he'd lined up twice to get that dose of severity. Donovan by way of contrast was a large man, with a stealthy sort of grace and a relaxed, almost furtive grin which threatened to break loose and run all over his face. He grew up in Gymea and served most of his cadetship around Cronulla where he'd rowed a rescue boat in the 1960s. I thought I recognised his passive, long-distance focus from the faces of old long-boarders out the back at Bondi.

Les briefly explained what I was doing in Mac Fields, how I wanted to watch an average station go through its paces, and I filled in the blanks for them as best I could. I'd have some hard things to say about the old force and to balance that, for myself as much as anyone, I wanted to see the conditions under which beat cops worked and try to understand the stresses on a command with such 'a difficult demographic'. We spoke frankly about the politics of my visit, about how nobody wanted another 'Cop It Sweet' and about how quickly the hammer could come down on them depending on what I wrote. Les was quite open about the political nature of his position. A good deal of his twelve-hour working day was spent handling community relations, the local establishment, the media and of course the government. 'We have dealt with the stresses and pressures coming from the executive team, from the Commissioner,' he said, 'and we all know they are responding to what comes out of Macquarie Street.' But what is Macquarie Street responding to, I wondered to myself. Mostly talkback radio, Newspoll and the obsessions of Col Allen, editor at the *Telegraph*.

Wales, who was working his way through the final semester of an MBA, was not an unthinking policeman. He despaired of the world into which he sent his officers every day, saying, 'I view some of those estates as the Third World. Some of the public housing in and around Minto, it's like Soweto in South Africa.' The unemployed on the estates have very little hope and public understanding of the symptoms and causes of crime in such areas are not, shall we say, encyclopaedic. Consequently much police work is reactive and crude. 'It's bandaid stuff,' Wales once told me. 'It's okay raiding drug houses and so on. But where mum's got no job, dad's disappeared and you have an education system which may not be competitive in twenty years' time ... Well, kids in twenty years' time, you can't imagine what the demands on them will be. What a job will look like. And the kids we're dealing now will be thirty, forty years old. They will be totally, absolutely hopeless, just bits of human flesh.'

The sixty-two faces pinned to the briefing room wall offered no argument. The command's frequent fliers, the 'recidivist offenders', stared out blankly from their photocopied CVs, their criminal histories sketching their own coarse interpretation of Mac Fields's vale of tears. It was all there. Hundreds, maybe thousands of break and enters, assaults and robberies. Car theft, domestic violence, GBH, attempted murder, drug offences, empty eyes and random fury. The radioactive glow of social meltdown almost hummed off the wall. If fifteen, twenty years of decay could produce these fine specimens, you had to wonder what another couple of decades would do.

Donovan and Shorrocks were somewhat at odds over the calibre of their patrons. 'We're not looking at the majors,' said Mick. 'I'll be quite candid. The sort of criminal we have in this area isn't capable of anything requiring too much intelligence. The best they can hope for is a stick-up on a building society or video store,

LEVIATHAN

some quick money and off they go. You're looking at jobs that don't take a lot of planning, a lot of intestinal fortitude or a lot of brains. As far as I can see we've got no real high fliers out here. There may well be people of that ilk who live in the area but they're not working here.'

Dave Shorrocks, however, was not as quick to give up on the local talent. Sure, he nodded, ninety per cent of Mac Fields armed robbery is opportunistic. 'A walk-in. Nobody around, four in the morning, give us your money. But we keep an eye on who's been arrested elsewhere and given our patch as their address. And when you look at it we've got some good crooks living here.' Dave cited a famous criminal clan, with the patriarch, his old mum and a couple of brothers all voting locally. 'They were organised criminals,' he said. Charged with murder and armed hold-ups. The real deal too, with shotties and fast cars, not syringes and a skateboard. Another cop said later that an old mate of Lennie McPherson reported as part of his parole conditions to the Eaglevale lock-up where he just shook his head in disgust at the antics of the junkie amateurs.

In a possible karmic payback for Mick Donovan's poor opinion of the area's talent pool, he received a call asking him to observe a search on a nearby speed lab that afternoon. I'd signed my release forms saying it wasn't their fault if I got my head shot off or anything, so Mick asked if I'd like to come and watch. In the face of my indecent enthusiasm he pointed out that the bust had already been made and we were just going to turn the place over for evidence. I must admit I was a little disappointed, having signed that release form and all.

The lab had exploded in a house across the road from an empty sports ground. It was cold when we drove over, with a persistent, drizzling rain obscuring the blank battlements of a

Pig City

housing estate which stared at us across the boggy oval from a small rise of ground maybe a kilometre away. The speed lab had been set up in the garage of a private house, one of a row of nondescript bungalows, of sixties or early seventies design, which hunkered down somewhat sullenly on the edge of the sporting field furthest from the housing commission land. The alleged cook, a guy we'll call Fat Aldo, lived in a wide-fronted brick number with a peeling white balustrade running across the front of the property. The front garden was covered with a lush green matting of grass from which emerged two palm trees, one potted plant and a slate mail box with an warning to junk mailers to stay the fuck away.

I chatted in a desultory fashion with Donovan as we waited in the cold car for the others to arrive. Customs were sending a guy with some piece of Stars War technology to run a scan for drug traces inside the house. A scientist from the government labs was coming to perform the test. A couple of detectives with carriage of the case were due along with a couple more who'd grabbed Fat Aldo off the street. He was a bit of a rat, they said, with a history of going for his guns when threatened with capture. It had been considered safer to put the bag on him when he was away from home and any possible weapons stash. The assorted stakeholders were coming from all over western Sydney it seemed, and the afternoon began to leak away while we waited for them. The police radio crackled into life every couple of seconds, putting cars onto burglar alarms, domestics and four Aboriginal youths smashing their way into a home at Parramatta with baseball bats.

After so many years Donovan seemed oblivious to it. He had joined the force as a cadet in 1965 and had been sworn in four years later. 'Being a cadet was like having an apprenticeship,' he explained. 'You learned shorthand and typing and served in various parts of the force until you were nineteen. I enjoyed it. I learned a lot from it. I do wonder whether I should have got a trade so I'd have something to fall back on, but I'm still here and I don't begrudge the time.' He said he'd moved out to the western suburbs early in his career and never really made it back to the sea. I agreed that was a bit of a shame.

A detective, nicknamed Scanners, arrived and pulled up next to us. He and Donovan knew each other and fell into conversation about that week's episode of 'Four Corners' on the State's outlaw motorcycle gangs. It was, all agreed, a bit of a blowjob for the gangs. Lots of bikies 'delivering pandas to sick kiddies in hospital', said Donovan. Scanners recalled a raid on one gang where they'd discovered 'a zoo with a roo' out the back. One detective had become the object of a big red's affections, the giant marsupial constantly nuzzling and licking the man who could only try and push the animal away. But love could not be denied. The roo grabbed the man from behind and tried to mount him, to the great amusement of his colleagues. The wildlife rescue service was called to put the animal in a bag and as they were leaving the victim asked, 'This him?' as he peeled off a round-house punch in revenge.

After nearly an hour of this, the last of the other cars arrived. Two cops cleared the house for boobytraps and lurkers while we waited outside in the chilly rain. Fat Aldo, who stood with us, did not live up to his fearsome reputation. He had red fleshy ears, drooping jowls, and unshaven he resembled a cartoon dog. Having been captured he gave the detectives no more trouble, shrugging and answering, 'Yeah, whatever,' to most of their queries. He

Pig City

arrived with a windcheater thrown over his handcuffs, a middle-aged man, maybe fifty or more, with a big Roman nose, an enormous gut, short black hair going grey in places, and a splotchy red mark on his chin which became fiery when he was upset. He wore old, white leather runners, black track pants, a white T-shirt with some indecipherable motif, and his cheap sporty windcheater which he put on after his cuffs were removed. It seemed the lock-up grub was not agreeing with Aldo as he burped, hiccupped, grunted and excused himself throughout the afternoon.

With the search for boobytraps complete, everyone moved into the garage where the lab had gone up. It was crowded, with Fat Aldo, Mick Donovan, the government scientist, the customs rep, myself and half a dozen detectives, including two who videotaped the whole procedure, squeezing into the small space. The place didn't present as any sort of secret HQ for a Mr Big of the drug trade. False pine panelling covered one wall, coming away from the ceiling at one point. It was neat, however, with an old spare tyre, a whipper snipper, a cricket bat, a punching bag and a knee-high copper statue of a Spanish knight all stored away tidily. If Fat Aldo had been making any sort of money cooking up amphetamines, he had not spent it on fitting out his home in the harsh, sterile fashion invariably favoured by your successful drug barons on TV. The lounge room was not so much 'Miami Vice' as 'Roseanne', its white-trash battler aesthetic pithily expressed in the brown four-seater modular couch, the beige carpet, a Harley Davidson wall clock and a wine rack stocked with a few lonesome and dusty bottles of Passion Pop and Spumante.

An Abdominator, an expensive and pointless device for performing sit-ups which is generally purchased over the phone from late-night telemall shopping ads, had been abandoned on the brown couch. It was just one of many pieces of exercise equipment scattered throughout the house. There were so many weight stations, running machines and discarded pairs of jogging shoes that Fat Aldo's jumbo girth initially struck me as something of a mystery, until Mick Donovan explained the equipment had been left behind by the other members of the drug ring who cleared out after the explosion. Aldo had tried to explain their presence by claiming he had simply sublet the spare rooms to some mystery guys who, unbeknownst to him, had immediately set about brewing up industrial-sized tubs of dangerous drugs in the laundry. Apart from the athletic gear, the mystery guys had left almost no trace of their presence. The searchers moved through the house finding nothing until somebody turned over two thousand dollars and three bullets in the doona on Fat Aldo's bed.

'Me savings!' he blurted out. 'You're not getting that. That's me life savings! They come in here last week, little bastards, and went through the place but they missed me savings!'

The cops tried to convince him his 'savings' were safe, Donovan saying, 'We're not gonna take your money, Aldo; we have to log it though.'

'But that's me savings,' he protested. 'You're not getting it. You can't have 'em. That's all I got. Just leave 'em in the doona when you counted it.'

Donovan refused. The house had been burgled a week earlier, probably by kids from the estate, and as Mick pointed out, it wouldn't look good if they put the money back in the doona only to have it disappear after another B&E. Aldo was suspicious but calmed down a little when they placed the cash inside his bumbag. The three bullets went into an evidence bag. They finished up in the bedroom and returned to the garage where the boffins were busy taking swabs from the walls and floor. The garage roll-a-door was open and local mums, picking their kids up from the nearby school, were wandering past and staring. Fat Aldo, worried what the neighbours might think, asked the cops to pull down the door. 'You know what people around here are like,' he muttered as the customs device chimed, alerting everyone to the presence of MDEA in the most recent swab. The cops brightened and Aldo slumped a little. When a few minutes later the computer toned an alert for THC, the active ingredient in marijuana, Fat Aldo made a play at suggesting his teenage son had been sneaking into the laundry for sly cones behind his back. Everyone smiled as if to say, 'Yeah, Aldo, whatever'.

The testing procedure ate up two or three hours, a major improvement on the twelve hours it used to take in the days before mobile crime labs and superpowerful laptop computers. But it was still cold and wet and after a while the cops began to shift from foot to foot, stamping as the chill crept up through their legs from the cement floor. The procedure was slow and painstaking, swabbing walls, doors and ceilings, running the test, dropping the swab into a bag with a note of the location where it had been taken. The swabs had to be handled with tweezers and could not be allowed to fall on the floor. During the many hours needed to tag and bag the evidence, the men grew bored and like any public servants they fell into discussing promotions and postings. When that petered out they were reduced to remarking on how much time this new technology saved, about how awful it had been having to stand around for up to twelve hours on jobs like this. 'Yeah,' said someone, 'it's great technology, but think how much trouble we'll be in when it can test for semen and lipstick.' Everyone laughed for the first time that afternoon. Even Fat Aldo.

Fat Aldo's place was what the cops and the tabloids call a 'drug house', which conjures up images of reinforced steel doors and firing loops to poke your AK-47 through. But Sydney's drug houses are not like crack houses in New York, said Donovan, where you have to drive a battering ram through the front door. 'Anywhere drugs are sold or stored is a drug house. There could be thousands out here. Most are very low level.' It's a righteous certainty that every one of the frequent fliers on the wall upstairs at Mac Fields lives in a drug house. Without the resources to send people in undercover, the command, like most others in the city, relies on a form of tactical harassment, sending squad cars past, parking random breath-test units outside the house, noting the details of everyone who comes and goes and passing the information on to Dave Shorrocks's intelligence section. 'We chase away the customers,' shrugged Donovan.

Most of the work done by the constables takes place at this bargain basement level. Although they are encouraged to follow through on simple investigations, they are rarely if ever involved in gigs like Fat Aldo's. Their shifts, which last twelve hours, are a catherine wheel of speed and movement. The command is huge and crisscrossed by thousands of kilometres of roads, streets and cul de sacs. They run through the sprawling blighted public housing estates, the newer denser private developments and even a tiny millionaires' enclave where the descendants of the Macarthur clan have circled their wagons. So large is the command that officers stationed there for three or four years still get lost. I was riding along in a wagon one afternoon when a call to assist a lone female officer wrestling with a man outside a bank came through. Our driver kicked in the afterburners for nearly ten minutes and still couldn't get to the scene before it was over.

Pig City

Misery's fallout generates the bulk of police business; break and enters, domestic violence and assaults. 'I have people here who've been victims of domestic violence fifteen times,' said Wales. 'I have two people out knocking on doors, looking at repeat victims. But some won't listen, won't talk to us, won't let us in the front door. I don't even know if we're scratching the surface. The community groups tell us the women accept it as a fact of life. Dad did it to mum, they just expect it themselves. There is a resistance to change.'

That resistance or apathy (or acceptance of 'a lot not now to be altered' to recall Watkin Tench's phrase), is one of the greatest frustrations of the uniformed constable. Late one afternoon, with the last of the day's warmth rapidly disappearing, two of them, Paul Doyen and Matthew Sheahan, were taking me through Mortimer Street, widely thought of as the worst in the command. Every New Year's Eve for the past couple of years the locals had stolen a car and burned it to celebrate. The blaze was usually so hot it melted the bitumen, and as we drove through I could see the outlines of previous bonfires in the surface of the road, like the ghosts of New Years past advancing down the street. Doyen, the senior cop, was trying to explain the learned helplessness so prevalent amongst the poor, telling me how, a few months after the Housing Commission installed smoke detectors in its properties, the police started taking calls to come fix them because the batteries had run down and the warning chirps were driving everyone crazy. His young partner, who had moved down from Queensland, was recounting a story about a guy who was always using his 'emergency dial out only' phone for requesting emergency pizza deliveries, when the radio crackled out a request for a unit to attend the first domestic of the evening.

We were nearby and there was something in the report which tugged at Doyen's memory so he took it, pulling up a few minutes later at a small house on a corner block across from a park. The whole family was waiting outside in the well-tended garden where plaster gnomes, frogs, donkeys and a swan hid amongst the flower-beds. A young, heavily pregnant blonde woman with a broken nose and a baby on her hip was fairly bursting out of her skin to tell us about her ex-boyfriend who had been ringing through death threats to her family. He had, she said, just killed her current boy-friend, making it look like a suicide, and was promising that she would be next. She stood in the failing twilight, thin knock-kneed shins and enormous thighs in black tights, wearing sandals with white socks and a grey shapeless top. She was defiantly controlled until Doyen, who had listened patiently to her story, said, 'I know you. You laid charges against your boyfriend before, then left me hanging at the courthouse when they came up.'

There was no real colour to drain from the girl's sallow face, but the nervous energy which had been coursing through her sud-denly seemed to run out of the holes in her socks.

'No,' she said. 'That's not right. I never done that. I never took any charges against him before.'

'You did,' he insisted. 'I grabbed him for assaulting you before and we took him to court and you didn't turn up. You left me hanging. I remember it.'

She suddenly burst into tears, bawling and sucking air and pro-testing her innocence for about two minutes. Nobody said any-thing. None of her family moved to support her and the two cops just stared, waiting out the performance. It was a hard, grinding passage of time, excruciating to watch as she died on the stage of her one act psychodrama. When at last she realised it was going nowhere, she stopped almost instantly and said, 'This has been going on for eight years. When are youse gonna done something about it? If you don't fuckin' do something soon, I'm gonna have to neck him meself.'

'No you're not,' said Doyen firmly. 'But I want to know that if we get a warrant this time you'll follow through. He's a slippery bastard, your boyfriend. The only reason we got him last time was because he got stoned and fell asleep on your patio. I'm not going to waste my time again if you won't follow through.'

Her father, a broken, middle-aged man with grey stubble and a sort of grey-green ducktail hairdo, pulled his brown windcheater tighter about him and said, 'Yeah, you done wrong on that one, luv. You gotta get the prick this time.'

'But I didn't get no warrant! I didn't!' she screeched.

Her mother, who looked more redoubtable by several orders of magnitude, weighed in by saying eight years was long enough and she had to do something this time. Doyen extracted a promise that if he located the boyfriend they would see any charges through, and with that we left.

'You gonna look for him?' I asked in the truck.

'Oh yeah. He is a slippery little prick, but he's a coward too. If we find him, he'll fold again.'

'Reckon she'll follow through?' I asked.

'Not a chance,' Doyen said.

The stresses which operate on the street patrol are more immediate and intimately threatening than the bureaucratic pressures which bedevil the senior command. 'We can't get people to come here,' complained Dave Shorrocks. 'Because they listen to the radio and all they hear is Mac Fields, Mac Fields, Mac Fields, domestics, domestics, domestics. Our detectives haven't been burdened with any murders for eighteen months but they're consistently over-worked because the uniforms are so busy they farm everything upstairs. I've only got twelve detectives and they have ten consta-bles on each shift dumping work on them every day. I continually send it back down again saying, "No, we can't do everything." But of course they say, "How can I do this this, this and this?" While they're doing one job another two others are backing up. They feel they're being burned out. They cannot cope with the volume of work.'

Every job creates paper, even false alarms – such as the regular visits to one service station where the attendant is notorious for hitting the armed robbery panic button every time a customer com-plains about the quality of their prefabricated microwave nachos. It doesn't matter how frivolous the call, as soon as a constable takes it they have to come back and write it up. In a simple domes-tic, which is the core business of uniformed police, they have to drive to the scene and assess the situation. A back-up crew will often be sent because of previous violence at the same premises.

'So then,' says Shorrocks, 'you got two crews tied up. They speak to the victim and take a statement. They may arrest the person who has assaulted the victim. They bring him back here, interview him, process him, ring up and get an interim court order for an apprehended violence order. If the offence took place at his house they have to find a suitable refuge for the woman and any children. They must take the victim there. A friend can't do it because the police cannot disclose the identity or the address to anyone.' After all that, chances are when the perpetrator arrives in court, the victim will not turn up to press the charges.

If, on the same shift, they take a call to a dog dispute, the officers must return to the station, put an entry on the computer, take out

Pig City

a summons application against the owner, take the papers to court, get them signed and stamped and then serve the summons. If on the way back from the canine dispute they snatch a tagger decorating the walls of Glenfield Railway Station, the same cops have to organise to photograph the area for the station's digital database. They have to interview the kid, but if he is under fourteen they must first contact the parents for approval. 'Most times,' says Shorrocks, 'the parents refuse to attend, forcing us to find an independent observer, say from the Salvation Army. If the tagger is Aboriginal the officers must contact the Aboriginal Legal Service and fax any documents to them. The ALS can and will demand that nobody speak to their client until one of their solicitors is present.' Three seemingly simple jobs thus develop their own complex, bureaucratic existence. If the tagger, dog owner or angry boyfriend have had any past experience with the police, or are simply obstreperous, perverse or hip to the system, they can further complicate the process by lodging an official complaint against the officer concerned.

These pressures, which would tell in a normal work environment, are accentuated by the unnatural conditions of police work. On night shift, a constable will pull twelve hours, three or four days in a row, for up to three weeks at a stretch. Shorrocks, who has a background in sports medicine, is only too aware of the dire effects on the human body of having its circadian rhythms constantly jerked in and out of sync.

'Me personally, I don't like them,' he said of the long shifts. 'I don't think they're healthy. I see my own daughter, she's in the job, and on the twelve hour shifts her whole life changes. She comes home from a shift, assuming she hasn't had to work back on anything. She has something to eat, she goes to bed, she goes

451

back to work, she comes home, eats, goes to bed, back to work. For three days all she does is work and sleep. She has no social life. No relaxation. No exercise. Nothing. She hasn't got time. She's too tired. She takes food which my wife cooks, but a lot of kids here don't. They eat KFC or McDonalds which has no nutritional value whatsoever. I don't think it's normal. But as a manager it's great because our overtime is down.'

This chronic abuse of the constables' bodies is regularly augmented by acute mistreatment at the hands of suspects. 'Some of the younger constables,' said Shorrocks, 'don't cope well with being spat on or bitten. When it happens I sit down and explain what they'll be going through because I can relate to it. I've been through the AIDS business, the non-support of the service. I provided mouth-mouth to a drug addict and he regurgitated. I copped a mouthful of fluids and got very sick. The service wrote it off until I produced medical evidence to show I was telling the truth. That was six months later, with no support for my family, no support for my wife.'

There sometimes seems to be a split in the minds of many police between the loyalty and trust they invest in fellow officers and their distrust of the service, which remains a remote and potentially hostile foreign power. The lack of resources, the trimming and cutting, the making-do and putting off and one hundred other improvised tactics of a hungry outfit are, however, only partly to blame for the sense of powerlessness and abandonment which periodically engulfs them. Royal Commissioner James Wood's comprehensive negation of the old ways and means may have swept hundreds of corrupt officers out of the system and demolished the structures which harboured them, but it also decapitated the service. New paradigms have had little time to evolve. The 13 000 cops who survived had to forget decades of institutional memory. For the older hands the attack on police culture, although understandable, was particularly galling because that culture, with its many ugly faults, was often the only thing standing between them and the abyss, as Greg, one of Shorrocks's detectives, put it to me.

'There are some positive sides of police culture,' he said. 'I know they're trying to get rid of blokes sticking up for each other, lying for each other, covering for each other and that's good. But it seems to me they're going too far, trying to stop us just being mates too. If you have to put your life on the line with someone, you want to know you can trust them. And a lot of the time, too, going down the pub and having a beer and a chat with your mates does help.'

Greg's eyes were red-rimmed and tired. He looked a bit lumpy, overworked and stale, as you would expect of a man trying to solve a possible murder, a heap of frauds, a couple of heavy armed robberies and a mixed bag of sex crimes. He nodded after another plain-clothes man who had just left the room. 'That detective who just walked out there did a job where a lady had killed her baby,' he said quietly. 'And when they did the autopsy it had no inners. There was nothing inside. So they sent him back to the house and under the griller was all the insides of the kid.' He paused and stared at the mess of papers on the desk in front of him, oblivious to my tape recorder for the first time. 'I don't know ...' he shrugged, biting his lip. 'How do you react to something like that? It's got to freak you out, and going to the pub and talking about it *does* help. I can't go home and tell my wife about that,' he said, looking up and shaking his head. 'Even though she's supportive she doesn't want to hear that because it's gonna freak her out too. So you talk to your mates who have been through it with you'.

Is it possible to maintain the faith in the face of experience which can only coarsen the soul? He insisted it is. Everyone has their way, he said. For him it was a retreat into professionalism. You get to a homicide and you turn off your emotions. You focus solely on what you need to make the case. Even so, the raw reality is sometimes strong enough to subvert these defences, if not breach them. 'I did a matter at Claymore where a lady killed her two kids,' Greg recalled. 'I had to go back and interview her and . . . at the end of it . . . it really freaked me out. I came back and had a blue with the boss, had a shit of a day and when I sat back and thought about it, it was that interview.'

On a run over to Campbelltown at four the next morning Wayne Hack, an old sergeant with a giant gravy-barrel stomach, reflected on the ruin police work can wreak on family and friends. 'No man is in a fit state to deal with his wife and daughters when he has spent half the night walking along a mile of train track picking up bits and pieces of body and brain,' he said. 'As soon as you put the uniform on you have to shift into a different way of thinking.'

An aggressive, mistrustful, sharply reactive frame of mind in which you cannot show weakness, in which there are few shades of grey, in which people are reduced to threats, perps, victims or witnesses.

'We don't see the nice mums and dads,' said Mick Donovan. 'We only deal with the shits.'

When I arrived at Campbelltown Station with Hack in the cold hours before dawn, he asked if I fancied a peek at 'a mad Irishman' we'd been hearing about on the radio for a few hours. This guy had been head-butting and punching the Catholic Club because they wouldn't serve him any more booze. It had taken three cops and a blast of capsicum spray to put him down. A Campbelltown sergeant named Errol – who would be played by Bryan Brown as laconic, slow-moving and amused by it all in the made-for-TV mini-series – told us the guy was simply 'mad on the piss'. That had always been just a phrase until they took me through to see him. I could hear his screams from the other end of the building. He stopped for half a second as we entered the room but on seeing Errol redoubled his efforts. He was a tall, well-built young man with a rat's tail haircut and no shirt. Tattoos, including an Irish flag, covered his torso and a lot of blood had soaked through his blue jeans. Errol was right. He was mad on the piss. They had locked him inside a plexiglass cube, a little bigger than a telephone booth, and he was jerking about, howling and throwing himself against the walls, raging to get out. Punching the brick walls of the Catholic Club had pushed his knuckles right back up his hand. A weary-looking custody officer and a very sorry-looking curly-haired drunk were the only other occupants of the room. The Irishman lit into Errol and 'his fat friend' with a ferocious torrent of abuse, stopping only when his eyes locked in on my own.

'Who's this tough-looking cunt think he is?' he sneered. 'Serpico?'

He pulled a face at me but then lost interest, preferring to bounce off the bulging plastic walls and roar like a bear.

'How often would you get something like that in the cage?' I asked Errol.

'Most nights,' he shrugged. 'Sometimes we get a whole bunch of them.'

Exposure to what Wood called 'the worst aspects of society' inevitably hardens the heart. But police are not alone in this. Journalism, for one, is another occupation in which the practitioners eventually develop a very scaly hide. But journalists do not carry guns. They are not permitted to use force or take lives in pursuit of their duties. Unlike police officers, they are not authorised to enter and search private homes and to seize personal belongings. Although they sometimes do, or at least try to. In common with police, journalists do occasionally form close relationships with criminal informants, and sometimes these working relationships become friendships. Like police, journalists are often exposed to the opportunity to benefit privately from their work, be it at a very low level such as taking freebies from companies during promotion drives, or more seriously through opportunities to engage in insider trading, or most harmfully through debauching the power of the media itself, as in the cash-for-comment talkback scandal of July 1999. At some stage almost all journalists indulge themselves in the milder forms of 'corrupt' practice. Nowadays most police do not. After I had been to Macquarie Fields I ran a trace through a CD-rom of the Wood Commission transcripts, looking for any references to the station or its senior officers. There were about forty or fifty all told, none of them negative and most concerned with the excellent manner in which the station managed its inform- ant program.

When exploring the nature of police work, to consider whether it was inherently corrupting, Wood also acknowledged that police officers find that many crimes, such as prostitution, gambling, drugs, porn and liquor licensing offences, are either victimless or in high demand by society. In working these areas a cop soon becomes 'acutely aware of the substantial difference between their take home pay and the financial opportunities available through crime'. They are rarely rewarded for ethical behaviour but quickly punished for disciplinary infractions. They are prey to the whims of politics, 'feel compelled to cut corners if they are to control the streets', and become cynical about the wider community which does not understand the dangers and difficulties they encounter. In the face of such strains it is surprising that corruption of the city's police is not universal.

Sydney had entered the Second World War as a fractured city, riven by class conflict, weak in any culture of civic responsibility which might curb the rapacity of its competing interests, and still carrying the incubus of its convict past. As late as 1946 it was still legally permissible for judges to hand out floggings, as one threatened to that year. The traditional antipathy of Sydney's inhabitants towards the police was likewise undiminished. One *Sydney Morning Herald* article lamented that bystanders could 'hoot and jeer at policemen struggling on a city pavement with a suspect for the possession of a loaded pistol'. So deep was this antipathy that more than fifty years later Stephen Knight identified a sympathetic fascination with the criminal as hero as a defining characteristic of Australian literature. There is, as Knight points out, something decidedly unusual 'about the readiness with which the Australian crime novel accepts the viewpoint of the criminal and outlines with sympathy the wrongs committed against him'. Almost as though his crime were a legitimate response to an unfair world. Whilst criminal heroes are occasionally celebrated in American and French culture, only Australian writing has observed a long, unbroken fascination for the prosaic, workaday concerns of the ne'er-do-well. Less dashing, less attractive and generally just much less inspiring than his foreign compadres, the criminal anti-hero of Australian literature has nonetheless proved more resilient. Knight describes him as a low-life plodder who is understood and sympathised with, but not for romantic reasons. 'Without glamour, usually rather unimpressive in personal terms, the criminal seems to see a life of lawbreaking as the only path open to him, is not particularly thrilled by it, yet has a reasonable range of antisocial skills and illegal procedures that are carefully and approvingly revealed by the story'. Two hundred years of affection for this dodgy Everyman speak to Knight of 'a deeply held and almost routinised sense that any move against conventional authority is to be admired'.

This may have made for an emptiness at Sydney's heart, a moral and structural vacuum which laid the city open to attack by the cancerous corruption it would become famous for. By the late 1970s the spread of that cancer was so advanced that key elements of the city's power structure and economy had drifted under the influence of a criminal counterstate; a dark alliance of corrupt police, businessmen, politicians and the underworld. Dr Al McCoy, an American specialist in the crosscultural analysis of crime, declared that 'no city in the world could rival Sydney's tolerance for organised crime'. So integrated was the system that the organised criminal milieu even began to take on political allegiances mirroring those of the legitimate world, and the political developments of the postwar era can be as easily read in its bloody, periodic realignments as in any volume of Hansard.

The war itself started the ball rolling. Just as the Second World War finally jump-started Sydney's economy out of depression, so too did it jolt the city's underworld out of the small-time pursuits of thieving, sly-grogging and prescription-drug rackets. Suddenly the city was awash with cash – an abundance of wage packets which hadn't been seen since the Depression hit – and Sydney's petty crims found themselves loose in a very big lolly shop.

Wartime rationing created an ideal environment for black market rackets – a sudden jump in demand by way of the increased cash circulation corresponded with a restriction of supply. Sydney's criminal milieu were not slow in nutting out hundreds of ways to insinuate themselves in the distribution chain. Coupon forging, waterfront pilfering and adulteration were the mainstays. A casual glance at the arrest records of any of the standover men of the 1950s and 1960s – infamous 'gunnies' like Chow Hayes, Richard Reilly or Johnny Warren – reveals how important the black market rackets were in nurturing the growth of Sydney's postwar organised crime. Most of them first graduated from petty thieving and thuggery at that time. Chow Hayes, the vicious heavy who later stood over illegal gambling enterprises like Thommo's two-up school and eventually did time for the murder of one of the school's bouncers, ripped off naive soldiers and greedy shopkeepers with the 'cabbage leaf racket' – selling sealed cartons of black market smokes which were in reality packed with cabbage leaves, the foliage which most closely approximated real tobacco weight. Richard Reilly, a strongarm king of the underground baccarat games in the Cross during the early sixties, whose 1967 murder threatened to expose the underworld connections of hundreds of society and political figures recorded in his contact books, ran a wartime racket printing forged clothing ration coupons. His killer, the late Johnny Warren, had a petrol coupon rort so profitable it allowed him to finance a phone-order stealing business and attempt to muscle in on the Kings Cross baccarat games with his own clubs. To the modern ear the black market rackets sound quaint, with their cabbage leaves, bodgie coupons and bottles of Scotch half-filled with water and sold to soldiers for a couple of quid profit. But they were the finishing school for a number of violent and fairly odious guys. The huge safari rifle with which Warren blasted a hole in Reilly's larynx, severing his carotid artery, hadn't been the upstart heavy's first choice of weapon. Still in the thrall of his wartime experience, Warren's original plan had been to kill Reilly by dousing him with petrol and setting him alight. He had only been dissuaded by a friend's insistence that the plan was impractical.

More important than the opportunities for black market entrepreneurship it created, however, was the effect the Second World War had on the trifecta of 'social' crimes that have been the staples of police corruption ever since – drinking, screwing and gambling. Drugs, the modern equivalent, were at that time almost unheard of, except for the relatively minor trade in cocaine to the city's prostitutes during the 1920s. The era's razor gangs, lineal descendants of the larrikin pushes, spent a few years frantically slicing and dicing each other in the fight to control that market. But back then grog was the thing. Tight opening hours and licensing restrictions in Sydney after the First World War created a thriving market for 'black' liquor vended after hours at exorbitant rates to legions of thirsty customers. Similarly prostitution and gambling were a standing inducement to police corruption.

Sydney police were unusually vulnerable to the corrupting influence of proscribed but publicly tolerated crimes. The peculiarities of Sydney's social and legal structure – the long shadow of her convict past – multiplied the points of temptation. The New South Wales criminal law encompassed an extraordinarily wide range of behaviour, equalled nowhere else in the Anglo-Saxon world. Drunkenness was a case in point. By 1948, fifty-five per cent of all arrests were for Inebriates Act violations. One Legislative

Pig City

Assembly member complained it was no longer safe for his constituents to frequent their local pubs due to the raids of the police 'trawler', which sometimes netted 800 arrests in a single weekend. The hangover of attitudes from the penal past can also be seen in the terminology of the pre-1970 versions of the Summary Offences Act. References to 'rogues', 'vagabonds' and 'incorrigible rogues' abound. What it all added up to was an unusually broad range of unenforceable laws unsupported by the general public but which the establishment expected to be policed.

Aggravating the equation was the heightened public disavowal of *any* control of the so-called 'social' or 'victimless' crimes. Drinking, whoring and gambling which, along with profanity, preoccupied the minds of that rabble disgorged from the First Fleet had, over the two centuries, indelibly stained the soul of the new city. This was the dynamic behind Sydney's unrivalled tolerance of organised crime, manifested in the peculiar spectacle of the city's postwar elite embracing the criminal element. Outside observers like McCoy were constantly amazed at the complacency with which political figures and high-ranking police not only associated with underworld figures but allowed themselves to be seen doing so. Fred Hanson, for example, Police Commissioner from 1972 to 1977, was fond of duck shooting with 'Aussie' Bob Trimbole, principal of the Calabrese marijuana operation in the Riverina district and a suspected conspirator in the murder of antidrugs campaigner Donald Mackay. Chief Stipendiary Magistrate Murray Farquhar stayed cool and hung loose when photographed with SP-betting operator George Freeman in the members' enclosure of Randwick Racecourse. And as David Hickie relates in his 1986 study of the New South Wales criminal milieu, *The Prince and the Premier*, one Labor premier even found himself elbowed out of his own home when partying crims, taking advantage of his hospitality, took to turning up with armloads of women for late-night roisters. The hapless leader was reduced to sitting out the night, alone on a park bench across the road, until the parties burned themselves out. Only when he complained personally to the Police Commissioner was a squad of detectives organised to turf out the heavies. United in the bonhomie of the track, the pub and the sly-grog dens, these establishment figures were simply playing out the national mythology of social crime. There was nothing wrong with it and only constipated wowsers and needledicks said otherwise.

Richard Hall, in his 1986 study of Australian 'disorganised' crime, argues that a political schism exaggerated the city's burden of unenforceable social legislation. At the turn of the century the newly formed Labor Party, uniting the numerically dominant working class behind it, had become a serious threat to the established political order. It was imperative middle-class opinion be mobilised, but the key to its support lay with those punishers and straighteners for whom drinking and gambling ranked alongside mixed marriages and goat fucking as threats to the nation. Their impost for averting a red takeover was a raft of laws to curb the debauchery of the lower orders. Pub closing time was cut from eleven p.m. to six p.m. and off-course betting was outlawed entirely. The Labor Party, smeared as the 'publican's party', bitterly decried the class bias of the movement, pointing out that none of the restrictions applied to the toffs in their racing clubs. Enduring political rancour in the racing world can be glimpsed in the 1976 complaint of Cliff Mallam MLA that racing in New South Wales was run by 'a bunch of amateurs and blue bloods who treat people in the industry like serfs'.

Like King Phillip II of Spain and modern day antidrug campaigners, no experience of the failure of the moral crusaders' prohibition policy could shake their belief in its essential excellence. In spite of the clampdown, sly-grogging was a steady earner for basement dives like the Ziegfeld Cafe in King Street. According to one Maxwell Liquor Royal Commission informer, prostitutes, male perverts, sly-grog and dope were all to be had at the Ziegfeld, along with the 'band and hot meal for six shillings six pence' the owner claimed to provide. The money was in after-hours sales; the commission heard of streets where hotels on one side followed the six o'clock close, while those on the other were inexplicably able to trade until late into the night. The situation changed with the outbreak of war. With hundreds of thousands of thirsty servicemen thronging the city, beer and liquor were in such demand that a quota system was introduced. The pubs, whose licences entitled them to a fixed ration every week, found themselves sitting on liquid gold. Liquor quotas quickly disappeared out the back door and onto the black market, where they were snapped up by unlicensed American-style nightclubs like Abe Saffron's Roosevelt Club or Sammy Lee's eponymous club ('If there's a girl you want to please, take her along to Sammy Lee's') in Woollahra Street. A frantic trade in bogus hotel licensees ensued – the Maxwell Commission stated flatly that, despite his denials, Saffron had 'a beneficial interest in a number of hotels using different persons as dummies'. Corruption of the vice squad accelerated. One of David Hickie's informants, a senior officer who joined the force in the early forties, confessed that one night-shift radio patrol car team was occupied full time touring the city's sly-grog, vice and gambling dens to collect kickbacks. Justice Maxwell expressed his displeasure that the Metropolitan Superintendent of Police, James Sweeney, should hold his retirement testimonial at Sammy Lee's, 'one of the most notorious offenders against the liquor laws', collecting £600 from the two or three hundred guests present 'in circumstances which lend themselves quite readily to suspicion and criticism'. Inevitably the dens began to attract the attention of standover merchants.

Prostitution likewise had been boosted by the war. The area around Palmer Street in East Sydney, informally zoned for brothel-keeping by the tacit consensus of police, public and government, soon exhibited a fantastic scene of industrial-age whoring. Hundreds of US servicemen queued outside hastily organised establishments, with MPs detailed to keep lines moving, and special clubs for Negro soldiers. One of these last, the Booker T Washington Club, created special problems for Sydney police; once word got out that black servicemen were paying double the going rates, East Sydney was inundated with women and girls – married, unmarried, some as young as fifteen and many from country areas – all keen to cash in. Confronted with the failure of the Brisbane vice trade to match Sydney's efforts, Prime Minister John Curtin authorised discreet approaches to underworld figures involved in Thommo's two-up school. Soon, writes Hickie, a trainload of 'warm, attractive females eager to assist the national war effort' was on its way north, with the women's tickets and a low weekly retainer paid for by the government.

Such playfulness was not long to characterise Sydney's vice trade, however. Despite an aversion amongst some status-conscious crims for 'living off the earnings' – a distaste with a solid basis in pragmatism given heavy jail terms for pimping – the exploding profits of the sex trade during and after the war attracted the city's gunmen and organised crime figures. These profits were not simply a matter of increased activity in the sex trade. A fundamental restructuring of prostitution from a freelance individual pursuit in the nineteenth century to a mass market service industry in the mid-twentieth century massively increased the profits available. Ironically, the cause of this restructuring was a series of laws, such as the Police Offences Amendment Bill of 1908, passed by socially conservative governments who claimed to be leading a moral backlash against vice. But by empowering the police to harass and persecute small-time street level operators, the God botherers simply laid the basis for a takeover by syndicated criminal groups which could organise the trade to be less visible but much larger and more lucrative. Thousands of street walkers were forced into the employ of brothel owners who concentrated their operations in East Sydney and Darlinghurst. Temperance legislation, the early closing laws, provided another income stream as did moves against narcotics in the 1920s. Cocaine was a popular drug amongst prostitutes and it had the added advantage for their controllers that, once addicted, the women would work for over-priced drugs, not money. This echoed the lament of Governors Hunter and Bligh that labourers who had become enslaved to alcohol would work punishing hours for a bottle of spirits which they would consume in a day, rather than taking their pay in grain by which they could support their families for a week.

Judith Allen, who analysed the shift of prostitution from cottage industry to mass production in Kay Daniels' *So Much Hard Work*, characterised the industry as just that, an industry, subject to the same laws and forces as any other. Brothelkeepers like Tilly Devine and Kate Leigh were simply capitalists, literally extorting the surplus value of their workers' labour. Encouraging demand for cocaine amongst prostitute employees, writes Allen, could be seen as just another strategy in the more longstanding and central underworld endeavour to appropriate an ever greater share of the profits from this immensely lucrative field. However, as Allen points out, because the coke trade played an 'internal function among underworld employees', unlike the popular vices of prostitution itself or sly grogging or off-track betting, it did not have the support required to withstand an assault from the state. That attack came when the violent struggle for control of the market, a battle popularly known as the razor gang wars, spun out of control. The multiple slashings were bad enough but when industry principals began placing hidden snipers atop buildings in Darlinghurst, even the Sydney police could no longer stand by. They crushed the trade with repressive consorting laws and aggressive policing.

While narcotics were driven from the sex industry, there was no change in the structure of that industry. The production line system of the brothels was still much more profitable for the criminals who controlled them than returning to the disorganised methods of the previous century. It also meant that with the return of affluence occasioned by the Second World War and the arrival of cashed up American soldiers, there was a system in place ready for massive expansion. Twenty years later another war, this time in Vietnam, would provide a similar growth impetus. But it would also mark a revolutionary and violent change in the underworld.

On the 28 May 1968 a Maltese man called Joe Borg turned the ignition key in his Holden ute and was just about ripped in half by the detonation of a nine-stick gelignite bomb. His right leg was severed and his car turned into a tangled heap of smoking metal. The attack was an opening salvo in the savage shake-up of the Darlinghurst vice rackets. Borg, sometimes tagged the King of Palmer Street, had been running girls from a stable of twenty houses in the labyrinthine laneways of the Doors area. Police estimated he was taking in $8000 to $10 000 per week at the time of his death. An orgy of beatings, stabbings, shootings and fire-bombings quickly followed, with even the veteran 'colourful identity' Tilly Devine burned out of her Palmer Street terrace. One of Borg's associates was car-bombed in Malta after fleeing there. The demise of Borg's contemporary, Stewart Johnny Regan, was even more illustrative of the anarchic feuding. Regan was running a string of girls and standing over a number of the city's SP bookies and illegal casinos when he inexplicably allowed himself to be lured to a killing ground in Marrickville. Trapped in Chapel Street, between a foundry and the Marrickville Infants' School, without his customary four bodyguards, Regan was dropped from behind by a single shot to the back. Three gunmen drove a patchily painted white car up to the dying hoodlum, alighted and popped another seven bullets into him.

What Regan and the other wanna-be vice lords who lost their lives failed to take into account was that there was already a gang of standover men operating in Sydney. They carried their weapons legally and enjoyed the atomic-powered advantage of legal sanction – problematic competitors could be loaded up or even murdered 'legitimately' in the course of an arrest. The gang which emerged as the heaviest, most ruthless criminal outfit in the city after the Second World War was not the mafia or the triads but the police force itself, and specifically the Criminal Investigations Branch. The accepted wisdom about Regan's death is that it was a police-inspired execution, carried out with police revolvers and organised by the legendary detective Ray 'the Gunner' Kelly, whom we first met beating seven kinds of hell out of Newtown anti-eviction protesters. Kelly had put his massive frame and hardened heart to good use in the intervening years. Working his way up through the CIB, he was appointed head of the prestigious Safe-Breaking Squad in the early 1950s – safe-crackers being considered the top of the criminal tree in those pre-narcotic days. In this position, Kelly created a fearsome reputation for himself, running down, and sometimes killing, some of Sydney's most infamous criminals – Darcy Dugan, Chow Hayes, James Hackett and Ronald Ryan among them. He also rose, along with his confederate bent copper, Frederick 'Froggy' Krahe, into a controlling position in the Sydney rackets.

Most observers agree the 1950s and 1960s saw the real flowering of police corruption in Sydney. McCoy, comparing the city with New York, Hong Kong and Marseilles, posited a five-stage growth cycle for corruption in police services culminating in criminal entrepreneurship on the part of police in stage four, and total syndication of all organised crime under a tight group of senior police officers in stage five. Though McCoy believes Sydney never made it to join Hong Kong in stage five, he was on firm ground in asserting that by the late 1970s the city's police were firmly locked into stage four – criminal entrepreneurship.

A snapshot of the transition from stage three – accepting regular retainers in exchange for failing to enforce the law – to four exists in a 1965 hearing of the bankruptcy court. The case, reported by Hickie, involved Aileen Donaldson, a Darlinghurst madam who was trying to conceal her interest in a number of brothels. The court was told that girls working the area commonly handed over substantial amounts to local police for the privilege of suffering only one arrest per week – stage three corruption in its pure form. But the court also heard allegations that the head of the Darlinghurst Vice Squad, Detective-Sergeant Harry Giles, had gone further, entering into a silent partnership with Donaldson in a Palmer Street brothel which he protected while police action drove other operators out of business. Giles's denials had suffered when his embittered wife filed for divorce, claiming he had lied about his relations with Donaldson and that his safe at home had at one stage held £10 500.

Froggy Krahe personified the commercialisation of official corruption. Celebrated as the king of the crooked cops, Krahe was described by one contemporary as 'a big brooding bastard with an aura of power and evil about him'. In photos he presents as an archetypal heavy-drinking, hard-charging blood-and-guts horror pig, which he was, with his eyes narrowed to slits and sandblasted skin folding around craggy features. Krahe was a stage four man through and through. His involvement in prostitution was just a one line item on an impressive portfolio of corrupt business dealings. With Gunner Kelly, Krahe ran Sydney's underworld as a personal fiefdom, raking in profits from abortion rackets, bribery, and 'green lighted' armed robberies. In 1970 he and Kelly even took a progressive interest in the emerging narcotics trade, reputedly leading to the death of their heir apparent, Superintendent Don Fergusson, who is supposed to have killed himself rather than follow his mentors over the abyss.

It was Krahe's connection with the sex industry that brought him undone. The first thread was pulled in 1971, when a prostitute named Shirley Brifman was charged with procuring a fourteen-year-old girl for the purposes of prostitution. Brifman was understandably pissed off – her weekly payments to the vice squad were insurance premiums taken out against just such an eventuality. She retaliated with a sixty-four page statutory declaration, circulated to both the police hierarchy and the press, detailing the business arrangements of her sometime lover and premier police contact, Fred Krahe. It was all there: regular payments to avoid prosecution and to keep the gunnies away, counterfeiting scams, partying with Shirley's hookers and planning robberies whilst at her premises (apparently Krahe had an arrangement with Brisbane detectives to exchange teams of crims for jobs on each other's turf). Fred's health took a dive, allowing him to retire 'medically unfit' in 1972. Brifman was not long to savour her revenge though. Realising the enormity of her sin, she fled north to escape. According to CIB legend, or myth if you will, Krahe tracked her down in March and, together with a Queensland police officer, forced a lethal dose of pills down her throat with a tube.

Krahe's career is worth studying as a metaphor of corruption. He joined a comparatively clean force in 1940 and progressed through the ranks as it mutated into a subterranean paracriminal fraternity by the 1970s; stage one to four in thirty-odd years. Krahe worked his way to prominence by sheer ability; as a CIB detective he broke some of Sydney's biggest cases – the thallium rat-poison murders and the 'bodyless' homicide of widow Phyllis Page among them. This was Krahe's Janus face, the mask which allowed him to foster his dark side. He was a genuinely good cop. According to Hickie he inspired such fear in the underworld that not even high-stepping crims like Chow Hayes or Darcy Dugan dared call him anything other than Mr Krahe. He ruled over them and they knew it. But in the anarchic expanding economy of the postwar city, such power was not long to stay within bounds. Krahe slid from curbing crime to managing and then promoting it. He personified the shift to criminal entrepreneurship. Even out of the force, and almost up to his death in 1981, he remained a figure of influence. In 1976 Sydney journalists Tony Reeves and Barry Ward raised his name in connection with the murder of Juanita Neilsen, the department store heiress and publisher of an independent community newspaper which bitterly opposed Frank Theeman's attempt to seize Victoria Street. They claimed Krahe had been one of three men to lure Neilsen to a motel in Kings Cross, where her throat was slit, her body dismembered and the remains fed down a garbage disposal unit. Krahe even figured in the collapse of the fantastically deviant Nugan Hand bank, being named in Parliament for intimidating the bank's auditors and organising bogus shareholders to oust those same auditors at an extraordinary general meeting.

The real engine of police and political corruption in Sydney was gambling which, like sly-grogging and prostitution, waxed fat on the rush of wartime spending. Not that it wasn't already entrenched. Thommo's famous two-up school had been roaring along since its inception in 1910. Just after the First World War its principal, George Guest (his ring name as a boxer had been Thomas, hence Thommo's), was thought to be pulling down £6000 a day. Of the three victimless crimes, gambling probably had the widest acceptance and the least social stigma attached to it. You get a sense of the importance of gambling in the city's democratic culture in a profile of Thommo's patrons published in the *Bulletin* in 1979.

> There were no colour, religious or political barriers between this rowdy classless assemblage of doctors, stockbrokers, graziers, public servants, jockeys, labourers, bookmakers, plumbers, butchers, pimps and criminals, either on bail, remand or released.

LEVIATHAN

Thommo's was a floating school and moved as token police raids required. Lit by naked, swinging lightbulbs, choked by a fug of smoke and sweat, men of all classes stomped the bare boards and threw their money down to the ratty green coir matting in ten, fifty and hundred pound wads, everything riding on the fall of the two spinning King Edward VII pennies, their heads polished and tails blacked for clearer viewing. It was probably as close as the city has ever come to the spurious fantasy of egalitarian mateship across the classes.

It was the Second World War which grossly distorted Thommo's margins. Hickie records the phenomenal amounts of cash which began to pass through the school in the 1940s, when American soldiers were the big punters and bets of £1000 were not unusual. The party continued into the fifties when celebrity punters like radio star Jack Davey could shrug off single spin losses of £2000. By that time the game had become an illicit staple of Sydney's night-life (for men only, women were strictly excluded) and was attracting the eclectic cross-section of crims, top hats and workmen the *Bulletin* noted. There was a Janus-faced quality about Thommo's too; on the one side the innocence of Runyonesque characters like the bouncer Big Itchy or the forty-five-kilo ring keeper Nixy the Flea with his coloured neckerchiefs and long cigars, and the backslapping bonhomie as when another radio man, 2KY's John Harper, kept his public promise to bare his arse to the ring when he failed to maintain his fourteen toss run of 'heading 'em'. On the other side, however, was the violent shadow, acknowledged in the school rule that nobody was allowed outside for fifteen or twenty minutes after the departure of a big winner to give him a sporting chance of getting away, and visible the night Big Itchy gave four men who had attempted to pass dud fivers a 'scrubbing' on the roadway outside, smashing their teeth out and pocketing £500 reward from George Guest; or again when an innocent punter took a bullet meant for Guest at the entrance to the school. And of course there was the corruption such a profitable operation allowed, in fact required. A police driver called Muir stated baldly in 1953 that he had often driven police to collect bribes from Thommo's and accepted them himself. The standard procedure was to just ignore Thommo's – in 1968 Police Commissioner Norman 'the Foreman' Allan gave Sydney a giggle by claiming Thommo's didn't exist – or, if public pressure grew too great, to collude in the setting up of a dummy game which could then be raided.

Baccarat, the European-style card game played in a host of illicit clubs which morphed into the casinos of the 1970s, followed a similar trajectory. Introduced early in the century by a former ship's steward, the game had spread to seven clubs in Kings Cross by 1940. Again the outbreak of war lifted them into the big league. In 1944 Siddy Kelly, a veteran of the razor gang wars, opened the first 'luxury' baccarat club in Victoria Street, Darlinghurst – an up market joint with plush carpet, luxurious fittings and complimentary buffet-style meals for patrons. Here mug punters could gamble from seven at night until eight the next morning, be plied with food to keep up their strength, drink to weaken their judgment, and eyedrops and 'patent medicines' to ward off the effects of fatigue. It was an instant success and the Cross was soon crowded with imitators. Kelly was making so much black money that when he died in 1948, Centennial Park was flooded with spade-wielding treasure hunters looking for £30 000 Kelly, who lived across the road, had supposedly buried there. When the windfall of returning servicemen's back pay ran out in 1947, the clubs were well enough established to continue and even expand, becoming a city-wide craze by the 1950s, and one enthusiastically adopted by women. One city alderman complained of the number of darts and chess clubs which were really nothing but baccarat schools, and a hundred-metre-long strip of Kings Cross where they flourished gained the appellation 'the rip-roaring Barbary Coast'. Sydney's infatuation with illicit gambling amazed visiting US judge Harold Buchanan, who said in 1958 that the legal gambling state of Nevada had nothing on the harbour city. A booming twilight industry inevitably attracted a substratum of criminal heavies, assuming they weren't already the club principals: bouncers working at $100 a week to turn away undesirables, floor men who patrolled for would-be bash and rob merchants; gunnies who gave no service for their money other than not unloading a few rounds on the club or its patrons. Just as inevitably, the flow of money gouged out deeper and wider channels of police and political corruption.

In *The Prince and the Premier* Hickie describes a meeting hastily organised by police, politicians and underworld figures to resolve a threatened crisis when a new luxury baccarat school, Club Enchantment, backed by gambling figures from Melbourne, opened in the Cross without consultation. A compromise deal evolved with the action being cut three ways between the club, its major competitor and the minor schools. If it seems remarkable that political figures and police should meet with crims in such circumstances (one of the items on the agenda was the level of protection to be paid) it has to be understood in the context of the times. The tacit acceptance of illegal gambling was a political phenomenon. At the start of the 1960s the Labor Party had been in power in New South Wales for twenty years and it was no accident that the man who emerged from the ruck as the baccarat enforcer extraordinaire in the mid-sixties had extensive party contacts. This was Richard Gabriel Reilly, whom you may recall as the guy getting his head blown off by would-be pyromaniac Johnny Warren. Reilly, an ex-boxer who had worked his way up from bouncing, thieving and violent extortion to a commanding position in the baccarat schools and abortion rackets, had links with many ALP members, including the old radical Eddie Ward, for whose meetings Reilly would provide squads of heavies to deal with hecklers. The extent of the connections between the Labor machine and the criminal milieu was exposed by the upheavals in the aftermath of Reilly's murder.

Despite the violence of his business life Reilly was a man of good habits and a tidy mind. The detectives who arrived at the dress shop into which his Maserati had rolled after Warren had capped him found two address books in his pockets. The books were crammed with the names, addresses and telephone numbers of everyone Reilly had ever dealt with. Along with the crims, brothel owners, hookers, lawyers, cops and abortionists, the books listed contacts for a number of A-grade political and society figures. This potential political bomb was defused through the simple expedient of immediately suppressing the details of the investigation. Hickie recalls a detective who worked on the case voicing his surprise that, 'as we checked the next groups of phone numbers each day the results were going straight to the Premier [by that time the Liberal Robert Askin]. It was the first and only time that happened on a murder case during my career and I thought it was most unusual.' Hickie, describing the fallout from Reilly's death relates an incident which illustrates how deeply corruption had soaked into the city's political fabric. Another detective working on the case said,

I was walking through State Parliament House with another detective ... [An MP] came running after us ... He wanted to know if another politician, a wealthy bloke from his own party, was listed in the notebooks. We said no. [The MP] said not to tell anyone that yet. He wanted to approach this other wealthy MP and tell him his name was in Reilly's books, but that if that wealthy MP paid [the MP], he could get it removed from the list ... [The MP] offered us part of the deal but I declined.

As Hickie notes, the incident spoke volumes, one MP so brazenly trying to shake down another. Why would it be so easy to bluff the wealthy politician into believing his name was in the books? And why was the potential blackmailer so confident of gaining the collaboration of the police in his obviously criminal venture?

As it happened, Reilly's death was not related to the political shake-up of 1965. Warren killed Reilly on a contract from a moneylender and in revenge for Reilly's having run him out of the baccarat rackets. But his death was emblematic. The underworld was realigning its power relationships at the same time as the State. The 1965 election, ironically the first modern law and order campaign, marked the end of Labor's hold on power. After twenty-four years the Liberal–Country coalition took office by dint of the centrist strategy hammered out by its leader, Robin (alias Robert) Askin. The change in the city and State's political superstructure also reshaped Sydney's criminal industries – streamlining and centralising them on the eve of an explosive period of growth, mirroring developments in the wider economy. At the start of Askin's administration Sydney was a city of easy virtue, crisscrossed by diffuse and *relatively* insubstantial currents of criminal enterprise which thrived on public tolerance and an absence of civic mores.

Pig City

Ten years later it was a city subverted, its politics enfeebled by the rise of a criminal counterstate.

In many ways Askin was as much a result of the shift in Sydney's politics as the cause. He was thought an anomaly – a battler who had ignored tradition to join the conservatives. To the Labor Party he was a class traitor, to the Liberals a freakish upstart. None of them understood that he was actually just representative of postwar political trends. Class-based politics were gradually being eaten from the inside out. All political parties were now bidding for the vote of an amorphous 'aspirational' class. Askin's centrist platform was merely the first crafted explicitly in recognition of this fact. His father had been a tram driver and his family so poor they used a packing case for a table and once had to sleep in a park when evicted from their home. Askin had clerked in the State Government Savings Bank and served in the infantry during the Second World War. He was totally relaxed with the two basics of Sydney's working-class culture – drinking and gambling – and had actually run an SP operation himself. In the army he had conducted his battalion's two-up school.

His laid-back attitude to gambling stood him in good stead in his quest for the working-class vote. In fact, Askin exploited the punting vote in more ways than one. He was the first political leader to perceive the SP betting community as a constituency itself, and he spent a great deal of effort massaging it in the lead up to the 1965 election. It is ironic then that one of Askin's noted accomplishments was the introduction of law and order campaigning to Sydney. He hammered the theme in his first two elections, using phenomena such as the pack rape scare that swept Sydney in the late 1960s. And Sydney *was* becoming a more dangerous place to live. Figures from police department annual reports recorded strong increases in all violent crime except homicide, and astronomical growth in acquisitive crime and sexual assaults. This was largely due to demographics. The baby boom made for an extra one or two hundred thousand eighteen to twenty-four-year-old males, the most crime-prone age group. Postwar affluence, of course, also made for a lot more material to steal. But even in this field of *disorganised* crime Askin had no remedy. Violent assault continued to rise throughout his tenure, even before the first waves of drug-related crime began to break in the early seventies. It could hardly be otherwise as the agencies tasked with fighting crime in the city instead commodified it and cut themselves in for a piece of the action.

The baccarat schools, for example, continued to flourish, albeit with some factional realignment. Hickie's detective-informer who had been surprised at Premier Askin's interest in Reilly's diaries also related a meeting he later attended where baccarat operators asked senior police whether they would be allowed to continue. That, the senior police said, was for the Premier to decide. Askin decided they could, provided they paid for the privilege. A bagman was designated to collect regular payments for the Premier and the Commissioner of Police. Thus was instituted the peculiar division of political patronage that characterised Sydney's illegal gambling industry through the late sixties and early seventies – the outer suburbs baccarat clubs maintained the ALP connections they had held before Reilly's death, while the inner city schools passed over to Askin's sufferance and protection. It was the latter which became the big money illegal casinos when baccarat lost its sheen in the early seventies and was replaced by roulette as the favoured game.

Pig City

These casinos – garishly plush leisure pits modelled on vulgar interpretations of European elegance, with drapes, circulating hors d'oeuvres, and scantily clad oriental babes – became a city-wide scandal in the seventies due to their brazen operations. Gambling dens like the Forbes Club, the Double Bay Bridge Club and its later incarnation the Telford Club marked their presence with prominent neon and painted signs and even circulated printed invitations to special events. Given their top-level political protection, there was little point in discretion. One female casino employee seemed surprised the casinos *were* illegal when the matter came up in a rape trial because, as she said, 'The police knew all about it. Detectives and others in uniform [were] always in and out of the place.' Meanwhile the gambling barons raked it in. Dr Geoffrey Lewis, a Sydney University economics researcher who conducted a year-long survey of Perce Galea's Double Bay Bridge Club, estimated that the former wharfie was turning over $110 million a year, and making a profit of $2.3 million. And that was but one of the city's many casinos. So vast was the illicit trade that the Launceston *Sunday Examiner-Express* wrote anxiously that Sydney's illegal industry would eventually doom Tasmania's Wrest Point Casino, at that stage the only legal casino in Australia. Protests were occasionally raised, most often when some gangland atrocity spilled into the public arena, forcing Askin to act. He would refer these concerns to his police commissioner – Norm Allan until 1972, and Fred 'Slippery' Hanson after that – for 'detailed study'. Since, by Hanson's time, the Commissioner and the Premier were allegedly splitting $5000 a week between them from Galea's clubs alone, this study probably took the form of throwing handfuls of banknotes into the air and dancing around under the money shower with their underpants on their heads.

The city's legitimate commercial realm was soon cross-pollinated with the can-do spirit of its outlaw milieu. Askin involved himself in the Comalco shares scandal of 1970 by accepting, through his wife, 1500 shares offered to him by the company. He also made a bundle on a package of 5000 shares he took in a company called Gem Exploration and Minerals Ltd, despite the fact that the company had mining lease applications in front of his government's Mines Minister at the time. Much comment arose over the Premier's close relationship with a development company when, in 1974, a federal MP revealed that Askin had signed a lease with the company for the College Street police headquarters for $930 000, a 'fabulous amount' at that time.

But Askin's government was not the only administration that played fast and loose. In September 1978 the *National Times* reported that a prominent council official had been engaged as a 'consultant' by the American company, Citibank, with the promise of a $75 000 bonus if he was able to secure a rezoning the bank desperately needed. In 1983 Senator Don Chipp, then leader of the Australian Democrats, expressed his astonishment in federal parliament that Neville Wran's State Labor government had chosen, upon discovering a Public Transport Authority building had been illegally sublet to Sydney's 'Mr Sin', Abe Saffron, and now contained a sex shop, a brothel and a gambling club, to pay out the lease to the tune of $2.6 million and had further declined to prosecute any of the enterprises involved.

The ruthlessness of people like Allan and Askin, and the way they protected criminal activity, was laid bare by the Arantz affair. Phillip Arantz was a detective-sergeant who had been appointed to head the police department's computer bureau in 1969. The department wanted to computerise its records but there was a problem. For many years the police had been running a two-track crime reporting system designed to maximise the official clear-up rate. This was the 'paddy book' scheme. Crimes which had little chance of being solved were kept out of official police statistics, being entered instead into the secret paddy book. Arantz had never been comfortable with the arrangement. At one point in his career at Ryde station only fifty crimes had been officially recorded while a thousand choked the paddy book. With computers the system would become unworkable. He demanded Commissioner Norm Allan release the real crime statistics for 1971, and when Allan didn't, Arantz released them himself. The reaction was swift and brutal. The Commissioner had Arantz proclaimed insane by a police medico and frog-marched to a psychiatric institution. When the doctors there refused to play along, Allan retaliated with instant termination of the detective-sergeant's employment. He and Askin then joined forces to intimidate the nascent computer industry into denying Arantz employment anywhere in the field. Given such a tightly contained and brutally maintained system, you could be forgiven for despairing that it would ever unravel. But it did, decisively, twenty-three years later with the coming of James Wood.

Any royal commission is likely to disrupt or even ruin the lives of those it investigates. Such inquiries are often a last line of defence when all the other safeguards of the State have failed. Their investigations and findings, unrestrained by the rules of evidence prevailing in a normal courtroom, are usually to be feared by someone. And the fearful nature of Wood's inquisition, the violence of the shock it delivered to the city, can be reckoned from the number of lives it took. It's possible that up to twelve men killed themselves after becoming enmeshed in Wood's deliberations. Nine certainly did. Among their number was Robert Tait, an acting patrol commander in Narrabri who blew his brains out after facing accusations of covering up the indiscretions of two other police officers; Clinton Moller, a former constable at Bondi station, who hung himself in a prison cell; Detective Senior Constable Wayne Johnson who shot his estranged wife then ate a bullet himself after he was named for cheating on his travel allowances; former Wollongong councillor Brian Tobin who gassed himself to death in a car after being approached by Wood's investigators; Peter Foretic who went the same way on the day he was scheduled to give evidence against a former mayor of Wollongong; and Ray Jenkins, a dog trainer, who came over all stiff and uncommunicative after earlier providing the commission with information about police corruption around Campbelltown. Many of these men passed quietly, unnoticed. The entire nation, however, was stunned by the suicide of former Supreme Court judge David Yeldham in November 1996 after he had been named in the upper house of the New South Wales Parliament by Labor member Franca Arena as someone who was being protected by the Wood Commission's pedophilia inquiry. Arena did not accuse Yeldham of being a pedophile, but he took it that way, as did many others. Some time on the afternoon of Monday 4 November, he connected the exhaust of his red Toyota Lexcen to a length of flexible piping, fed the hose through a window, climbed into the driver's seat and put himself beyond the reach of Arena's parliamentary privilege.

Pig City

No evidence emerged of Yeldham's ever being involved in child abuse. At most he seems to have been a man whose unacknowledged homosexuality or bisexuality led him to furtive encounters with like-minded men in the city's train stations and public toilets. An unexpected casualty of Arena's speech was the police Special Branch which was found to have protected Yeldham from exposure, thus leading to the possibility of blackmail. When Wood sent his finders into the branch, it quickly gave up the information that for years it had been keeping files on parliamentarians, civil liberties activists and lawyers. The Police Commissioner disbanded the unit within hours. The shockwaves continued spreading though, with government departments such as education and community services exposed as being virtually complicit in child sexual abuse, so pathetically inadequate was their response to the quite amazing number of pedophiles revealed within their employ. And then the cancer spread beyond them into what could be thought of as the moral core of society, with revelations that the churches had protected child molesters within their ranks for decades.

The Wood Commission ran for so long that the endless revelations eventually had something of a numbing effect. It is probably only now, some time after the event, that a dry recitation of its findings carries some emotional potency. Leaving aside the results of his pedophilia inquiry and concentrating only on the police, Wood detailed 'a state of systemic and entrenched corruption' within the service which encompassed bribery, fraud, illegal violence and the abuse of police powers, subversion of prosecutions, theft and extortion, protection of the drug trade as well as active drug trafficking, protection of illegal clubs and brothels, protection of illegal gambling operations and interference with internal investigations.

A form of 'noble cause' corruption, also known as process corruption, involved breaking the law to enforce it, with officers engaging in perjury; the planting of evidence such as drugs and weapons; tampering with evidence; inventing fictitious confessions; denial of basic rights such as a caution; assaults, including baton whippings and macing to induce confessions; posing as lawyers to advise suspects to cooperate with police; and ripping off criminals seen to be beyond the law.

Traditional forms of corruption included bribes from illegal clubs and gambling dens, taken in the form of money, free booze and meals at the clubs or free sex in brothels. Such bribes were sometimes extracted through direct extortion, but more often they simply formed the basis of unhealthy friendships with criminals. The limitless supply of free grog and drugs inevitably led to problems of substance abuse with Wood exposing serious levels of alcoholism within the service and the use of speed, dope, steroids and coke among younger officers. Drinking on duty frequently resulted in car crashes and violent assaults on both suspects and members of the public. In an illustrative case one officer working around Penrith, St Marys and Fairfield admitted

to a graphic history of alcohol abuse, opportunistic theft from the scene of break and enters, the sexual exploitation of a prostitute and a prisoner in police cells, tow truck scams, insurance fraud, the 'flowering of facts' and the sale of handguns surrendered to police ...

The connections formed between police and criminals during long lunches and visits to brothels and illegal casinos often perverted the justice system when officers interfered with the prosecution of such figures, through 'watering down' their criminality by reducing the amount of drugs or money involved in any case against them, by selecting lesser charges or supporting bail applications by withholding relevant details, by losing track of evidence or witnesses and creating loopholes in records of interviews or court testimonies. Some favoured informants were virtually given a ticket to ride through the system; for instance, one group of detectives sat on electronic surveillance of one of their informants pulling off an armed robbery.

Not everyone got off so lightly of course. Wood also wrote that theft and extortion of criminals had become 'regular features of policing' by the late 1980s. In its simplest form this consisted of shaking down street level drug dealers, a practice which evolved into something of an art form at Kings Cross. Relieving unimportant crooks of their drugs and cash 'generated vast amounts of money for those police who engaged in it', some of them developing such rapacious appetites that they unwittingly helped suppress the drug trade by simply walking out the front door of the station. When they were on the streets, said one officer, 'word quickly spread amongst the runners who suspended operations until they had left the area'. Major drug dealers, in contrast, were not all that concerned about shake-downs and rip-offs because the money was very easily replaced and every dollar extorted or stolen by the cops during a raid was a dollar which couldn't be used against them as evidence in court.

Some stings took place at the highest levels of the drug industry, with correspondingly greater problems should the sting turn bad. In December 1983, for example, an operation run by both the Victorian police and a joint task force of the New South Wales and federal police targeted two suspects who were followed from

Sydney airport to the northern beaches after a drug sale. A search of their car uncovered plastic bottles full of cocaine and two bags stuffed with over forty grand in cash, all of which was formally booked up as evidence. Missing from the evidence list, however, was $6000 two NSW detectives found in the dealers' car, another stash of cocaine and somewhere between $150 000 and $285 000 discovered in the garage. This windfall was parcelled out between eight NSW cops but, like the paranoid goldminers in *The Treasure of the Sierra Madre*, they knew for a stone fact they could not trust each other and bad blood soon developed over the carve-up. An even greater problem arose when it emerged that the dopey but honest Victorian cops had logged some of the money their Sydney colleagues had trousered. An almost Seinfeldian episode ensued, with 'strenuous efforts' being made to recover the money. Unfortunately 'this was made difficult by the fact that the bundle of notes originally booked up had already been photographed by the Police Scientific Section'. Detective Trevor Haken, who later turned informant for the commission, 'had to return the stolen notes to that bundle and organise to have it rephotographed'.

More disturbing than mere opportunistic freelance banditry was overwhelming evidence of alliances between police and drug lords, with officers taking bribes to ignore the trade, or rendering active assistance to dealers in the form of tip-offs about raids, undermining their trials and even driving out the competitors of favoured dealers; a win-win situation, as the protected criminals thrived and the cops looked like they were doing their job. Police, wrote Wood, were actively involved in the supply of cocaine, heroin and cannabis, mostly through recycling drugs seized in various operations but not booked up as evidence. So cosy were the links with some traffickers that they actually supplied money for the service to use in buy-bust ops against their competitors. On one such occasion a bungled operation resulted in the loss of $12 000 which had been lent to the police by a dealer. The detectives compensated by cutting the drugs and giving some to the dealer to make good his loss. In another case four and a half kilograms of cannabis were stolen in a job set up by police informants, and resold by them, the proceeds being shared between the crims and their controlling officers. One detective even bought a consignment of heroin from one criminal associate for resale to another because the latter was having trouble obtaining the stocks he needed at a competitive price from his usual supplier.

In something of a twist to this, the usual supplier gave evidence of supplying the end buyer for a time through yet another detective, his purpose being to hide his role as he feared that the buyer was a police informant. The last mentioned detective collected a commission on these sales, further evidencing the entrepreneurial spirit of the detectives working in this area. A third detective admitted that he too had arrangements with the end buyer for the supply of drugs to him which included, on one occasion, their joint financing of a purchase of a quantity of heroin for resale.

Another dealer turned snitch for the police in order to close down a rival, on the basis that he would take a half share of any heroin the cops might find.

The competitor was raided and one pound of heroin was found. This was taken back to the Drug Unit office where it was cut with glucose. A small quantity of the cut drug was given to the informant who was not advised of the amount which the police had located. The remainder was sold by the police to a major heroin dealer who subsequently handed the first mentioned detective $80 000 in payment. According to that detective, this was shared with some of the other police associated with the raid. Other officers, who were not aware of the amount of heroin seized, were given smaller amounts of cash.

There was no honour, it seems, amongst thieves or bent cops. The real victims in all this of course were the likes of that fourteen-year-old girl who sat next to me on the steps outside of Woolworths in Kings Cross, or the emaciated Aboriginal boy who needed us to stick the syringe into his arms, or the sad, stiffening transsexual on the slab at the Glebe Morgue.

How far back would you have cast your gaze to understand why things went so wrong? In 1900, the editor of the *Truth* and member of parliament, John Norton, called for a Royal Commission into the police force, some of whom, he alleged, were in the pay of brothel keepers and 'in league with some of the worst scoundrels ever let loose on society'. Al McCoy argues that Sydney compared very poorly with Melbourne. The southern capital had its fair share of scandals, and the sort of thriving vice trade you would expect to find in any large port city. But unlike Sydney it never succumbed to rule of criminal syndicates. Once established, he writes, syndicates cannot survive without an understanding with police and political power. 'It is at this point that a city's fundamental character comes into play.' Sydney's organised criminals of the 1960s and 1970s courted premiers, distributed heroin across the country and entered into joint ventures with the American mafia. Melbourne's were confined to the docks and corralled

Pig City

within the waterfront unions. For McCoy, it was a case of Melbourne having much stronger commercial and industrial sectors than Sydney. There the establishment held firmly onto 'the reins of social control' and strove to block any rise of the nouveau, 'criminal or otherwise'. Sydney by contrast did not have such resources. The pastoral-commercial elite who had seen it as nothing more than a transit point for their shipments to European markets 'created an opportunity for Sydney's syndicate lieutenants to gain political influence'.

In Melbourne the Victorian Parliament, controlled by the city's financial and industrial burghers, demanded that police crush the upstarts of the criminal milieu when they first appeared in the 1920s. Through periodic pressure upon criminals and their police allies [eg. through royal commissions], Melbourne has since checked the growth of powerful syndicates. In Sydney, by contrast, a more pliable parliament has adopted a tolerant attitude and thereby allowed the emergence of strong criminal syndicates; repeatedly corrupt constables and rising criminals have forged alliances which have helped them both rise to the top in their respective fields.

According to McCoy the informal alliance of the underworld and the city's political superstructure became evident in 1967 as men like Borg and Reilly began to die. The very nature of this violence was a measure of the new system. Between 1944 and 1963 there were, writes McCoy, only eight murders in Sydney's criminal milieu, an average of one killing every 2.25 years. Many of these were the result of personal vendettas and involved such intimate methods of murder as combat with knives, chains and pistols. The five killings of 1967, however, occurred at the rate of one every five weeks, and were 'impersonal liquidations involving machine guns, sniper rifle and dynamite'. The victims had set themselves against the new regime by refusing to recognise its authority. Most significantly 'none of Sydney's new syndicate leaders were indicted or even investigated for their role in these killings. When it became apparent to the milieu that the new syndicate "powers" had an immunity to police investigation, vice traders either sold out their business to the syndicate or retired'.

The central business of organised crime has always been extortion, mostly on the supply side of any illicit economic activity. Like any other capitalist enterprise the ultimate objective, explains Judith Allen, is to maximise profits by the greatest possible control of the market, 'a striving towards the ideal of monopoly'. Here perhaps, we can find the genesis of the city's fall; that ceaseless, shifting dissonance within Sydney's history, that will to power in a place without history, long-lived institutions or a moral centre. There is something so familiar in the way the likes of George Freeman and Lennie McPherson consolidated their hold over the city in the 1960s. Something so ordinary in the ferment of violence and ruthlessness directed towards establishing their monopolistic power. John Macarthur would have understood.

But in the end, of course, understanding counts for little when measured against consequence and the sorrows of the dead.

Gordon Gallagher was a good cop. And that, said his wife Wendy, was the problem. The politics, she said, the politics were well and truly there. 'Yeah, well and bloody truly,' whispered Gordon beside her. I had to lean forward to hear him and keep my own voice low, concentrating hard on what he was saying, because Gordon was dying. The cancer which had taken Wendy's brother just a few years before had come back to claim another of her men, and although the pain had not yet disordered his mind, it had reduced him to a husk who could only murmur his last thoughts into my tape recorder. He was fifty-one years old when I spoke to him, fifty-two when he died.

We sat at the kitchen table in their simple home on the city's south western fringe. 'You'll have to excuse the mess,' said Wendy as I tried not stare at the cleanest house I had ever seen. Empty display homes in model estates could only aspire to be this immaculate. The crumbs which spilled from the plate of fruitcake she served me were the only unruly element, unless you wanted to count the bursts of uncontrolled muscle spasms which seized poor Gordon every now and then. He was a bald, kindly, round-shouldered man, with none of the hardness or scarring of the soul you might expect to find in a veteran of the force. He wasn't hard enough, said Wendy. That was his problem. He wasn't hard enough and tough enough. He had a conscience, she said, leaning forward, wanting me to understand. 'Gordon never lost his humanity,' she said, 'and I'm pleased about that, John. He always stayed a person, a fair person, I'm proud of him.'

Gordon joined the force in 1965 looking for a job with a bit of security. He worked as a tyre-fitter in Liverpool after leaving school, meeting his wife-to-be when she was a fifteen-year-old office girl with the same outfit. He never burned to be a policeman, unlike many of them. He was just getting a little old to learn a trade and looking for a job he could settle into for the rest of his life. The tyre game wasn't much money, he reckoned. You'd work your arse off all day for next to nothing. Wendy didn't want him anywhere near the force, though. She wanted him to go into the fire brigade if he absolutely had to get involved in that sort of thing. 'My next-door neighbour was a police officer,' she said, 'and he used to say to me, "Tell him not to do it." He didn't understand the implications.'

There were 120 or so in his class at the academy. Only two of them were women. They were a pretty good bunch, as he remembered. A few footballers, some tradesmen, ex-screws, a few poms, a couple of blokes just out of the army. They all had similar reasons to him for going in and most were his age. They did six weeks initially, returning for a week's secondary training every two months out of the next twelve. There was a lot of physical stuff, every morning and afternoon. Sit-ups, push-ups, weights and punching bags. The classroom work was basic, mostly paper shuffling. Gordon looked at it and shook his head and thought, 'I don't think I'm up for this.' He used to hate paperwork. Still did, when I spoke to him.

They sent him out to Regent Street to walk a daylight beat for a couple of weeks, completely lost, freaking out, 'praying to Christ nobody was gunna ask me anything cos I didn't know what to bloody do'. He got his first break when he was transferred to Glebe to work under an old cop named Joe Walker, a senior constable who'd been there since the First Fleet came in and who went by the name of the Doctor, because if he couldn't fix something, it couldn't be fixed.

'Most of the work over there was street accidents,' murmured Gordon. 'Brawls in pubs and deceased persons, suicides. I had heaps of them. Every day you went to work you'd get at least one.'

Wendy placed a hand on his arm and interrupted, 'I remember one time he came home and we couldn't let him inside the house because the bodies had exploded and they were all over him.' They had to burn the uniforms, nodded Gordon. He was living out at Campbelltown then and had to drive all the way home with the stench seeping into his clothes, his hair, the folds of his skin. And not just the stench but other stuff too. Stuff you don't talk about with the wife. I asked him how long it took to harden up. About twelve months, he answered. After about twelve months you ignore it. You say it's nothing to do with me. Still, when you came to the end of the job it could get to you.

'A lot of people go into the job and after about six months on the street they find somewhere to hide or run,' he said, pausing, and then sighing. 'Aaah ... you go into places and everything's splattered everywhere ... you know, time and time again ... especially the kids, cut up, you know.'

Gordon and Wendy were married in 1972. Gordon spent six months with prints, a few weeks at Liverpool, then ten years in Green Valley, at that time the toughest of the city's public housing estates. The Valley was mostly the haunt of the welfare generations, as he called them without any trace of judgment. Hundreds of thousands of hopeless souls forced to the edge of settlement, the last tidal outflow of the underclasses which Arthur Phillip set in motion when he despatched the convicts to the western side of the Cove. Marooned in estates where the architects had planned for everything except grinding poverty and inherited ennui, successive generations of the city's poor devolved into modern variants of the 'loathsome reptiles' the *Herald* found in nineteenth-century slums like Durands Alley where 'careless of life, and heedless of death, they sink into the grave leaving nothing behind them but a vicious example'. Gordon spent nearly two decades trawling through the wreckage of these lives. The distaste in his voice was palpable even with his low, murmuring delivery.

'The suicides ... oh, it was unbelievable the suicides out there. You'd get one at least every second day, one way or another, hanging or drugs, and they had this habit of blowing their bloody heads off with shotguns out there.'

Wendy leaned forward and stroked his arm which had begun to shiver again. 'Tell John about that time that fellow sat his kids down,' she said, desperate that I should understand what Gordon had seen and done for twenty years. I doubt he was even seeing me when he replied in his soft, haunted voice, 'One bloke got round the side of his house and held the shotgun under his mouth to blow his head off. He had his young blokes sitting there to watch him while he did it.'

Wendy and Gordon had a strange sort of interlude then, during which they spoke in their own personal shorthand, quick snatches and fragments of phrases conjuring up a vision of a shared hell. They repeated each other's words like talismans. Much of the time Gordon would just moan or groan or say, 'The stink' or 'The stench', while remembering something. His left arm would fall and hang limp at his side until Wendy noticed and gently picked it up and replaced it on the table. His other hand, which was okay most of the time, would rise unsteadily to his forehead during a hard moment and begin to twitch and tremor as though with the onset of Parkinson's.

'The Green Valley Hotel,' he said quietly, as though confiding a secret, 'you'd go in to get someone ... blokes there'd belt the living hell out of you ... arms on them like this. Everyone had to have a fight ... Christ, I couldn't fight my way out of a paper bag, you know.' He wasn't lying. He seemed the antithesis of a hard-riding Sydney cop, even in photographs taken before the onset of his illness. He was not physically imposing. Threat did not emanate from him like a scent, the way it does with a lot of cops. 'It was a new pub, this pub,' he said. 'Top ten pub in the State for a long time because it sold so much grog. It was even number one at one stage. It was the centre of social life out there.' Wendy interrupted again to explain that the people had nothing else. It was miles away from Liverpool shopping centre, she said, with no rail line. 'Yeah, the old pub, she was the centre of attention,' laughed Gordon softly but without mirth. 'I got some floggings ... but gee did I get some floggings out there. I got one, I was in hospital for three months. I copped a bloody good kickin' ... touch and go for about three months.'

His eyes grew distant again, lost in the memory. 'They just wouldn't leave the pub,' he said. 'They had a baby. We went over to try and get them out of the pub but as we were trying to get rid of the father, the two sons jumped us. Me mate had glasses on and as soon as they smashed his glasses that was the end of him, he couldn't see. At least he got back to the truck and got to the radio. I copped a bloody flogging on the ground, I did. From the four of them. Mum, dad and the two sons ... You'd get belted up just about every night. Everywhere you went, domestics, everything. No-one's going to go along easy, it's always, "Come on, take me," you know.'

Gordon had an old Australian voice which still had a lot of residual power but it failed him frequently, trailing out long silences which were often more eloquent than words.

'One of my mates ... shot in the guts ... shitbox bloody domestic ... lucky to be alive.'

At one point he transferred to Liverpool for two or three years but Green Valley called him home. Wherever he went in the west, however, the drugs were always there. It was a shame he said as his own life sputtered out of him, it was just a shame to see those kids going down the same shitty path. 'Remember Ashcroft High?' he asked Wendy. 'They had that good football team. Lot of sports kids out there. It was a shame to see some of them go down. You'd look at them, six months later they'd be dead. OD. Shockin' it was ... hangin' themselves ... never seen so many hangings in me life,' he muttered, reminding me of Brando's Colonel Kurtz at the end of *Apocalypse Now*, so much tightly contained horror coiled up in the voice.

Mostly I'm pretty good at keeping my distance during these interviews. Doesn't matter how sad or outrageous the story might be, I just nod along, waiting for that telling detail, that awesome quote I know is going to nail the story for me. With Gordon and Wendy, however, I found myself worrying less about the interview and more about the subjects. They were simple folk, as Wendy stressed more than once. But their mutual regard, their love, and their unobtrusive pride in that love, was painful to observe. This man was obviously seeing out the closing weeks of his life and although his job had conspired to keep them apart so often – Gordon told me he had spent only one Christmas with Wendy in twenty years – they were closer than almost any married couple I knew. Perhaps the lack of children contributed to that. With many couples, childlessness seems to loom as a void with the passage of time, but these two seemed to have filled any emptiness with a heightened sense of each other's worth. I had only recently been married myself and the strength of their bond was reassuring, just as its inevitable sundering by Gordon's cancer would be wrenching and traumatic.

It was his fight with the police service that was keeping him alive, even as it ruined their last days together. Some years before, Gordon had arrived at work to be told the district commander wanted him to transfer to Liverpool. Another sergeant was scheduled for the move but refused, having been entangled in an affair with another policeman's wife over there. 'He couldn't move because this bloke was going to kill him,' explained Gordon, who went in his place. The biggest mistake of his life, he now believed. In Liverpool he ran afoul of one of the rising stars of the force, a shameless self-promoter with a flair for massaging the media.

'This bloke just didn't like uniformed police to start with,' explained Gordon. 'He just hated uniformed police ... no-one knows why ... just an absolute bastard that's all. His mentor was Attila the Hun ... he took his leave once and wrote this little book. He was going to boost morale at the station. He took all these sayings from Attila the Hun.'

When word came through from Queensland that Wendy's brother had cancer, they decided to leave Sydney to look after him. 'And John, I was happy for him to leave,' said Wendy, 'because those eighteen months he was under that man ... Gordon's always been an even-tempered ... He's not an easily provoked person ... And he's not a malicious person ... And that last eighteen months under that man ... Gordon would return to the house *ropeable* and *ashen grey*. I said it's just no good for you, leave the stinking job, because I could see by that time it was really having a toll on him. Little did we know that he had a malignant melanoma on him. We'd sold the house. We're in between the move. And in June Gordon gets diagnosed with a malignant melanoma. It was just one hell of a time. I saw Gordon's health go down. And I think it was the stress. Because Gordon's a straight person. And I don't think this bloke could handle that attitude. The sergeants weren't there to lick his boots. They were there to do a job. I mean, if the guy has a persecution number that's his problem. You tell John what your opinion was, Gordon. What you joined the police force for.'

Gordon, who was shaking quite a lot now, drew in a long shuddering breath. 'Just to go to work and do your job,' he breathed. 'And to be left alone, and not be hampered by stupid bloody bosses about bloody stupid things when they knew that all this shit was going on.'

His voice began to speed up and become more emphatic. What he meant by all this shit was the corruption exposed by the Wood Commission. 'That's what got him at the end,' Wendy nodded emphatically. 'It was blatant to a lot of them what was going on.'

Unprompted, Gordon suddenly launched into a bitter speech, fired by an intense energy which had been missing up to that point. 'You used to tell them things what were going on in the bloody cells and shit,' he spat. 'Why people were hanging themselves, you know, and some bloody things that might have helped. And they'd do bloody nothing about it! All they did was get up after some bastard was dead ... You could bail bloody most of them ... Get rid of them. Was only stupid little things they were kept in there for. They could have been bailed out and gone. That was just their procedure then, filling up the bloody cells with bloody people.'

'The politics is there,' said Wendy. 'The black knights and the white knights, whatever you call them. The politics are there well and truly, John.'

'Well and bloody truly,' nodded her husband.

'And if you're not in, you're gone.'

'They've all come through the system,' Gordon said. 'They're all ex-detectives. They've all been involved in the quid coppin' and everything else. They're all bosses. And if they didn't know, they should have bloody known. That was their bloody job, to know, to dig it out ...' This seemed to disgust Gordon more than anything. He bore the scars of doing his job for more than twenty years but the bosses had not done theirs. 'The people who bloody complained ...' he continued. 'Soon as you mentioned anything ... Christ they came down on you like a bloody ton of bricks. Telling people to come forward ... yeah come bloody forward all right.'

'It's like politics,' said Wendy. 'You pick on the easy one, don't you? It's the same system. Pick on the guys that can't really defend themselves while the heavies, they keep going.'

'It's better off handing out a hundred bloody parking tickets than grabbing some bloody crook,' muttered Gordon.

Wendy leaned forward with an imploring look on her face. 'You guys would know this, you're round it all the time, aren't you?' she said, meaning journalists. 'You're seeing it. You must see it better than dumbos like us. God only knows what goes on in some places. You would have seen it up in Queensland. What can you do about it? Will anything ever be done?'

'Some blokes, they try to do their bloody job ...' Gordon whispered to himself.

'And they're worse off for doing it, aren't they?' said Wendy. 'To be fair and have a good police service you've got to have it from the top down, don't you? Maybe I'm very naive in my talkings ... But I think it's the only way that people are going to gain confidence ... Why are they frying the little guy, and the big guy who is responsible keeps getting off the hook all the time? Nobody is going to address that in my opinion, John. That's the game, isn't it ... it's so political. And that's why the police force will never be what the public would like it to be … because it's so political … I presume from the detectives up is where it kicks in. You look at the royal commission, that seems to be where it's coming from. Not that Gordon or myself would ever know about those levels.'

'Ryan, the [Police] Commissioner, he's an educated man,' said Gordon, more softly now. 'He knows what's going on … Christ, he should be doing something! But he's not doing anything about it. He's just talking about it. He's gunna do this, gunna do that … gunna gunna gunna.'

'How does it make you feel?' I asked, hating myself just a little bit for such a braindead question but wanting to know anyway.

'Absolutely sick to the stomach,' said Gordon Gallagher, the dying policeman. 'Sick to the stomach that you were ever involved in it.'

Gordon sued the police service in March 1998, alleging disability discrimination. He had tried to take up his old job in 1994 but had been rejected because his previous sick leave had been 'excessive'. In fact, his sick leave throughout his many years of physically gruelling and dangerous work had been well within his entitlements, but the service refused to explain the basis for its decision. Legal aid flogged them in the Equal Opportunity Tribunal with his former tormentor, Attila the Hun Jr, having to squirm his way through nearly an hour's excruciating testimony as he tried to justify his part in the exclusion. When Gordon won, the tribunal ordered the service to pay damages and publish a full apology in the *Police Service News* 'forthwith'.

Pig City

I attended his funeral and burial service at Sutherland on a bitterly cold day in mid-winter. It was wet and bleak and steam plumed from the mouths of dozens of police officers who had come to pay their respects. Most of them arrived in cheap, rusting cars. They were just workers. As Gordon had been. They sang their hymns, said their prayers and committed their friend to the earth. Months had passed since the tribunal's decision, but the service had never found time to publish that apology.

So Much for the Afterglow

LEVIATHAN

I t was a weird feeling. Really weird. Ten past four on a Saturday afternoon, one week before my birthday, I shut down my Powerbook and stretched back from the desk I'd made my own over the previous four years. The Mitchell Library was quiet, sleepy and warm. Nothing unusual there. It was about this time most afternoons I could be caught flaked out for a little covert nap action. On the next table a couple of high-school kids were already snoozing atop their stack of HSC papers. Half a dozen or so of the Mitchell's resident freaks and trainspotters were scattered through the huge reading room. I stood and stretched and tried to shake off that weird feeling like a big old dog emerging from a pond. But there was nothing for it. It was too weird.

I had just written the last line of my last chapter and although another few weeks of editing, revising, defamation checking, foot stamping and tantrum throwing stretched in front of me, the long, long run was over and the fat times were coming. For two months I'd been forcing myself through the barbed wire entanglements of my deadline with promises of unimaginably indulgent bludging afterwards. During breaks I'd sit on the steps of the Mitchell washing down mouthfuls of M&Ms with paper cups of instant coffee dreaming of my personal big rock candy mountain. When

So Much for the Afterglow

this baby was delivered to the printers I planned to play quite a few video games, catch more than my fair share of waves and smoke way too many cones. Basically, dear reader, my plan was to boogie oogie oogie until I just couldn't boogie no more.

It had been such a long journey that now the end was near I wasn't quite sure of what to do next – after surfing, thrashing my Playstation to death and pulling heaps of cones, that is. And it was only in the last few months, looking up from the line or paragraph immediately in front of me and scoping out the book as a whole for the first time that I realised just how far I'd strayed from my intended destination since 13 April 1995, the day I'd signed on for this King Hell road trip. At eleven a.m. that day I'd pitched Random a history of Sydney in the style of Michael Pye's *Maximum City*. The difference between these sorts of books, I explained, and your more conventional histories is partly based on content and partly on technique. Essentially the author brings the methods of American magazine journalism, once known as the New Journalism, to a much longer format.

In Pye's case this involved writing what he termed a 'biography' rather than a standard history of New York. Pye's story of New York advances through themes as much as through time. It follows a rough line from the founding days of the colonies through to the end of the twentieth century. However, by organising his material in thematic chapters rather than in a more rigid chronological order, he shows how present-day New York is a child of its past. Within each chapter he deploys standard historical techniques of archival research, alongside the journalistic methods of interview, narrative, biography, personal observation and shifting points of reference. In this way his history becomes richer than a standard textbook and accessible to a much wider audience.

LEVIATHAN

I had planned to write a celebration of my city. Some obvious themes in her story suggested themselves; migration; environment; money; power; leisure and culture. I planned to open with an essay called 'Creation Myths', covering prehistory to convict transportation and including Aboriginal history. I also intended writing a whole chapter on women and actually mapped out a long section on the city's gay history. But none of these things happened.

Four years later I sat hunched over my laptop, tapping out the ghoulish details of corpse ratting at the Glebe morgue. 'At one point I stopped typing, sat back and smiled my most lopsided, fatalistic smile. Well here we are, I said to myself, the emotional low point of the book. Ladies and gentlemen, I think we have bottomed out.

How the hell did we end up there?

Not only had the chapter on Sydney's women disappeared, the women themselves, apart from a few cameos, had gone MIA. And the gays? The burbs? The celebration? The good vibes of living in the greatest city in the world? Forget it. Sometime back in 1995 I wandered off the bright, teeming thoroughfares and down into a very dark alley. I never came back.

I think Arago's journals might have drawn me down there, all that grim business about the opulent merchants of olde Sydney towne tossing some blackfellas a bottle of rum and some mouldy bread to beat each to death for whitey's entertainment. I'd always known we'd done those blackfellas wrong but it had never really come home to me before. When I started researching the Gundy shooting and the subsequent Redfern raids I began to understand how little the mindset of white authority had changed, and when I read the story of Gundy to an audience at the Brisbane Writers'

So Much for the Afterglow

Festival I realised I wasn't the only one who'd been wearing a white blindfold.

It was a strange gig on which to lay such a heavy reading. A comedy night in fact. Dirk Flinthart and I had just released *How To Be A Man* and the festival organisers rang to see if we'd like to do a little dog and trumpet routine for the new book. Flinthart was up for it but I wasn't. They sort of pecked at me a bit, teased out that I was working on *Leviathan* and asked whether I'd like to read from that instead. I would, I said, but not at a comedy night. Oh, it's not all comedy, they assured me. We have some really heavy-going performance poetry too. That should bring down a suitably gloomy atmosphere. Oh well, I said, in that case ...

I hired a young Aboriginal actor to read out the longer quotes, practised an appropriately grave persona for reading such depressing material and arrived to discover I'd been billed as something like 'Crazy John Birmingham, Queensland's favourite funny man'.

Hmmm, good deal.

Anyway, the actor and I took the stage, or rather the couch, from which we would be reading. I gazed across the dreadlocked, nose-ringed, pin-eyed audience and understood with a sick sinking feeling that they were there to hear some hilarious anecdotes about bucket bongs and mad flatmates. I started to read.

Well, you could actually see the pain in their eyes when they realised this was not about the funny things which happened to Crazy John the last time he pulled too many cones. But that was nothing compared to the discomfort and the urge to flee which ran through the room when it dawned on them that the topic for the night was, oh no – oh God no please don't – Aborigines.

It's a hell of thing to perform in front of a room full of people who suddenly don't want to be there. But I had faith in this story, and I had faith in my reluctant listeners too, so I ploughed on and after a few minutes a really cool thing started to happen. In spite of themselves they were drawn in. Not in a good way of course. They stopped and attended the same way you can't help but look at a bad road accident as you drive by. But the boredom, the agitation and even the hostility which had been there evaporated. At first curiosity took over, then active interest and finally horror. I could see it in the way their faces went sort of slack, their eyes widened and a few folks lost control of their mouths, letting them fall open.

It was the shotgun that did it. I had slowed the reading right down and reached the line, 'The Remington 870 is a big heavy-hitting piece of artillery.' My own voice hitched at that point, which was a surprise, I can tell you. I looked up to catch my breath and composure and saw that for the first time every pair of eyes was boring in on me. As I worked through what happened next some people began to shake their heads slowly, some gave out little groans and one or two began to dab discreetly at their eyes. I think at last the story had come home for them as well.

After that, I don't know, it was all just a bit difficult to embrace the Good Living Sydney of laughter and forgetting. I was deep inside the alleyway now, perhaps Durands Alley or Abercrombie Lane, and although I knew there was a world of light somewhere above, I only wanted to push further into the gloom. So let me apologise if you think I've been too dark, or biased, or unfair; if you think I've dwelt too much on violence and alienation and not enough on the triumphs and virtues of this great city. Perhaps I

So Much for the Afterglow

have written a black armband biography and have been unjustly selective in my choice of material. I am guessing, for instance, that Prime Minister John Howard would not approve. But then, John Howard can go fuck himself. And the horse he rode in on.

History is never bloodless. Someone always gets hurt. And I guess, in the end, I couldn't draw my eyes away from that. Perhaps then, I should it make clear that I love Sydney. She took me in and made me her own when I was just a starving baby writer, living on friends' brown couches and bludging meals off the Hare Krishnas to get by. I love it that she didn't care, dirty trollop that she is. She just threw her arms around me and cried, 'Here I am baby, come an' get it!' I love her beaches, her sunshine, her food and her art. I love her arrogance, her greed and promiscuity. I love her parties and the hangovers that inevitably follow. I love it that she loves a good fight. That she knows she is better than anyone else. That you can do things her way or you can shove it.

If I could take the ghost of Arthur Phillip on a tour of the city he founded, I'd want him to be proud. I'd take him to the highest towers and shout him the most expensive lunch. I'd tell him that all things considered, he'd done well. I'd say a free people now live where he pitched his camp so long ago. The city he helped raise is one of the finest in the world. Its treasures would make the London of his day seem like a mean and muddy little village. I'd want him to know that it was all worth it.

The only dark spot I could imagine might come if Phillip asked what had become of his old friend Bennelong's people. I could take him down to Circular Quay, warp his mind with the Opera House and tell him we now celebrate the memory of his friend in the name Bennelong Point. But of his people? The Iora and all the other tribes? Well, surrounded by the city's staggering wealth and progress, I suppose that question might prove a little embarrassing.

I could imagine so many things I'd want to say to Phillip if his ghost did turn up. But if he brought his friend Bennelong with him, what would I say then?

Perhaps sorry might be a good place to start.

Bibliographic Notes

Hey there. How you doing? You'll probably be doing a lot better if you choose to skip this little section. Believe me, you've got better things to do. You could have a cup of tea and a nice sit-down, play a video game, toss the old tennis ball around for Rover perhaps. All much better than plowing through an essay on my major sources.

I don't have much of a choice, however, because I chose not to make you fight your way through a barbed wire tangle of citations and footnotes in the main text. I did that because nobody but pointy-heads (and of course the good folk being cited) ever read the footnotes and because, frankly, I think they look kind of ugly.

Before plunging into a discussion of everyone else's work I should write a quick note on self-plagiarism. *Leviathan* took over four years to write, during which time I tried to keep my journalistic commitments to a minimum. Occasionally, however, an editor would offer me a commission which related to research I was already doing, and in such circumstances I'd take the job and write the story because it helped the cause. Hence there are a few minor sections of *Leviathan* which have been published in embryonic form elsewhere. In the very first edition of the *Australian*'s *Review of Books* I held forth on the nature of violence, a discussion which I refined in chapter three of this book. Later, in reviewing Stephen Knight's *Continent of Mystery* for the same publication, I drew on some work I had already done on the working conditions of early Sydney. When Peter Craven asked me to contribute to *Best Australian Essays 1998* I did so because it allowed me to work out some ideas I'd been having about the appeal of Pauline Hanson, which also appear in here. The linked discussion of Sydney's neo-Nazis was first published in *Rolling Stone* under the title 'Hearts of Darkness', while some of chapter four's examination of the 5T first appeared in *Juice* magazine as 'Exit Wounds'. Ten years ago I embarked on what I hoped would be a ground-breaking piece of writing for *Rolling Stone*, living on the streets for a month to document the life of some street kids. The story was a failure largely because I was too immature to make it work. It's been bugging me ever since and I rescued a few snatches of that feature to use here in the hope that I might redeem the time I otherwise wasted. The abusive episode which opens 'Pig City' is taken from that piece.

Wherever I have drawn directly on somebody else's work, I have either said so or tried to make it obvious. But sometimes the same ground might have been covered by four or five different writers, each with a subtly different spin and, once again, I wasn't about to make you wade through half a dozen names every couple of lines just for the sake of good form. Which brings us here, at the end of my own personal Vietnam, to this awkward, disjointed sort of essay where I'm going to try to put myself right with all of those guys in whose books, articles, essays and theses I've been buried for the past four years or so. The following isn't really exhaustive in the same way as the formal bibliography, but I hope this does cover everyone whose diligence and hard work I profited from. If, God forbid, you've been reading *Leviathan* and have suddenly leapt from your dusty old armchair in the commonroom, spittle flying and temperature rising because you think I've swiped your life's work without sufficient acknowledgment, well, uh, sorry. Give me a bell or drop me an email and I'll see you're cited properly in any later editions.

1. *The Long Goodbye*

Additional details of the last days of Saigon were drawn from *The Fall of Saigon* by David Butler, *Vietnam at War* by Davidson, Tim Bowden's *One Crowded Hour*, Neil Sheehan's *A Bright Shining Lie*, and *Time* magazine's special issue commemorating the twentieth anniversary of the war's end, 'Saigon: the final 10 days'. I found Dinh Tran after reading his story in the *Herald*.

When researching conditions in Georgian London, besides those works cited in the text, such as those by Engels and Mayhew, I also referred to *Selections from Cobbet's Political Works*, AGL Shaw's *Convicts and the Colonies* (specifically chapters seven and eight) and MD George's *London Life in the Eighteenth Century*, from which came some of the great detail about the effects of the gin trade. Manning Clark's 1956 articles in *Historical Studies* were a good source of data and tips for further reading in this section. Shaw also did sterling service in the re-creation of the First Fleet voyage, along with Bateson's *The Convict Ships*, John Cobley's 'The Crimes of the First Fleet Convicts', Hazel King's 'Villains All?', Anne Conlon's 'Convict Narratives' and of course Robert Hughes's *The Fatal Shore* (which I still think is really cool, even if lots of pointy-heads don't). The best source of information about the First Fleet however, remains the foundation journals. If the government is looking to throw some money at digital ventures, perhaps it could think about putting these babies on a single CD-rom.

I re-created the Gundy shooting and its aftermath from the investigation by the Royal Commission into Black Deaths in Custody and the New South Wales Ombudsman's report into 'Operation Sue'.

The section on Australia becoming an El Dorado for the English poor drew on dozens of different authors' work and they are so closely woven it is difficult to tease out the most important; but if I had to point the finger at the culprits responsible, you'd be looking at Townsend's 'The Molesworth Enquiry: Does the Report Fit the Evidence?' in the *Journal of Australian Studies* and 'Document: Sir Richard Bourke's Afterthoughts, 1838' in *Push From the Bush* and 'The British Parliament and Transportation in the Eighteen-Fifties' in *Historical Studies*. Ritchie's 'Towards Ending An Unclean Thing: The Molesworth Committee and the Abolition of Transportation to NSW, 1837–40' got a good workout, as did Conlon's 'Mine is a Sad Yet True Story'. Margaret Kiddle's research on Chisholm forms the basis of my version of that great story. Hayden's 'The NSW Immigration Question and Responsible Government, 1856–1861' provided a useful starting point in understanding early anti-migrant feeling, while Pyke's 'Some Leading Aspects of Foreign Immigration to the Goldfields' provides the description of the Chinese arrival on the goldfields. As I mentioned in the text, Curthoy's chapter in *Who Are Our Enemies?* was my template for laying out the ensuing anti-Chinese movement, with lots of material provided by contemporary press reports, the Final Report of the Committee to Enquire into Crowded Dwellings, which you will find attached to the Eleventh Progress Report of the Sydney City and Suburban Sewage and

Bibliographic Notes

Health Board, Appointed 12 April 1875, and the Report of the Select Committee on Common Lodging Houses, V&PNSWLA, 1875–6, Volume 2.

Rennie's 1982 article in the *Journal of the Royal Australian Historical Society*, 'The Factor of National Identity: An Explanation of the Differing Reactions of Australia and the United States to Mass Immigration', was where I first encountered the argument that postwar migration in Australia contributed to a sense of national identity and security.

A few minor details about National Action, such as the sharehouse meeting in Glebe, were drawn from Greason's *I was a Teenage Fascist*. Most of that section, however, is based on my own article for *Rolling Stone* called 'Hearts of Darkness'. Former National Action leader James Saleam obviously has a different view of the events in the 1980s. Those interested in this unique take on far-right politics could visit National Action's website, as I did to check details of the Funde incident. You'll find it at www.adelaide.net.au/~national/

2. *The Virgin's Lie*

Most of the cool tsunami stuff came from Bryant and Young. The *Australian Dictionary of Biography* supplied the bio of Carl Sussmilch. Wherever I seem to display a formidable knowledge about the obscure achievements of long-dead Australians such as Sussmilch or Dr J Ashburton Thompson, you can be pretty sure it was the *Australian Dictionary of Biography* I cribbed the good gear from. An insanely great resource, it's a damn shame those guys have to struggle so hard to turn a buck.

The geological history of the Sydney basin, although quite a short section, was one of the hardest parts of this book to write because, let's face it, I didn't have a clue what I was talking about. Chris Herbert, who is The Man where the basin is concerned, really helped out with his 1:100 000 Sheet and Guide to the Sydney Basin. Stanbury's *10 000 Years of Sydney Life* was a huge help with the bio side, and I leaned heavily on Proudfoot's *Seaport Sydney* because it was written in English rather than propellor-head. Robinson's *Journal of the Royal Australian Historical Society* article 'Geographical Aspects of Land Settlement in the Sydney District, 1788–1821' was very useful but even with all these champion references I couldn't have put a sentence down were it not for Penguin's *Dictionary of Geography* and the *Britannica* on CD-rom. Kids, did I mention how cool that thing is? I kept those suckers open and at hand during the whole three weeks it took me to write my three or four paragraphs. Without them, well, this book would be three or four paragraphs shorter. Of course, having lost fistfuls of hair teaching myself all about geology, I put the last full stop in place only to find that bloody Tim Flannery in the *Herald* a week later had written the whole story, probably off the top of his gigantic throbbing head. Doh! If only I'd procrastinated a little while longer. Mr Flannery's *The Future Eaters*, by the way, contributed a bit to my understanding of the evolutionary effects of geological change.

The short section on the Aboriginal use of fire was drawn largely from Rosen's *Losing Ground* of 1995 and Flannery's *Future Eaters*, with a tip o' the beanie from Tim to Professor Rhys Jones's seminal 1969 article on the uses of fire amongst Australian Aborigines. Flannery provided the reference to Sir Thomas Mitchell's comments on the change in Sydney's vegetation brought about by the altered fire regime. The State Coroner's NSW Bushfire Inquiry

Bibliographic Notes

Findings Volume 3 laid out the facts of the Como-Jannali disaster which I fleshed out with interviews with survivors. Bob Beale, writing a feature in the *Herald* on 8 January 1994 (coincidentally the day of the disaster), provided the neat explanation of what gum trees do in a bushfire.

I learned most of what there is to know about ancient and mediaeval conceptions of Terra Australis in Wood's entertaining *Journal of the Royal Australian Historical Society* article about, uhm, ancient and mediaeval conceptions of Terra Australis, supplemented by the Bicentennial History. John Cobley's *Sydney Cove* series proved a very useful starting point for tracking down primary sources, especially within the First Fleet diaries, and the State Library's Cobley collection got a real workout while I was researching early English perceptions of Australia. Graeme Aplin's contribution to *A Difficult Infant* also played a big part in anything smart I might have said about the environment of Sydney as experienced about 200 years back, as did Peter Bridges's *Foundations of Identity* and the rambunctious *Botany Bay Mirages* by Alan Frost. All that flapdoodle and balderdash about the Romantic and Picturesque movements would have been nonexistent without Proudfoot's 'Botany Bay, Kew, and the Picturesque' and, again, the *Britannica* on CD.

I'm not sure now why I got so carried away with trying to explain El Niño. Possibly because I could after reading all about it at the web page of the National Oceanic and Atmospheric Administration Pacific Marine Environmental Laboratory. The Environmental News Network Special Report of 22 September 1997 and the US News and World Report's online El Niño reports are also largely to blame.

The material on Sydney during and after Macquarie was drawn from Bridges's *Foundations of Identity*, Jahn's *Sydney Achitecture*;

Norman Edwards's chapter in Kelly's *Nineteenth Century Sydney*, 'The Genesis of the Sydney Central Business District 1788–1856'; James Broadbent's chapter in Kelly's *City of Suburbs*, 'The Push East: Woolloomooloo Hill, the First Suburb'; and Paul Ashton's *Accidental City*.

Details of James Barnet's career came from the *Australian Dictionary of Biography*, Jahn, and the bio article in the *Journal of the Royal Australian Historical Society* by McDonald. Jahn's beautifully realised book was a godsend for a bloke with a whole chapter to write about Sydney's built environment and nary a clue as to how to go about it. Written clearly, without the impenetrable bombast which renders a lot of architectural literature completely unreadable, it gets my Big Tick as one of the coolest funny-shaped books to be published in the last couple of years.

Birch and Macmillan's *Sydney Scene* provided neat summaries as well as great first-hand accounts of the city's physical growth. I drew heavily upon them, along with Shirley Fitzgerald's *Rising Damp* and Maisy Stapleton's chapter in Jahn, to describe the city's expansion in the later half of the 19th century. Stapleton's article in particular was useful for getting my head around the Rubik's cube of suburban growth and terrace housing, and my explanation of how the city fanned back along transport routes is really down to her. Good old Freddy Engels supplied the info on the disgusting eating habits of the English poor. He might have been partly responsible for the emergence of a couple of vicious, totalitarian dictatorships, but jeez he could write. Mayne's 'City Back-slums in the Land of Promise', an article from *Labour History*, provided the damning quote about the city's lack of poverty from the *Herald* on Australia Day 1876, along with the government statistician's comment on infant mortality in the 1870s. Kelly is cited in the text but I feel I should mention his

Bibliographic Notes

'Picturesque and Pestilential: The Sydney Slum Observed' chapter in *Nineteenth Century Sydney* again.

I took most of the gaudy detail of the plague which struck Sydney in 1900 from Dr J Ashburton Thompson's excellent reports. Simply and lucidly written, they even achieve the occasional flight of poetry. His recommendations for keeping man and rat separate appear in the appendix to his 1907 report. Max Kelly's much quoted slum article also reared its head in this section.

Peter Spearritt's *Sydney Since the Twenties* neatly summarised the growth of the city after the Great War and I owe the description of changes to suburbia from that period to his work. He also did the research on the 1920s land boomers which I profited from in the same section, supplemented by the *Australian Dictionary of Biography*'s entry for Sir Arthur Rickard. Whitham's quote about Lane Cove was snipped from Spearritt too. Jahn's mini-essays on the Astor and the Macleay Regis, and Richard Cardew's chapter in Roe's *Twentieth Century Sydney* did good-cop-bad-cop duty for me while I was looking at the apartment boom of the 1920s and 1930s. The biographical details for Portia Geach came from the *Australian Dictionary of Biography* and an unpublished manuscript in the Mitchell Library (ref A 920.7 G). The description of de Groot's attack on the ribbon-cutting ceremony at the opening of the Harbour Bridge is taken from contemporary reports in the *Herald* and the *Daily Telegraph*.

Jahn was the starting point for the brief section on high-rise Sydney with small diversions in Birch and Macmillan's *Sydney Scene*, Ruth Park's *Companion Guide to Sydney* and *Haskell's Sydney* by John Haskell. My description of the Australia Hotel is derived from the hotel's own guide for guests, held in the Mitchell Library. When writing this book I often wished I could transport myself back into Sydney's sepia-toned days. Had that wish been granted, I think the Australia would have been one of my first ports of call. It's one of the many great tragedies of this city that we let it slip away. Harold Cazneaux's photographic tributes to this lost city are a powerful reminder of what was lost, and for anyone interested I recommend Philip Geeves and Gail Newton's collection and study of 1980 or Phillip Adams and Helen Ennis's more recent *The Quiet Observer*. It was in the former I found Cazneaux's beautiful photograph of the old Royal Exchange. Geeves's simple prose, which I drew on, was an appropriate counterpoint to the photographer's elegant style. From him comes the droll information about the need for early car owners to always carry a potato and a description of Rowe Street before the MLC Centre buried it. Jahn provided the info for the brief treatment of high-rise Sydney.

3. *Only the Strong*

All that juicy bayonet stuff comes from the BBC documentary series 'Decisive Weapons'. Details of Bligh's last hours in government came from the transcript of George Johnston's court martial with a bit of cribbing from Fitzgerald and Hearn's *The Rum Rebellion* when I just couldn't see through the bullshit and spin-doctoring any more. The wry detail of Bligh's daughter attacking the main guard with her parasol is mentioned by GC Mundy decades later in *Our Antipodes*. He probably got the story first-hand from her as she was back in Sydney in the late 1840s, having long before married the colony's then military commander Sir Maurice O'Connell.

As you might guess I tend to favour Bligh's version of events, a bias which will no doubt earn me a good head-kicking from some Macarthur loyalists when the reviews come out.

Bibliographic Notes

SJ Butlin's *Foundations of the Australian Monetary System* turned out to be much more interesting than you'd ever imagine and it forms much of the basis for my discussion of the city's infant economy. The journey down the long and winding road through the colony's power structure before the rebellion was made much simpler by constant reference to Fitzgerald and Hearn (again), to Kercher's *Debt, Seduction and Other Disasters*, and to David Neal's *The Rule of Law in a Penal Colony*. It's a helluva job writing an interesting treatise on the relationship between money, power and the legal system, but these boys all stepped up for a shot at the brass ring, Fitzgerald and Hearn in particular.

The re-creation of the riots of 1843 was brought to you by the good journalists at the *Sydney Morning Herald*, the *Chronicle* and the *Colonial Observer*, with a little help from Mr Brewer's extract in *Sydney Scene*. The journal of William Wills, secretary to the first mayor of Sydney, provided some fascinating colour. I don't recall seeing it referred to anywhere in the literature, which isn't surprising seeing as how I stumbled across it while searching for weather reports amongst the log books of those ships moored in Sydney during election week. Anyone who's interested in delving more deeply can find the manuscript in the Mitchell Library at ref M934. See entry 165 Part 8, AJCP handbook. The gritty detail of the depression that year comes from press reports and a series of Legislative Council enquiries which can be found in the British Parliamentary Papers, session 1842–4.

Details of Wentworth's life are largely drawn from the *Australian Dictionary of Biography*, with a pinch of Manning Clark's iconoclasm thrown in for balance. Wentworth's early attacks on the landed and wealthy are from his own book, *A Statistical Account of the British Settlements in Australia*. The small diversion into the early industry of Sydney, contained within the discussion of JW McCarty's ideas, was made possible by the work of Brian Fletcher in *Sydney: A Southern Emporium*. The ensuing discussion of the rich draws on a wide range of sources, threading data and argument from numerous writers in and around each other. Briefly, the main players are Michael Roe's *Quest for Authority in Eastern Australia*, Rubinstein's two papers on the wealthy of New South Wales, GC Bolton's 'The Idea of a Colonial Gentry', Sandra Blair's 'The Felonry and the Free', Barrie Dyster's 'The Fate of Colonial Conservatism on the Eve of the Gold Rush', and Shirley Storrier's *Journal of the Royal Australian Historical Society* article 'Colonial Society' from which I snipped the James Henty extract. Roe's book was particularly useful and I drew repeatedly on it, first in the discussion of James and Edward Macarthur's ideas and then in the general discussion of gentry characteristics which followed.

Shirley Fitzgerald's history of the city council and Paul Ashton's *Accidental City* were both, as cited, principal sources for the discussion of conflict between the colonial and municipal levels of government.

Wendy Lowenstein's fantastic *Weevils in the Flour* was a great souce of first-hand acounts of the Depression, supplemented by newspaper accounts, David Hickie's bio/interview with Chow Hayes, Lydia Gill's memoir and Trevor Sykes's chapter on the collapse of the Government Savings Bank in *Two Centuries of Panic*. I found Sykes a great help in coming to grips with the premiership of Jack Lang, but also drew on Lang's entry in the *Australian Dictionary of Biography* and sections of Gavin Souter's *Company of Heralds* and Paul Barry's *Rise and Rise of Kerry Packer*, both of which contain interesting discussions of the role played by the

Bibliographic Notes

city's leading media dynasties at that time. The re-creation of the antieviction crusade draws heavily on Nadia Wheatley's pioneering work in *Twentieth Century Sydney*, contemporary press reports for what they are worth, and Lowenstein. Wendy's young lad Richard made a short film based on that section of her book and I watched it in the State Reference Library one afternoon to get a feel for the grit of the period. A footnote in Wheatley's essay led me to the Australian National University in Canberra where the Noel Butlin Archive Centre holds the legal files of Christian Jolly Smith, a female solicitor, a rare breed in the 1930s, who took on a lot of cases for the International Class War Prisoner's Aid group. She must have been quite a take-charge babe, but somehow I doubt she got to spend a lot of time down at the Australian Club with the other lawyers knocking back the brandies and bullshitting about the glory days of the Sydney bar. Smith's witness statements are all on file and we can only thank the person who saw the historical significance of her work and donated it to the ANU. The great quote about the explosion and fireworks of the Russian Revolution was cribbed from *Cities in Civilization* by Sir Peter Hall.

Until I read MT Daly's *Sydney Boom Sydney Bust* I knew nothing about the building and finance boom of the 1960s and early 1970s. I still don't know very much, but by judiciously drawing on Daly's work and closely studying Trevor Sykes's essays on the period in *Two Centuries of Panic*, I was hopefully able to conceal the bottomless well of my ignorance. The green bans of the early 1970s have been extensively documented but I found Meredith and Verity Burgmann's history of the BLF the most informative, whilst Anne Coombs's dissection of the Sydney Push in *Sex and Anarchy* has a top section on the battle for Victoria Street. An AFC doco called 'Woolloomooloo' and readily accessible at the State Reference Library in Macquarie Street has some really nice interviews with street-level participants, including Mick Fowler whose passing, like that of my friend Pat Bell, left the city all the poorer. All of Mick's quotes and the grabs from Val Hodgson and Frank Theeman are taken from this documentary. Theeman's paraphrasing of Norm Gallagher is from the same source.

4. *Pig City*

The quote from Manning is taken from *Running the Risks* by Lisa Maher et al, a truly amazing piece of investigation. The structure of the Kings Cross heroin trade in the late 1980s came from Dobinson and Poletti's report, *Buying and Selling Heroin*.

The statistics on arrests for drunkenness in New South Wales in 1948 are from Peter Grabosky's *Sydney in Ferment*, as are references to the Summary Offences Act of 1970 and various information on social crime in Sydney and the breadth of New South Wales criminal law. He also contributed information about the pack rape scares of the late sixties and the so-called 'Age of Lawlessness'. The quotes from Dr Alfred McCoy are taken from Evan Whitton's work on New South Wales crime, *Can of Worms*. As I hope is obvious from the text, a great deal of the information on postwar crime in Sydney is taken directly from David Hickie's exhaustive survey of the period *The Prince and the Premier*; some of the information on black-market rackets also comes from his work *Chow Hayes*. No doubt a lot of real historians come over all sniffy at Hickie's work, but having waded through millions of words on Sydney I'm willing to lay hard money that next century his bio of Hayes becomes one of the most important sources on

Bibliographic Notes

the criminal history of the city. A debt is owed to Richard Hall for the valuable insights into the political dimensions of gambling and vice in Sydney in his book *Disorganised Crime*. The information on Phillip Arantz, his dismissal and the 'paddy book' system of crime statistics is taken from his self-published work, *A Collusion of Powers*. Information on royal commissions leading up to the Wood Royal Commission is taken from Athol Moffit's book, *A Quarter to Midnight*.

Any information about the Wood Commission not drawn directly from the official reports, such as details of the related suicides, was provided by the *Herald*'s eight page special report of 1 May 1997.

Bibliography

Bibliographies

Bettison, M. and Summers, A. (comps). *Her Story: Australian Women in Print 1788–1975*. Hale & Iremonger, Sydney, 1980.

Borchardt, D.H. *Australian Bibliography: A Guide to Printed Sources of Information*. Pergamon, Sydney, 1976.

Borchardt, D.H. *Checklist of Royal Commissions, Select Committees of Parliament and Boards of Inquiry*. Stone Copying Co (pt 1), Sydney; Wentworth Press (pts 1a, 2, 3), Sydney; La Trobe University Library (pts 4, 5), Melbourne, 1958–78. 5 pts in 6 vols plus consolidated index by J. Hagger and A. Montanelli.

Crittenden, V., et al. *Index to Journal Articles on Australian History*. History Project Inc., Sydney, 1980–82.

Ferguson, J.A. *Bibliography of Australia*. Angus & Robertson, Sydney, 1941–69.

Hogan, T., et al. *Index to Journal Articles on Australian History*. University of New England, Armidale, NSW, 1976.

Irish University Press. *Index to British Parliamentary Papers on Australia and New Zealand, 1800–1899* (2 vols). IUP, Dublin, 1974.

Mira, W.J.D. *Coinage and Currency in New South Wales, 1788–1829; and an Index of Currency References in the Sydney Gazette 1803–1811*. Metropolitan Coin Club of Sydney, Sydney, 1981.

Mitchell Library, Sydney. *Catalogue of Manuscripts of Australasia and the Pacific in the Mitchell Library* (2 vols). Trustees of the Public Library of NSW, Sydney, 1967–69.

Mitchell Library, Sydney. *Early Sydney Newspapers, Collation Notes*.

Monie, J. *Index to English Language Journal Articles on Australia Published Overseas to 1900*. History Project Inc., Sydney, 1983.

National Library of Australia. *Guide to Collections of Manuscripts relating to Australia*. NLA, Canberra, 1965– .

Bibliography

White, O., et al. *Our Heritage: A Directory to Archives and Manuscript Repositories in Australia*. Australian Society of Archivists, Canberra, 1983.

Books

Aird, W.V. *The Water Supply, Sewerage and Drainage of Sydney: An Account of the Development and History ... From Their Beginnings with the First Settlement to 1960*. Sydney Metropolitan Water, Sewerage and Drainage Board, 1961.

Aplin, G. *A Difficult Infant: Sydney Before Macquarie*. New South Wales University Press, Sydney, 1988.

Arantz, P. *A Collusion of Powers*. Arantz, Dundedoo, 1993.

Arendt, H. 'On Power', in *The First Anthology, Thirty Years of the New York Review of Books*, The New York Review of Books, New York, 1993.

Ashton, P. *The Accidental City*. Hale & Iremonger, Sydney, 1993.

Barry, P. *The Rise and Rise of Kerry Packer*. Bantam, Sydney, 1994.

Barton, G.B. and Britton, A. *History of New South Wales from the Records*. Hale & Iremonger, Sydney, 1980.

Bartrum, Mr. *Proceedings of a General Court Martial ... of Geo Johnston*. Sherwood, Neely & Jones, London, 1811.

Bateson, C. *The Convict Ships, 1787–1868*. Library of Australian History, Sydney, 1983.

Bentham, J. *A Plea for the Constitution of New South Wales*. Mawman, Poultry & Hatchard, Piccadilly, 1803.

Berry, A. 'On the Geology of Part of the Coast of New South Wales', in B. Field (ed.). *Geographical Memoirs on New South Wales*. John Murray, London, 1825, pp. 231–54. (First Geology Paper Presented to Philosophical Society of Australasia.)

Birch, A. and Macmillan, D.S. (eds). *The Sydney Scene: 1788–1960*. Melbourne University Press, Melbourne, 1962.

Bowden, T. *One Crowded Hour*. Collins, Sydney, 1988.

Boyd, R. *Australia's Home: Its Origins, Builders and Occupiers*. Penguin, Victoria, 1978.

Bradley, W. *A Voyage to New South Wales: The Journal of Lieutenant William Bradley RN of HMS Sirius, 1786–1792*. Trustees of the Public Library of New South Wales in asssociation with Ure Smith, Sydney, 1969.

Bridges, P. *Foundations of Identity: Building Early Sydney*. Hale & Iremonger, Sydney, 1995.

Broome, R. *Aboriginal Australians: Black Response to White Dominance, 1788–1980*. Allen & Unwin, Sydney, 1982.

Burgmann, M. and Burgmann, V. *Green Bans, Red Union*. University of New South Wales Press, Sydney, 1998.

LEVIATHAN

Burnley, I. H. *The Australian Urban System: Growth, Change and Differentiation*. Longman Cheshire, Melbourne, 1980.

Butler, D. *The Fall of Saigon*. Simon & Schuster, New York, 1985.

Butlin, S.J. *Foundations of the Australian Monetary System*. Melbourne University Press, Melbourne, 1953.

Butlin, N.G. *Our Original Aggression: Aboriginal Populations of Southeastern Australia, 1788–1850*. Allen & Unwin, Sydney, 1983.

Chappell, D. and Wilson, P. *The Australian Criminal Justice System*. Butterworths, Sydney, 1994.

Clark, R. *The Journal and Letters of Lt Ralph Clark, 1787–1792*. (ed. by P.G. Fidlon and R. J. Ryan). Australian Documents Library in association with the Library of Australian History, Sydney, 1981.

Cobbett, J. M. and Cobbett, J. P. *Selections from [William] Cobbett's Political Works*. London, 1835.

Cobley, J. *The Crimes of the First Fleet Convicts*. Angus & Robertson, Sydney, 1982.

Cobley, J. *Sydney Cove, 1788–1792* (revised edition) 3 vols. Angus & Robertson, Sydney, 1980.

Coghlan, T.A. *Labour and Industry in Australia from the First Settlement in 1788 to the Establishment of the Commonwealth in 1901*. Oxford University Press, London, 1918.

Collins, D. *An Account of the English Colony in New South Wales* (2 vols). T. Cadell Junior & W. Davies, London, 1798.

Coombs A. *Sex and Anarchy: The Life and Death of the Sydney Push*. Viking, Ringwood, 1996.

Cresiani, G. *Fascism, Anti-fascism and Italians in Australia, 1922–1945*. Australian National University Press, Canberra, 1980.

Curthoys, A. and Markus, A. (eds). *Who are Our Enemies? Racism and the Australian Working Class*. Hale & Iremonger in association with the Australian Society for the Study of Labour History, Sydney, 1978.

Daly, M.T. *Sydney Boom Sydney Bust*. Allen & Unwin, Sydney, 1982.

Daniels, K. *So Much Hard Work*, Fontana, Sydney, 1984.

Davidson, P. *Vietnam at War*. Presidio Press, Novato, 1988.

Easty, J. *Memorandum of the Transactions of a Voyage from England to Botany Bay, 1787–1793: A First Fleet Journal*. Trustees of the Public Library of New South Wales in association with Angus & Robertson, Sydney, 1965.

Edelman, M. *Politics as Symbolic Action*, Markham, Chicago, 1971.

Engels, F. *The Condition of the Working Classes in England* [1844]. Progress Publishers, Moscow.

Fitzpatrick, D. *Oceans of Consolation*. Melbourne University Press, Melbourne, 1995.

Fitzgerald, R. and Hearn, M. *Bligh, Macarthur and the Rum Rebellion*. Kangaroo Press, Sydney, 1988.

Fitzgerald, S. *Rising Damp*. Oxford University Press, Melbourne, 1987.

Bibliography

Fitzgerald, S. *Sydney 1842–1992*. Hale & Iremonger, Sydney, 1992.

Flannery, T. *The Future Eaters*. Reed, Sydney, 1994.

Flynn, M. *The Second Fleet*, Library of Australian History, Sydney, 1993.

Frost, A. *Botany Bay Mirages*. Melbourne University Press, Melbourne, 1994.

Geeves, P. and Newton, G. *Philip Geeves Presents Cazneaux's Sydney 1904–34*. David Ell Press, Sydney, 1980.

George, M.D. *London Life in the Eighteenth Century*. Kegan Paul, London, 1925; London School of Economics and Political Science, London, 1951.

Gill, L. *My Town: Sydney in the 1930s*. State Library of NSW Press, Sydney, 1993.

Glynn, S. *Urbanisation in Australian History, 1788–1900*. Nelson, Melbourne, 1975.

Gott, K. D. *Voices of Hate: A Study of the Australian League of Rights and its Director, Eric D. Butler*. Dissent Publishing Association, Melbourne, 1965.

Grabosky, P.N. *Sydney in Ferment: Crime, Dissent and Official Reaction, 1788–1973*. Australian National University Press, Canberra, 1977.

Greason, D. *I was a Teenage Fascist*. McPhee Gribble, South Yarra, 1994.

Hainsworth, D.R. *The Sydney Traders: Simeon Lord and his Contemporaries, 1788–1821*. Melbourne University Press, Victoria, 1981.

Hall, P. *Cities in Civilization*. Pantheon Books, New York, 1998.

Hall, R. *Disorganized Crime*. University of Queensland Press, St Lucia, 1986.

Haskell, J. *Haskell's Sydney*. Hale & Iremonger, Sydney, 1983.

Hickie, D. *The Prince and the Premier*. Angus & Robertson, Sydney, 1985.

Hickie, D. *Chow Hayes: Gunman*. Angus & Robertson, North Ryde, 1990.

Holt, J. *A Rum Story: The Adventures of Joseph Holt*. (ed. by P. O'Shaughnessy). Kangaroo Press, Sydney, 1988.

Holt, P. (ed.). *A City in the Mind: Sydney Imagined by its Writers*. Allen & Unwin, Sydney, 1983.

Howitt, A.W. *The Native Tribes of South-East Australia*. Macmillan, London, 1904.

Hughes, R. *The Fatal Shore*. Collins Harvill, London, 1987.

Hunter, J. *An Historical Journal of the Transactions at Port Jackson and Norfolk Island*. Stockdale, London, 1793.

Jahn, G. *Sydney Architecture*. Watermark Press, Sydney, 1997.

Jeans, D.N. and Spearritt, P. *The Open Air Museum: The Cultural Landscape of NSW*. Allen & Unwin, Sydney, 1980.

Johnson, R. *An Address to the Inhabitants of the Colonies Established in New South Wales and Norfolk Is*. London, 1792.

Kelly, M. *City of Suburbs*. New South Wales University Press, Sydney, 1987.

Kelly, M. (ed.). *Nineteenth Century Sydney: Essays in Urban History*. Sydney University Press in association with the Sydney History Group, 1978.

Kelly, M. *Plague Sydney 1900: A Photographic Introduction to a Hidden Sydney, 1900*. Doak Press, Sydney, 1981.

Kercher, B. *Debt, Seduction and Other Disasters: The Birth of Civil Law in Convict New South Wales*. The Federation Press, Sydney, 1996.

LEVIATHAN

Kiddle, M. *Caroline Chisolm*. Melbourne University Press, Victoria, 1957.

King, P.G. *The Journal of Phillip Gidley King: Lieutenant RN, 1787–1790*. (ed. by P.G. Fidlon and R.J. Ryan). Australian Documents Library, Sydney, 1980.

Knight, S. *Continent of Mystery*, Melbourne University Press, Melbourne, 1997.

Larcombe, F.A. *A History of Local Government in New South Wales* (3 vols). Sydney University Press, Sydney, 1973–78.

Levi, J.S. and Bergman, G.F.J. *Australian Genesis: Jewish Convicts and Settlers, 1788–1850*. Rigby, Adelaide, 1974.

Loveday, P. and Martin, A.W. *Parliament, Factions and Parties; The First Thirty Years of Responsible Government in New South Wales, 1856–1889*. Melbourne University Press, Victoria, 1966.

Lowenstein, W. *Weevils in the Flour*. Scribe, Melbourne, 1998.

Madgwick, R.B. *Immigration into Eastern Australia, 1788–1851*. Longman, London, 1937.

Martin, G. (ed.). *The Founding of Australia: The Argument About Australia's Origins*. Hale & Iremonger, Sydney, 1978.

Martin, J.I. *The Migrant Presence, Australian Responses 1947–1977: Research Report for the National Population Inquiry*. Allen & Unwin, Sydney, 1978.

Mayhew, H. *London Labour and the London Poor*. Frank Cass & Co., (republished) 1967.

McCarty, J.W. and Schedvin, C.B. (eds.). *Australian Capital Cities: Historical Essays*. Sydney University Press, Sydney, 1978.

McCoy, A., in Davidson, J. *The Sydney–Melbourne Book*. Allen & Unwin, Sydney, 1986.

Moffit, A. *A Quarter to Midnight, the Australian Crisis: Organized Crime and the Decline of the Institutions of the State*. Angus & Robertson, Sydney, 1985.

Mundey, J. *Green Bans and Beyond*. Angus & Robertson, Sydney, 1981.

Mundy, G.C. *Our Antipodes*. Richard Bentley, London, 1852.

Mundy, G.C. *Sydney Town 1846–1851*. Review Publications, 1971.

Murray, J. *Larrikins*. Landsdowne Press, Melbourne, 1973.

Neal, D. *The Rule of Law in a Penal Colony*. Cambridge University Press, Sydney, 1991.

Park, R. *The Companion Guide to Sydney*. Collins, Sydney, 1973.

Pearl, C. *Wild Men of Sydney*. Angus & Robertson, Sydney, 1977.

Phillip, A. *The Voyage of Governor Phillip to Botany Bay with an Account of the Establishment of the Colonies and Norfolk Island*. Stockdale, London, 1789.

Poulson, M.F. and Spearritt, P. *Sydney: A Social and Political Atlas*. Allen & Unwin, Sydney, 1981.

Proudfoot, P. *Seaport Sydney*. New South Wales University Press, Sydney, 1996.

Reece, R.H.W. *Aborigines and Colonists: Aborigines and Colonial Society in New South Wales in the 1830's and 1840's*. Sydney University Press, Sydney, 1974.

Reynolds, H. *The Other Side of the Frontier: Aboriginal Resistance to the European Invasion of Australia*. Penguin, Victoria, 1982.

Bibliography

Robson, L.L. *The Convict Settlers of Australia: An Enquiry into the Origin and Character of the Convicts Transported to New South Wales and Van Dieman's Land, 1787–1852*. Melbourne University Press, Melbourne, 1976.

Roe, J.I. (ed.). *Twentieth Century Sydney: Studies in Urban and Social History*. Hale & Iremonger, Sydney, 1980.

Roe, M. *The Quest for Authority in Eastern Australia*. Melbourne University Press, Melbourne, 1965.

Roseby, T.J. *Sydney's Water Supply and Sewerage, 1788–1918*. Government Printer, Sydney, 1918.

Rosen, S. *Losing Ground*. Hale & Iremonger, Sydney, 1995.

Rude, G.F.E. *Protest and Punishment: The Story of the Social and Political Protesters Transported to Australia, 1788–1868*. Oxford University Press, Oxford, 1978.

Sandercock, L. *Cities for Sale: Property, Politics and Urban Planning in Australia*. Melbourne University Press, Melbourne, 1977.

Shaw, A.G.L. *Convicts and the Colonies: A Study of Penal Transportation from Great Britain and Ireland to Australia and other parts of the British Empire*. Melbourne University Press, Melbourne, 1977.

Sheehan, N. *A Bright Shining Lie*. Cape, London, 1988.

Sherington, G. *Australia's Immigrants, 1788–1978*. Allen & Unwin, Sydney, 1980.

Souter, G. *Company of Heralds*. Melbourne University Press, Melbourne, 1981.

Spearritt, P. *Sydney Since the Twenties*. Hale & Iremonger, Sydney, 1978.

Stanbury, P. (ed.). *10 000 Years of Sydney Life*. Macleay Museum, Sydney, 1979.

Steven, M. *Trade, Tactics and Territory: Britain in the Pacific, 1783–1823*. Melbourne University Press, Melbourne, 1983.

Stone, S.N. (ed.). *Aborigines in White Australia: A Documentary History of the Attitudes Affecting Official Policy and the Australian Aborigine, 1697–1973*. Heinemann Educational, Melbourne, 1974.

Sturma, M. *Vice in a Vicious Society: Crime and Convicts in Mid-Nineteenth Century New South Wales*. University of Queensland Press, Queensland, 1983.

Sudjic, D. *The 100 Mile City*, Flamingo, London, 1992.

Sykes, T. *Two Centuries of Panic: A History of Corporate Collapses in Australia*. Allen & Unwin, Sydney, 1998.

Taylor, G. *Sydneyside Scenery*. Angus & Robertson, Sydney, 1958.

Tench, W. (ed. Flannery, T), *1788*, Text Publishing, Melbourne, 1996.

Viviani, N. *The Indochinese in Australia, 1975–1995*. Oxford University Press, Melbourne, 1996.

Wentworth, W.C. *A Statistical Account of the British Settlements in Australia*. Whitaker, London, 1824.

White, J. *Journal of a Voyage to New South Wales*. (ed. by A.H. Chisolm). Angus & Robertson in association with the Royal Australian Historical Society, Sydney, 1962.

Whitton, E. *Can of Worms*. Fairfax Library, Sydney, 1987.

Willey, K. *When the Sky Fell Down: The Destruction of the Tribes of the Sydney Region, 1788–1850s*. Collins, Sydney, 1979.

Wills, W. *Journal of William Charles Wills, Oct 1841–Jan 1844*. Australian Joint Copying Project. (Manuscript in Mitchell Library M934. See entry 165 Part 8, AJCP handbook).

Wotherspoon, G. (ed.). *Sydney's Transport: Studies in Urban History*. Hale & Iremonger in association with the Sydney History Group, Sydney, 1983.

Journals

Abbott, G.J. 'The Formation of Joint Stock Companies in Sydney in the Second Half of the 1830s', *Push from the Bush*, no. 14, pp. 4–27, 1983.

Ajax. 'Larrikinism', *Sydney Quarterly Magazine*, January, pp. 207–215, 1884.

Andrews, A. 'Sydney's Lamp-Lighting Entrepreneur: John White and the Blazing Star', *Journal of the Royal Australian Historical Society*, vol. 67, no. 2, pp. 132–149, 1981.

Anon. 'The Holey Dollar and the Dump', *Journal of the Royal Australian Historical Society*, vol. 2, no. 4, pp. 93–96, 1909.

Ashworth, H.I. 'The Sydney Opera House', *Journal of the Royal Australian Historical Society*, vol. 59, no. 3, pp. 153–161, 1973.

Atkinson, A. 'The British Whigs and the Rum Rebellion', *Journal of the Royal Australian Historical Society*, vol. 66, no. 2, pp. 73–90, 1980.

Atkinson, A. 'The Ethics of Conquest, 1786', *Aboriginal History*, vol. 6, nos 1–2, pp. 82–91, 1982.

Atkinson, A. 'Four Patterns of Convict Protest', *Labour History*, no. 37, pp. 28–51, 1979.

Atkinson, A. 'Marriage and Distance in the Convict Colonies, 1838', *Push from the Bush*, no. 16, pp. 61–70, 1983.

Atkinson, M. 'Notes on the Early Economic History of Australia', *Journal of the Royal Australian Historical Society*, vol. 3, no. 11, pp. 530–545, 1917.

Auchmuty, J.J. 'The Background to the Early Australian Governors', *Historical Studies*, vol. 6, no. 23, pp. 301–314, 1954.

Austin, M. 'Victoria Barracks, Paddington', *Sabre*, vol. 21, nos 1–2, pp. 13–27, 1981.

Aveling, M. 'Gender in Early New South Wales Society', *Push from the Bush*, no. 24, pp. 30–40, 1987.

Baalman, J. 'Gubernatorial Land Jobbing', *Journal of the Royal Australian Historical Society*, vol. 48, no. 4, pp. 241–254, 1962.

Bach, J. 'Sea Communication Between Sydney and Melbourne before 1860', *Journal of the Royal Australian Historical Society*, vol. 41, no. 1, pp. 1–22, 1955.

Basham, R. 'The Supportive Environment of Asian Organised Crime', AustAsian

Bibliography

Paper No. 3, Research Institute for Asia and the Pacific, 1995.

Beever, A. 'From a Place of "Horrible Destitution" to a Paradise of the Working Class: The Transformation of British Working Class Attitudes to Australia, 1841–1851', *Labour History*, vol. 40, pp. 1–15, 1981.

Bergman, G.F.J. 'Phillip Joseph Cohen (1802–1864)', *Journal of the Australian Jewish Historical Society*, vol. 8, no. 2, pp. 48–81, 1975.

Bergman, G.F.J. 'The Bizarre Life Story of Mordecai Moses: The Shamaas of the York Street Synagogue', *Journal of the Australian Jewish Historical Society*, vol. 8, no. 3, pp. 100–108, 1977.

Bergman, G.F.J. 'The (Sydney) George Street Synagogue: Australia's First Synagogue', *Journal of the Australian Jewish Historical Society*, vol. 8, no. 5, pp. 272–276, 1978.

Bersten, H. 'Jewish Sydney: The First Hundred Years', *Journal of the Australian Jewish Historical Society*, Sydney, 1995.

Bertie, C. 'Old Pitt Street', *Journal of the Royal Australian Historical Society*, vol. 6, no. 2, pp. 69–96, 1920.

Bertie, C. 'Old Castlereagh Street', *Journal of the Royal Australian Historical Society*, vol. 22, no. 1, pp. 42–68, 1936.

Bertie, C. 'The Street Names of Early Sydney and Some Street History', *Journal of the Royal Australian Historical Society*, vol. 36, no. 10, pp. 15–60, 1950.

Bladen, F.M. 'The Deposition of Governor Bligh', *Journal of the Royal Australian Historical Society*, vol. 1, no. 10, pp. 192–201, 1908.

Blainey, G. 'Climate and Australia's History', *Melbourne Historical Journal*, vol. 10, pp. 5–9, 1971.

Blair, S. 'The Convict Press: William Watt and the *Sydney Gazette* in the 1830s', *Push from the Bush*, no. 5, pp. 98–120, 1979.

Blair, S. 'The Felonry and the Free? Divisions in Colonial Society in the Penal Era', *Labour History*, vol. 45, pp. 1–16, 1983.

Blair, S. 'Patronage and Prejudice, Educated Convicts in the NSW Press, 1838', *Push from the Bush*, no. 8, pp. 75–87, 1980.

Bland, F.A. 'City Government by Commission', *Journal of the Royal Australian Historical Society*, vol. 14, no. 3, pp. 117–199, 1928.

Bolton, G.C. 'The Idea of a Colonial Gentry', *Historical Studies*, vol. 13, no. 51, pp. 307–328, 1968.

Bridges, B. 'The Aborigines and the Land Question: New South Wales in the Period of Imperial Responsibility', *Journal of the Royal Australian Historical Society*, vol. 56, no. 2, pp. 92–110, 1970.

Bryant, E.A. & Young, R.W., 'Bedrock-Sculpting by Tsunami, South Coast, New South Wales, Australia,' *Journal of Geology*, vol. 104, pp. 565–582, 1996.

Burke, J. 'Sydney's Style: The Home and Homogeniety Command', *Meanjin*, vol. 40, no. 1, pp. 35–51, 1981.

LEVIATHAN

Burley, K.H. 'The Organisation of the Overseas Trade in NSW Coal, 1860–1914', *Economic Record*, vol. 37. (Sept.), pp. 371–381, 1961.

Burnley, I.H. 'Greek Settlement in Sydney, 1947–71', *Australian Geographer*, vol. 13, pp. 200–214, 1976.

Butlin, S.J. 'The Beginnings of Savings Banking in Australia', *Journal of the Royal Australian Historical Society*, vol. 32, no. 1, pp. 1–87, 1946.

Burroughs, P. 'The Fixed Price Experiment in NSW, 1840–1841', *Historical Studies*, vol. 12, no. 7, pp. 389–404, 1966.

Byrne, P.J. 'Women and the Criminal Law: 1810–1821', *Push From the Bush*, no. 21, pp. 2–19, 1985.

Cable, K. 'The Eastern Suburbs Railway, Early Plans and Politics', *Journal of the Royal Australian Historical Society*, vol. 51, no. 4, pp. 317–340, 1965.

Cain, N. 'Financial Reconstruction in Australia 1893–1900', *Australian Economic History Review*, vol. 6, no. 2, pp. 166–183, 1966.

Campbell, E. 'Prerogative Rule in NSW, 1788–1823', *Journal of the Royal Australian Historical Society*, vol. 50, no. 3, pp. 161–190, 1964.

Campbell, J. 'Smallpox in Aboriginal Australia', *Historical Studies*, vol. 20, no. 81, pp. 536–556, 1983.

Campbell, J.F. 'The Valley of the Tank Stream', *Journal of the Royal Australian Historical Society*, vol. 10, no. 2, pp. 63–103, 1924.

Campbell, J.F. 'Notes on the Development of Macquarie Street South', *Journal of the Royal Australian Historical Society*, vol. 23, no. 3, pp. 194–205, 1937.

Campbell, W.S. 'A Matrimonial Encouragement in the Early Days', *Journal of the Royal Australian Historical Society*, vol. 16, no. 4, pp. 260–263, 1930.

Campbell, W.S. 'Some Old Cries, Old Customs and Old Practices in the Middle Ages of Sydney, 1848–1861', *Journal of the Royal Australian Historical Society*, vol. 14, no. 2, pp. 105–116, 1928.

Campbell, W.S. 'The Use and Abuse of Stimulants in the Early Days of Settlement in New South Wales', *Journal of the Royal Australian Historical Society*, vol. 18, no. 2, pp. 74–99, 1932.

Church, G. J. 'Saigon: The Final 10 Days', *Time*, April 24, vol. 145, no. 17, pp. 24–36, 1995.

Churchward, L.G. 'Australian–American Trade Relations, 1791–1939', *Economic Record*, vol. 26 (June), pp. 69–86, 1950.

Clark, M. 'The Origins of the Convicts Transport to Eastern Australia, 1787–1852 (Part 1)', *Historical Studies*, vol. 7, no. 26, pp. 121–135, 1956.

Clark, M. 'The Origins of the Convicts Transport to Eastern Australia, 1787–1852 (Part 2)', *Historical Studies*, vol. 7, no. 27, pp. 314–327, 1956.

Cobley, J. 'The Crimes of the First Fleeters', *Journal of the Royal Australian Historical Society*, vol. 52, no. 2, pp. 81–93, 1966.

Conlon, A. 'Mine is a Sad Yet True Story: Convict Narratives 1818–1850',

Bibliography

Journal of the Royal Australian Historical Society, vol. 55, no. 1, pp. 43–82, 1969.

Corris, P. 'Racialism: The Australian Experience', *Historical Studies*, vol. 15, no. 61, pp. 750–759, 1973.

Cowburn, P. 'The Attempted Assassination of the Duke of Edinburgh, 1868', *Journal of the Royal Australian Historical Society*, vol. 55, no. 1, pp. 19–42, 1969.

Cresciani, G. 'The second awakening: The Italia Libera movement', *Labour History*, vol. 30, pp. 22–37, 1976.

Cresciani, G. 'The Proletarian Migrants: Fascism and Italian Anarchists in Australia', *Australian Quarterly*, vol. 51, no. 1, pp. 4–19, 1979.

Cresciani, G. 'Italian Immigrants in Australia, 1900–22', *Labour History*, November, pp. 36–43, 1982.

Crough, G. 'Transnational Banks and the World Economy', *Australian Quarterly*, vol. 51, no. 2, pp. 66–80, 1979.

Crowley, F.K. 'The British Contribution to the Australian Population: 1860–1919', *University Studies in History and Economics* vol. 2, no. 2, pp. 55–88, 1954.

Currey, C.H. 'The Law of Marriage and Divorce in New South Wales (1788–1858)', *Journal of the Royal Australian Historical Society*, vol. 41, no. 3, pp. 97–114, 1955.

Dallas, K.M. 'Transportation and Colonial Income', *Historical Studies*, vol. 3, no. 12, pp. 297–312, 1949.

Dallas, K.M. 'Commercial Influences on the First Settlements in Australia', *Tasmanian Historical Research Association Papers and Proceedings*, vol. 16, no. 2, pp. 36–49, 1968.

Dallas, K.M. 'Slavery in Australia – Convicts, Emigrants, Aborigines', *Tasmanian Historical Research Association Papers and Proceedings*, vol. 16, no. 2, pp. 61–76, 1968.

Denoon, D. 'Understanding Settler Societies', *Historical Studies*, vol. 18, no. 73, pp. 511–527, 1979.

Dickey, B. 'Charity in NSW 1850–1914, Outdoor Relief to the Aged and Destitute', *Journal of the Royal Australian Historical Society*, vol. 52, no. 1, pp. 9–32, 1966.

Dickey, B. 'The Evolution of Care for Destitute Children in NSW, 1875–1901', *Journal of Australian Studies*, no. 4, pp. 38–57, 1979.

Dixon, W. 'Sydney Street Lighting 115 Years Ago', *Journal of the Royal Australian Historical Society*, vol. 27, no. 4, p. 307, 1941.

Dixson, M. 'Class Struggle and Ideology During the Great Depression in New South Wales', *Armidale District Historical Society Journal*, no. 15, pp. 72–76, 1972.

Dowd, B.T. 'Town Planning in New South Wales 1829', *Journal of the Royal Australian Historical Society*, vol. 36, no. 6, pp. 318–320, 1946.

Dowling, J.A. 'Potts Point, Darling Point and Neighbourhood – In the Early Days', *Journal of the Royal Australian Historical Society*, vol. 2, no. 3, pp. 52–70, 1909.

LEVIATHAN

Driscoll, F. 'Macquarie's Administration of the Convict system', *Journal of the Royal Australian Historical Society*, vol. 27, no. 6, pp. 373–433, 1941.

Dunlop, N.J. 'Who's Who in the First Elective (1843) Parliament of New South Wales', *Journal of the Royal Australian Historical Society*, vol. 13, no. 30, pp. 172–201, 1927.

Dyster, B. 'The Fate of Colonial Conservatism on the Eve of the Gold Rush', *Journal of the Royal Australian Historical Society*, vol. 54, no. 4, pp. 327–355, 1968.

Earnshaw, B. 'The Colonial Children', *Push from the Bush*, no. 9, pp. 28–43, 1981.

Edward, H.R. 'Employment in NSW Manufacturing Industries, 1877–1938–39', *Economic Record*, vol. 26 (Dec.), pp. 270–277, 1950.

Edwards, N. 'The Sydney Business Frontier, 1856–92: A Building Stock', *Australian Geographical Studies*, vol. 19, no. 1, pp. 78–98, 1981.

Ellis, M.H. 'Some Aspects of the Bigge Commission of Inquiry into the Affairs of New South Wales, 1819–1821', *Journal of the Royal Australian Historical Society*, vol. 27, no. 2, pp. 93–126, 1941.

Ellis, M.H. 'Governor Macquarie and the Rum Hospital', *Journal of the Royal Australian Historical Society*, vol. 32, no. 5, pp. 273–293, 1946.

Ellis, M.H. 'Rum Rebellion Reviewed', *Quadrant*, vol. 2, no. 1, pp. 13–23, 1957–58.

Encel, S. 'The Concept of the State in Australian Politics', *Australian Journal of Politics and History*, vol. 6, no. 1, pp. 62–76, 1960.

Fairfax, J. 'Some Recollections of Old Sydney', *Journal of the Royal Australian Historical Society*, vol. 5, no. 1, pp. 1–37, 1919.

Fisher, S. 'The Mobility Myth: Some Sydney Evidence', *Australia 1888 Bulletin*, no. 2, pp. 81–84, 1979.

Fitzhardinge, V. 'Sydney: Translated from the Russian of Pavel Mukhanov', *Journal of the Royal Australian Historical Society*, vol. 51, no. 4, pp. 296–316, 1965.

Fitzpatrick, D. 'Irish Immigrants in Australia: Patterns of Settlement and Paths of Mobility', *Australia 1888 Bulletin*, no. 2, pp. 48–54, 1979.

Fletcher, B.H. 'The Hawkesbury Settlers and the Rum Rebellion', *Journal of the Royal Australian Historical Society*, vol. 54, no. 3, pp. 215–237, 1968.

Forde, J.M. 'Genesis of Commerce in Australia', *Journal of the Royal Australian Historical Society*, vol. 3, no. 120, pp. 559–593, 1917.

Forde, J.M. 'Some Comments on Interpretations of the Origins of the 1890s Depression', *Historian*, no. 23 (April), pp. 7–10, 1971.

Foster, A. 'Odd Bits of Old Sydney', *Journal of the Royal Australian Historical Society*, vol. 7, no. 2, pp. 57–92, 1921.

Foster, A. 'Some Early Homes and Epitaphs', *Journal of the Royal Australian Historical Society*, vol. 11, parts 5 and 6, pp. 288–321, 1925–26.

Foster, W. 'Francis Grose and the Officers', *Journal of the Royal Australian Historical Society*, vol. 51, no. 3, pp. 177–199, 1965.

Fry, E.C. 'Outwork in the Eighties: An Examination of Outwork in the Infant

Bibliography

Industries of the Eastern Australian Colonies, c.1880–90', *University Studies in Politics and History*, vol. 2, no. 4, pp. 77–93, 1956.

Gallagher, J.E. 'The Revolutionary Irish, 1800–1804', *Push from the Bush*, no. 19 (April), pp. 2–33, 1985.

Gandevia, B. 'Socio-medical Factors in the Evolution of the First Settlement at Sydney Cove, 1788–1803', *Journal of the Royal Australian Historical Society*, vol. 61, no. 1, pp. 1–25, 1975.

Gibbons, P.C. 'The Administration of Governor Hunter', *Journal of the Royal Australian Historical Society*, vol. 26, no. 50, pp. 403–418, 1940.

Gilchrist, H. 'Australia's First Greeks', *Canberra Historical Journal*, March, pp. 1–4, 1977.

Gill, J.C.H. 'The Hawkesbury River Floods of 1801, 1806 and 1809: Their Effect on the Economy of the Colony of New South Wales', *Royal Historical Society of Queensland Journal*, vol. 8, no. 4, 1968–69.

Gray, A.J. 'Peter Burn: The First Convict Officially Presumed Killed by Natives at Sydney Cove', *Journal of the Royal Australian Historical Society*, vol. 45, no. 2, pp. 96–104, 1959.

Gray, A. 'Social Life at Sydney Cove in 1788–1789', *Journal of the Royal Australian Historical Society*, vol. 44, no. 6, pp. 379–398, 1958.

Hainsworth, D.R. 'In Search of a Staple: The Sydney Sandalwood Trade 1804–09', *Business Archives*, vol. 5, no. 1, pp. 1–20, 1965.

Hamann, C. 'Nationalism and Reform in Australian Architecture, 1880–1920', *Historical Studies*, vol. 18, no. 72, pp. 393–411, 1979.

Hammerton, A.J. 'Without Natural Protectors: Female Immigration to Australia, 1832–36', *Historical Studies*, vol. 16, no. 65, pp. 539–566, 1975.

Harris, H.L. 'The Financial Crisis of 1893 in New South Wales', *Journal of the Royal Australian Historical Society*, vol. 13, no. 6, pp. 305–344, 1927.

Harris, J. 'Governor's Errors Silly but Colossal', *Canberra Historical Journal*, no. 7 (March), pp. 1–5, 1981.

Hartwell, R.M. 'The Australian Depression of the Eighteen Twenties', *Historical Studies*, vol. 3, no. 11, pp. 209–216, 1947.

Hartwell, R.M. 'Australia's First Trade Cycle', *Journal of the Royal Australian Historical Society*, vol. 42, no. 2, pp. 51–67, 1956.

Havard, W. 'The First Beacon in Port Jackson', *Journal of the Royal Australian Historical Society*, vol. 20, no. 4, p. 272, 1934.

Havard, W.L. 'Francis Howard Greenway, Macquarie's Architect', *Journal of the Royal Australian Historical Society*, vol. 22, no. 3, pp. 137–190, 1936.

Havard, W. and Havard, O. 'A Frenchman Sees Sydney in 1819' (Translated from the letters of Jacques Arago), *Journal of the Royal Australian Historical Society*, vol. 24, no. 1, pp. 17–42, 1938.

Hayden, A. 'The New South Wales Immigration Question and Responsible

Government, 1856–1861', *Journal of the Royal Australian Historical Society*, vol. 46, no. 6, pp. 343–352, 1960.

Hayden, A. 'The Anti-immigration Movement, 1877–1893', *Journal of the Royal Australian Historical Society*, vol. 48, no. 1, pp. 25–43, 1962.

Heath, L. 'A Safe and Salutory Discipline: The Dark Cells of the Parramatta Female Factory 1838', *Push from the Bush*, no. 9, pp. 20–27, 1981.

Heney, H. 'Caroline Chisolm Pioneer Social Worker', *Journal of the Royal Australian Historical Society*, vol. 29, no. 1, pp. 21–34, 1943.

Heney, H. 'The First Generation of Australians', *Journal of the Royal Australian Historical Society*, vol. 29, no. 3, pp. 157–161, 1943.

Herman, M. 'A Hundred Years of Continuity and Australian Architecture', *Journal of the Royal Australian Historical Society*, vol. 40, no. 2, pp. 117–125, 1954.

Hicks, N. 'Theories of Differential Fertility and the Australian Experience, 1891–1911', *Historical Studies*, vol. 16, no. 65, pp. 567–583, 1975.

Hogue, J.A. 'Governor Darling, the Press and the Collar', *Journal of the Royal Australian Historical Society*, vol. 2, no. 12, pp. 308–323, 1907–09.

Holder, R.F. 'The History of the Bank of NSW', *Journal of the Royal Australian Historical Society*, vol. 43, no. 2, pp. 97–120, 1957.

Hopkins, A. 'Power, Elites and Ideology: A Commentary on "Elites in Australia" ', *Australian and New Zealand Journal of Sociology*, vol. 16, no. 1, pp. 73–78, 1980.

Houison, J.K.S. 'Robert Campbell of the Wharf', *Journal of the Royal Australian Historical Society*, vol. 23, no. 1, pp. 1–28, 1937.

Hume, L.J. 'Working Class Movements in Sydney and Melbourne Before the Gold Rush', *Historical Studies*, vol. 9, no. 35, pp. 263–278, 1960.

Hyslop, R. 'War Scares in Australia in the 19th Century', *The Victorian Historical Journal*, vol. 47, no. 1, pp. 23–44, 1976.

Jackson, R.V. 'Owner Occupation of Houses in Sydney, 1871–91', *Australian Economic History Review*, vol. 19, no. 2, pp. 138–154, 1970.

Jeans, D.W. 'Some Literary Examples of Humanistic Descriptions of Place', *Australian Geographer*, vol. 14, no. 4, pp. 207–214, 1979.

Jervis, J. 'The Road to Parramatta – Some Notes on its History', *Journal of the Royal Australian Historical Society*, vol. 13, no. 2, pp. 65–85, 1927.

Jervis, J. 'The Tread Mill', *Journal of the Royal Australian Historical Society*, vol. 31, no. 5, pp. 337–9, 1945.

Jose, A. 'Sydney and District in 1824 as Described by a French Visitor', *Journal of the Royal Australian Historical Society*, vol. 10, no. 4, pp. 215–227, 1924.

Kelly, M.J. 'Eight Acres: Estate Subdivision and the Building Process, Paddington 1875–1890', *Australian Economic History Review*, vol. 10, no. 2, pp. 155–168, 1970.

Kemp, R.E. 'Commercial Life in Australia a Century Ago', *Journal of the Royal*

Australian Historical Society, vol. 4, no. 3, pp. 131–161, 1917.

Kent, D. 'The Orange Order in Colonial Australia', *Push from the Bush*, no. 26, April, pp. 73–78, 1988.

Ker, J. 'The Macarthur Family and the Pastoral Industry', *Journal of the Royal Australian Historical Society*, vol. 47, no. 3, pp. 131–155, 1961.

Kerneck, S. 'Australian and American Characteristics: The Influence of Differences in Economic Prosperity and the Power of Private Business', *University Studies in Politics and History*, vol. 5, no. 3, pp. 1–32, 1969.

King, G.A. 'Old Sydney – Grave and Gay', *Journal of the Royal Australian Historical Society*, vol. 21, no. 5, pp. 216–287, 1935.

King, H. 'Some Aspects of Police Administration in NSW, 1825–1851', *Journal of the Royal Australian Historical Society*, vol. 42, no. 5, pp. 205–230, 1956.

King, H. 'Problems of Police Administration in NSW, 1825–1851', *Journal of the Royal Australian Historical Society*, vol. 44, no. 2, pp. 49–70, 1958.

King, H. 'The Struggle for the Freedom of the Press in New South Wales, 1825–31', *Teaching History*, no. 13, pp. 19–22, 1965.

King, H. 'Villains All? A Review Article', *Journal of the Royal Australian Historical Society*, vol. 53, no. 1, pp. 72–86, 1967.

King, H. 'Lt. John Watts and Macquarie's Improvements to Parramatta', *Journal of the Royal Australian Historical Society*, vol. 59, no. 2, pp. 148–152, 1973.

King, H. 'An Upper Crust Colonial Widow, Elizabeth MacArthur: 1834–50', *Push from the Bush*, no. 3, pp. 26–32, 1979.

King, R.J. 'Eora and English at Port Jackson: A Spanish View', *Aboriginal History*, vol. 10, no. 1, pp. 47–57, 1986.

Knight, K. 'Patronage and the NSW Public Service: The 1894 Royal Commission', *Australian Journal of Politics and History*, vol. 7, no. 2, pp. 166–185, 1961.

Lamb, P.N. 'Crown Land Policy and Government Finance in NSW 1856–1900', *Australian Economic History Review*, vol. 7, no. 1, pp. 38–68, 1967.

La Nauze, J.A. 'A Social Survey of Sydney in 1858', *Historical Studies*, vol. 2, no. 8, pp. 264–269, 1943.

Leroy, P.E. 'The Emancipists, Edward Eager and the Struggle for Civil Liberties', *Journal of the Royal Australian Historical Society*, vol. 48, no. 4, pp. 270–300, 1962.

Levi, J.S. 'The Tale of Australia's First "Rabbi": Joseph Marcus 1767–1828', *Journal of the Australian Jewish Historical Society*, vol. 8, no. 2, pp. 29–36, 1975.

Lewis, M. 'Some Infant Health Problems in Sydney, 1880–1939', *Journal of the Royal Australian Historical Society*, vol. 68, no. 1, pp. 67–73, 1982.

Lyons, W.J. 'Prominent Business Figures of Sydney in the 1850s', *Business Archives*, vol. 1, no. 3, pp. 1–11, 1957.

Lyons, W.J. 'Notes on the History of the Royal Exchange of Sydney', *Business Archives*, vol. 1, no. 2, pp. 1–7, 1956.

MacCallum, D. 'The Alleged Russian Plans for the Invasion of Australia, 1864',

Journal of the Royal Australian Historical Society, vol. 44, no. 5, pp. 302–321, 1958.

McCarthy, J.M. 'All for Australia: Some Right Wing Responses to the Depression in NSW, 1929–1932', *Journal of the Royal Australian Historical Society*, vol. 57, no. 2, pp. 160–171, 1971.

McCarty, J.W. 'Australian Capital Cities in the Nineteenth Century', *Australian Economic History Review*, vol. 10, no. 2, pp. 107–137, 1970.

McConville, C. '1888 – a Policeman's Lot', *Australia 1888 Bulletin*, no. 11, pp. 78–87, 1983.

McDonald, D. 'Carving Furore Underlined Cultural Cringe in Colonial New South Wales', *Canberra Historical Journal*, no. 8, pp. 23–30, 1981.

McDonald, D.I. 'Child and Female Labour in Sydney, 1876–1898', *ANU Historical Journal*, Nos 10 & 11, pp. 40–49, 1973–74.

McDonald, D.I. 'James Barnet – Colonial Architect, 1865–1900', *Journal of the Royal Australian Historical Society*, vol. 55, no. 2, pp. 124–140, 1969.

MacDonald, W.A. 'The Boundary Stones of Sydney', *Journal of the Royal Australian Historical Society*, vol. 16, no. 2, pp. 81–102, 1930.

McGuanne, J.P. 'The Humours and Pastimes of Early Sydney', *Journal of the Royal Australian Historical Society*, vol. 1, no. 3, pp. 34–42, 1901.

Machray, R. 'Gates and Pillars of the Empire: Sydney and Melbourne Illustrated', *Pearsons Magazine*, no. 2, pp. 243–253, 1896.

Mackaness, G. 'Exiles from Canada', *Journal of the Royal Australian Historical Society*, vol. 50, no. 6, pp. 429–432, 1964.

McMartin, A. 'The Payment of Officials in Early Australia, 1786–1826', *Public Administration*, vol. 17, no. 1, pp. 45–80, 1958.

McMartin, A. 'Aspects of Patronage in Australia; 1786–1836', *Public Administration*, vol. 18, no. 4, pp. 326–340, 1959.

Macnab, K. and Ward, R.B. 'The Nature and Nurture of the First Generation of Native Born Australians', *Historical Studies*, vol. 10, no. 39, pp. 289–308, 1962.

Maiden, J.H. 'History of the Sydney Botanic Gardens', *Journal of the Royal Australian Historical Society*, vol. 14, no. 1, pp. 1–43, 1928.

Marks, P.J. 'Rum and Wheat Economy in New South Wales', *Journal of the Royal Australian Historical Society*, vol. 26, no. 6, pp. 511–515, 1940.

Markus, A. 'Jewish Migration to Australia, 1938–49', *Journal of Australian Studies*, no. 13, 1983, pp. 18–31.

Matthews, T. 'The All For Australia League', *Labour History*, no. 17, pp. 136–147, 1970.

Mayne, A. 'City Back-slums in the Land of Promise: Some Aspects of the 1876 Report on Overcrowding in Sydney', *Labour History*, no. 38, pp. 26–39, 1980.

Mayne, A. 'The Question of the Poor in the Nineteenth Century City', *Historical Studies*, vol. 20, no. 81, pp. 557–573, 1983.

Bibliography

Meaney, F.J. 'Governor Brisbane and the Freedom of the Press in NSW, 1824–25', *Armidale and District Historical Society Journal*, no. 12, pp. 67–78, 1969.

Megaw, R. 'Australia and the Great White Fleet 1908', *Journal of the Royal Australian Historical Society*, vol. 56, no. 2, 1970, pp. 121–133.

Metcalfe, J.W. 'Governor Bourke or the Lion and the Walrus', *Journal of the Royal Australian Historical Society*, vol. 30, no. 1, pp. 44–79, 1944.

Miller, J.D.B. 'Greater Sydney, 1892–1952', *Public Administration*, vol. 13, no. 2, pp. 110–122; no. 3, pp. 192–200, 1954.

Millin, B. 'Sydney Harbour and some Shipping Reminiscences', *Journal of the Royal Australian Historical Society*, vol. 23, no. 40, pp. 310–316, 1937.

Murphy, D. 'Religion, Race and Conscription in World War I', *Australian Journal of Politics and History*, vol. 20, no. 2, pp. 155–163, 1974.

Nairn, N.B. 'A Survey of the History of the White Australia Policy in the 19th Century', *The Australian Quarterly*, vol. 28, no. 3, pp. 16–31, 1956.

Norrie, H. 'John MacArthur', *Journal of the Royal Australian Historical Society*, vol. 15, no. 4, pp. 189–215, 1929.

Norrie, H. 'Sydney's Ferry Boats', *Journal of the Royal Australian Historical Society*, vol. 21, no. 1, pp. 1–27, 1935.

O'Callaghan, T. 'Police Establishment in New South Wales', *Journal of the Royal Australian Historical Society*, vol. 9, no. 6, pp. 277–309, 1923.

O'Donnell, D. 'Sectarian Differences and the Inclusion of History in the Curriculum of NSW Public Schools', *Journal of the Royal Australian Historical Society*, vol. 54, no. 3, pp. 283–298, 1968.

Packham, G.H. (ed.). 'The Geology of New South Wales', *Journal of the Geological Society of Australia*, vol. 16, no. 1, pp. 1–654, 1969.

Palfreeman, T. 'Non-European Immigration into Australia', *Australian Outlook*, vol. 29, no. 3, pp. 349–354, 1975.

Parker, R.S. 'Power in Australia', *Australian and New Zealand Journal of Sociology*, vol. 1, no. 2, pp. 85–96, 1965.

Parsons, G. 'The Cato Street Conspirators in New South Wales', *Labour History*, no. 8, pp. 3–5, 1965.

Parsons, T.C. 'Governor Macquarie and the Economic Crisis in NSW 1810–1815', *New Zealand Journal of History*, vol. 2, no. 2, pp. 178–200, 1968.

Parsons, T.G. 'The Social Composition of the Men of the New South Wales Corps', *Journal of the Royal Australian Historical Society*, vol. 50, no. 4, pp. 297–304, 1964.

Parsons, T.G. 'The New South Wales Corps – A Rejoinder', *Journal of the Royal Australian Historical Society*, vol. 52, no. 5, pp. 239–240, 1966.

Parsons, T.G. 'Governor Macquarie and the Assignment of Skilled Convicts in New South Wales', *Journal of the Royal Australian Historical Society*, vol. 58, no. 2, pp. 84–88, 1972.

Philipp, F.A. 'Notes on the Study of Colonial Australian Architecture', *Historical Studies*, vol. 8, no. 32, pp. 405–411, 1959.

LEVIATHAN

Philipp, J. 'The Function of Land in a Colonial Society', *Victorian Historical Magazine*, vol. 39, nos 1–2, pp. 46–51, 1968.

Polden, K. 'The Collapse of the Government Savings Bank of NSW, 1931', *Australian Economic History Review*, vol. 12, no. 1, pp. 52–70, 1972.

Pope, D.H. 'Contours of Australian Immigration', *Australian Economic History Review*, vol. 21, no. 1, pp. 29–52, 1981.

Pratt, A. 'Push Larrikinism in Australia', *Blackwoods Magazine*, February, pp. 27–40, 1901.

Price, C.A. 'Overseas Migration to and from Australia, 1947–1961', *Australian Outlook*, vol. 16, no. 2, pp. 160–174, 1962.

Proudfoot, H.B. 'Botany Bay, Kew, and the Picturesque: Early Conceptions of the Australian Landscape', *Journal of the Royal Australian Historical Society*, vol. 65, no. 1, pp. 30–45, 1979.

Pyke, N. 'Some Leading Aspects of Foreign Immigration to the Goldfields', *Journal of the Royal Australian Historical Society*, vol. 33, no. 1, pp. 1–25, 1947.

Pyke, N.O.P. 'An Outline History of Italian Immigration into Australia', *Australian Quarterly*, vol. 20, no. 3, pp. 99–109, 1948.

Rennie, S. 'The Factor of National Identity: An Explanation of the Differing Reactions of Australia and the United States to Mass Immigration', *Journal of the Royal Australian Historical Society*, vol. 68, no. 2, pp. 133–143, 1982.

Reynolds, H. 'Aborigines and European Social Hierarchy', *Aboriginal History*, vol. 7, no. 2, pp. 124–133, 1983.

Reynolds, H. 'Racial Thought in Early Colonial Australia', *Australian Journal of Politics and History*, vol. 20, no. 1, pp. 45–53, 1974.

Richmond, K. 'Reaction to Radicalism, Non-labour Movements, 1920–29', *Journal of Australian Studies*, no. 5, pp. 50–63, 1979.

Ritchie, J. 'Towards Ending an Unclean Thing: The Molesworth Committee and the Abolition of Transportation to NSW, 1837–40', *Historical Studies*, vol. 17, no. 67, pp. 144–164, 1976.

Robinson, K.W. 'Geographical Aspects of Land Settlement in the Sydney District, 1788–1821', *Journal of the Royal Australian Historical Society*, vol. 48, no. 1, pp. 60–79, 1962.

Robson, L.L. 'The Origin of the Women Convicts Sent to Australia, 1787–1852', *Historical Studies*, vol. 11, no. 41, pp. 43–53, 1963.

Rogers, D. 'A Saga of Two Hundred Years: The Families of Governor King and Captain John Macarthur', *Victorian Historical Magazine*, vol. 33, no. 4, pp. 422–441, 1963.

Rose, L.N. 'The Administration of Governor Darling', *Journal of the Royal Australian Historical Society*, vol. 8, nos 2 and 3, pp. 49–176, 1922.

Rowland, E. 'The Illumination of Sydney', *Journal of the Royal Australian Historical Society*, vol. 38, no. 1, pp. 47–48, 1952.

Bibliography

Rubinstein, W.D. 'The Top Wealth-holders of NSW, 1817–1939', *Australian Economic History Review*, vol. 20, no. 2, pp. 136–152, 1980.

Rubinstein, W.D. 'The Top Wealth-holders of NSW in 1830–44', *Push from the Bush*, no. 8, pp. 23–49, 1980.

Rude, G. 'Early Irish Rebels in Australia', *Historical Studies*, vol. 16, no. 62, pp. 17–35, 1974.

Rutland, S. 'Jewish Immigration to New South Wales, 1919–1939', *Journal of the Australian Jewish Historical Society*, vol. 7, no. 5, pp. 337–347, 1973.

Saclier, M. 'Sam Marsden's Colony: Notes on a Manuscript in the Mitchell Library', *Journal of the Royal Australian Historical Society*, vol. 52, no. 2, pp. 94–114, 1966.

Scott, E. 'The Canadian and United States Transported Prisoners of 1839', *Journal of the Royal Australian Historical Society*, vol. 21, no. 1, pp. 27–44, 1935.

Schultz, R.J. 'Land Policy in New South Wales 1831–1850', *Historian*, vol. 24 (October), pp. 17–23, 1972.

Selfe, N. 'A Century of Sydney Cove and the Genesis of Circular Quay' (Part 1), *Journal of the Royal Australian Historical Society*, vol. 1, no. 4, pp. 55–68, 1906; (Part 2) vol. 1, no. 5, pp. 69–72, 1907.

Sharman, C. and Suart, J. 'Premier's Department: Patterns of Growth and Change', *Politics*, vol. 17, no. 1, pp. 46–58, 1982.

Shaw, A.B. 'Fort Denison Sydney Harbour', *Journal of the Royal Australian Historical Society*, vol. 23, no. 5, pp. 382–7, 1937.

Shaw, A.B. 'Port Jackson – Its Romantic Growth', *Journal of the Royal Australian Historical Society*, vol. 35, no. 6, pp. 305–338, 1949.

Shaw, A.G.L. 'Rum Corps and Rum Rebellion', *Melbourne Historical Journal*, vol. 10, pp. 15–23, 1971.

Short, A.D. and Wright, L.D. 'Beach Systems of the Sydney Region', *Australian Geographer*, vol. 15, no. 1, pp. 8–16, 1981.

Smith, B. 'Architecture in Australia', *Historical Studies*, vol. 14, no. 53, pp. 85–92, 1969.

Spearritt, P. 'Sydney Slums: Middle Class Reformers and the Labour Response', *Labour History*, no. 26, pp. 65–81, 1974.

Stephen, E.H. 'Darwin's Prophecy the Bridge', *Journal of the Royal Australian Historical Society*, vol. 16, no. 6, pp. 463–465, 1931.

Steven, J.E. 'Robert Campbell and the Bligh Rebellion, 1808', *Journal of the Royal Australian Historical Society*, vol. 48, no. 50, pp. 344–359, 1963.

Steven, M.J.E. 'The Changing Pattern of Commerce in New South Wales, 1810–1821', *Business Archives*, vol. 3, no. 2, pp. 139–155, 1963.

Stilwell, F. 'The Current Economic Depression and its Impact on Australian Cities', *Australian Quarterly*, vol. 51, no. 20, pp. 5–16, 1979.

Storrier, S.A. 'As Others Saw Us: Two Papers on Colonial Society as seen by Overseas Visitors, 1880–1900', *Journal of the Royal Australian Historical Society*, vol. 51, no. 3, pp. 232–248, 1965.

LEVIATHAN

Sturma, M. 'The Eye of the Beholder: The Stereotype of Women Convicts, 1788–1852', *Labour History*, no. 34, pp. 3–10, 1978.

Sturma, M. 'Public Executions and the Ritual of Death', *Push from the Bush*, no. 15, pp. 3–11, 1983.

Sullivan, M. 'Master and Servant in NSW before 1850', *Push from the Bush*, no. 3, pp. 44–63, 1979.

Sussmilch, C.A. 'Note on Some Recent Marine Erosion at Bondi, *Journal and Proceedings of the Royal Society of New South Wales*, vol. 46, pp. 155–158, 1912.

Swann, M. 'Caroline Chisolm', *Journal of the Royal Australian Historical Society*, vol. 6, no. 3, pp. 134–150, 1920.

Textile, Clothing and Footwear Union of Australia, 'The Hidden Cost of Fashion', *Report of the National Outwork Information Campaign*, March 1995.

Townsend, N. 'The Molesworth Enquiry: Does the Report Fit the Evidence?', *Journal of Australian Studies*, no. 1, pp. 33–51, 1977.

Townsend, N. 'Document: Sir Richard Bourke's Afterthoughts, 1838', *Push From the Bush*, no. 12, pp. 61–75, 1982.

Vipond, J. 'The Impact of Unemployment on Areas Within Sydney', *Journal of Industrial Relations*, vol. 22, no. 3, pp. 326–341, 1980.

Walker, E. 'Old Sydney in the Forties', *Journal of the Royal Australian Historical Society*, vol. 16, no. 40, pp. 292–320, 1930.

Walsh, G.P. 'Factories and Factory Workers in NSW, 1788–1900', *Labour History*, no. 21, pp. 1–16, 1971.

Walsh, G.P. 'The Geography of Manufacturing in Sydney, 1788–1851', *Business Archives*, vol. 3, no. 1, pp. 20–52, 1963.

Ward, R. 'Black and White Australians: Race Relations in History', *The Australian Quarterly*, vol. 55, no. 2, pp. 160–167, 1983.

Waterman, J.C. 'Recollections of Sydney', *Journal of the Royal Australian Historical Society*, vol. 8 (supp.), pp. 359–362, 1923.

Watson, J. 'The Early Fortifications of Port Jackson', *Journal of the Royal Australian Historical Society*, vol. 3, no. 8, pp. 385–402, 1916.

Watson, J. 'Notes on Some Suburbs of Sydney', *Journal of the Royal Australian Historical Society*, vol. 13, no. 1, pp. 21–41, 1927.

Watson, J. 'Sydney Harbour Bridge', *Journal of the Royal Australian Historical Society*, vol. 18, no. 1, pp. 44–47, 1932.

Webster, D. 'Terminolgy, Hegemony and the Sydney Press, 1838', *Push from the Bush*, no. 10, pp. 31–46, 1981.

Weingarth, J. 'The Head of Sydney Cove', *Journal of the Royal Australian Historical Society*, vol. 10, no. 5, pp. 298–300, 1924.

Williams, G. 'Far More Happier than We Europeans: Reactions to the Australian Aborigines on Cook's Voyage', *Historical Studies*, vol. 19, no. 77, pp. 499–512, 1981.

Bibliography

Wood, G.A. 'Ancient and Mediaeval Conceptions of Terra Australis', *Journal of the Royal Australian Historical Society*, vol. 3, no. 10, pp. 455–465, 1916.

Wood, G.A. 'Governor Hunter', *Journal of the Royal Australian Historical Society*, vol. 14, no. 6, pp. 344–362, 1928.

Wood, G.A. 'Governor Macquarie', *Journal of the Royal Australian Historical Society*, vol. 16, nos 5 and 6, pp. 323–463, 1930.

Woodward, P. 'The NSW Premier's Department', *Politics*, vol. 17, no. 1, pp. 29–35, 1982.

Government reports

Australian Bureau of Crime Intelligence. *Australian Illicit Drug Report 1996–97*, December 1997.

Australian Bureau of Statistics. *Census of the Commonwealth of Australia Taken for the Night between 2nd and 3rd of April 1911*, Canberra.

Australian Bureau of Statistics. *Sydney, A Social Atlas*, Canberra, 1993.

Despatches from the Governor of New South Wales, Transmitting Reports of the Legislative Council Relative to the Monetary Depression in the Colony, and the Petition of the Distressed Mechanics and Labourers, in *British Parliamentary Papers, Session 1842–4*.

Dobinson, I. and Poletti, P. *Buying and Selling Heroin*, New South Wales Bureau of Crime Statistics and Research, 1988.

Eleventh Progress Report of the Sydney City and Suburban Sewage and Health Board, Appointed 12 April 1875.

Herbert, C. (ed.). *Geology of the Sydney Region 1:100 000 Sheet*, New South Wales Department of Mineral Resources, Sydney, 1983.

Independent Commission Against Corruption. *Report on the Investigation into the Glebe Morgue*, March 1998.

Landa, D. *Public Interest in Releasing the Ombudsman's Report on Operation Sue*, New South Wales Office of the Ombudsman, 1991.

Maher, L., Dixon, D., Lynskey M. and Hall, W. *Running the Risks: Heroin, Health and Harm in South West Sydney*, National Drug and Alcohol Research Centre, Monograph No. 38, 1998.

Muirhead, J.H. and Johnston, E. (Commissioners). *Royal Commission into Aboriginal Deaths in Custody*, 1991.

New South Wales Department of Prisons. *Annual Report for the Year 1896*, Government Printer, Sydney, 1897.

New South Wales Ethnic Affairs Commission. *Not a Single Problem, Not a Single Solution: A Report to the Minister for Ethnic Affairs on the Recent Clashes Between Youth in Bankstown and Marrickville*, July 1986.

New South Wales Ethnic Affairs Commission. *The People of Sydney: Statistics from the 1991 Census*, Sydney, 1994.

New South Wales Legislative Assembly. Report of the Select Committee on Common Lodging Houses, *Votes and Proceedings*, 1875–6, vol. 2.

New South Wales State Coroner. *Inquest into the Death of David John Gundy*, Glebe, 1990.

New South Wales State Coroner. *New South Wales Bush Fire Inquiry*, Westmead, 1995.

Report of the Royal Commission for the Improvement of the City of Sydney and its Suburbs, Government Printer, 1909.

Wood, J. (Commissioner). *Royal Commission into the New South Wales Police Service*, vols 1–6, May 1997.

Wooten, J.H. (Commissioner). *Report of the Inquiry into the Death of David John Gundy, Royal Commission into Aboriginal Deaths in Custody*, Canberra, 1991.

Index

Index

Index

Index

Index

Index

Index

Index

Index